TALKS WITH SRI AUROBINDO

Talks with Sri Aurobindo

Volume 2

Nirodbaran

SRI AUROBINDO ASHRAM
PONDICHERRY

Previous editions
Volume I 1966, 1986
Volume II 1971
Volume III 1973
Volume II-III 1985
Volume IV 1989

Present edition
Volumes 1 and 2 2001

Volume 1
Second impression 2009
Volume 2
Second impression 2013

Rs 275
ISBN 978-81-7058-635-7

© Sri Aurobindo Ashram Trust 2001
Published by Sri Aurobindo Ashram Publication Department
Pondicherry 605 002
Web http://www.sabda.in

Printed at Sri Aurobindo Ashram Press, Pondicherry
PRINTED IN INDIA

NOTE

These talks are from my notebooks. For several years I used to record most of the conversations which Sri Aurobindo had with us, his attendants, and a few others, after the accident to his right leg in November 1938. Besides myself, the regular participants were Purani, Champaklal, Satyendra, Mulshankar and Dr. Becharlal. Occasional visitors were Dr. Manilal, Dr. Rao and Dr. Savoor.

As these notes were not seen by Sri Aurobindo himself, the responsibility for the Master's words rests entirely with me. I do not vouch for absolute accuracy, but I have tried my best to reproduce them faithfully. I have made the same attempt for the remarks of the others.

NIRODBARAN

TALKS WITH SRI AUROBINDO

Volume 2

1 MARCH 1940

Nirodbaran was twisting a letter in his hands. Sri Aurobindo, hearing the faint noise, looked back.

SRI AUROBINDO: What's that?

NIRODBARAN: Z's letter. He wants guidance.

PURANI: Any more of Dutt's stories?

NIRODBARAN: No more. He has stopped.

SRI AUROBINDO: His story of my meeting him at Baroda Station may be true, as I used to go very often to the Station. And about his earthen tumbler incident, there may be some foundation to it, but I object to the shooting incident. Ask him the names of those two Marathi youths. There was no one I knew who was quite capable of doing such things, going to the Consuls, the Czar, the Kaiser.

PURANI: Does Barin's article show any change in his attitude?

SRI AUROBINDO (*smiling, stretching out both hands in a half-hanging position and then pausing a little*): It is difficult to say about Barin. After having failed in whatever he tried, he may look back now in a different light. He says whatever suits him at the moment. There may be some change in his attitude, but how far he has made inner progress is difficult to say.

PURANI: A change in attitude doesn't indicate inner progress?

SRI AUROBINDO: Not always, because it may be simply a mental change and it may be due to his having failed in everything after going from here, while the Ashram has grown ever since. That may have impressed him.

PURANI: To realise and say that he has deviated from the path is rather strong for Barin, I thought.

SRI AUROBINDO: He says whatever is uppermost in his mind, according to his moods, and he says it with force.

NIRODBARAN: X is trying to boycott the Calcutta Nationalist papers, especially the *Jugantar.*

SRI AUROBINDO: Why?

NIRODBARAN: It seems that this paper criticised X and supported the Working Committee. The editor of the *Hindustan Standard* has been dismissed through his influence.

SRI AUROBINDO: What for?

NIRODBARAN: Because the editor made a joint declaration with other editors against X's move to muzzle the press. It is a Leftist paper.

SRI AUROBINDO: Is that the only Leftist paper?

NIRODBARAN: I think so.

SRI AUROBINDO: Doesn't X talk of democracy and its rights?

NIRODBARAN: Yes, when he is flung down, I suppose. Y seems to have said that fair and just criticism is welcome even of people serving the country.

SRI AUROBINDO: But anybody can say he is serving the country and then do whatever he likes.

PURANI: X is serving more his personal ambition, I should say.

NIRODBARAN: Fazlul Huque gave the same argument when he restricted the *Hindustan Standard*, saying that fair and just criticism is always welcome but when it brings in the name of Allah, then –

SRI AUROBINDO: Allah?

NIRODBARAN: Yes, attacking Allah. I believe he means religion. X says that the public have every right to boycott a paper if they find it is going against the national interest.

SRI AUROBINDO: The public also have the right to buy any paper they like or to boycott it, but why should anybody advise or dictate to them? The public are not fools.

NIRODBARAN: That is exactly what the *Patrika* says. It declares that the Bengal public are not fools. Let them decide as they wish. Why should X hold meetings from park to park to boycott a particular paper?

SATYENDRA: He is holding an anti-compromise conference.

SRI AUROBINDO: But who is going in for a compromise?

SATYENDRA: It is the impression both of the Leftists and of X that Gandhi will compromise. Gandhi said, "I am not against compromise if that is for the good of the national interest. Satyagraha doesn't preclude compromise." But Gandhi won't betray the country – that is quite certain. Everybody is attacking the Congress: X, the Muslims, the Justice Party.

NIRODBARAN: M. N. Roy too.

SRI AUROBINDO: And X is attacking M. N. Roy. Such is the universal movement. Look at Europe.

SATYENDRA: Ours is a reflection of that, perhaps.

NIRODBARAN: X says he was an idealist; how was he a political leader?

SRI AUROBINDO: That sort of leadership is nothing. He was just beginning his career. If you have the gift of the gab, the power of ideas and the ability to put them into form, you can always be a leader. All politics is a show. In the British Parliament it is the Civil Service people who are really behind everything and these people whose names are never known do the real work. The Ministers are only their mouthpieces, except for a few rare cases like Churchill and Hore-Belisha. The Civil Servants have been at their job for their lifetime and they know everything about it.

The Mother's brother, for instance, organised Congoland in Africa and did a lot of work. He was one of the best colonial governors and administrators – but all the credit went to the Minister who was only a figurehead at the top. Even when he was an officer in Equatorial Africa, sometimes as Governor and sometimes as Governor-General, the whole job was done by him. He hardly had a bed but used to lie down in an easy-chair. He is nearly seventy now but as soon as the war broke out he went to the office and asked for work. Now he is working eighteen hours a day.

EVENING

Krishnalal had done a painting of a buffalo. The Mother had been overheard remarking to Sri Aurobindo that it looked a bit sentimental.

SRI AUROBINDO (*from his bed, to Purani*): I have been looking at the buffalo. It looks as if it were undergoing a psychic change. (*To Satyendra*) What is your opinion?

SATYENDRA: I don't know, Sir. I don't know what the idea behind it is. It doesn't appeal to me. The white elephant plucking lotuses from a pond was all right. The elephant is said to be Durga's vehicle. But why the buffalo?

SRI AUROBINDO: The buffalo is also the vehicle of someone.

PURANI: Of Yamaraj.

At this point the Mother came in.

SATYENDRA (*to the Mother*): We have been wondering what the meaning of this buffalo could be.

THE MOTHER: Meaning? Did Krishnalal want to give it any meaning? I thought it was only a buffalo, like his cats. One year we had flowers, last year birds and this year beasts.

Satyendra narrated some Gujarati stories about buffaloes.

SRI AUROBINDO (*to Nirodbaran*): Sarat Chatterji also has written a story, hasn't he?

NIRODBARAN: I think it was about a bullock.

SATYENDRA: It is supposed that while cow's milk is good, buffalo's milk makes the brain dull. Doctors don't prescribe it. Why don't you take milk, Sir?

SRI AUROBINDO: Because I don't care to.

SATYENDRA: It is very good for the blood.

SRI AUROBINDO: I have plenty of blood, I think.

DR. BECHARLAL: Milk is said to be good for spirituality.

SRI AUROBINDO: It is no better than Nirod's brinjal. (*Laughter*) The Mother and I don't take milk. There are many people who have taken milk for many years – even ten years – but I don't know that they have progressed spiritually. Punnuswamy, who was suffering from an ulcer, took nothing but milk.

DR. BECHARLAL: Milk is believed to be an ideal food.

SRI AUROBINDO: I have no idea.

NIRODBARAN: Dr. Becharlal is rather fond of milk.

SATYENDRA: I also don't disfavour it.

SRI AUROBINDO: But that is for the sake of your blood. (*Laughter*)

SATYENDRA: There are stories of buffaloes being used as sacrifice.

SRI AUROBINDO: Ah, then this buffalo must be one which is to be so used!

NIRODBARAN: Nishikanto is having his old trouble – pain, vomiting, etc.

SRI AUROBINDO: Has he been eating anything?

NIRODBARAN: I don't think so. No resources.

SRI AUROBINDO: No resources?

NIRODBARAN: No pocket money, but he took some sweets which people had brought during the Darshan period.

SRI AUROBINDO: Ah, I thought so.

NIRODBARAN: But they were nothing much –

SRI AUROBINDO: Nothing much?

NIRODBARAN: I mean, not so much in quantity – about three or four, he said.

SRI AUROBINDO: How was he cured last time?

NIRODBARAN: By your Force, he says.

SRI AUROBINDO: And now he is brought back to his old condition by his own force?

NIRODBARAN: It seems Dutt's story about Prafulla Chakravarty's death is not all correct. Nolini himself was one of the party. They never approached Dutt. But the boy's death by a bomb explosion is quite true.

PURANI: Nolini said that Barin was carrying the bomb in his hand with the cap on.

SRI AUROBINDO: Cap on? Just like Barin.

PURANI: And when Prafulla threw the bomb, it exploded in the air before touching the ground.

NIRODBARAN: Chakravarty thought that as soon as it would touch the ground he would hide himself behind a rock. He didn't expect it would explode before.

SRI AUROBINDO: Even so, it was very risky to watch like that. I think it was Nevinson who said that the Indian revolutionaries were as good as the Russian. But this incident is hardly an encouraging one. Time is needed to become efficient. It took the Russians more than a hundred years to throw off the Czar. Among the Indian revolutionaries Rashbehari Bose was an exceptional man – very clever in every way. Pulin Das was also very good.

PURANI: Rashbehari was really remarkable. He was a linguist. He used to speak Punjabi just like a Punjabi. He escaped just the night before the arrests. All the others got arrested.

2 MARCH 1940

THE MOTHER (*coming into Sri Aurobindo's room at 11.00 a.m.*): Do you want to hear a story?

SRI AUROBINDO: Yes, what is it about?

THE MOTHER: About the theft in Aroumé. It seems that a man was lying drunk against the wall with a bag of husk by his side. The time was about 8.30 a.m. Some sadhaks saw him and found that he was the Dining Room's sanitary servant. They showed compassion for him but didn't know what to do. They came to Amrita. He went there, hired a rickshaw, put the man in it and sent him home. In the morning Dyuman found that a bag of husk was missing from the Dining Room, and he saw traces of footprints on the wall. This man evidently climbed the wall, fell down and lay there in a drunken condition. So now these people have first lost the thief and then paid money for him to go home along with the bag of husk! (*Sri Aurobindo started laughing.*)

Later, during his sponging, Sri Aurobindo spoke to Purani who had not been there in the morning.

SRI AUROBINDO: Have you heard the story of Buddhist compassion in Aroumé?

PURANI: No; is it about some theft? I saw Amrita bustling about.

SRI AUROBINDO (*after recounting the story to Purani*): Amrita out of Buddhist compassion paid the man's rickshaw fare.

SATYENDRA: I too was there at that time.

SRI AUROBINDO: Oh, you were also one of the Buddhists?

SATYENDRA: No, Sir. I was only a spectator. The whole story sounds like one of Dutt's.

SRI AUROBINDO: Yes – only it has the disadvantage of being true. It seems there have been thefts in the house of Benabellis and of the Inspector of Police. It has proved the inefficiency of the Police.

SATYENDRA: Dutt's stories have shed a flood of light on old events.

SRI AUROBINDO: Yes, the light that never was on sea or land.

PURANI: May I recount a tale about Barin now? Sudhir told me that once Barin came to his house as a guest. Sudhir asked him straight why he had left Pondicherry and to his straight question wanted a straight answer. "When all are turning towards Pondicherry," he said, "how is it that you have come away? You had many experiences, stayed a long time. Still why have you come away? Tell me frankly."

SRI AUROBINDO (*enjoying the story*): And then? What was the reply?

PURANI: The first day Barin evaded Sudhir. The second day he again was asked and then Barin told him that he had come away because of his personal difficulties. The Mother had asked him repeatedly not to go; even while going away he was having experiences right up to Villipuram, as if he were being carried in a golden egg by the Mother and he was all the time hearing, "Don't go, don't go." But he wouldn't listen. He had fallen from the path and was getting the consequences of the fall.

EVENING

PURANI: I asked Krishnalal whether he had any idea behind his buffalo.

SRI AUROBINDO (*smiling*): Yes? What was his answer?

PURANI: He says he wanted to paint a goat first. As he had heard that somebody was presenting a goat to the Ashram, he waited for confirmation. In the meantime he did this buffalo in a single day.

SRI AUROBINDO: All the same he has done it well.

PURANI: He wanted to show, as you said, a psychic change.

SRI AUROBINDO (*breaking into laughter on hearing about the confirmation of his own joke*): It looks like a well-disposed cow and a bit of a dog too. But there is more psychic sorrow in it than joy – sorrow over the sins of the world. (*Laughter*)

Have you heard that the thief has paid rather heavily for a little bag of husk? He has been handed over to the Police; he will lose his job and has also lost two rupees. Perhaps it is the rickshawalla who has deprived him of the money.

SATYENDRA: I suspect more the servant, Sir, who accompanied him and was taking care of him. (*Laughter*) But why did he scale the wall when the door was quite open?

SRI AUROBINDO: He was too drunk to know that.

PURANI: Some other things were found in the bag, they say.

SRI AUROBINDO: Amrita's old shirt, which was presented to the man according to his own story. He has confessed to the Police about the bag but said that he was too drunk to know what he was doing. What will be the law of Karma in his case? He has paid heavily for his Karma in this life, and will he pay still more heavily in the next?

SATYENDRA: No, Sir, it is more than cancelled. (*Laughter*)

A man loiters regularly near the wine shop by the side of our Dining Room and makes rather free use of the liquor available. Dr. Becharlal is anxious about him and says, "This poor man will die of his liver."

PURANI: He may die without it as well.

SRI AUROBINDO: With no liver! (*Laughter*)

3 MARCH 1940

NIRODBARAN: Dutt was much impressed, it seems, by the Ashram, and much moved.

SRI AUROBINDO: How?

NIRODBARAN: Don't know; that is what they are saying.

PURANI: Nolini was telling his last story.

SRI AUROBINDO: What is it?

PURANI: It seems it was when he was interned somewhere.

SRI AUROBINDO: Was he interned?

NIRODBARAN: Yes, in Cooch Bihar, he said.

PURANI: His father was anxious to reinstate him in his job. So he thought the best way would be to make him see Sir Andrew Fraser who might then think that Dutt was quite innocent. Dutt had to be coaxed to agree but on the condition that he would only see him in his Bengali dress and wouldn't wait in the Governor's antechamber. It was agreed. Dutt then put on a dirty dhoti and shirt and kept his slippers on. In that condition he went straight to Fraser whose legs were shaking out of fear, and his right hand was slightly thrust forward. A bodyguard stood behind Fraser with a revolver pointed at Dutt. Dutt could even see the metallic point of the revolver.

SRI AUROBINDO (*laughing*): Nonsense. He could see the metallic point of his own imagination.

PURANI: After the interview, while he was coming away, he said, "My father has asked me to offer his thanks to you," to which Fraser laughed aloud.

SRI AUROBINDO: What has Fraser got to do with his job? He was at Bombay.

PURANI: Perhaps Fraser could cast some influence.

SRI AUROBINDO: You don't know Dutt's other story? What Fraser said about me?

PURANI: No.

SRI AUROBINDO: Fraser, after seeing me in jail, said to Dutt, "I have seen him. He has the eyes of a madman." Dutt replied, "No, he has the eyes of a Karmayogi." (*Laughter*)

NIRODBARAN: Dutt wanted to write to Mother, but it seems he has a false idea that Mother has told him not to write anything.

SRI AUROBINDO: Mother told him it was not necessary to write for permission of darshan for his wife.

NIRODBARAN: Yes, they told him so.

SATYENDRA: Now he will tell all sorts of stories about Pondicherry. (*Laughter*) Nobody will contradict him.

NIRODBARAN: T may now say, "Dutt is sentimental."

SRI AUROBINDO: And he may also say, "Why are all these people going to Aurobindo Ghose?" T is very childlike in some ways.

PURANI: He will get another shock.

SRI AUROBINDO: And will say that the world is getting sentimental.

EVENING

DR. BECHARLAL: There is a superstition that by looking at the moon one goes mad. Is there any truth here?

SRI AUROBINDO: Ramachandra says that. According to him Premshankar went mad by concentrating on the moon. Poets are said to be influenced by the moon, but, I suppose, poets are mad people anyway.

DR. BECHARLAL: I personally get much peace by looking at the moon.

NIRODBARAN: But do you have a fear of going mad? (*Laughter*)

SRI AUROBINDO: If you simply look without concentrating on it, it is all right! (*Laughter*)

PURANI: In a journal K gives an explanation for the earthquake in Turkey. He says that it is due to the war-fever in Europe.

SRI AUROBINDO: How? What has Turkey got to do with the war-fever?

PURANI: His argument is queer. He says, "When the stomach is upset, the head aches; when the hand steals, the back gets a beating."

SRI AUROBINDO: That doesn't always hold. The head may ache without any stomach upset or the hand may indulge in stealing without the back getting beaten.

PURANI: In his view the question is whether the moral law is partially active or absolutely active. Is there any room for accident or chance?

SRI AUROBINDO: Why take for granted that these are the sole alternatives? There may be so many other factors.

PURANI: He speaks of fate.

SRI AUROBINDO: There may be things like that.

PURANI: Gandhi's explanation of the Bihar earthquake is similar. He said it was due to the sins of the people.

SRI AUROBINDO: That at least is more reasonable than K's idea. The sins are Indian and the earthquake is Indian. But why should the war-fever in Europe make Turkey have an earthquake? I don't understand, in any case, why people always associate outer events with morality and interpret them in terms of sin and punishment. It is a question I have raised in *The Life Divine*. If, for instance, a man gets knocked on the head by some accident, why bring in the question of morality and say that it must be due to his sin or Karma? And what have the peasants dying in Anatolia by earthquake got to do with the sins of people arming and fighting in Europe? The disaster is due simply to the movement of Nature's forces.

PURANI: K says it is a question of faith, not intellectual explanation.

SRI AUROBINDO: Then why argue about it and give reasons? We might as well say that S is suffering because of the sins of mankind. According to the Hindu Shastras, four generations suffer for the sins of the father.

SATYENDRA: That is hereditary syphilis. (*Laughter*)

SRI AUROBINDO: And according to the Mahabharata, the king is responsible for the sins of his subjects. In that case, Mustapha Kemal would be responsible for the earthquake because he abolished the Caliph, religion, etc. If the headache is due to the stomach, what about Gandhi's blood-pressure? Is it due to the stomach also? It would be more correct to say that it was due to the sins of Jinnah. (*Laughter*)

SATYENDRA: Moral law is not the creator and upholder of creation.

SRI AUROBINDO: No, prior to man there was no moral law. In the material or vital world, moral law doesn't exist. It comes in with man, and at a certain stage of his development it is useful. Even then, it is a social necessity, because without some kind of moral law society can't exist. But to say that the world is regulated by moral law is to deny the facts of existence. That is absurd. There are two ways: one can either go beyond moral law as we seek to do by spirituality or one can uphold moral law as an ideal to be realised. This is understandable. If there is a moral legislator of the world, why does he give the same punishment for different sins?

PURANI: K says man ought to learn lessons from these things. Vinoba Bhave maintains that one must even starve to death.

SRI AUROBINDO: For nothing?

PURANI: For non-violence, Ahimsa.

SRI AUROBINDO: Perhaps that's nothing. (*Laughter*) Even then it won't solve the problem, for you will be killing so many germs in your body by starvation.

PURANI: He says one has the right to take one's own life.

SRI AUROBINDO: That is questionable. You have no right to take the life that has been given to you for a particular purpose.

4 MARCH 1940

NIRODBARAN: How far can withdrawal be useful in sadhana?

SRI AUROBINDO: Mere withdrawal is not enough. A man may separate himself from the contacts of the world but it doesn't mean that all his desires and hankerings have ceased. If you simply withdraw without throwing away the seeds of attachment and don't replace the ordinary by the spiritual consciousness, the problem remains unsolved. If you permit the seeds to remain, they may keep quiescent for a time but as soon as circumstances present themselves they may come up. Withdrawal may lead to a neutral state but that is not our Yoga. We want spiritual dynamism as the source of action.

NIRODBARAN: If one writes about metaphysics or philosophy with a spiritual attitude the spiritual consciousness must be there.

SRI AUROBINDO (*laughing*): Must it? Attitude is not enough. There must be an inner change too. Of course if one wrote from his personal experience and vision it would be different. But remaining withdrawn need not lift one into the spiritual consciousness: one may very well be in the mental consciousness. Philosophical writings are of the mental plane.

NIRODBARAN: Calm and peace may be there behind.

SRI AUROBINDO: That is not sufficient. There must be the spiritual dynamism too, which would be projected into all the activities.

SATYENDRA: There are many people who have peace or have experienced a descent of peace into them – solid peace which is the peace of Brahman. (*To Nirodbaran*) You had it yourself.

NIRODBARAN: No, I didn't.

SRI AUROBINDO: He is indignantly denying it.

SATYENDRA: At least the experience of light and force.

NIRODBARAN: Not of light.

SATYENDRA: He is speaking about his own problem, Sir. (*Laughter*)

SRI AUROBINDO: His own problem? Is it to get to the Brahman or to the psychic being?

SATYENDRA: His psychic has emerged.

SRI AUROBINDO: Simple emergence will not do, the psychic must come forward.

NIRODBARAN: I am a little surprised. When you said that there are five or six people in the Ashram who are living in the Brahmic consciousness, I thought X was one of them.

SRI AUROBINDO: The Brahmic consciousness? I must have used the term loosely. Peace and calm is only a part of that consciousness and not the whole of it. One may be in contact with it or able to go into it at will or there may be the reflection of it in the mind and the vital. All that is partial. One has to go further, into the higher consciousness above the head and remain there.

NIRODBARAN: Then I suppose one won't be disturbed by these things.

SRI AUROBINDO: Even if they come, one won't be touched by them. They will be on the external surface, coming and passing away, or one may look upon them as if they belonged to somebody else. This Brahmic consciousness decends first into the mental and then the peace and calm remains in all the activities of the mind. The test comes when it descends into the vital. Unless the vital is purified, one may fail. This is called falling from yoga, *yogabhrashta*, as happened here in the early years. When the Brahmic consciousness descended into the vital, all broke down.

NIRODBARAN: But one can keep it in the mind. It need not come into the vital.

SRI AUROBINDO: No, but that would be the old Yoga, in which people want to depart from the world, living in their highest mental consciousness. But when they come into contact with the external world, they can't keep that poise and silence. The seeds have not been thrown away: they have only remained dormant. There are also cases where people leave the vital to do as it likes. You know the story of the Vedantin and Ramakrishna. The Vedantin came to the

Math with a concubine. Ramakrishna asked why he was moving about with her. He replied, "What does it matter? Everything is Maya." "Then I spit on your Vedanta," Ramakrishna exclaimed.

SATYENDRA: There are many Yogis with this consciousness, who live in the world and have contact with the world and yet are in that consciousness.

SRI AUROBINDO: Yes, one may exercise a sufficient mental control over the vital.

NIRODBARAN: Then the question is: are they controlling the vital with the mind or has the Brahmic consciousness actually descended into the vital so that all their activities come from that higher dynamism.

SATYENDRA: Of course their activities are of a limited kind. They accept life only as much as is necessary for their purpose.

NIRODBARAN: Then that is different from what we are speaking of.

SATYENDRA: Some people here say that such a realisation is imperfect.

SRI AUROBINDO: Not imperfect. They mean incomplete, and that too from our standpoint. From the standpoint of others it is complete and perfect.

SATYENDRA: It is only you, Sir, who have brought in this idea of acceptance of life, descent and transformation. Others wanted liberation.

SRI AUROBINDO: Liberation is all right. Everybody wants it and must have it.

SATYENDRA: Even the Vaishnavites and Tantrics wanted an extraterrestrial Goloka or an escape into Shiva. In the South, Ramalinga Swami had the idea of physical transformation and immortality.

SRI AUROBINDO: In the South such an idea is more common.

SATYENDRA: I have also come in contact with Yogis who have lived up to an old age. One was about a hundred and two years old. He died a few years after I saw him and another died at eighty or so. That was also one or two years after my contact.

SRI AUROBINDO: How is it that people who have lived up to an old age died soon after you have come in contact with them? Brahmanand who is said to have been more than two hundred, died soon after I met him and Sakharia Baba who was about eighty, died from dog-bite soon after my meeting him.

SATYENDRA: In reference to Dr. Becharlal's mention of getting peace by looking at the moon, I may say that some people whom I know get peace by concentration on breath and by repeating a mantra – say, Ramanama – with each breath.

SRI AUROBINDO: Yes, that is quite a well-known method. Any kind of concentration that quiets the mind gives peace.

SATYENDRA (*looking at N and smiling*): If Nirod's path had been of Brahmic consciousness he would have got it by now. His is of the psychic, perhaps.

NIRODBARAN: I may get it unconsciously one day.

SRI AUROBINDO: Unconsciously you may have got it already. (*Laughter*)

NIRODBARAN: I couldn't quite follow the first part of your answer about the replacement of the ordinary consciousness by the spiritual.

SRI AUROBINDO: What I said was that withdrawal is not enough. The seeds of the ordinary life have also to be thrown away and one has to get the spiritual consciousness; one has to get to the true spiritual dynamism which is the source of right action.

EVENING

SATYENDRA: There is a difference between the reflection of peace and the descent of peace, isn't there?

SRI AUROBINDO: Yes. The descent of peace is more intense and powerful. Besides, the descent opens the way.

SATYENDRA: For other things?

SRI AUROBINDO: Yes, and also for the ascent.

SATYENDRA: Another question: how can one be free from ego, have a complete release from ego?

SRI AUROBINDO: What do you mean by a complete release?

SATYENDRA: I mean that the sense of individuality will be lost.

SRI AUROBINDO: When one gets into the cosmic or the transcendent, then the sense of ego is lost. Complete release is difficult unless the nature is transformed. When the sense of ego is lost, still the habits remain, the habits of the old nature. Of course, there is no I-ness. One is not egoistic in one's actions, etc., but the habits persist. Even when everything is rejected from all the parts, the subconscious remains and it carries the stamp of all the old things. But one is not affected or touched by these habits. One can see that they are something exterior, not properly belonging to one's being. People sometimes think and say that they have no ego, that their ego has disappeared. But others can see quite clearly the egoistic movements or actions which are not clear to themselves. Y, who is dead now, used to say the same thing, that he had no ego. The more we contradicted him and pointed out to him the truth, the more he would insist. He used to say that he was moved by some Force. That was true, but he was moved by it because it flattered his ego; if it had not flattered his ego, he wouldn't have been moved. He was lacking in self-criticism. You can judge from one statement of his whether he had ego or not. He said, "I alone possess the Truth." (*Laughter*) He was of a rajasic nature and it is very difficult with that nature to get rid of ego.

After this, Sri Aurobindo lay down and addressed Champaklal.

SRI AUROBINDO: Champaklal, I am going to be Gandhi-like tomorrow. I will wear a dhoti high enough to make my walking easy and from tomorrow I will sit in the chair and write.

CHAMPAKLAL: And what about going for bath?

SRI AUROBINDO: Everything will come step by step. You don't want me to be like Subhas Bose, do you? (*Laughter*)

5 MARCH 1940

PURANI: While talking on the world situation yesterday, did you say that the Indian problem is no less complex or did you mean our Ashram problem?

SRI AUROBINDO: I said nothing about the Ashram and I didn't use the word "complex". I said "extremely confused" and added that the Indian situation is no less so with its Muslims, Parsis, X, Y, etc.

SATYENDRA: When one has attained to the higher consciousness and is firmly seated in that consciousness, then one can slowly take up any activity without getting disturbed.

SRI AUROBINDO: Quite so.

NIRODBARAN: In the transitional stage till the mind is replaced by the spiritual consciousness, with what attitude should one do his work?

SRI AUROBINDO: What work?

NIRODBARAN: Say, philosophical or political.

SRI AUROBINDO: It is not necessary to do political work. About the philosophical, one has to reject what ought to be rejected from the nature, for example, the habit of disputation, considering one's own idea alone as true and not seeing the truth in other's ideas and taking up an idea because one likes it, not because it is true. That is the nature of the mind in general.

(*After a pause*) In my own case so long as I was in the mind I couldn't understand philosophy at all. I tried to read Kant but couldn't read more than one page. Plato, of course, I read. But it was only when I went above the mind that I could understand philosophy and write philosophy. Ideas and thoughts began to flow in, visions and spiritual experience. Insight and spiritual perception, a sort of revelation built my philosophy. It was not by any process of mental reasoning or argument that I wrote the *Arya*.

NIRODBARAN: Then you didn't try by the mind to understand?

SRI AUROBINDO: As I said, I read only one page of Kant and then gave it up, because it wouldn't go in: that is, it didn't become real to me. I was like Manilal grappling with *The Life Divine*. Plato I could read, as he was not merely metaphysical. Nietzsche also because of his powerful ideas. In Indian philosophy I read the Upanishads and the Gita, etc. They are, of course, mainly results of spiritual experience. People think I must be immensely learned and know all about Hegel, Kant and the others. The fact is that I haven't even read them; and people don't know I have written everything from experience and spiritual perception. Modern philosophers wrap their ideas up in extraordinary phraseology and there is too much gymnastics of the mind – even then they don't seem to have gone deeper than the Greeks in their ideas and theories. I read some of the commentaries of Ramanuja, Shankara, etc. They seemed to me mere words and phrases and at the end Ramanuja says that nobody has experienced Pure Consciousness – a most amazing statement, absurd.

NIRODBARAN: In your case it was an opening then, like the one to painting?

SRI AUROBINDO: Yes; but with painting, it was a moment's sudden opening while this one was a result of spiritual experience.

NIRODBARAN: Then I can hope to understand philosophy some day.

SATYENDRA: You want to understand Kant?

NIRODBARAN: Oh, no, no!

SRI AUROBINDO: It would be a sheer waste of time for him.

SATYENDRA: Then Sri Aurobindo's philosophy?

NIRODBARAN: Yes, and Indian philosophy..Even here there is too much complication; there are so many Purushas and Prakritis.

SRI AUROBINDO: There is only one Prakriti.

NIRODBARAN: Para and Apara Prakriti.

SRI AUROBINDO: What is difficult there? Para Prakriti is nature higher than your own.

EVENING

NIRODBARAN: Will you now have time to finish *Savitri?*

SRI AUROBINDO: Oh, *Savitri* will take a long time. I have to go over all the old ground.

NIRODBARAN: How?

SRI AUROBINDO: Every time I find more and more imperfections.

NIRODBARAN: Jatin Bal is preparing some notes for you on Einstein's relativity.

This led to a talk on relativity between Sri Aurobindo and Purani who brought in Riemann's name as a famous mathematician.

SRI AUROBINDO: Euclid was bad enough. When Riemann came in, it was time for me to give up mathematics.

6 MARCH 1940

In the Prabartak *of January 1940, M translated into English his article "Life's Companion" in which there is reference to Sri Aurobindo. Purani read out portions of the article.*

PURANI: "He (Sri Aurobindo) used to raise the topic of Vasudeva, Pradyumna, etc., and explain the subject with emotion."

SRI AUROBINDO: I didn't know that I had any emotion during my explanation.

PURANI: "I used to read all my articles to him. *Udbodhan,* a dramatic composition, I read from start to finish."

SRI AUROBINDO: Good Lord! It would have been a wonder if I could stand it to the end.

PURANI: "He would freely relate how he stayed in the air in meditation."

SRI AUROBINDO: Good Lord! That legend seems to be going to last.

PURANI: "I heard from his lips that Ramakrishna sat before him consoling him when he was arrested at Grey Street."

SRI AUROBINDO: When? That is another story.

PURANI: "He would relate how the hard iron bars of the prison felt soft like butter..."

SRI AUROBINDO: Romantic!

PURANI: "... and the devilish figures of thieves."

SRI AUROBINDO: Devilish? I never used that word. It is his imagination. They were not devilish figures, but like human beings. He is an imaginative fellow, of course not like Dutt.

PURANI: "We feared that if he stayed long in one place, his concealment would come to light."

SRI AUROBINDO: That is true.

PURANI: "He was removed unexpectedly. People knew that he had gone to the Himalayas for Sadhana."

SRI AUROBINDO: Good Lord!

PURANI: "I was charged with taking him in a carriage to the southern border of the town. It was midnight. I found that the coachman was asleep. With great caution I brought out the horses etc... I handed over Sri Aurobindo to the gentleman as already arranged."

SRI AUROBINDO: I don't remember about all that; it may be true. I know that I was to be handed over to somebody in whose house there was Saraswati Puja.

PURANI: "Then I drove back home and informed my wife of the whole affair. She asked, 'The coachman didn't know?' 'No', I replied. 'A serious thing,' she said; 'then a thief might take away the carriage.' 'All this due to Sri Aurobindo's saintliness.' I added. She concluded saying, 'Everything is a big event with you. Do go to sleep.'" (*Laughter*)

SRI AUROBINDO: She has more common sense. I knew that he was imaginative, but not inventive. I thought that inventiveness was reserved for Dutt.

SATYENDRA: He must have achieved something in order to be able to hold so many people together.

SRI AUROBINDO: Yes, it was the vital force that he got from me and he had some experiences too. He claimed to have gone above the head but there was no manifestation in his expression, there was no mental result. He wanted to go for the Supermind but when the demands were made on him he drifted away.

NIRODBARAN: We heard that his Adhar was small. How could he then receive your Force?

SRI AUROBINDO: Why not? Do you mean to say that because a man is small, he will always remain small? "Small" means he got no expansion.

NIRODBARAN: He was in contact with you for a short period only; about three or four years, wasn't he?

SRI AUROBINDO: No; I stayed in his house for a month; he came here three or four times.

PURANI: He was in contact for more than ten or twelve years. The last time I met him, in 1918 perhaps, he said that he was getting direct guidance and inspiration from you.

NIRODBARAN: Was it as a result of the development of his spiritual consciousness or by your Force that he achieved so much?

SRI AUROBINDO: It was his vital opening to the Force I gave him.

NIRODBARAN: And spiritual?

SRI AUROBINDO: Very mixed.

NIRODBARAN: Then you gave him the Force for the vital?

SRI AUROBINDO: I gave it for both.

SATYENDRA: But his vital opened.

SRI AUROBINDO: Yes, it was an opening into a larger consciousness, the cosmic vital, the force for action and movement. It was all my plan and idea I gave him when I left that he worked out.

PURANI: Yes, he got all the help from your name and association.

SRI AUROBINDO: Yes, he described himself as my spiritual agent in Bengal.

SATYENDRA: Everybody knew that he was connected with you.

SRI AUROBINDO: He said at one time that his body was burning and his head was on fire – it was true – and that disappeared by
his contact with me.

CHAMPAKLAL: When the Mother first saw him, she is supposed to have said that he was wonderful.

SRI AUROBINDO: Wonderful? I don't know about that; at least
Mother didn't tell me. R said that he would be wonderful in
America.

SATYENDRA: That takes away much of the compliment.
(*Laughter*)

SRI AUROBINDO: It was because of his energy and eloquence
that R said that.

NIRODBARAN: There is authentic evidence about the Hanu-
mant Rao cures. He himself has written a letter.

SRI AUROBINDO (*seeing the address*): It is Mother's letter. It has
been addressed to her.

NIRODBARAN: Yes; it has been sent to be read to you.

SRI AUROBINDO: Who has decided that? Mother's letters
should go to her.

CHAMPAKLAL: Isn't it the same?

SRI AUROBINDO: Read it.

*Nirodbaran read the letter and there were instances of Rao's miraculous
cures of madness, snakebites, etc., by using the Mother's Force, by the
stretching of his right and left hands.*

SRI AUROBINDO: There is no mention of leprosy.

NIRODBARAN: No.

SRI AUROBINDO: It is the vital force. There were many such
cases of cures by placing the hand on the head. They used to call it
the passage of fluid magnetism into the body.

CHAMPAKLAL: He says it is the Mother's Force.

SRI AUROBINDO: Why shouldn't it be?

NIRODBARAN: You said vital force.

SRI AUROBINDO: Yes, force acting through the vital. It is the
vital-physical force; being nearer the physical it has a more powerful
effect in such cases. One can cure by mental power also, but that
requires more power of concentration.

PURANI (*smiling, from behind*): Nirod wants such a force!

SRI AUROBINDO: Stretching the right hand and the left?

NIRODBARAN: My problem is solved. Sri Aurobindo has said that the vital has to be pure first in order to get intuition.

PURANI: That is for intuition but this is cure by the Force, not by medicine.

NIRODBARAN: For both, purity, seems to be necessary.

SRI AUROBINDO: Without purity you may become egoistic. Otherwise plenty of people cure without purity.

NIRODBARAN: That's what I was going to ask – why should it be necessary?

SRI AUROBINDO: To have vital purity? (*Laughter*)

NIRODBARAN: No, to have that first to be able to cure. Both can go together.

EVENING

SRI AUROBINDO (*addressing Purani*): What has become of your thief?

PURANI: Which thief? The one with the bag of husk?

SRI AUROBINDO: Yes.

PURANI: He has been released. It was not important. The police said that it was done under the effect of wine. (*Laughter*)

SRI AUROBINDO: He felt inspired? (*Laughter*)

PURANI: Perhaps. Mother has again taken him into service. (*Sri Aurobindo laughed.*)

PURANI: Amrita's servant has stood guarantee for him.

SATYENDRA: And who stood guarantee for Amrita's servant? (*Laughter*)

PURANI: They have made a good collection for the Red Cross. Dr. André and his chief were members. It is Rs. 8000.

SATYENDRA: It depends on who collects.

SRI AUROBINDO: And if the Governor writes the names of persons, they can't but pay.

SATYENDRA: Have we paid anything?

SRI AUROBINDO: No, they didn't come to us. Mother set apart a sum for them.

NIRODBARAN: How much did André contribute?

PURANI: I don't know. He can't pay much. He has bought a plot of land beside his house.

SRI AUROBINDO (*smiling*): You don't want to insinuate that he gathers money in this way for his personal use? (*Laughter*)

PURANI: No, I meant that he can't pay much just now.

SRI AUROBINDO: The incident coming just after the collection made me think that you wanted to suggest that. (*Laughter*)

PURANI: No, no.

SATYENDRA: I don't see why people should contribute to this war. One doesn't know when it will end or what results it will bring to people. These people themselves are responsible for the war. Germany is more bitter against England.

SRI AUROBINDO: Yes, it is mainly England who is responsible. After the conquest of the last war it was England who set Germany on foot again to play against France, it being the biggest power in Europe. Now England will again court Germany after this war.

7 MARCH 1940

NIRODBARAN: A letter from Charu Ghose. Do you remember he wrote asking your blessings and you inquired, "Who is he?"

SRI AUROBINDO: Yes, who is he?

NIRODBARAN: He replied, "I am an ordinary man, a clerk, aged fifty-one. I have no other relation except my wife. I could get no learning."

SRI AUROBINDO: Ideal condition for Yoga. He is extraordinary in having no learning but ordinary in having no children.

NIRODBARAN: Then a question comes, "Is there anything more than what I have understood after reading Sri Aurobindo's books? I want to practise the Yoga of surrender by the help of his force and knowledge." So what's the answer?

SRI AUROBINDO: Has he done any Yoga? He speaks of surrender. So he may know something. He can be asked what he has understood of my works.

NIRODBARAN: That is a question difficult to answer.

SRI AUROBINDO: I mean what he has understood practically and not philosophically of the Yoga of self-surrender.

NIRODBARAN: While in England I read your book *The Yoga and Its Objects*. I thought, "Why, it is very easy." (*Laughter*)

SATYENDRA: That book is merely a general statement about Yoga. It was only afterwards, when the Supermind came in that everything was made difficult. In this Yoga there is a perpetual progression, no fixed goal or end.

SRI AUROBINDO: There is an end at present.

NIRODBARAN: What?

SRI AUROBINDO: Supermind.

SATYENDRA (*to Nirodbaran*): How do you find it now?

NIRODBARAN: Well, I am paying for that facile thought about Yoga being easy.

SATYENDRA: For me it is still more difficult because I have been accustomed to look at the world as unreal and at Brahman as real. Now I have to accept the world, which the mind refuses to do, having been trained for such a long time in the other principle.

SRI AUROBINDO: For that reason I had to write three volumes of *The Life Divine*. Otherwise, as Nirod says, Yoga would be easy.

NIRODBARAN (*to Satyendra*): It is no less difficult for us. To you Brahman is real, the world is unreal and for us it is the other way round. (*Laughter*) So the difficulty is the same.

SATYENDRA: No, Sri Aurobindo has said that the denial of the materialist is not so hard to overcome as the refusal of the ascetic.

Since your talk on X in connection with politics, Dr. Becharlal has given up reading newspapers. He reads only the headlines.

CHAMPAKLAL: Is that why Satyendra is always putting papers by his side?

SRI AUROBINDO (*laughing*): I didn't mean it for him, I myself read newspapers and enjoy whatever is interesting. For instance, Abdulla Haroon says that each minority is an independent nation. Of course Muslims first – but Harijans are also a nation. (*Laughter*)

SATYENDRA: Dr. Alam also seems to be going over to the League. He says now it is a question of distribution.

SRI AUROBINDO: Yes, he says the fight is now not against the Government but between Hindus and Muslims. The cake is already there; the question is how to distribute it.

SATYENDRA: He says that all Muslims should join the League to combat the Congress objection that the League is not the only Muslim organisation.

SRI AUROBINDO: It is like the fox which had lost its tail asking others to do the same.

K3

8 MARCH 1940

NIRODBARAN: Nishikanto has passed a distressing night. He says that whatever little faith and devotion he had has left him. Now the physical also, with which he wanted to serve the Divine, is out of gear. So he is getting depressed.

SRI AUROBINDO: Why depression? The thing is to get cured.

NIRODBARAN: He doesn't believe he will be cured. He was thinking he would go where his eyes took him.

SRI AUROBINDO: In English they say: "To follow your nose." But what is his complaint at present?

NIRODBARAN: Pain. Pain is constant though he doesn't feel it. (*Laughter*)

SRI AUROBINDO: How is that? If he doesn't feel it, how can there be pain?

NIRODBARAN: I don't understand either. He says that with any jerk the pain comes.

SRI AUROBINDO: Oh, he means that. But one can get spiritual experiences in illness too. The illness doesn't stand in the way of getting spiritual experiences.

PURANI: Besides, what is there to be depressed about? Punnuswamy had ulceration and he lived only on milk for quite a number of years and yet he has been doing Yoga.

NIRODBARAN: Yes, he has faith. Nishikanto has lost his faith. His faith comes with a cure and goes with an illness. (*Laughter*)

CHAMPAKLAL: How can permanent faith be established?

SRI AUROBINDO: By having it permanently. (*Laughter*)

CHAMPAKLAL: I mean, does it depend on experience, growth of consciousness and other things, or is it inborn?

SRI AUROBINDO: All that. Some people have full faith from the beginning.

CHAMPAKLAL: How? Acquired from a previous birth?

SRI AUROBINDO: Yes, or owing to Karma or consciousness. Some have faith at the end. Some go on doubting even after having experiences.

CHAMPAKLAL: All have faith in that way.

SATYENDRA: If all had faith, everybody would come to do Sri Aurobindo's Yoga. (*Laughter*)

SRI AUROBINDO: Or they have faith but they don't feel it — like Nishikanto's pain. That is a splendid statement.

NIRODBARAN: Somebody had a vision in meditation. Above his head was projected the cornice of a building and the cornice was covering the sun far up high but the rays of the sun had illuminated the sky on the opposite side of the cornice. Any meaning?

SRI AUROBINDO: It is very simple. The vision is symbolic. The building is the mental construction. The cornice is the roof. The mental building is coming between the mind and the sun of Truth.

PURANI (*pointing at Nirodbaran from behind Sri Aurobindo and laughing*): It is his own vision probably.

SRI AUROBINDO (*to Nirodbaran*): Is the "somebody" yourself?

NIRODBARAN: Yes.

SRI AUROBINDO: That is very promising.

NIRODBARAN: How?

SRI AUROBINDO: It means the crust is going away.

NIRODBARAN: But the sun is far, far away. (*Laughter*)

A wasp had built a nest behind one of the paintings in Sri Aurobindo's room and it was constantly coming and going. P broke the nest and threw away two pupas. Sri Aurobindo remarked that the Jains would object to it. P said, "Yes, violently."

9 MARCH 1940

SATYENDRA: Do ascent and descent of consciousness take place only through the head?

SRI AUROBINDO: No, they can take place through the lower centres also.

SATYENDRA: Nirod had the idea that they happen only through the head. I was thinking of Sahana's experience of ascent and descent.

SRI AUROBINDO: Did she have that experience?

NIRODBARAN: The one we told you about.

SRI AUROBINDO: Oh that? Her usual ascent-descent?

NIRODBARAN: Yes.

SRI AUROBINDO: That is different. That is common among most people who have an opening. That is the ascent and descent of one's own consciousness, while what I am speaking of is the whole being going up to the Divine Consciousness and coming down with it.

NIRODBARAN: The distinction is still not very clear.

SRI AUROBINDO: In the usual experience, it is one's habitual consciousness that rises: it may be any part of the being, the mental, vital or physical, that goes up to the higher planes above the mind and stays there for a time; some organisation takes place and then the consciousness comes down with some result. In the ascent and descent about which I have written in *The Life Divine*, the whole being – you may call it the Self – goes up, say, to the Overmind, settles there and meets the Divine and then the descent of the Divine takes place. Obviously this is more difficult.

SATYENDRA: Is descent easier than ascent?

SRI AUROBINDO: Yes.

NIRODBARAN: I thought it was through the head alone that both happen.

SRI AUROBINDO: It is usually through the mind, when the mental consciousness goes up, but it can happen otherwise also, the vital or physical consciousness directly going up without passing through the mental.

NIRODBARAN: Sahana's experience of ascent and her feeling of nothingness and then her return with the sense of a flame in the heart – is it an experience of an ascent through the heart?

SRI AUROBINDO: I don't remember well. In her case it wouldn't be through the mind. But all the same it is a major ascent into the spiritual consciousness.

SATYENDRA: I had also the experience of ascent through the Muladhara Chakra before doing any Yoga.

SRI AUROBINDO: That is the physical consciousness ascending.

NIRODBARAN: It would be nice to have this experience of ascent and descent.

SRI AUROBINDO: Remove that "cornice"!

PURANI: One Pradhan, an M.L.C. of Bombay, has written a letter asking for darshan and wanting to meet you. He says he had the privilege of translating your speech at the Surat Congress and that you may know him.

SRI AUROBINDO: How can I know him? Anyone could stand up and translate my speech. You can tell him that I give only silent darshan three times a year. It won't be true to say that I don't talk with my disciples. (*Laughter*)

EVENING

SATYENDRA: If the Supermind is involved in matter, why should the divine intervention and descent be necessary? It can evolve by itself.

SRI AUROBINDO: There was intervention in the evolution of the mind too and so will there be for the Supermind. The forces of the Inconscience are too strong. That is why the intervention is needed. Otherwise in the ordinary course of evolution it would take a very long time. The forces of the Inconscience are there to prevent any premature evolution and they exert a strong downward pull. There is also an upward pull. Mind and Supermind are involved in matter just as they are in the Superconscience. It is by waking up their corresponding forces below by the upward pull and the corresponding force mounting up and meeting those from above that the evolution can be complete.

PURANI: Is spiritual experience possible without the awakening of the psychic?

SRI AUROBINDO: What do you mean by the awakening? The psychic may be simply awake or it may take command of the being. But spiritual experience is not possible without the psychic awakening – occult experience can occur without it.

NIRODBARAN: Then, when the experiences stop, it means that the psychic has gone to sleep.

SRI AUROBINDO: It may be the overactivity of the other parts that stops them.

NIRODBARAN: In our own case I don't see any overactivity due to which they could have stopped.

SRI AUROBINDO: In your case it may be underactivity. (*Laughter*) But you had the experience of the "cornice"!

NIRODBARAN: Is there some decision by the Higher Force to stop experiences in this or that fellow because they may be bad for him? (*Laughter*)

PURANI: He thinks his experiences have been intentionally stopped.

NIRODBARAN: But can't it be true that when work goes on in some plane, for example, the subconscient, experiences may get suspended?

SRI AUROBINDO: Of course. Not only the subconscient but also the physical. It all depends on how far one has gone.

10 MARCH 1940

PURANI: A Kashmiri Brahmachari has come for Darshan. He was lying near the gate at night. He seems to have done Rajayoga and had some experiences.

SATYENDRA: He seems to be a fine personality.

NIRODBARAN: Person or personality?

SATYENDRA: Personality – the physical –

SRI AUROBINDO: Oh, the physical?

SATYENDRA: I was more concerned about his belongings. Somebody could have taken them away while he was sleeping outside the gate.

SRI AUROBINDO: You mean some of our innocent servants who don't know what they are doing? (*Laughter*)

PURANI: He says he has lost his peace and has come in search of it.

SRI AUROBINDO: For peace he can go to Ramana Maharshi. When people come here for peace I always ask them to go to him.

NIRODBARAN: Why? Can't they get peace here?

SATYENDRA: They may even lose whatever peace they have!

SRI AUROBINDO: They may get disturbed by the complex working here.

SATYENDRA: Here peace is not the main object. In the Mother's *Conversations*, the first thing she says is: "What do you want Yoga for? For peace? It is not enough." At the Maharshi's place it is different. People do get peace there because it is almost the main thing.

CHAMPAKLAL: One really can't get peace here if one wants it?

SRI AUROBINDO: It depends on the person. Europeans who come here get peace, they say. It is because they come with an agitated mind, I suppose.

DR. RAO: I am so glad, Sir, to see you sitting and writing. In August you will be able to give us blessings.

SRI AUROBINDO: I am giving them even now.

SATYENDRA: He is speaking of all the people, as in the past.

CHAMPAKLAL: There is no more chance for that.

SATYENDRA: Why? Why do you close the door like that? (*Sri Aurobindo smiled.*)

CHAMPAKLAL: How can it be possible with so many people? Even without an accident the blessings would have been stopped some day. The accident served as an excuse.

SRI AUROBINDO: Do you mean I broke my leg to stop the blessings? (*Laughter*)

CHAMPAKLAL: No, no, I don't mean that.

NIRODBARAN: It's like Dr. Becharlal's remark. He said that he had been aspiring and aspiring to hear you, to talk with you, and now with your accident he has been lucky.

SRI AUROBINDO: Dr. Manilal also wanted to hear my voice.

SATYENDRA: I too and everyone wanted that. We all hope that some day you will come out; everybody will hear you talk and see you.

SRI AUROBINDO: Supermind – that has to come first.

NIRODBARAN: But who knows – after Supermind comes you may busy yourself with something else.

SATYENDRA: The Mother also is gradually withdrawing. There is practically no physical contact.

SRI AUROBINDO (*looking at Nirodbaran*): Wasn't it Dilip who said that after the withdrawal of the contact he was progressing more?

NIRODBARAN: Progressing? He seems to have said that the physical contact is not the main thing. At first he was very upset, then got accustomed perhaps.

SATYENDRA: One gradually gets accustomed to anything.

SRI AUROBINDO: Like getting accustomed to blackouts? (*Laughter*)

PURANI: In blackouts it is the blind men who are the most useful. Being accustomed to darkness they know all the ways and so they can lead the others.

SRI AUROBINDO: So it is a case of the blind leading not the blind but the seeing!

CHAMPAKLAL: I know a blind Sadhu who could recognise by the sound whether it was a one-anna piece or a two-anna one.

SATYENDRA: He acquired a money-sense.

SRI AUROBINDO: Was it the only sense he was aware of?

CHAMPAKLAL: By their footsteps he could know persons.

SRI AUROBINDO: Footsteps, of course. Everybody has his own peculiar way of walking.

SATYENDRA: There is a talk of the Darshan taking place in April now. People are asking us about it. If we say, "We don't know," they get angry and retort, "Oh, you are having Darshan every day and so you don't care." (*Laughter*)

SRI AUROBINDO: I don't know myself. Maybe. (*Purani was signalling from behind to Nirodbaran that there would be Darshan.*)

SATYENDRA: Purani knows.

SRI AUROBINDO: He does?

PURANI: There is a chance. The Mother perhaps doesn't want to say anything because many people may ask for permission.

SATYENDRA: If the sadhaks know, it's sure to leak out.

SRI AUROBINDO: Yes. Spreading news has become a yogic siddhi. (*Laughter*) Even before anything is decided it leaks out!

NIRODBARAN: We tell friends and say, "Don't tell it to anybody else." The friend repeats the same to his friend and everybody keeps his secret except from one friend.

SRI AUROBINDO: So it becomes a universal secret.

DR. RAO: The swelling of the leg is about the same as when I saw it last.

SRI AUROBINDO: Yes, that is because I am doing the exercises now. At one time it became almost normal like the other leg.

DR. RAO: Perhaps the circulation hasn't been fully established yet and that may also be the cause of deficient flexion to a certain extent.

SRI AUROBINDO: Yes.

NIRODBARAN: What has circulation to do with flexion?

SRI AUROBINDO: It has something to do with it, because after the exercise I feel the joint getting stiff and feel there is no circulation.

NIRODBARAN: That may be to a certain extent.

EVENING

PURANI: The *Hindu* has published a review by Varadachari of *The Life Divine*. Have you seen it? He seems to have reviewed it well.

SRI AUROBINDO: Yes, I was afraid they might send the book to X. Varadachari couldn't have said more within the space given him.

DR. BECHARLAL: Wouldn't X's review have been favourable?

SRI AUROBINDO: No. He is orthodox and not open to new ideas.

NIRODBARAN: A writes that K has sent you a request through Suren Ghose to save him.

SRI AUROBINDO: Save him? What is the matter?

NIRODBARAN: He means spiritually. Kazi Nazrul has also approached with the same request.

SRI AUROBINDO (*smiling*): When K was here he stayed a long time. He used to say, "The movement won't grow, won't grow." (*Laughter*)

NIRODBARAN: It seems his movement is still not growing.

SRI AUROBINDO: He has asked for permission to stay here. But the Mother hasn't approved.

PURANI: The Mother has given permission.

SRI AUROBINDO: Oh?

PURANI: For Darshan.

SRI AUROBINDO: No, he wanted to be a disciple. He was here during the mysterious stone-throwing without any apparent physical agency. He was very frightened and said that Barin and Upen didn't understand the seriousness of the matter.

PURANI: I remember his joke about a Tamil servant. He didn't know Tamil. A servant said, "Terima?" He replied, "What *terima?* I am *tera baba.*"[1] (*Laughter*)

SRI AUROBINDO: He is a very humorous fellow.

NIRODBARAN: Is he Bengali?

SRI AUROBINDO: Yes, his people have been settled in Bengal for a long time, like Motilal Roy's.

PURANI: Prithwi Singh and some others are also practically Bengali.

NIRODBARAN: But they don't follow Bengali customs. They speak Hindi at home.

PURANI: That is not Hindi, I can tell you.

SRI AUROBINDO: Then neither Hindi nor Bengali. One of their ladies wrote a letter to the Mother. It was a queer affair. People become Bengalis very easily. The Mahrattas whom I knew were practically Bengalis – except for their stubbornness.

(*Addressing Purani after some talk on political subjects*) Gandhi has declared that he is not going to be hustled into a struggle. The country is not yet ready. Some paper has remarked that if Gandhi

---

[1] In Tamil "*Terima*" means "Do you know?" but in Hindi, "Your mother?" In Hindi "*Tera baba*" means "Your father."

won't launch the struggle before the country is ready according to his demands, then the country will never be ready. There is some truth in that.

PURANI: Yes, it is very difficult.

SRI AUROBINDO: Not very difficult – as good as impossible.

11 MARCH 1940

SATYENDRA: Jayantilal was asking if a glossary was going to be prepared for *The Life Divine*.

SRI AUROBINDO: Glossary for what? Sanskrit terms?

SATYENDRA: He didn't tell me exactly. It may be: for the new Yogic terms also. Perhaps he wants it more for himself than for others. He finds it difficult, for instance, to catch the distinction between extraterrestrial and extra-cosmic.

SRI AUROBINDO: If it is for Sanskrit terms I can understand. You can't write of Yoga without using Sanskrit terms.

There followed a short talk on R. Purani showed Sri Aurobindo a poem of R's in answer to Yeats' poem "The Lover Tells of the Rose in His Heart".

SRI AUROBINDO (*after reading the poem*): These people write now and then very fine lines. Here's an example: "Embrace the malice in the dragon's fold." It is a really fine line.

PURANI: Here are four lines of J's, as if in answer to R.

SRI AUROBINDO (*on reading them*): There is a poetic competition between Yeats, R and J! When R was sending me his poems, I found some fine lines amidst a mass of nonsense. With his wonderful vital energy he could have succeeded in any line he took up, but his vital being was rather undisciplined.

PURANI: When he showed me his poems I told him to try to improve his form and advised him to see Amal's poems. He saw them and said, "That chip of a boy – what does he know of poetry?"

SRI AUROBINDO: That chip of a boy knows how to write and R doesn't.

After this, Nirodbaran read out two letters. One was from Buddhadev Bhattacharya. Buddhadev had written that he had talked about Sri Aurobindo in his class.

SRI AUROBINDO: How do I come into a class of botany?

SATYENDRA: Perhaps as an example of evolution?

SRI AUROBINDO: From the red lotus known as "aurobindo"? (*Laughter*)

Then everybody enjoyed Charu Dutt's letter in which he said that he would very soon let loose a flood of stories about Pondicherry. This was just what Satyendra had predicted before Dutt's departure.

E VENING

SATYENDRA: I hear that the glossary to *The Life Divine* is going to be prepared by Sisir Mitra. I don't know what precisely he intends doing. Perhaps he will give a definition of every term.

PURANI: It can't be a definition. For the meaning of a term will vary in different contexts.

SRI AUROBINDO: Yes, the meaning has to be taken with reference to the context. A definition ties down the meaning.

SATYENDRA: Other philosophers have well-defined terms of their own.

SRI AUROBINDO: That is why their philosophies are so rigid. One can give only an indication. In spiritual subjects, one can't give anything more.

SATYENDRA: There will be so many commentaries on *The Life Divine* in the future.

PURANI: There won't be much room for them. There is a sufficient body of mental reasoning in the book for everyone to be able to understand it. If the book had been like the Sutras, there would have been more room.

SRI AUROBINDO: Even so, I suppose different interpretations will be made, just as there are Hegelians and Neo-Hegelians. Shankara wrote a brief commentary on the Gita and then there were many commentaries on his commentary. But in *The Life Divine* some of the chapters run to sixty or seventy pages of exposition.

12 MARCH 1940

NIRODBARAN: The Yuvaraja of Mysore is dead.

SRI AUROBINDO: Yes. He had double pneumonia. We had a wire two days back. He had been suffering from high blood-pressure for a long time. There seems no chance now of our getting the goat we had been promised. Krishnalal will be disappointed. Who will succeed the Yuvaraja?

PURANI: His son.

SRI AUROBINDO: Oh, then the son may fulfil his father's promise.

CHAMPAKLAL: They will send the goat all right since they have made the promise.

SRI AUROBINDO: There seems to be a strain of weakness in these Yuvarajas. Sukul, who wanted to bring the late Yuvaraja here, appears to be an unlucky fellow. He had wanted to bring one of the Rockfellers but the man died. And now that he wanted to bring the Yuvaraja he too is dead. The present Maharaja is said to be a pious person.

SATYENDRA: Yes, Sir.

SRI AUROBINDO: In what way?

SATYENDRA: He has no vices, observes religious ceremonies, etc.

SRI AUROBINDO: A moral man?

SATYENDRA: Yes.

SRI AUROBINDO: Is he really an able man or is the credit for the well-organised State due to one of the Dewans? Sir Albion Banerji was the Dewan, wasn't he? He was a very able man.

PURANI: Shivaswami Ayer also.

SRI AUROBINDO: Oh, then he has had a succession of able Dewans.

SATYENDRA: During the recent Mysore University centenary celebrations, one of their boasts was that they had supplied many Dewans to Mysore.

SRI AUROBINDO: I see.

SATYENDRA: Somebody has disputed the date of the centenary. He says that it has been held thirteen years too early.

SRI AUROBINDO: How is that? He must have been an archaeo-logist and has perhaps unearthed an inscription?

PURANI: Mysore is a highly developed industrial State.

SRI AUROBINDO: Are there any private industries?

PURANI: Yes, some are State-aided and some are run by the State itself.

SRI AUROBINDO: It is the private industries that make for the prosperity of the State. The State can only show the way.

PURANI (*after a while*): Belisha is crying himself hoarse!

NIRODBARAN: Purani's raising this topic is rather strange, because I was just thinking of asking you about the same thing. Hore-Belisha is pleading strongly for Allied intervention in favour of Finland.

SRI AUROBINDO: The situation is risky from all standpoints. If they intervene, Russia will send military aid to Germany. So far it has not done so. Only an economic agreement has been made. But if the Allies don't intervene, then after taking Finland, Russia will wait for an advantageous moment to strike at the Allies.

PURANI: Besides, one does not know what Italy will do.

SRI AUROBINDO: Yes, Italy's position is still uncertain.

PURANI: It may decide to join Russia and Germany.

SRI AUROBINDO: Quite so. But if Italy joins them, the stalemate in the Siegfried Line will come to an end. France will be able to launch a direct attack through Italy. The Italian defence is well-known to be defective.

NIRODBARAN: But Germany and Russia seem to have a common understanding.

SRI AUROBINDO: Probably. Even then, if the Allies intervene, they will have to face an attack in the Near East. Russia may attack Turkey and send forces to India. The Allies, though they have some armies there, are not abounding in strength. Of course, they can also attack Russia through Asia Minor. In any case it is a very risky game.

NIRODBARAN: Russia won't stop at Finland. She may try next for Sweden.

SRI AUROBINDO: No – the Balkans more likely. If she had any intentions against Sweden she would not leave the Finland struggle half-finished.

NIRODBARAN: People say that Hore-Belisha may have resigned over Finnish policy.

SRI AUROBINDO: Possibly, though they were said to have had entire agreement there.

13 MARCH 1940

Satyendra brought some photographs of Brahmananda, Balananda and Purnananda.

SRI AUROBINDO (*looking at Brahmananda's picture*): He was not so haggard when I saw him. (*About Balananda's*) He was young when I saw him. In this photo he looks very jolly. (*About another photo of him*) Yes, this is more like him. Who is Purnananda?

SATYENDRA: His disciple perhaps.

SRI AUROBINDO: Oh yes, I seem to have heard his name.

SATYENDRA: Balananda had his Ashram in Deoghar. So Anilkumar and Jayantilal were asking if you knew him and what you thought of him.

SRI AUROBINDO: I saw him only once. He was doing much Tapasya.

SATYENDRA: Our Keshav Shastri has taken a vow of silence and Madangopal's friend has broken his. Ravindra gives me all these stories. When our sugar was being rationed, Ravindra said to me, "Take from Shastri's tin. He is silent, he can't protest." (*Laughter*)

PURANI: He can write, and write stongly, I can tell you.

SRI AUROBINDO: He will consider the sugar-taking an outrage on his silence, but the vow of silence should include writing. Why speech only? Plenty of people don't speak, but they write. Gandhi is one, isn't he?

SATYENDRA: Yes, Sir. Meher Baba too.

SRI AUROBINDO: You can tell Shastri that sugar is not necessary for a life of silence but only for calorific speech.

SATYENDRA: Radhananda also observes silence.

CHAMPAKLAL: But he talks with particular people.

SRI AUROBINDO: Yes, Sarala[1] used to talk a lot with him during their French lessons, till they quarrelled over Communism.

CHAMPAKLAL: Radhananda said Sarala was a newspaper.

SRI AUROBINDO: But not a very reliable one. (*Laughter*)

PURANI: She quarrelled with Kanai also.

SRI AUROBINDO: She quarrelled with everybody.

PURANI: She seems to be staying in a Protestant home in France.

SATYENDRA: I had heard she was staying with a friend.

SRI AUROBINDO: She was, but they started beating each other. So she went to a home where she could talk of Communism and plot against Daladier.

---

[1] The Ashram name of an old French lady.

NIRODBARAN: She departed from India, it seems, because she was afraid of dying here.

SRI AUROBINDO: Yes.

NIRODBARAN: And if she died here she would be reborn here.

SRI AUROBINDO: Do all Europeans who die here get reborn in India?

NIRODBARAN: She wanted to die in a free country.

SRI AUROBINDO: I understand living in a free country – but dying?

PURANI: She was a great eater.

SRI AUROBINDO: Both Suchi[1] and Sarala were great eaters.

NIRODBARAN: They say the French usually are.

SRI AUROBINDO: Not like the Germans. The Germans eat three times more. They are fond of good food. Plenty of French people are abstemious and temperate. The Nordic races are good eaters while the Latins are temperate.

PURANI: The English also are good eaters.

SRI AUROBINDO: Yes, but not so much as the Germans. True, they eat four times a day, but each meal is not large.

EVENING

SRI AUROBINDO (*addressing Purani*): Are the Russo-Finnish peace terms confirmed?

PURANI: Yes.

SRI AUROBINDO: Why did the Finns fight then?

PURANI: They perhaps expected that the Western Powers would help them.

NIRODBARAN: The Allies say there was no official approach from the Finns.

PURANI: That is nonsense. According to the League Covenant, they are obliged to help.

SRI AUROBINDO: If Norway and Sweden object to the passage of troops across their territory, then nothing can be done.

PURANI: The Finns had plenty of ammunition and arms. There was a dearth of men.

SRI AUROBINDO: Yes, both England and France have supplied them with plenty of ammunition.

[1] The Ashram name of Sarala's husband.

NIRODBARAN: By this treaty the Russians will be at an advantage.

SRI AUROBINDO: Of course. What will happen next is the
question. Perhaps Russia will now turn south against Rumania
and Turkey. And that will be world war. For the Allies have
guaranteed Rumania, and already Turkey is allied to them. Then
India too will have to fight Russia.

NIRODBARAN: What about Hungary?

SRI AUROBINDO: Hungary depends on Italy.

NIRODBARAN: Perhaps Norway and Sweden have been threatened by Germany?

SRI AUROBINDO: Yes, it is a frightened self-interest that has
overtaken these people. Each of them thinks that he will be safe,
whereas actually each will be swallowed up in turn. It seems the
Allies will have to fight single-handed, if there is world war, against
Russia and Germany – a formidable combination! As Hore-Belisha
has pointed out, the blockade can't be successful. There are so many
neutral countries on the German border and the resources of Russia
will be available to Germany.

NIRODBARAN: Will Germany tolerate a Russian attack on
Rumania? Germany itself is in need of Rumanian oil.

SRI AUROBINDO: They are both working in agreement. What
Russia wants is Bessarabia, control in the Black Sea, and in the
Balkans, over Turkey. In exchange for that she can agree to let
Germany have Rumanian oil. Russia has plenty of oil for herself.
So she doesn't need it.

NIRODBARAN: What about Italy? She doesn't want Russian
influence in the Balkans.

SRI AUROBINDO: If the Allies are clever enough, they can win
over Italy. If Italy gets Yugoslavia and Greece, she will come round.
If Russia is clever enough, she may attack Rumania first. Turkey has
reserved the right of peace with Russia. But if she does keep peaceful
she will be swallowed up next.

NIRODBARAN: Russia will meet with a stiffer resistance in the
south.

SRI AUROBINDO: Yes, both Rumania and Turkey are prepared.

PURANI: But if Turkey remains neutral, then the Allies can't
help Rumania. They have to pass through Turkey.

SRI AUROBINDO: Yes. The same situation will arise as with
Norway and Sweden in connection with Finland.

NIRODBARAN: What will India do if Russia attacks? India has no army.

SRI AUROBINDO (*after raising both his hands*): Of course it will take time, England will have to shift ammunition and army to India and give training little by little. There will be recruitment in India.

SATYENDRA: Recruitment may not be very successful in the face of Britain's present attitude.

SRI AUROBINDO: But Britain will be more accommodating.

NIRODBARAN: Russia will have to attack through Afghanistan.

SRI AUROBINDO: Yes, of course it will be difficult.

PURANI: Afghanistan, Gabriel says, is afraid of Russia.

SRI AUROBINDO: Yes, she has always been afraid of a Russian attack. There is no chance for the world unless something happens in Germany or else Hitler and Stalin quarrel. But there is no such likelihood at present.

NIRODBARAN: No. That may happen at the end. Hitler thinks perhaps that he can handle Stalin easily afterwards.

SRI AUROBINDO: And Stalin thinks he can deal with Hitler.

NIRODBARAN: German soldiers are better fighters than the Russians.

SRI AUROBINDO: Yes, but Russia has tremendous resources and immense manpower.

PURANI: Somebody said that the Allies have a chance if they fight Russia in the north.

SRI AUROBINDO: Of course. As has been shown, the Russian forces are inefficient. Even the Finns gave them a good resistance. The Allies would have some chance of success – unless they tried to attack Moscow, which would be difficult.

PURANI: Norway and Sweden made it all impossible. Of course the Allies couldn't help through Latvia.

SRI AUROBINDO: Oh, no. That would have been sheer madness. With the combined forces of German and Russian submarines, fleet, etc., they would have been crushed.

PURANI: Did you read Hitler's speech? He seems to have given a sermon.

SRI AUROBINDO: I don't read his speeches. They are the same thing repeated.

PURANI: He seems to see God's hand in everything.

K4

SRI AUROBINDO: Yes, but would he do that if he were knocked down? That would be the test. So far it is the hand of Hitler's God that is in everything.

14 MARCH 1940

NIRODBARAN: Pothan Joseph, editor of the *Indian Express*, has written his impressions of the Darshan of February 21.

PURANI: I didn't know he is the brother of George Joseph. George is said to have read all your works.

SRI AUROBINDO: Yes. But I can't understand this editor's position. He says he is an impenitent rationalist and yet calls Jesus the only Avatar!

PURANI: And he is an agnostic too!

SATYENDRA: He doesn't know himself what he is.

PURANI: A lady of an aristocratic family in Broach has written to you for help. She is the wife of an England-returned man who squanders all her money and doesn't give her any religious freedom. She is a devotee of Krishna and sees him in visions. Once Krishna asked her, "What do you want?" She replied, "I want to have darshan of Goloka." Krishna answered, "That is very difficult." And from that time her difficulties in family life have increased. She also hears voices. Now she asks you to help her to see the integral Being of Krishna.

SRI AUROBINDO: If she hears voices and has guidance, she can ask Krishna himself. (*Laughter*) Do these family difficulties trouble her mind?

PURANI: I should think so.

SRI AUROBINDO: That is why she finds it difficult to have darshan of Goloka.

SATYENDRA: Somehow I distrust these voices.

SRI AUROBINDO: Because it reminds you of "specially favoured people"? There is a true voice that comes, but it is not so common as people make it out to be. Gandhi hears voices only during crises.

PURANI: In times of conflict when he himself can't decide the pros and cons.

NIRODBARAN: X has written, asking for some advice. It seems some Muslim fakir gave him a mantra – OM Hring – twenty years ago. He has been repeating it since then and sometimes 20,000 times a day.

PURANI and SATYENDRA: A Muslim fakir gave him such a mantra?

SRI AUROBINDO: I must say the result has been catastrophic.

NIRODBARAN: Now he wants to know whether he should repeat it any more. He meditates on the Mother in the heart and goes on repeating the mantra.

SRI AUROBINDO: What is the use of repeating a mantra if he remains what he is? He can't have any realisation if he goes on like that.

NIRODBARAN: Shall I write that?

SRI AUROBINDO: No, I don't want him to stop the mantra if he has been using it for such a long time. You may write that there is no need to stop it but he must not forget the other parts of Yoga.

NIRODBARAN: To the mantra he himself added "Salutations to the Guru."

SRI AUROBINDO: Dovetailed it with the mantra? (*Laughter*)

SATYENDRA: He will spoil both.

NIRODBARAN: A has asked to clear some English constructions in *The Life Divine* which he couldn't understand.

PURANI: Olaf also doesn't understand *The Life Divine*. He was telling Amrita, "'Or rather; or rather' – what does all that mean?"

SRI AUROBINDO: He doesn't know English, and what he writes is Swedish English. He says reading *The Life Divine* is all sadhana. Sadhana of hunger and incapacity. (*Laughter*)

PURANI: He says it should be like the Bible: "O ye!"

SRI AUROBINDO: "Suffer the little children to come unto me"?

PURANI: Yes.

EVENING

NIRODBARAN: O'Dwyer has been shot dead in an East London hall by a Punjabi, and Zetland and others have been hit.

SRI AUROBINDO: The Punjab seems to have a predilection for shooting in London. The previous time it was Dhingra.

PURANI: Yes. But this has no political significance, it seems.

SRI AUROBINDO: The right man has been shot but at the wrong time.

NIRODBARAN: All the same, it is good in a way.

SRI AUROBINDO: How?

NIRODBARAN: He has paid for his crime.

SATYENDRA: Moral retribution?

PURANI: It is too late now.

SRI AUROBINDO: Yes, he should have been shot after the Jallianwalla incident.

NIRODBARAN: Perhaps there was no opportunity.

SRI AUROBINDO: Why? There was plenty of opportunity in London.

PURANI: But he was guarded all the time.

SRI AUROBINDO: He would not have been guarded by detectives during lectures. If Zetland had died, there would have been a sensation. And if the Punjabi could have had all three in the bag, that would have been something – ex-Governors, ex-Secretaries of State!

PURANI: O'Dwyer used to write in *The Times* against Congress and Reforms, saying, "I told you so," etc.

SRI AUROBINDO: If after being shot he could say, "I told you so," it would be quite appropriate. (*Laughter*)

15 MARCH 1940

PURANI: Sisir Mitra was praising highly the style of the revised chapters of *The Synthesis of Yoga*. He asks when you will complete it.

SATYENDRA: Its completion should logically follow that of *The Life Divine*.

SRI AUROBINDO: I have to finish *The Psychology of Social Development* and *The Ideal of Human Unity*. Herbert showed the former to his friends. They said it would have a very good sale in Europe if translated. But the danger is that it might be translated in a rather rigid style.

NIRODBARAN: I hear the Mother's French style is very fine.

SRI AUROBINDO: Of course. And it is also very clear. Haven't you seen it in the *Conversations*?

NIRODBARAN: I know too little French to judge.

SRI AUROBINDO: French style is always clear. It is very difficult to translate *The Life Divine* into French.

PURANI: *The Life Divine* will be difficult to translate into any language.

SRI AUROBINDO: Except German. German is the language for philosophy.

SATYENDRA: How?

SRI AUROBINDO: It is hard and abstract.

NIRODBARAN: Kant's language!

PURANI: *The Future Poetry* also may sell well in England and America.

SRI AUROBINDO: Not in England. There the age of modernism is on, and my stand is quite different.

PURANI: Amiya Chakravarti also praised the style of *The Life Divine*.

NIRODBARAN: Dilip finds the second volume finer than the first. He sees the proofs with Sisir and says to him, "Wait, wait. Let me quote this." (*Laughter*) Amiya said to Sisir, "We want something new. Has Sri Aurobindo written anything recently?" Sisir asked, "Have you read *The Life Divine?*" Amiya replied, "No." So Sisir said, "Then it is new for you." (*Laughter*)

SATYENDRA: Has he got it?

NIRODBARAN: He has bought a copy.

SATYENDRA: No, I mean: has he got the divine life?

SRI AUROBINDO: Oh, you mean that?

SATYENDRA: Do you have to change much in the *Psychology*?

SRI AUROBINDO: No – only adding a passage here and there, and one or two new chapters at the end. The *Ideal* I have to recast because of Hitler. He has brought new problems.

16 MARCH 1940

NIRODBARAN: Sahana has given me two letters of yours to her explaining her experience of ascent and descent. She wants to know if the ascent and descent spoken of is the usual one or the major ascent and descent we heard about from you the other day.

SRI AUROBINDO (*after reading both the letters*): The first one is the usual ascent and descent. The consciousness has not got fixed above in the higher planes. It is the mental opening through the head and going up. The second one is the major ascent, rather the beginning. It has to become fixed above and the descent of the higher consciousness has to take place and transform the nature. Her later experiences are a continuation of this, I suppose.

NIRODBARAN: The first letter is dated 1931, the second 1936.

SRI AUROBINDO: Yes; in between she had a lot of troubles and disturbances.

NIRODBARAN: Can't one have experiences during such troubles and disturbances?

SRI AUROBINDO: One can but they may not be of the higher ascent and descent because when such movements take place there comes a turn in the sadhana and these troubles and disturbances do not occur.

NIRODBARAN: She says that now she doesn't get disturbed.

SRI AUROBINDO: Then she has taken a decisive turn perhaps. In the struggle between the vital and the psychic, the vital may have submitted and the psychic may have triumphed. Unless the psychic is not only in front but also strongly established to take control of the other parts, the decisive descent does not occur. There are cases in which even without the psychic opening there may be the ascent. Then the course is a more chequered one. If the psychic is strong, the mind and the vital submit; but it doesn't mean that one has no more difficulties. There will still be difficulties but they are superficial, they don't disturb one so much, and there are no major difficulties in which one is on the point of giving up Yoga. The mind and vital then yield. That is what I call a decisive turn. When the psychic is strongly established the Divine Consciousness can descend and do the work.

SATYENDRA: Her first experience of this kind was in 1931. Nine years have passed. She still speaks of egoism.

SRI AUROBINDO: Oh, egoism! Even spiritual people have some sort of egoism. Egoism goes only after absolute Siddhi. Do you think nine years too long?

SATYENDRA: Life is too short. (*Laughter*)

SRI AUROBINDO: A period of nine years is not too long for sadhana.

SATYENDRA (*addressing Nirodbaran*): What was Sahana's method?

NIRODBARAN: I don't know.

SRI AUROBINDO: Like everybody else she was making an effort and falling down.

NIRODBARAN: She was having experiences in meditation before she came here.

SATYENDRA: I can't meditate.

SRI AUROBINDO: Meditation is a great help because you can get into the inner being and work on the other parts. Not that the work can't be done from the surface, but it is more difficult. That is why people lay stress on meditation.

SATYENDRA: I also had a few experiences. One of ascent, as I have told you. Another of death. I knew that my breathing was going to stop and I felt that I was going to die, while my consciousness was above the head in a sort of an egg-shell.

SRI AUROBINDO: That is not death. It is the rise of consciousness from the body.

SATYENDRA: I had also the experience of Light above the head.

SRI AUROBINDO: The Light has to come down. Then the vital troubles will disappear.

SATYENDRA: The difficulty is that I am still not settled here. Others have accepted this path as their own. I have a great desire for Moksha.

SRI AUROBINDO: In spite of her experiences Sahana was also on the point of going away about two years ago.

SATYENDRA: Of course I didn't have such acute crises.

EVENING

SRI AUROBINDO: About Indumati I may say that Purna "God-meeting" is possible by Purna devotion, full self-giving, so that nothing else matters to her, although she can get guidance from and communication with Krishna without that.

SATYENDRA: She seems to be a Vaishnavite.

SRI AUROBINDO: How?

SATYENDRA: She speaks of Goloka darshan.

SRI AUROBINDO: How does one get it?

SATYENDRA: I don't know.

SRI AUROBINDO: By intensity of devotion, isn't that so?

SATYENDRA: She may be holding Mirabai before her as an example.

SRI AUROBINDO: Yes, Mirabai had the intensity of love.

CHAMPAKLAL: Is there anything like Goloka? Is it real?

SRI AUROBINDO: It is real but it depends on how one sees it.

PURANI (*showing a book by Laurence Binyon*): Binyon praises Chinese art and says about Indian art that its subject matter appeals indirectly, not through the lines and moods of the painting itself, while Chinese art is synthetic.

SRI AUROBINDO: That is not true. I don't agree. Western critics call Indian subject matter conceptual, by which they mean intellectual. Take for instance these two Javanese figures.[1] Javanese art is practically Indian. They express very clearly the attitude of devotion and prayer through the lines and moods of the figures. No doubt, if one paints a man in an attitude of prayer without conveying any such feeling, it is different. Europeans like Chinese art the best among the Eastern arts.

PURANI: He says that in Chinese art there is the expression of the Spirit in Nature.

SRI AUROBINDO: Europeans have no clear idea of the Spirit and the spiritual. What Binyon mentions is the expression of the Spirit of universal Nature and nothing truly spiritual. As I have said, Far Eastern art expresses the Spirit as Nature, as Prakriti, while Indian art expresses the Spirit as Self, the spiritual being, Purusha. That is too subtle for the European mind to understand.

17 MARCH 1940

There was a letter from an outside sadhak regarding his election affair. Nirodbaran read it to Sri Aurobindo.

NIRODBARAN: "You may not be interested in politics..."

PURANI: We are interested.

SRI AUROBINDO: We are very much interested though we don't take part in it.

NIRODBARAN: "The allegation of newspapers is not true that I voted against the release of political prisoners. I voted for it. Neither is it true that I sided with the Government against the censure motion by Congress."

SRI AUROBINDO: Why doesn't he contradict the allegation then? It is absurd to remain quiet when the papers are spreading false news.

---

[1] Wood-carvings which stood on a table in Sri Aurobindo's room.

NIRODBARAN: "I have spoken to my friends and other members about it."

SRI AUROBINDO: He may have spoken to them but he didn't speak to the papers.

Then the letter elucidated why he had taken part in politics, etc. On this there was no comment from Sri Aurobindo.

PURANI: You seem to have relaxed the rule that the disciples shouldn't take part in politics.

SRI AUROBINDO: It is meant for inmates, not for those who are outside. But there also, if they take part in politics, they shouldn't join any revolutionary activities, as that would bring trouble to the Ashram.

EVENING

DR. BECHARLAL: Can one get liberation with desire still present in the lower nature?

SRI AUROBINDO: Yes, why not? One can realise the Self and attain Moksha or liberation in spite of desires.

DR. BECHARLAL: Won't one have to take birth again because of the desires?

SRI AUROBINDO: No, the desires fall off with the death of the body.

CHAMPAKLAL: When one snores in meditation, does it mean that one is sleeping instead of meditating?

SRI AUROBINDO: One may be meditating. One's consciousness may have gone within – it is not quite Samadhi – while the body falls asleep.

CHAMPAKLAL: I ask because very often I have felt that I have gone somewhere and am feeling nice, calm and peaceful but when I wake up I myself find I was snoring or others tell me I was doing so.

SRI AUROBINDO: When you feel peace and calm it means you have gone within. But aren't you conscious of where you have gone?

CHAMPAKLAL: No, only a feeling of going very deep into a pleasant region. And this has been happening for many years. What is the further stage and how is one to get it?

SRI AUROBINDO: The further stage is to be conscious and there is no device for it. One has to aspire and to will in one's waking moments to be conscious. (*Looking at Nirodbaran*) You are wondering how they feel calm and peaceful?

NIRODBARAN: No, because you have already told me that first my physical crust has to go. (*Laughter*)

PURANI: In my case, when I dream, I am very conscious but just as I wake up I forget all about it. But if some clue remains, I can work it out and get back the full dream.

SRI AUROBINDO: One has to acquire the habit of keeping the mind quiet after waking. Then the memory comes back.

NIRODBARAN: X accosted me suddenly and said, "Do you know the cause of Sri Aurobindo's accident? It is due to our mistakes, our egoism."

SRI AUROBINDO: She means I broke my leg and took the sins of all of you upon my thigh?

SATYENDRA: That is the general belief. It seems that the Mother also said something to that effect.

PURANI: If this was said of Universal Nature, it would be more correct, perhaps. Of course we also come in there.

SATYENDRA (*to Sri Aurobindo*): What do you say, Sir?

SRI AUROBINDO: Even in the old Yogas there is such a belief. Some Yogi in the South told another, "If you take disciples, then you will have the difficulties of your disciples to take up, added to your own." Christ said that he took up the sins of the world.

NIRODBARAN: But the accident appears to have come as a blessing because, X says, everybody is now feeling a push, there is a tremendous progress.

SRI AUROBINDO: They couldn't feel the push without my breaking my thigh? (*Laughter*)

NIRODBARAN: X herself is flying.

SRI AUROBINDO: Flying where?

NIRODBARAN: She says she feels free now because of a great suffering she went through soon after the accident: her egoism seems to have become ripe and burst!

SRI AUROBINDO: Oh, an abscess? Does she actually say her egoism has disappeared?

NIRODBARAN: Yes. It has burst, she says.

SRI AUROBINDO: Burst in what sense? (*Laughter*)

PURANI: She seems to be trying to cure Y of his egoism. I told her that it would be a big job for her.

SRI AUROBINDO: Too big an abscess, spread all over the body? (*Laughter*)

Champaklal again brought up the subject of snoring.

CHAMPAKLAL: Except for causing disturbance to others, does snoring harm one in any way?

SRI AUROBINDO: Harm? You mean, is it immoral? (*Laughter*) There is no harm; while the body sleeps, the inner being meditates. It does not mean this happens in all cases. All cases of snoring are not meditation.

CHAMPAKLAL: Why does one snore?

SRI AUROBINDO: You mean why does the physical body snore? For that you have to ask a doctor. Ask Nirod. Why should others get disturbed by snoring?

PURANI: One doesn't if one can get into the rhythm of the snoring. I disturb Nirod when he goes out of rhythm.

SRI AUROBINDO: You mean when he doesn't snore but snorts – and goes from mental into Overmind rhythm or from lyrical to epic rhythm? (*Laughter*)

18 MARCH 1940

PURANI: Hitler's sudden meeting with Mussolini and the postponement of Sumner Wells' return seem to suggest a peace move again from their side.

SRI AUROBINDO: Yes, but if the Allies sell out to Hitler, Hitler will only wait for an advantageous time to strike again.

PURANI: Have you heard of the prophecies of Leonard Blake? A Parsi who had come here has offered to present a copy of Blake's book if we are interested.

SRI AUROBINDO: You can ask for it. Buying won't be worthwhile but if someone offers it we can accept.

SATYENDRA: Among Parsis there are no spiritual men. But the Parsis seem to be quite catholic: wherever they find anybody spiritual, they accept him, whether he is a Jnani or a Bhakta. It is strange they themselves have nobody markedly spiritual.

PURANI: Haven't they got Meher Baba?

SATYENDRA: Oh yes, one example.

SRI AUROBINDO: But this one example is considered the Saviour of the world! Zoroastrians claim to have had seers and magi among them. They ought to have some spiritual figures.

NIRODBARAN: Have you read of J. L. Banerji's death during the Congress election?

SRI AUROBINDO: I thought he had been long dead and I took this Banerji for a different person. Or has he risen from the dead to fight the election? At one time he was a Moderate and stood for compromises. Of course he changed many times. First he attacked me vigorously and then became a strong devotee of mine. Afterwards he turned a Moderate. Perhaps he has come to the Congress now.

NIRODBARAN: Now here are some letters sent by A from his friends. One new friend of his writes that he is very often dreaming about you and, if things go on like this, he will have to forsake his children and start for Pondicherry.

SATYENDRA: It is going to be like the Sannyasins.

NIRODBARAN: Why? People can come here with all their children.

SRI AUROBINDO: Bah!

SATYENDRA: Somebody said to me that you have no sympathy for Sannyasins. I replied that we are practically Sannyasins ourselves, leading a Sannyasin's life, though of course it may be a temporary phase, for our lifetime only, because you want a new creation, don't you?

SRI AUROBINDO: Yes, but a new life has to be based on spiritual experience. I have dealt with that in *The Life Divine*.

SATYENDRA: The very fact that we have an Ashram means that we have to keep aloof from the world for a time. Else we could as well establish ourselves in the world.

SRI AUROBINDO (*smiling*): "Ashram" is only a conventional term. As I said, we can't start a new creation except on the basis of spiritual experience. The starting of a new life has been a strong idea among many people for a long time. Anukul Thakur, Radhashyam and Dayanand had all the same idea.

EVENING

NIRODBARAN: In the *Amrita Bazar Patrika* there is a report that Surendra Mohan Ghose is unanimously going to be chosen as the President of the new B.P.C.C.

SRI AUROBINDO: I am rather surprised. Let me see the report.

NIRODBARAN: Suren Ghose seems suddenly to have come into prominence.

SRI AUROBINDO: Yes, he was so disgusted with dishonesty and intrigue that he wanted to give up politics.

19 MARCH 1940

As usual, Nirodbaran was meditating during Sri Aurobindo's walk. He was in a sort of trance and so he did not know that the walking was over and the Mother had been waiting. After she left and Nirodbaran opened his eyes, Sri Aurobindo commented:

SRI AUROBINDO (*smiling*): Deep trance?

NIRODBARAN: Just at the last moment. But I don't know if it can really be called a trance: something was happening inside.

SRI AUROBINDO: It is a trance all the same: you know that you were somewhere but don't know where. That alone is not enough; you must know where you went.

NIRODBARAN: I tried again for intuition but as usual failed.

SATYENDRA (*smiling*): Nirod is trying the straight path through intuition.

NIRODBARAN: To Supermind?

SATYENDRA: Yes.

SRI AUROBINDO (*laughing*): I am afraid the straight path is the longest.

NIRODBARAN: Satyendra tells me that instead of trying for the Supermind I should try to realise the Self first. The other is a very long path. (*Sri Aurobindo began to smile.*)

SATYENDRA: I was just going to say that again. You are trying for intuition but you don't get it.

NIRODBARAN: But I get the trance.

SRI AUROBINDO: And it may lead to intuition.

NIRODBARAN: My trance is only for a short time.

SRI AUROBINDO: How do you know? In a trance one has no sense of time.

NIRODBARAN: Yes, but here I was quite awake and saw the time: 11.20 a.m., and I expected that you would stop walking at any moment. Then suddenly I went off and woke up at 11.25.

SATYENDRA: The word "trance" is rather vague; it doesn't convey the real sense.

SRI AUROBINDO: Why? In English that is the only word. "Trance" means the loss of outer consciousness and going within. One can't say all that every time. Of course, as with Samadhi, there are many kinds of trances.

NIRODBARAN: I read somewhere that a patient under chloroform was watching his own operation from above.

SRI AUROBINDO: That is the rising of the consciousness out of the body. In hypnotism the subjects can know all their experiences and under chloroform they can do the same. During fever one can have vital experiences.

NIRODBARAN: How? There is no loss of outer consciousness then.

SRI AUROBINDO: The non-physical centres get excited. We can use our favourite term, "physical crust", and say that it temporarily becomes thin and the centres just below it become active.

PURANI: The English writer Hilaire Belloc has said that Germany will make a strong attempt to break through the Maginot Line. Once it breaks through it, France will be vulnerable.

SRI AUROBINDO: It was German generals who were against any such attempt.

PURANI: But after breaking Poland so easily they have got confidence.

SRI AUROBINDO: But there was nothing to break in Poland. The Poles couldn't offer any resistance to speak of.

NIRODBARAN: Finland had some defence.

SRI AUROBINDO: Yes, the Mannerheim Line, though nothing equal to the Maginot Line. The Russians could only make a dent.

20 MARCH 1940

PURANI: In Sweden public opinion seems to be in favour of Germany.

SRI AUROBINDO: Yes.

PURANI: That is why no help was given to Finland.

SRI AUROBINDO: Norway and Sweden have become pacific. Of course the Norwegians are not said to be particularly good fighters, though once the Norwegian Vikings went even up to Sicily. The Swedes are known to be good fighters, and in the earliest periods they were a great power; they ravaged the whole of Northern Europe.

EVENING

PURANI: The French Cabinet has resigned. But it seems Daladier will again be asked to form the Ministry.

SRI AUROBINDO: They passed a vote of confidence the other day.

PURANI: But this may have happened yesterday. Some three hundred members remained neutral. They seem to be dissatisfied with the war policy and also the dictatorial power of Daladier. Daladier refused to appoint new ministers.

SRI AUROBINDO: What do they expect in war-time? One has to be dictatorial.

PURANI: They also want a more vigorous action.

SRI AUROBINDO: What vigorous action? Attacking the Siegfried Line?

SATYENDRA: But how long can this go on? Sitting on the fence like this?

SRI AUROBINDO: What else can be done? It is the nature of this war. What is the use of breaking your heads against a stone wall?

SATYENDRA: That may be, but like this the war will prolong itself endlessly. England and France declared war and yet they are on the defensive.

SRI AUROBINDO: Do you mean to say that for that reason they should lead an invasion against the Siegfried Line? Already Germany has more men than the Allies. And if one million men are sacrificed to Hitler by trying to break the Siegfried Line, then the war is finished. There is no sense in that.

PURANI: Perhaps they are dissatisfied with the treatment of the Communists since the Government has put them in detention camps.

SRI AUROBINDO: Bah! What do they want then? To let them go free and spread a revolution behind the lines? They were plotting against France, taking orders from Stalin and trying to help Hitler. What else could be done to such enemies of the country? Allow them to betray France? The Socialists also agree to the Government policy. When Blum went to London he said that he would have done the same to the Communists – only in a different way.

PURANI: Some people may be saying that Daladier is led too much by Chamberlain.

SRI AUROBINDO: If a quarrel starts between England and France, the war is done!

SATYENDRA: Every day they are spending six million pounds.

SRI AUROBINDO: That can't be helped. It was the same during the last war.

PURANI: The Allies did not want to prosecute a vigorous war by helping Finland. Only Sweden refused to allow passage to their troops.

SRI AUROBINDO: Yes, but the Labour Party was dead against war with Russia. Now they have published that they had kept one hundred thousand soldiers ready to send to Finland under the plea of "non-intervention" – a queer phrase invented by Mussolini.

NIRODBARAN: Sweden says England promised help too late.

SRI AUROBINDO: How can that be? Chamberlain has said that the soldiers were kept ready and they were to be asked for in May by Finland but Finland didn't call because of Scandinavia's refusal to allow them passage.

21 MARCH 1940

NIRODBARAN: I was having a discussion on Avatarhood.

SRI AUROBINDO: With whom?

NIRODBARAN: In a trance, with my own inner and outer selves. The only thing I remember is: "How can the Avatar –?"

SRI AUROBINDO: This is the first time you remember something!

NIRODBARAN: I met X today.

SRI AUROBINDO: Ah! What does he say?

NIRODBARAN: He says he still can't do much physical work. Any strain gives him difficulty in breathing and a feeling of compression in the chest. It seems he was not feeling up to the mark and spoke of "lowered vitality" to a semi-medical friend. The friend gave him a powerful, dangerous drug. He had mistaken the sense of the words "lowered vitality".

SRI AUROBINDO: How? He thought the vitality had been exhausted by numerous erotic actions?

NIRODBARAN: Yes–and he gave him yohimbin hydrochloride with incorrect directions. X took a huge quantity of it and hence the drastic consequences. X says, "It was by a special divine intervention that I was saved."

SRI AUROBINDO: Yes.

NIRODBARAN: A letter from Y. This time Y versus Z. Z has written to Y asking some questions and Y has replied.

SRI AUROBINDO (*after reading the two letters*): When you are doing mental work there is of course no silence in the mind, but things can come to you when the mind is silent and then it won't be mental work. After my meeting with Lele, when I used to give speeches or write articles for the *Bande Mataram*, my mind was silent and things came from above. The mind didn't take any part.

CHAMPAKLAL: You seem to have written to Z that the *Essays on the Gita* was written in this manner.

SRI AUROBINDO: Yes.

SATYENDRA: In fact, the whole of the *Arya* was so written.

SRI AUROBINDO: Yes. Y says that the mind can become truly silent by the touch of Supermind. Why does he bring Supermind in? The mind can become silent long before–without its touch.

NIRODBARAN: If we have to wait for Supermind in order to get the mind silent, we shall all be gone before any silence comes!

SRI AUROBINDO: Quite so. I had the experience long before I knew anything about Supermind. And when the mind becomes silent, things may come from anywhere: from the Cosmic Vital or Cosmic Mind, from above–Intuition–or from within. Some people think that everything comes from the Mother or the Divine. It is a little dangerous to think, as the writer of one of these letters does, that whatever comes to us or passes through us has its source in the Mother.

NIRODBARAN: How to differentiate the sources?

SRI AUROBINDO: You can only know by experience.

SATYENDRA: Why does Y bring in Supermind to get silence? One can get it even by going a little within.

SRI AUROBINDO: That won't be silence but quietude. One can get silence even by concentration. When one is concentrated on a subject, the rest of the mind falls silent and it is only one step more to make the whole mind silent. Of course, to keep it permanently silent is a different matter and is very difficult. When the mind is silent one can get spiritual experiences.

NIRODBARAN: Whatever comes to the silent mind – is it necessarily correct?

SRI AUROBINDO: No. (*Then with a little smile*) People make two common mistakes. Whatever they hear within themselves, whatever comes to them, they say, is all from the Mother – and whatever they receive, they say, comes from above. If things were like that, it would all be very easy.

22 MARCH 1940

NIRODBARAN: Adhar Das has reviewed A's *Songs from the Soul* in the *Calcutta Review* and compared it with Saint Augustine's *Confessions.*

SRI AUROBINDO: It is not a very great compliment.

NIRODBARAN: About the poetry, Das writes that it is too much burdened with mysticism and philosophy.

SRI AUROBINDO: Objection to philosophy I can understand but how can one object to mysticism in poetry?

PURANI: There are many mystic poets.

NIRODBARAN: Das objects to too much of it.

SRI AUROBINDO: But the question is whether the writing is poetic or not. Maybe the book is overburdened with mysticism but if the mysticism is expressed poetically, I don't see how there can be any objection.

NIRODBARAN: Y has sent another letter. He says that the distinctions between the quiet mind, the calm mind and the silent mind are not clear.

SRI AUROBINDO (*after reading the letter*): A quiet mind is not necessarily free from thoughts. Thoughts can come but the mind is free from disturbance. The mental activity can go on in a quiet mind without the mind getting disturbed in any way. It is a negative state, you may say. In the silent mind also, thoughts can come but they are on the surface, while the silence remains behind, watching the thoughts without taking part in them.

NIRODBARAN: In the quiet mind thoughts can come; they can also come in the silent mind. What is the distinction then?

SRI AUROBINDO: In the silent mind, the mind may be completely silent without allowing any thoughts to enter at all or, if they come, they remain on the surface and the activity goes on on the surface while the silence remains intact behind. You can say that what is behind is silent while the surface is quiet. Do you understand? You can call the quiet mind a negative state whereas the silent mind is a positive one. The silent mind is the Purusha and the quiet is the activity of energy or Prakriti in a particular way. My mind is now silent. If I allow thoughts they will come in: they will be just on the surface without touching the silence behind. Of course, if the silence is not strong enough, the activity may disturb the silence.

The calm mind too is a positive state. It is the whole stuff or substance of the mind that is silent in the silent mind. In the calm mind also activity goes on on the surface without disturbing the calmness. It is a sort of fundamental stillness. Peace of the mind is still more positive.

NIRODBARAN: All these seem then to be differences in degree.

SRI AUROBINDO: Yes, but very great differences. I have explained all of them somewhere. The silence of the mind is the final stage.

NIRODBARAN: And the vacant mind?

SRI AUROBINDO: The vacant mind may not be necessarily Yogic. It may be an inert mind, a neutral state and in that condition it may open to anything. Peace and silence in the mind are the result of Yoga.

NIRODBARAN: Y says that he has more or less a quiet mind, not a silent one which can only be had by some descent from above.

SRI AUROBINDO: Peace and silence in the mind are either a descent from above or a welling up from within. But they do not necessarily come from Supermind. They can come from the spiritual planes.

NIRODBARAN: Since he finds silence something very difficult to get, he says it can't be had by any effort but by a descent.

SRI AUROBINDO: That is so, but the descent is not from Supermind.

PURANI: One can have the experience of silence by experience of Sachchidananda in the mind.

SRI AUROBINDO: Of course. Didn't he have the experience?

NIRODBARAN: I don't know. He doesn't understand how the mind in transmitting things, can be passive. He says some activity must be there.

SRI AUROBINDO: What activity?

NIRODBARAN: Thoughts, for instance; say, in writing. A descent of light or peace can come directly without going through the mind.

SRI AUROBINDO: In writing also thoughts may not pass through the mind at all. While I was writing for the *Bande Mataram*, they didn't pass through the mind; they either came directly to the pen and I didn't know beforehand what I was writing or they came just like that (*gesture from the head downwards*). Sometimes they passed through the mind which was quite passive. If the mind takes part, then the whole thing gets spoiled. In poetry, it is the activity of the mind that meddles.

NIRODBARAN: The quiet or silent mind I can make clear to myself, but not the calm mind. Perhaps it is a matter of experience?

SRI AUROBINDO: Yes, you have to know the stuff of the mind. Calmness has strength in it. It is the strong man who can be calm, a weak man can be quiet. The gods are calm; you can't say they are quiet.

NIRODBARAN: In occupied moments, various loose thoughts come in. They don't disturb. What is that state?

SRI AUROBINDO: That is the quiet mind. Vivekananda says that one should allow the mind to run on like that and ultimately it will by itself get tired. I don't think it is always successful.

PURANI: When I used to be disturbed, I would read *The Life Divine* and other books of yours. The mind would grow quiet and I would suddenly experience the mental representation of the ideas expressed.

SRI AUROBINDO: Yes, it was the same with me when I was reading the Gita and the Upanishads in jail.

CHAMPAKLAL: People say that Krishna gave the Gita into your hand.

SRI AUROBINDO (*after laughing*): I think I said or wrote something like that. I didn't know that they would give a material interpretation to it.

NIRODBARAN: Y says he has tried for ten to twelve years to get silence but hasn't succeeded.

SRI AUROBINDO: I don't know whether one can get it by trying. It is by a descent that one can get it.

NIRODBARAN: But a descent will only be occasional.

SRI AUROBINDO: Yes, but its effects go on.

23 MARCH 1940

PURANI: Laurence Binyon says that the dragon is a symbol of water. Water is everything; it forms into clouds and comes down as rain and therefore the dragon is a symbol of the Infinite.

SRI AUROBINDO: Why "therefore"? The dragon may symbolise the Infinite by being a symbol of the sky.

PURANI: In China the Infinite is symbolised by the dragon.

SRI AUROBINDO: Yes, as we have Anantanag, the symbol of infinite Time. That symbolism has come from prehistoric animals like the dinosaurs.

PURANI: Binyon says that what Wordsworth has realised in poetry, China and Japan have done in art, manifesting the Spirit in Nature.

NIRODBARAN: China also?

SRI AUROBINDO: Yes, both have the same source of inspiration. Chinese art is greater, Japanese more subtle and perfect in detail.

PURANI: Binyon writes that they lay a strong emphasis on hues.

SRI AUROBINDO: All oriental art does that. The Japanese of course have made beauty the standard in their life. Now European civilization is spoiling everything. Outside people judge the art of the Japanese by their exports, but they export only mediocre things, saying these are good enough for barbarians. Only people who return from Japan bring genuine articles.

PURANI: Binyon also says about European religious paintings by Tintoretto and others that there is too much action in them. In a picture of heaven, for instance, one feels quite outside heaven!

SRI AUROBINDO: That is just what I recently said. Mrs. Raymond, hearing it, remarked that I knew nothing of art.

PURANI: She doesn't see anything in Indian art.

SRI AUROBINDO: She is a modernist. But Raymond is a fine artist. He has something more than modern.

PURANI: Yes, he appreciates Indian art. But both of them like Moghul and Rajput art.

SRI AUROBINDO: Yes, because it has become established. They go by the authorities.

PURANI: Raymond gave up painting for architecture.

SATYENDRA: He has so many plans of the buildings he has done.

SRI AUROBINDO: He doesn't seem to be very practical. Somewhere he built a hotel which was not very comfortable to live in. The owner complained to him that it was not comfortable. And Raymond replied, "Comfortable? Comfortable? An architect is not concerned with comfort. He is concerned with beauty." (*Laughter*)

SATYENDRA: Modern interior decorators also have that mentality. They don't look to the comfort of the people but to their own art.

EVENING

PURANI: Two justices of Nagpur have come on a visit – one Bengali and the other Marathi perhaps. They have brought some books and are acquainted with a bit of Yoga. They say this Yoga is so new that they don't understand it.

SRI AUROBINDO (*smiling*): The newness is a disputed point.

PURANI: They inquired if there were any Marathis here.

SRI AUROBINDO: We have none.

NIRODBARAN: Charu Dutt won't be surprised. He says the Marathis are practical people.

SRI AUROBINDO: So Yogis are unpractical? And can a people influenced by Ramdas be of an unyogic nature?

SATYENDRA: They are said to be very provincial. They will go only to Marathi saints.

SRI AUROBINDO: That would be rather queer. Yogis are above province or country. Yogis can't think of such things.

PURANI: There has been a sudden change in the French Ministry. Reynaud has become Prime Minister in place of Daladier.

SRI AUROBINDO: This unsteadiness looks like a bad sign.

NIRODBARAN: It is said Reynaud is more efficient, has more drive.

SRI AUROBINDO: He is certainly more intelligent. In fact he is the only intelligent minister, they say.

NIRODBARAN: And I hear that he was handicapped by the French capitalists, while Daladier was much under their influence.

SRI AUROBINDO: The French capitalists are very powerful. The Senate is backing them.

PURANI: Have you seen Leonard Blake's book on astrology and his predictions?

SRI AUROBINDO: What I have read of the summary seems to be almost the same as the French astrologer's prophecies. The Frenchman also says that there is a chance of peace in May, but because of some contrary indication it may come about only in September. After the peace there will be a Leftist influence in France and then France and England will turn communist.

PURANI (*after reading a few extracts from Blake's book*): Blake calls Hitler a devil.

SRI AUROBINDO: There lies the difference from the French man. The Frenchman calls Stalin a devil and Hitler human. One can say that Hitler is not a devil but is possessed by one.

24 MARCH 1940

PURANI: Jinnah speaks of two Indian States – one Hindu and one Muslim.

SRI AUROBINDO: Why two and not several?

PURANI: Armando Menezes, the Goan poet, has come. He is publishing another book called *Chaos and a Dancing Star*.

SRI AUROBINDO: The dancing star will be taken for a cinema star. (*Laughter*)

PURANI: Yes, he himself fears so.

NIRODBARAN: One criticism of Nishikanto's book is out.

SRI AUROBINDO: I was wondering why no criticism had been made by anybody. What does it say?

NIRODBARAN: It is by Buddhadev. He says that Nishikanto, by using fine images and rhythms, gives us pictures as well as sound-patterns so that both eye and ear get plenty of joy.

SRI AUROBINDO: Well, what more does he want?

NIRODBARAN: He is lamenting over Nishikanto's exclusion of his prose-poems and also his previous poetry. Bengalis think that his early work was wonderful.

SRI AUROBINDO: I didn't see anything in it. Does Nishikanto think like them?

NIRODBARAN: Perhaps not. Buddhadev says that there are seeds of a great poet in him but they are likely to be spoiled if he remains secluded in the Pondicherry Ashram. The complaint is that he writes in the same way and on the same subject all the time.

SRI AUROBINDO: He surely doesn't write in the same way. As for the subject, others also write on the same subject, their own, though other than Nishikanto's.

NIRODBARAN: These people seem to be too much enamoured of their prose-poems. They think prose-poetry is a great creation.

PURANI: Yes. I wonder how Tagore could take it up.

SRI AUROBINDO: To keep up with the times. Nobody has really succeeded in prose-poetry except to some extent in France. Whitman has succeeded in one or two instances – but only when he has approached nearer poetic rhythm. I read somewhere that modern poets are giving up prose-poetry now and going more towards irregular free verse.

PURANI: Tagore says that his works of this kind must be read aloud to catch the rhythm.

SRI AUROBINDO: Anything read aloud can have a rhythm, even prose.

25 MARCH 1940

On the radio there was news that Alla Bux had been shot at while returning from Ramgar.

SRI AUROBINDO (*to Purani*): Have you found out why he was shot at?

PURANI: No.

SATYENDRA: Alla Bux says that there was a European in his compartment. So it can't be said that Alla Bux was really shot at.

SRI AUROBINDO: Who would shoot such an inoffensive man? One may as well shoot Malaviya or Pattabhi Sitaramayya. (*Laughter*)

SATYENDRA: In Sind the Muslim League seems to have been dissolved and a Nationalist Party formed.

SRI AUROBINDO: There was no Muslim League in Sind. The Sind Ministers appear to be as fluid as the French ones.

SATYENDRA: The French Ministers seem to last about nine months. Only Daladier remained a little longer.

SRI AUROBINDO: About two and a half years. The shortest period of a Ministry was one day. (*Laughter*)

NIRODBARAN: It couldn't be shorter perhaps.

SRI AUROBINDO: Then they can write "ex-Ministers" and hope by that to govern some day.

PURANI: There was a joke in the *Indian Express*. Somebody in England during the air raids wanted to camouflage his house with palm leaves over the chimney. He was asked: "Why palm leaves?" He replied: "The German pilot will then think he is in Africa."

SRI AUROBINDO: There is another joke somewhat similar. Somebody went up in an aeroplane and was trying to learn things. He was calculating where he could be at the time. Then suddenly he told the pilot: "Take off your hat". "Why?" asked the pilot. He replied: "Don't you see we are under the dome of St. Paul's Cathedral?"

26 MARCH 1940

NIRODBARAN: You have said in *The Synthesis of Yoga*, Volume II, in the chapter entitled "The Difficulties of the Mental Being", that there are divine planes in the mental being just as there are divine planes above into which one ordinarily enters in Samadhi. What are these planes? Higher Mind, etc.?

SRI AUROBINDO: But there are divine planes everywhere. It depends on the context.

NIRODBARAN: Here is the passage.

SRI AUROBINDO (*after reading it*): I must have meant the reflections of the higher planes in the mind. Thus, for instance, one may receive a reflection from the Overmind. One may not oneself know it. What is called genius is the reflection from the higher planes – from the Intuitive Mind, for example. But it does not mean that one is living in that plane. There may be reflections in the vital being also.

27 MARCH 1940

PURANI: Professor Attreya of Benaras has brought some "psychic" photographs.

SRI AUROBINDO: Is he a spiritualist?

PURANI: Looks like one.

SRI AUROBINDO: But what is the good of photographs of these things? You know about the famous photograph of fairies by Conan Doyle. I don't know how it was done, because fairies don't lend themselves to photography.

PURANI: There has been one good result of Attreya's visit. KS has broken his silence and was talking with him.

SRI AUROBINDO: It was not due to that. Nolini spoke to the Mother about the silence and afterwards told KS: "Sri Aurobindo doesn't like silence." He at once started talking. It seems he was fading away into the Ineffable – couldn't talk or walk or do anything. Such things happen to those who force themselves before they are ready. They either go into that condition or become rajasic. One kitten of ours became like that. Whenever we used to concentrate, it came and lay down near us and afterwards it couldn't move or walk. With great difficulty it had to be pulled out of that condition. It was a remarkable cat.

PURANI: It was Baby perhaps?

SRI AUROBINDO: No, it was Goldie. Baby was possessed by a devil. While a procession was passing, she got a sudden fit. Perhaps a devil came from the procession and entered her. It is always the kittens that are affected. Old cats are too much fixed in cathood.

29 MARCH 1940

Satyendra was smiling at Nirodbaran without any apparent reason.

NIRODBARAN: What is the matter? What makes you smile?

SATYENDRA: I was thinking, "Nirod thinks himself so important but if he knew how much empty space there is in his body, he wouldn't."

SRI AUROBINDO: It is because of the empty space that he feels important.

NIRODBARAN: What empty space?

SATYENDRA: I was reading a popular book of science where it is said that the empty space between protons and electrons is comparatively greater than between the stars and that the table which looks so solid has more empty space than we know: the very earth we stand on is mostly empty space!

SRI AUROBINDO: But somewhere in the *New Statesman*, perhaps in an article by Haldane, I read that the empty space of the infinite cosmos is not of the same kind as that within the atom. But how do they know that the space between protons and electrons is empty?

NIRODBARAN: Because they can't find anything there.

SRI AUROBINDO: Science is full of emptiness then.

Jinnah has proclaimed his Muslim India and Hindu India scheme which has brought out numerous protests. Savarkar is touring all over India and is getting a tremendous reception.

SATYENDRA: Savarkar says Hindus have never been conquered by the Muslims after 1677.

SRI AUROBINDO: What about Panipat?

PURANI: He mentions Panipat but doesn't call it a conquest. Nadir Shah, he says, couldn't.

SRI AUROBINDO: Because he didn't want to, perhaps. Savarkar has suddenly shot up into a powerful personality. And how does he call Shivaji an emperor? He is no more an emperor than Fazlul Huque. (*Laughter*)

31 MARCH 1940

NIRODBARAN: Nishikanto says that Becharlal has asked for his poems.

SRI AUROBINDO: Why does he want them when he says they are too philosophic and thus unfit for publication?

NIRODBARAN: Nishikanto asks the same question and, besides, he wonders why one who speaks against the Ashram should want them.

SRI AUROBINDO: But since he is asking for them Nishikanto can send them. Criticism is no reason why poems shouldn't be sent. And Becharlal himself doesn't want his criticism to be taken seriously: otherwise why should he ask for poems he doesn't like?

PURANI: Yes, and if the poems are published the public will see that Becharlal is himself going against his own criticism.

NIRODBARAN: According to Bhattacharya, there seems to be a section of the public in Calcutta that says Nishikanto lacks a little refinement in poetry.

SRI AUROBINDO: In what way?

NIRODBARAN: In the use of some expressions like "womb".

SRI AUROBINDO: What is wrong with it? Why do they find it vulgar or unrefined? Is it because it is sexual?

NIRODBARAN: I don't know.

SRI AUROBINDO: But I want to know. The word has been used in all Indian languages for a long time. If you say that such expressions should not be used, that is different. But how are they vulgar? Since when has Bengal become so puritan? It seems to be a Brahmo Samaj influence.

NIRODBARAN: Tagore never uses such words. In Sanskrit they are used extensively.

SRI AUROBINDO: Has Bhattacharya been to Shantiniketan?

NIRODBARAN: But he is a Sanskrit scholar. Why then does he object? Some people object to Nishikanto's use of the word "prostitute" also.

SRI AUROBINDO: Bah! That is too much. In English they use "harlot" and "whore". At one time in Europe, particularly in England, such words were considered vulgar and they were not used. But now everybody is using them. The pre-Brahmo Bengal was also to a certain extent puritan. Moni said that he was not allowed by the teachers to sing in school: it was considered immoral. If music is immoral, then there can be no question about dancing, and yet in ancient India even the princesses were taught dancing and used to dance before the public. Music, painting, dancing, all these were publicly encouraged. These objections have no substance in them: they are just finicky.

NIRODBARAN: Dilip doesn't like the use of "worm, insect, phlegm". He gets a repugnant sensation because he is reminded of their associations.

SRI AUROBINDO: Madhusudan has used such words, I think. In English they use the word "worm"; I myself have used it.

NIRODBARAN: He may not object to it in English.

PURANI: Why? It doesn't give those associations?

SRI AUROBINDO: Should one write only of aesthetic things in poetry?

NIRODBARAN: "Buttocks" too is regarded as vulgar.

SRI AUROBINDO: It is frequently used in Sanskrit. In English one wouldn't use "buttocks" but that is because of the prosaicness of the word itself: the English say "posterior".

NIRODBARAN: Have you seen Nishikanto's song sent to you the other day by Dilip?

SRI AUROBINDO: Yes, what about it?

NIRODBARAN: There is one expression in it – "own dream" – about which there is a dispute. Nishikanto says he has used the first part of it in the sense of the Self, which Dilip says nobody will understand and so should be changed.

SRI AUROBINDO: Yes, it can't be taken as the Self; but I understood it to mean one's self-dream which one can't get away from. It is one's own creation and has not been imposed upon one and one has to fulfil it. In that sense it is all right.

NIRODBARAN: Dilip says that what the poet has tried to express is not important: what is important is whether the expression has come right and people will understand it in that sense. According to him, Nishikanto's word will be understood as "own dream".

SRI AUROBINDO: It is not a question of understanding only. The feeling too has to be considered. We must see whether one feels something even if one does not understand.

NIRODBARAN: Nishikanto says that we have to see the drift of the whole poem instead of considering a single expression taken separately. His whole poem's idea, he says, is that what appears as "illusion" or "dream" is not "dream", it is something real of one's own Self. If that word is changed, the entire meaning will be spoiled. The two words coming together have produced the emphasis.

SRI AUROBINDO: He is quite right. If the word is changed, the lyrical beauty of the poem will be spoiled. One has also to see the implication.

NIRODBARAN: Nishikanto seems to agree with Dilip. Dilip goes too much by the mind: what is intellectually not clear to him is suspect.

SRI AUROBINDO: Yes, he follows the old tradition of his father and others. Here the poetry is trying to be suggestive. In his own poetry intellectuality is quite in place.

NIRODBARAN: Satyendra said that X employed the expression "own shore" in a recent poem; by "own" she meant the Self, but Nishikanto objected and told her that it couldn't have that meaning in Bengali and so she changed it.

SRI AUROBINDO: It depends on the context. (*After a pause*) I don't see how it can be taken in any other way. It seems a fine suggestion.

1 APRIL 1940

PURANI: A poet friend of mine has written that he met X and was impressed by him. He found X to have illimitable Bhakti for the Mother and you.

SRI AUROBINDO: Illimitable? Well, X had a strange way of showing it.

PURANI: Then my friend writes that X has gone very deep down in his consciousness.

SRI AUROBINDO: It is always possible to go down. (*Laughter*)

PURANI: Here is a letter from Indumati. She asks whether or not her Bhakti for Krishna is genuine and how she can dedicate herself to Krishna and pray to him to free her from all bonds.

SRI AUROBINDO: It is a little dangerous to pray for that.

PURANI: Then she says that sometimes she sees Krishna's picture moving. Once she saw that he was very far away.

SRI AUROBINDO: You may say to her that Bhakti is all right but it has to be complete and when it is complete she won't suffer from any troubles. The picture seen as moving means the Presence is there.

NIRODBARAN: Why do you say it is dangerous for her to pray to be freed from bonds?

SRI AUROBINDO: Because Krishna has extraordinary ways of freeing one, and she may not like them. You know the story of Nolineshwar and his father. Because his father used to persecute him, he prayed for his father's death. But when his father was on the point of dying, Nolineshwar prayed again to Krishna to spare him. The father recovered and then he started his old persecution again! (*Laughter*)

NIRODBARAN: Dilip has made two more objections to Nishikanto's expression: first he says that "own" is a pronoun and here it has been used as an adjective, which is not permissible with "dream".

Nishikanto's objection seems to have gone. He has agreed that by implication it can be taken in the sense of "self-dream".

PURANI: Yes, he says that if a hyphen is put, then it will be clear.

SRI AUROBINDO: If a hyphen solves the problem, then put it.

NIRODBARAN: The other objection of Dilip is that the dream is called "disagreeable". How could a disagreeable dream be asked to fulfil itself? Why should a dream of which one is afraid be fulfilled?

SRI AUROBINDO: The poet is not afraid. He thinks he is afraid. That is not an objection at all. The whole argument of our philosophy is that what seems disagreeable is really not disagreeable. It is an emanation of the Self and it can't be an illusion. One has to find one's fulfilment in it or through it.

PURANI: After all, a poet has the right to take some liberty.

NIRODBARAN: Dilip says that this kind of liberty is not permitted.

PURANI: Why not? He himself has taken liberties with the language in his *Anami*, that are grammatically impossible. About one expression, I had to explain to him with all the force possible that it couldn't be allowed and he dropped it.

SRI AUROBINDO: I see. In a novel of Stevenson's a character says, "Opulent orotunda Dublin," and argues: "Why should I say 'Rotunda Dublin' like the others and not as I please?" Now modern writers invent new words: for "beautiful and lucid" they say "blucid". (*Laughter*)

PURANI: That is fine. It can also mean "blue acid".

SRI AUROBINDO: And I have seen "hithery-thithery movement", which, of course, is expressive.

EVENING

DR. BECHARLAL: How to distinguish between self-respect and egoism?

SRI AUROBINDO: There is no general rule. You have to become conscious. If you get angry or hurt, it means that it is your egoism and not self-respect. Otherwise there is no rule by which it can be distinguished.

PURANI: Krishnalal has painted a dog, a Kabuli dog belonging to Jwalanti's son. The colour has not come out properly because the model is velvety black.

SRI AUROBINDO: It is not necessary to make an exact copy of the model. Talking of Kabuli animals, I remember my mother had a Kabuli cat. She had asked a Kabuliwalla to bring her a cat; he brought one, the size of a small tiger. The first thing it did was to kill all the chickens in the neighbourhood. (*Laughter*) I don't know what happened to it afterwards.

PURANI: The second volume of your *Life Divine* is likely to come out in August. Many chapters have already been sent to the Press.

SRI AUROBINDO: Who puts all the interrogation marks on the proofs?

PURANI: If it is the first proof, then somebody from Calcutta may be putting them. Otherwise people who see the proofs here may be doing it.

SRI AUROBINDO: Sometimes the marks are very puzzling. Once I saw a vertical line against four or five lines and one interrogation mark beside it. That's all. No questions are asked. Just a mark is put. I don't know what it means – whether the English is considered incorrect or some omission is felt or there is an objection to the whole statement. (*Laughter*)

SATYENDRA: Perhaps they object to the whole philosophy?

PURANI: Amal was asking if you would be publishing any poetry.

SRI AUROBINDO: Poetry? Perhaps after thirty years. Considering the criticism of Nishikanto's poetry it seems better to write for private reading than for publication. Besides, English publishers say that nobody reads poetry now.

2 APRIL 1940

A critic named Nagaraj wrote an unfavourable review of *The Life Divine* in *The Aryan Path*. We were wondering how he came to do so – whether *The Aryan Path* had asked him to review it or he himself had sent it to the journal.

SRI AUROBINDO: Usually *The Aryan Path* sends my books to Krishnaprem for review.

NIRODBARAN: As the article has appeared in the review columns the journal must have sent the book to Nagaraj. We know what kind of thing to expect because his ideas are well known to us. Our attitude is, "Oh, Nagaraj!"

SATYENDRA: From the very beginning of the review it seems the writer has not understood Sri Aurobindo at all.

PURANI: Possibly he had not even read the book.

SATYENDRA: Even if he has read it, he doesn't appear to have understood it. Who is this Nagaraj?

PURANI: Don't you know him? He is the critic of The *Hindu.* He is a Madhwaite.

SRI AUROBINDO: He can't understand any new ideas or any new interpretation of the old. He considers it a violation of the truth. The *Hindu* has given him prominence.

SATYENDRA: If one understands and then disagrees, the disagreement may be worth considering. But without understanding, disagreement is foolish.

PURANI: May I read out Jayprakash Narayan's statement in court from The *Harijan?* No other paper has published it for fear of the Indian Defence Act. He says that both Germany and the Allies are fighting for new colonies.

SRI AUROBINDO: That is not true for the Allies because they have more at present than they can chew and they are content with what they have.

PURANI: He says that England is fighting to preserve her empire.

SRI AUROBINDO: That is true.

PURANI: "To us Indians," he continues, "both Nazism and British Imperialism are the same. There is no difference between the two."

SRI AUROBINDO: That is humbug.

PURANI: "So why should we fight for an Imperialism which denies our freedom, which holds the same domination over us? It is good that I have been arrested for my speech at Jamshedpur, for it is an important industrial centre. And if by my arrest the workers get more war bonus, I will be satisfied."

SRI AUROBINDO: After getting the war bonus, can they fight for the Allies? If they can't, it seems inconsistent.

NIRODBARAN: Dilip is seeing the proofs of *The Life Divine* and he gets great joy out of it.

SRI AUROBINDO: I see.

SATYENDRA: Obviously – but ask him to see the account sheets and let us know if he gets any joy.

SRI AUROBINDO: They will kill him. (*Laughter*)

NIRODBARAN: Usually he finds proof-reading a dull business.

PURANI: But if one is an author, one has to do it – at least the first proofs.

NIRODBARAN: He has done it and he does it, but he finds it dull.

SRI AUROBINDO: Of course writing is more pleasant than proof-reading. Even in my second reading I missed an obvious mistake like "cact" for "act". (*Laughter*)

EVENING

SRI AUROBINDO (*looking at Purani with great amusement as he came in*): Have you seen the report of the All India Sweepers' Conference at Lahore under Sardul Singh's presidentship?

PURANI: No.

SRI AUROBINDO: They have protested against Jinnah's Moslem India scheme and said that if India was going to be divided they must also have a separate India. I was not quite wrong when I said that barbers also would now start an agitation for an India of their own. (*Laughter*)

(*Still greatly amused*) Chhotu Ram has said that the Sikhs will resist partition at any cost. They will not live under Muslem domination, be it under a Khoja Baniya (Jinnah) or a Hindu Baniya (Gandhi). (*Laughter*) Jinnah is now piping down and saying; "Ah, I didn't mean this or that. They have misunderstood me. I didn't want the transference of Muslim minorities," etc., and he is all praise for the Sikhs.

PURANI: He knows he will get it hot from the Sikhs. If Jinnah maintains his theories he will create difficulty in the Punjab. Sikander Hyat Khan will lose all his support.

SRI AUROBINDO: The Sikhs have very strange names: "Tiger Lion", "Water Lion", "Fire Lion".

3 APRIL 1940

EVENING

NIRODBARAN: B. C. Chatterjee seems to have been defeated by the Bose group.

SRI AUROBINDO: Yes. The Hindu Sabha has got about fifteen seats. Considering that it is their first attempt, it is not bad.

PURANI: The corporation election seems to me more a personal issue.

SRI AUROBINDO: How personal? When the Congress fought the election it was on a political issue, to capture the corporation for the Congress. There was no personal question involved.

PURANI: Bhai Paramanand has protested against a joint electorate in Sind at present.

SRI AUROBINDO: Yes, he has said that a joint electorate, unless established all over India, won't turn out to be good for a single place like Sind where the Muslims are in a majority, because the Muslims being in a majority will get all the seats. Of course there is a provision that ten percent of the votes must be secured from the opposite community but ten percent is not enough. When a joint electorate is established all over India, a minority in one province will be counterbalanced by the majority in another province; so it will serve as a check against majority rule in a province. At present the Hindus may be at a disadvantage there. Of course they depend on their majority districts where they hope to turn the scale. Otherwise unless some provisions are made for minorities, difficulties may arise.

4 APRIL 1940

In the morning, the radio gave the news that Lord Zetland had declared that no reforms could be given to India unless Congress and Muslims came to a compromise.

SRI AUROBINDO (*looking at Purani*): So there won't be any more reforms?

PURANI: No.

SRI AUROBINDO: But why does Zetland stop where he does? He can say that even after an agreement between Congress and Muslims there will be no reforms. For there is the Hindu Mahasabha, the Khaksars have to be considered, C. R. and Nyekar, Nehru and the Socialists have to be dealt with, and then the Harijans!

NIRODBARAN: There doesn't seem to be any way for Gandhi but to fight.

PURANI: Already the Government has started arrests. Ranga Iyer is arrested.

NIRODBARAN: That is the Defence Act.

PURANI: Others will follow now.

NIRODBARAN: Yesterday Nishikanto gave a triplet banana to show to the Mother and asked if he could take it. The Mother laughed and inquired, "Is he starving? He can take it with milk after mashing it sufficiently." This morning he said he couldn't take the whole. Even then there was some heaviness. I said I would report it to you.

SATYENDRA: But why does he want to attract Sri Aurobindo's notice? To have pity on him because he can't take even a banana? (*Laughter*)

SRI AUROBINDO: He seems to be forced into yogic austerity! (*Laughter*)

NIRODBARAN: The vision he had some time back seems to have come true. Once during his sleep he saw a vital being pointing to his abdomen and saying, "That is the source of your strength. I am going to finish it." Then the being struck at the pit of his stomach like a bull with his head down. Nishikanto groaned and retaliated by suddenly giving a sharp squeeze to the being's scrotum. At this the being fled. (*Laughter*)

SRI AUROBINDO: The being appears to have been right about Nishikanto. The pit of the stomach is the vital-emotional centre, which is the source of his strength. But it would be interesting to know what happened to the scrotum of the vital being. (*Laughter*)

After this, Satyendra gave Sri Aurobindo a Bengali poem to see, as requested by Mridu. The poem was written by Jyoti on the presentation copy of her book Red Rose *to Mridu.*

SRI AUROBINDO: She says that Mridu's business is cooking and hers is writing. The "friend" finds the cooking sweeter than poetry.

NIRODBARAN: An old correspondent, a victim of asthma, writes that he is the worst sufferer: he hasn't seen a single asthmatic patient suffering like him, day and night without any respite.

SRI AUROBINDO: Every sick person says that of his own disease. He should be made to live with Suren. (Laughter)

SATYENDRA: And then it will be seen whose suffering is worse!

NIRODBARAN: The correspondent has asked X to write an article on the 'results of Karma' based on the points which he himself has asked him. The questionnaire has many points. The first is: By whom is Karma recorded?

SRI AUROBINDO: By whom? There is our office upstairs.

PURANI: Chitragupta does that.

NIRODBARAN: Point 2: Many people die in an earthquake or a train disaster. Is it to be inferred that all had acted in the same way in their previous births?

SRI AUROBINDO: He means the same way in the past because they all had the same experience now – quaked together? (Laughter)

NIRODBARAN: Point 3: Sri Aurobindo has said that physical death is followed by vital and mental deaths hereafter.

SRI AUROBINDO: I have never said that. I have spoken of the dissolution of the several sheaths. I have already answered such things in The Life Divine. Let the correspondent have a copy of it for ten rupees.

5 APRIL 1940

In the morning news came of C. F. Andrews' death.

SRI AUROBINDO (*looking at Purani after his sponging was over*): These doctors are wonderful. They had given out the news that the operation was successful. Now Andrews is dead.

PURANI: There is the famous joke that the operation was successful but the patient died.

SRI AUROBINDO: This is not a joke but a reality. This is the second case of late. The other was Brabourne.

NIRODBARAN: I don't know why Andrews went to Presidency Hospital. Major Drummonds who seems to have operated on him doesn't have a very high reputation. There were other leading surgeons – even among the Indians.

SRI AUROBINDO: Europeans have a prejudice against Indians but Andrews should have known better. Arjava had a very poor opinion of the Indian Medical Service. He said only third rate people come here as I.M.S.'s.

NIRODBARAN: Why should first-rate people come here when they are well provided for at home?

SATYENDRA: Surgeons sometimes diagnose wrongly and re-move an organ only to find that there was nothing wrong with it.

SRI AUROBINDO: And they can't put it back! (*Laughter*)

NIRODBARAN: There are also differences among doctors. Venkataraman was told by one oculist that needling was not safe for a second cataract. Another said there was nothing wrong with needling. One said saline injections might be tried, another that they should have been tried at the outset only. One oculist said, "A very broad iridectomy has been done; the old-fashioned method was a bad one."

SRI AUROBINDO: And the old-fashioned will say that the modern people are faddists. Who did the operation?

NIRODBARAN: A relative.

SRI AUROBINDO: Relatives will do like that. (*Laughter*)

PURANI: The Secretary of the Muslim League states that the Muslims were originally Hindus. Sikander Hyat Khan comes from Rajput stock and the Secretary himself had Brahmin ancestors, and so they can all claim a separate Muslim India.

SRI AUROBINDO: If they were Hindus, why do they claim anything separate?

PURANI: He also says that the British took India from Muslim hands. So they were the more recent rulers. Somebody from Madras has replied that India was taken from the Sikhs, Rajputs and Mahrattas. The Muslims were already decadent at that period.

SRI AUROBINDO: That is true, though there was still some Muslim rule.

PURANI: The Madras man also says that the argument about being rulers is funny. The Harijans, who are converts to Christianity, may after fifty years claim that because they have the same religion as the British, they were the rulers. (*Laughter*) Somebody else said that if only one district from U.P. was included in Punjab and one from Bihar in Bengal, then the Hindus would become a majority. This present division is fictitious and not natural.

SRI AUROBINDO: In Assam it is like that. Sylhet has been included in Assam only for the Muslim majority there. Some parts of Bengal are included in Orissa deliberately and so also are Birbhum and Manbhum.

EVENING

PURANI (*showing some paintings*): Here is the work of a Chinese painter who has come to India.

SRI AUROBINDO (*looking at them*): They are very powerful and very Chinese.

PURANI: A picture of Chinese generals by this painter has been done in European style. It appeared in the *Visvabharati*.

SRI AUROBINDO: Poor imitation of Europe. When Chinese painters imitate, they produce a very weak result.

PURANI: It is said that the Chinese are the world's greatest artists. Their handwriting is such as to make an artist.

SRI AUROBINDO: Yes, their calligraphy is a good training for the mind and for art. Arabic calligraphy also is very delicate and thorough in detail. The letters and the writings of other nations are too utilitarian.

6 APRIL 1940

PURANI: Nirod didn't quite understand how calligraphy –

NIRODBARAN: First of all, what is calligraphy? Good handwriting?

SRI AUROBINDO: All good handwriting is not calligraphy. Calligraphy is artistic handwriting. Haven't you heard of illuminated manuscripts?

PURANI: Chinese and Arabic books are very artistic, with beautiful borders. It seems William Morris tried to produce Homer's epics like that.

SRI AUROBINDO: The Roman script is too utilitarian to produce a good effect. In England they are trying oriental calligraphy now.

EVENING

As often happened, Champaklal suddenly burst into laughter, looking at Nirodbaran.

SRI AUROBINDO (*turning in Nirodbaran's direction*): Laughter of yogic communion?

PURANI: There is an idea that D. M. Sen of Shantiniketan will be reviewing *The Life Divine* in the *Hibbert Journal*. But Jayantilal tells me that he is a scholar of Western psychology. He hasn't read much of Eastern philosophy. It will be difficult for him to speak on yogic psychology and philosophy.

SRI AUROBINDO: Then how can he do the reviewing? Of course there is plenty of mental psychology in *The Life Divine*, as well as yogic.

PURANI: It is very difficult for these people to grasp yogic psychology. I once wrote that the seat of the emotions is the heart, and a critic sarcastically said, "Now we are to believe that the heart is the seat of the emotions!"

SRI AUROBINDO: Well, where then is the seat? Outside the body? Or in some gland?

NIRODBARAN: In the mind.

SRI AUROBINDO: Mind is an abstract term.

PURANI: They will say, "In the subconscient".

SRI AUROBINDO: That is psychoanalysis. There is also a gland psychology and another that runs everything together.

PURANI: Jayantilal met Jung in Ceylon. He gave him your books to read, but he couldn't find much in them. Maybe because he considers himself too great.

SRI AUROBINDO: Jung has said that India has plenty of psychology.

NIRODBARAN: Amal intends to bring out a book of his poems.

SRI AUROBINDO: But he must not expect to be hailed as a great poet or even to have a good sale.

NIRODBARAN: No, he expects to sell about one hundred copies among friends and realise the cost. He asks if you could write a foreword.

SRI AUROBINDO: Oh, no.

NIRODBARAN: "Foreword" is a misnomer, he says; it is a sort of blessing he wants.

SRI AUROBINDO: A puff of blessing?

PURANI: In order to sell well he must be modern.

SRI AUROBINDO: Yes, and publish in England, and moderns like Spender must recommend him.

PURANI: Amal said he listened to H's radio talk on the Ashram. If one good statement was made, it was immediately counteracted by something quite opposite. For example, he said, "I hear Sri Aurobindo is busy writing an epic – a very good thing, but what shall we do with an epic when people are starving?"

SRI AUROBINDO: When epics were being written in the past, were there no people starving? And surely poetry was not written only for the proletariat? It is the same type of argument as, "Don't get rich when people are poor; don't be happy when people are miserable."

PURANI: Gandhi uses the same argument. He writes against machines, art, etc. Once he wrote from a train to somebody decrying machines and the addressee replied, "I see that you wrote the letter from the train and yet you decry machines." Mahadev Desai, of course, defended Gandhi.

SRI AUROBINDO: He is as inconsistent.

7 APRIL 1940

NIRODBARAN: X wants to bring out a selection from your books and he corresponded with his English publishers, asking if they would publish it. They have said that such a book would have a very small sale in England but they wanted to know whether it would sell in India.

SRI AUROBINDO: A selection is not much use at present. It may have some sale in India but not as much as a whole book on one theme. Selections are all right if one's books are widely read and appreciated. Selections from either a popular book or a popular writer would have a good sale.

8 APRIL 1940

NIRODBARAN: X is asking if *The Psychology of Social Development* and *The Ideal of Human Unity* couldn't be published in England – at least one of them – by his publishers there.

SRI AUROBINDO: Will they take them?

NIRODBARAN: He can write and find out. Allen and Unwin have already included one chapter from *The Ideal of Human Unity* in one of their books.

SRI AUROBINDO: It doesn't follow that they will publish whole books.

SATYENDRA: *The Psychology of Social Development* is being translated into French. If it sells well in France, then in England also there may be a demand.

SRI AUROBINDO: Again it doesn't follow. The French are more plastic and they are interested in these things. Besides, I have already promised these books to the Arya Publishing House. Let them be on their way first.

NIRODBARAN: It seems Dilip also is coming out to fight against Meghnad Saha. He has written a thesis of fifty-four pages!

SRI AUROBINDO: Good Lord! I don't see the use of arguing with a man who is shut up in his science. He is at the same stage where Europe was fifty years ago. Except for Russia and perhaps some Socialists, Europe gave up the old scientific standpoint long ago. We are fifty years behind.

NIRODBARAN: We are always taking up what they give up.

SRI AUROBINDO: Yes, we may turn Fascist when they have done with it. The Khaksars are trying to do that.

PURANI: Yes. And J seems to be financing their movement.

SRI AUROBINDO: Now he has asked them to suspend it and is communicating with the Government to remove the ban.

PURANI: Yes, it is he who was behind the trouble in Hyderabad. He stood against Sir Akbar Hydari.

SRI AUROBINDO: Yes.

PURANI: Sir Akbar says that Hyderabad had no Hindu-Muslim trouble before. It has been brought in from outside.

SRI AUROBINDO: That is true. Muslims from the North and the Arya Samaj brought it there. The British Government can't allow the Khaksars to become powerful, for they want to drive out the British.

SATYENDRA: It is said that the Government is behind the present Hindu-Muslim disunity. Somebody said that this Muslim India scheme won't survive Jinnah.

NIRODBARAN: A hint to do away with him? (*Laughter*)

SRI AUROBINDO: By sending him to the war? How old is he?

PURANI: About sixty.

SRI AUROBINDO: Oh, then no chance. (*Laughter*)

PURANI: But his health is rather weak and poor.

SRI AUROBINDO: Diseased people often live long.

NIRODBARAN: There's a letter from Y to Nishikanto. Y objects to Nishikanto's use of words like womb, prostitute, etc. and says they are unrefined, though he adds that they are found in plenty in Sanskrit. And his own family has Sanskrit culture.

SRI AUROBINDO: Then why does he object?

NIRODBARAN: Can't say. He continues that such sensibility about poetry may be due to European influence from which Tagore also is not free. "Why should Ishwar Gupta be our ideal when he is not even a greater poet than Tagore?" he asks.

SRI AUROBINDO: What about Bengali prose? Are there no such expressions there?

NIRODBARAN: I think there are, especially in modern books. At least in one book which was proscribed for obscenity.

SRI AUROBINDO: Then if they can copy Europe in prose, why not in poetry? European prose contains any number of such things. What Y says smacks of the Victorian period. Europe has moved far away from it. In fact, it has gone to the other extreme. Now they use these expressions for the sake of using them. I don't see why we should be confined to the Victorian period. The point is: if such words are necessary for one's expression, then they have to be used.

NIRODBARAN: Even Z objected to the word "prostitute" and asked Nishikanto to change it.

SRI AUROBINDO: Change it and put "a woman of bad character"? It is not the words so much as the way of expression that should matter.

NIRODBARAN: Nishikanto was asked by his friends not to send any more poems to Z after such criticism.

SRI AUROBINDO: If criticisms are resented like that –

NIRODBARAN: No, not because of the criticism; they say that he has attacked you and the Mother and spoken against the Ashram.

SRI AUROBINDO: He has not spoken against us. Speaking against the Ashram is not an attack on us.

NIRODBARAN: But he has said that by being confined to the limited Ashram atmosphere, the germ of Nishikanto's greatness will be killed and he has also referred to "religious propaganda", the Ashram philosophy, etc.

PURANI: That can't be called "abuse"; it is a criticism of our philosophy, made just as by other people.

SRI AUROBINDO: The book has been published from the Ashram and contains our philosophy. So he has every right to criticise that philosophy. Of course, if the criticisms are hostile and malignant, it is a different matter or, if one attacks us, the question of loyalty and of serving one's Guru comes in. It would be serious even in case of repeated attacks on spirituality. Otherwise, if there are simple criticisms, they are not enough to stop sending poetry to the critic.

NIRODBARAN: Is there any such criticism in Gujarat against Pujalal?

PURANI: No, not yet.

SRI AUROBINDO: You mean Gujarat is not modern enough?

PURANI: Perhaps not. Besides, two modern Gujarati poets have come here and they are impressed by what they have seen.

Purani then gave a long description of the modern tendency of Gujarati poetry.

EVENING

PURANI: Dara has a novel suggestion for solving the Hindu-Muslim problem.

SRI AUROBINDO: What is it?

PURANI: He says that in the South the Hindus are in the majority, so they can be given self-government. In the North-West Frontier the Muslims are in the majority, and they can be given self-government there. In the rest of the places where they are almost equal, let them fight it out among themselves.

SRI AUROBINDO: Fight till they come to a solution? Not quite without sense. For short of the threat of a decisive fight, people will go on talking and talking. If there was the possibility of such a fight, then they would come round.

9 APRIL 1940

SATYENDRA: Senapati Bapat has been arrested. He was asked not to enter Bombay.

SRI AUROBINDO: No, he was asked to "remove himself".

SATYENDRA: Not only did he not do so but he addressed a meeting.

SRI AUROBINDO: That's all very well, but why on earth is he called Senapati?

PURANI: Because he led a Satyagraha movement against the Tatas' extension of their dam.

SRI AUROBINDO: Oh, commander-in-chief of passive resistance?

PURANI: Yes, but not quite, because they had swords with them.

SATYENDRA: He seems to try being spectacular.

SRI AUROBINDO: But the spectacle doesn't always come off.

SATYENDRA: That is not his fault.

SRI AUROBINDO: How? Is it because once, when he would have died by drowning, it was his friends who saved him and thus prevented him from being spectacular?

SATYENDRA: Probably. That reminds me of a friend of mine who took more than a lethal dose of opium to commit suicide. But he didn't die; he was quite conscious though he couldn't move his limbs. He was an intellectual and a rationalist and was fed up with the world.

SRI AUROBINDO: It was an intellectual attempt at suicide then, but some part in him that was not rationalist saved him. (*Laughter*)

EVENING

NIRODBARAN: Germany has entered Denmark.

SRI AUROBINDO: Oh! The war has begun then. Was this the measure they were considering? It is the direct result of British mine-laying.

SATYENDRA: Germany will now have two fronts.

NIRODBARAN: But why did they choose Denmark?

SRI AUROBINDO: Because then they can control the Baltic and the North Sea and from there they can enter any time into Norway and Sweden.

NIRODBARAN: So that was the reason for their troop-concentration there?

SRI AUROBINDO: Yes. The Germans have the power to foresee and act accordingly, while the British act from hour to hour: "If this happens, we will do that – if that, then this."

NIRODBARAN: Rumania has been saved.

SRI AUROBINDO: Yes, she is lucky. The attack on Finland saved her the first time and now the entry into Denmark has done it the second time.

NIRODBARAN: Unless Russia takes this opportunity and spreads her net.

SRI AUROBINDO: Now Finland will look on at them sharing the same fate.

NIRODBARAN: Poor countries! They wanted to preserve strict neutrality.

SRI AUROBINDO: Even now perhaps Norway and Sweden will say, "We must safeguard our neutrality at any cost." (*Laughter*)

NIRODBARAN: The Allies have pledged their support in case they are attacked.

SRI AUROBINDO: Yes, but they must invite the Allies.

PURANI: Well, the Allies will first send 500 men, then 1000, then 2000 – like that.

SRI AUROBINDO: Step by step. (*Laughter*)

PURANI: The eleventh of this month seems to be an auspicious day. Something is going to happen.

SRI AUROBINDO (*Laughing*): Something is happening all right.

PURANI: There is the combination of Sun and Jupiter, Saturn and Mars. Sun and Jupiter being more powerful will counteract the evil influence of the others. There will be a dash for peace.

SRI AUROBINDO: Peace? Peace has been dashed all right, in Norwegian waters by the Allies and in the Baltic by Germany. Saturn and Mars are said to have dashed, aren't they? They seem to be more powerful than Sun and Jupiter.

PURANI: They may have the start.

SRI AUROBINDO: I see. The other two will come at the end or are working together now to run them out at the end? (*Laughter*)

It was afterwards learnt that the Germans had captured some ports in Norway.

SRI AUROBINDO: The British also should occupy other ports.

10 APRIL 1940

PURANI: It seems that Germany collected all its navy, merchant ships and trawlers to carry its army to Norway. And the British navy is firing on them.

SRI AUROBINDO: If the whole German fleet is out and gets attacked and intercepted by England, then it will be Germany that will have to turn back. Hitherto the Germany navy has not proved itself superior to the British navy. But it depends on what proportion of the navy is there. If it is only a part or if they have to collect it from various places, then it will be difficult for them. Of course, if the French fleet is also there, then it will be all right. If they had possessed foresight, they would have gathered their fleet nearby. It seems they knew that Germany thought of making some such move. At least Denmark and Norway ought to have known. It is their imbecility that is responsible. If they knew, they should have made some secret agreement with the Allies.

SATYENDRA: Germany has given the fine reason that if it hadn't taken these countries, the Allies would have done it. So it has taken them under its protection.

SRI AUROBINDO (*laughing*): Too entire a protection.

PURANI: If England occupies part of Norway –

SRI AUROBINDO: That depends on her sea-power. If she can, it will be a tremendous economic blockade of Germany.

PURANI: And then the Allies can try to invade Germany through this front.

SRI AUROBINDO: That is difficult because just as they have the Siegfried Line in the west, the Germans have here the Kiel.

EVENING

NIRODBARAN: It is reported that about five of England's destroyers were damaged and one ran ashore, while there were few losses on the German side.

SRI AUROBINDO: It couldn't have been a big battle then and the battle must have been near the shore.

11 APRIL 1940

SRI AUROBINDO (*suddenly to Nirodbaran*): What is all this that
Dilip writes about sadhaks siding with Meghnad Saha against X in
the controversy between the two? And what is this discussion about
Aldous Huxley?

NIRODBARAN: It seems that in his controversy with Saha, X
made a mistake, for which he got a licking from Saha. Some sadhaks
were glad about X's defeat. At this, two other sadhaks were very
puzzled. They couldn't understand how anybody could feel elated
at one's own people being beaten. Y said that he hadn't seen such
feelings even at Shantiniketan.

SRI AUROBINDO: That may be true, but what was the point at
issue?

NIRODBARAN: I don't know. I haven't read the writings.

PURANI: I believe it was the philosophic interpretation of the
theory of relativity and the change that is coming in among scientists – for instance, Jeans and Eddington.

SRI AUROBINDO: But scientists don't recognise any metaphysics – except perhaps some scientists in America. On the Continent
no recognition is given to the metaphysical views of Jeans or
Eddington. The scientists there say that Science is concerned only
with explaining the processes of the universe; as for the rest, it is not
their business. You can no more say that Science is turning towards
metaphysics from Jeans' example than that fiction is becoming yogic
from Huxley's.

NIRODBARAN: The point about Huxley seems as follows: Y
told Z that Huxley had undergone a great change, becoming a Yogi
and having spiritual experience. Z denied it, saying, "What is there
of Yoga here? It is all mental." Then Y spoke of Huxley's experience of peace as described in *Eyeless in Gaza*. This again was contradicted by Z. Y asked him, "But have you read the description? Have
you gone through Huxley's latest books?" Z replied, "No." At this,
Y said, "How then can you speak like that?" Y was pained that
without reading about the man Z had passed judgment. Z does not
believe that there can be any change in Huxley.

SRI AUROBINDO: Why? Just because a man has once been one
way, can there be no change in him?

NIRODBARAN: Y told him what you had said to me – that
Huxley might have had some experience in the mind. To this,

Z replied, "People interpret in their own way what Sri Aurobindo says."

SRI AUROBINDO: I don't remember what exactly I said. It may have been to the effect that Huxley had some mental experience.

NIRODBARAN: But mental experience is quite different from spiritual, isn't it?

SRI AUROBINDO: No, not quite different. For, it is not something obtained by mental discussion or understanding. It is an experience of the Truth in the mind.

PURANI: To go back to your statement about the change in Science, that we are fifty years behind Europe and that, except for the Russian Communists and perhaps a few scientists elsewhere, Science does not hold its old position any more. I think even the Russian Communists may be getting disillusioned with the old position.

NIRODBARAN: Yes, but not our Indian Communists. Possibly because they are Communists as a fashion only. As Suhrawardy says, they call themselves Communists but build fine houses in Ballygunj.

SRI AUROBINDO: That is because real Communism hasn't come here yet. Their standpoint may be: "It is better that we Communists rather than non-Communists should have fine houses." (*Laughter*)

AFTERNOON

Dilip had sent Sri Aurobindo an extract from Huxley describing his experience of peace. As soon as the door opened, Sri Aurobindo started to speak.

SRI AUROBINDO (*to Nirodbaran*): You have to take this extract back to Dilip and tell him I have read it. Say that it is a big yogic experience – a psycho-spiritual one. It shows a going through the psychic down into the vital being and finding there the unitarian principle, the principle of oneness with everybody. Huxley speaks of "dark peace" because it is down below that he goes and from there opens to the Light above. All the details are quite recognisable, and they cannot be a mental construction. This experience must have changed his life.

K7

EVENING

Sri Aurobindo saw in the afternoon that Nirodbaran was reading the extract from Huxley.

SRI AUROBINDO: Have you read it? Remarkable and significant, isn't it?

NIRODBARAN: Yes, very much so – a fine description.

SRI AUROBINDO: It is no poor mental imagination at work here.

PURANI: Is the extract from *Ends and Means*?

SRI AUROBINDO: No, it is from the last chapter of *Eyeless in Gaza*.

PURANI: In *Ends and Means* he more or less describes the remedy for the present troubles of the world, and speaks of non-violence as a means.

SRI AUROBINDO: He also discusses the future of the world and speaks of Mohenjodaro and says that the people of those ruins must have been doing Yoga.

NIRODBARAN: Huxley has a powerful self-expression.

SRI AUROBINDO: Yes, he has a remarkable style and a subtle and plastic mind. He must have done Yoga for some time to get that experience.

NIRODBARAN: I wonder how from being a cynic and atheist he got converted to this.

SRI AUROBINDO: Cynicism and atheism were the inheritance of the age. Even then he was dissatisfied with world conditions and there was some psychic aspiration for better things.

NIRODBARAN: Joad seems to be veering round again.

SRI AUROBINDO: He is floating. He had come to a spiritual standpoint but he gave it up, he said, owing to the hard knocks of the philosophers. Now he sees that it can be upheld; so he is changing.

NIRODBARAN: Einstein seems to have said that cosmic religious feeling is an incitement to Science.

SRI AUROBINDO: I see. But what does he mean by "cosmic religious feeling"? If Einstein could use such words, Meghnad Saha can't say that he is not a scientist. Or perhaps he will say that Einstein is only giving his personal views.

NIRODBARAN: By the way, who are the Chaldeans?

SRI AUROBINDO: They are the ancient Babylonians who came to be known as Sumerians. In the places they occupied, archaeologists have found several things like those at Mohenjodaro.

12 APRIL 1940

NIRODBARAN: Authorities in England say that the Allies have captured Bergen and Trondjheim, but the official circles don't confirm the news.

SRI AUROBINDO: If they have captured them, why should they conceal the fact?

NIRODBARAN: Bose's group has indulged in rowdyism against the new Bengal Provincial Congress by hurling stones and shouting violently.

SRI AUROBINDO: And the B. P. can't retaliate because they are non-violent. This creed of non-violence is very funny when put into practice. Gandhi perhaps thinks that Bose's heart will melt by it.

PURANI: In Denmark, Germany has restricted all food-stuff, even the use of fodder by the Danish people, somebody said. I said, "Will the Germans eat fodder now?" (*Laughter*)

SRI AUROBINDO: Perhaps they want to export fodder to Germany for their cattle. In that case, they can't have butter from Denmark.

PURANI: Germany thought it would have an easy victory over Norway, as in Poland, Czechoslovakia and Denmark.

SRI AUROBINDO: Denmark was easy, for geographically it is a sort of suburb of Germany. The Germans had practically to walk in. Poland they conquered because the Allies had no chance of helping it directly. Czechoslovakia was different. The Czechs could have offered good resistance but for the Allies who betrayed them. If the Allies had agreed to help them at that time in combination with Russia, the Czechs could have given an effective fight to Hitler.

NIRODBARAN: The Allies didn't want to combine with Russia probably.

SRI AUROBINDO: No, that was not the reason. The reason was that they were not ready for the war. They were not even mobilised and all their war machinery was insufficient. In the case of Norway, Germany's power will depend on the control of the sea. It will have to transport troops and mechanised units across the sea. If the British navy can intercept them, then it will be difficult for Germany. It is a very well-arranged coup by the Germans. Once they have occupied the main ports and landed troops, it will be difficult to turn them out.

PURANI: The British seem to be landing troops at Narvik.

SRI AUROBINDO: That won't help much because it is far off and there is no proper transport facility for mechanised units. If they can capture one of the ports, then it will be very easy for them. Or if Sweden, instead of foolishly guarding its neutrality, joins the Norwegians, then by the time they make a combined resistance the Allies can land their troops in Sweden. Sweden does not seem to realise that it is its turn next to be swallowed up by Germany.

After this, a quotation from Einstein given by Dilip was read to Sri Aurobindo, in which Einstein said that a cosmic religious feeling was an incitement to Science.

SRI AUROBINDO: That doesn't come to much. All depends on what he means by religious feeling. It may be simply a sense of reverence at the sight of the universe or a feeling of worship.

EVENING

SRI AUROBINDO (*looking at Purani*): All this news seems to be travellers' tales and rumours. There is no official statement. There are various contradictory assertions. Some say Oslo is pressed upon by the Allies, others that Bergen is captured and the only truth seems to be that a battle is going on but the result is not yet known. The British navy hasn't scored any great success yet. What they seem to have is only organisation, strong and efficient organisation, but no military genius and, in this organisation, there is no room for initiative. It reminds me of the Italian historian who said that organisation is the only thing that matters. Napolean's successes were considered to be due to sheer luck.

PURANI: And any individual initiative is likely to be crushed under organisation. If the Allies can't do anything, they will lose all the moral sympathy of the world. Already they are on the point of losing it.

SRI AUROBINDO: Quite so.

PURANI: If they could take Norway, they could even attack Germany through the North.

SRI AUROBINDO: That is not easy. Germany has its Kiel fortress, which is one of the strongest in the world.

14 APRIL 1940

PURANI: It seems the Germans are carrying their guns and machines in aeroplanes to Norway.

SRI AUROBINDO: Why can't England do the same? They don't seem to want to do anything that involves work. They want to capture or conquer without doing anything. They don't have any initiative. In individual actions they have so far shown superiority, but in group actions what they have is organisation and they have perfected only that. Even Gamelin has organised his army perfectly but he has not shown any military genius. So long as Chamberlain is at the helm, nothing will happen. He applies only business intelligence to politics.

PURANI: They have captured the Faroe Islands which appear to be strategically important.

SRI AUROBINDO: Where are they?

PURANI: Somewhere between Orkney and Norway.

SRI AUROBINDO: Then they are of no importance. Hitler is not such a fool as to go and occupy Iceland or Greenland.

NIRODBARAN: Does Chamberlain direct the military operations?

SRI AUROBINDO: No, he supervises all the departments and is advised by the military, but if the Ministry is against any move of the military, they can't do anything. If Hore-Belisha had been there, he could have done something.

SATYENDRA: He was the man we were thinking of the other day and, on this very point you have mentioned, he resigned. Somebody remarked about the occupation of the Faroe Islands that the Governor there had only six guns. The British had no difficulty in occupying it. (*Laughter*)

SRI AUROBINDO (*after some time*): I can't understand the moves of the British. As soon as they heard of the German occupation, they could have occupied Bergen. Bergen would have been far away from Oslo and yet within striking distance. If Germany had six destroyers, they could have brought twenty. Even if a great part of their fleet had been lost, they would have gained a lot. They seemed to be enamoured of the idea of blockade, the navy's starvation of Germany and they are daunted by the presence of the Siegfried Line on their east. They don't want to risk anything. They are tied up by their organisation, while Hitler fixes himself to nothing. He considers all possibilities and strikes according as it suits him.

PURANI: Yes, the British must have their plans and moves fixed beforehand: "If such things happen, then we shall do this or that." Instead, they appear to do things too late and decide only after a move has been made by the enemy. The countries still remaining neutral are already scared and can't rely very much on the Allies.

SATYENDRA: There was something in the papers about the Balkans — some threat to the Allies.

SRI AUROBINDO: And I suppose the Allies said they were watching the situation. (*Laughter*)

NIRODBARAN: Without Norway, can the Allies' blockade be effective?

SRI AUROBINDO: It can be. They can impose it with their navy. If they can smash the German fleet now, then there is a chance of peace as was prophesied by the London astrologer Blake.

NIRODBARAN: If the Germans have only 20,000 troops in Norway, scattered in various places, they can be easily routed.

SRI AUROBINDO: If the Norwegians could have fought like the Finns, there would have been some resistance.

EVENING

SRI AUROBINDO (*looking at Purani*): The French news says that one German officer was shot by Hitler's order because he criticised Hitler's invasion of Norway, saying that it was a blunder which would bring economic ruin to Germany and all sorts of faults and crimes would be imputed to Germany.

PURANI: The German people will perhaps like it as a deserved punishment.

SRI AUROBINDO: Many people must be thinking like this officer, only they won't dare to speak out. He, being a military man, was outspoken. His conviction got the better of his prudence. The news report also says that one more major left the puppet ministry and joined the Norwegians. Perhaps he has become wiser. This puppet ministry is composed not only of professors: there are many majors in it. The German fleet seems to have lost heavily – two big battleships have been destroyed. If the whole navy is destroyed, the Germans will be in a very bad position. They will be quite isolated in Norway.

PURANI: They are said to be carrying troops in aeroplanes.

SRI AUROBINDO: That can't come to much. Only ships can carry enough.

PURANI: If the Allies can set up a base somewhere there, it will be very advantageous for them: they can then attack German bases.

SRI AUROBINDO: Of course.

PURANI: In Denmark the Germans can't do much because Denmark has to depend on import for foodstuff. It has very scanty resources of its own.

SRI AUROBINDO: Yes, Germany will have to support the Danes when it can't even support itself.

PURANI: It seems the Norwegian industrialists and landowners are in favour of Germany.

There's news that the Russian fleet is in the Arctic.

SRI AUROBINDO: Fleet? Only some ships perhaps. Their fleet is either in the Baltic, the Black Sea or at Vladivostok. And if it is in the Baltic it will be noticed if it comes out.

15 APRIL 1940

SRI AUROBINDO: If the radio news is correct, the Germans have only one pocket battleship left, two being destroyed, two big battleships also being sunk and many cruisers. By cruisers are meant battlecruisers perhaps; they have then some light cruisers. So half their cruisers are also destroyed and many merchant ships – a heavy loss.

PURANI: It is reported that the Allies have broken through the line and penetrated into the Baltic.

SRI AUROBINDO: If they enter the Baltic, then the Germans are done for.

NIRODBARAN: So it seems true then that Hitler has blundered by extending the war front.

SRI AUROBINDO: It was a very rash thing to do. These things depend in the end on sea-power. Without sea-power you can't transport supplies, mechanised troops, etc.

PURANI: They counted on the aeroplanes.

SRI AUROBINDO: Hitherto aeroplane attacks have not been a success except in Poland and Finland. Aeroplanes are only a powerful aid. You can't conquer a country with them.

PURANI: No, except in places like Abyssinia, perhaps. There too the Italians were hard put.

SRI AUROBINDO: Some French general said that Hitler's move was well-planned, well-executed but not well-judged. If the prohibition of the use of petrol, etc., is true, then Germany's condition is pretty bad. Hitler seems to succeed only where there is not much resistance.

EVENING

Devata, Dr. André's lab assistant, was on the point of dying from heart failure. André said, "If he is dead, I will resuscitate him," and by giving him injections he brought him back to life. This was related to Sri Aurobindo.

SRI AUROBINDO: This attitude reminds one of Oscar Wilde's definition of life – happy anticipation of the future.

NIRODBARAN (*after some time*): There have been fifteen election suits in the Calcutta corporation election: three by the Bose party, one by the Hindu Sabha and one or two by the Muslims. In one of the suits the charge by the Bose group was that the Hindu Sabha candidate tried to coerce the voters with fanatical religious threats, divine displeasure, wrath of God, etc.

SRI AUROBINDO: God is angry with Bose because he is a Socialist?

PURANI: In Dacca also there was a clash between the student federation and the Bose party students, in which one student of the federation died.

SRI AUROBINDO: What did the other party do? Did they not fight?

PURANI: Yes, they did.

SRI AUROBINDO: That's better.

PURANI: Here in Pondicherry schoolboys were asked to write an essay on the war. A boy of fifteen wrote against the Allies, saying that it was an imperialist war. The teacher foolishly sent the essay to the Director, then to the Governor. The boy's scholarship was suspended.

SRI AUROBINDO: Naturally. When it was forwarded to them, they had to take action on it. They could not do otherwise even if they wanted to.

PURANI: In France the rules are still more severe for such crimes.

SRI AUROBINDO: It is treason and one must bear the consequences. If India were free and had to fight she would do the same.

CHAMPAKLAL: Mithran said some boys were shot.

SRI AUROBINDO: Shot? Can't be. How old were they?

CHAMPAKLAL: Below twenty perhaps.

SRI AUROBINDO: I can't believe it. They couldn't have been shot. They may have been given some other punishment. This Quisling of Norway should have been shot. Do you know what he has done? When the Norwegians were defending Trondjheim with their coastal batteries, Quisling sent them directions to stop fighting and by the time they realised that he had betrayed them it was too late. Also in Holland I don't know why they keep their traitors under supervision instead of shooting them.

16 APRIL 1940

NIRODBARAN: Dr. André was so happy last evening, thinking he had saved Devata. The poor man is dead today.

SRI AUROBINDO: He was too optimistic. The attack was too strong for the man. I did not expect him to survive tonight.

PURANI: André also said that if he survived a seizure last night, he would recover.

NIRODBARAN: I don't understand why the attack came in the early morning on three successive occasions.

SATYENDRA: It is said that one's vitality is at its lowest in the early morning.

SRI AUROBINDO: Yes.

NIRODBARAN: Could it be an attack of some force as he had just returned from visiting various places?

SRI AUROBINDO: What places?

PURANI: Kumbhakonam, Trichinopoly, etc.

SRI AUROBINDO: Oh, then it is quite possible. Sacred places are the places for such forces, also the places of priests and Pandas.

PURANI (*after some time*): The British have landed troops at different points, leaving the occupied areas.

SRI AUROBINDO: Of course. But what is their manoeuvre? They seem to intend to occupy Bergen and Trondjheim because they are concentrating their attacks on them.

PURANI: The *Indian Express* says that one third of the German navy is gone.

SRI AUROBINDO: May be true. The radio says half, but it may be one third.

PURANI: Have you read the report of the officers in the Khaksar shooting enquiry? They have made some amazing disclosures – that Allama Mushriqui intended to enlist twenty-five lakhs of volunteers and be a dictator.

SRI AUROBINDO: Twenty-five lakhs! That means all the Muslim adults.

PURANI: After this, Sikander will hesitate to lift the ban – especially after Sir Chimanlal's accusation that he was also a party to the Pakistan scheme.

SRI AUROBINDO: But, in the scheme, if the Sikhs and Hindus were separated, they would have poor success. They may try to bring in Afghanistan. But Afghanistan is not wealthy and its people have a certain contempt for Indian Muslims. And in Bengal the West Bengalis will want a separate province.

After this Purani out read a letter from a correspondent of his, a man eighty years old. He had been doing some sadhana for a long time, such as reading Shastras, mentally seeing the Divine in everybody, etc. Now he wanted some direct guidance from Sri Aurobindo.

SRI AUROBINDO: The difficulty is that he is too old. It is like X trying to learn Greek at eighty. These things take too long and before he has taken a few steps he may be off.

Then Purani gave Sri Aurobindo a typed review of The Life Divine *by N. C. Brahma. Sri Aurobindo read it and kept silent.*

PURANI: He says that what you have said is what Shankara has said. (*Laughter*) It is all Adwaita philosophy.

SRI AUROBINDO: Adwaita, yes, but not Shankara's Adwaita. And so many people have interpreted Shankara in so many ways that had he been alive he would himself have been shocked at what they had made of him.

17 APRIL 1940

PURANI: The French army seems to have landed in Norway.

SRI AUROBINDO: The French army also?

PURANI: Yes. Narvik is said to be in Allied hands.

SRI AUROBINDO: Nobody knows what is happening there. Have the officials said that?

PURANI: No, not the officials. They say that the situation is quite clear now.

SRI AUROBINDO (*shaking his head and smiling*): It is not at all clear. It may be clear to Chamberlain but not to us.

SATYENDRA: Chamberlain is doubly convinced that the Allies are going to win.

SRI AUROBINDO: Yes, now he finds that right is on their side. He had suspected perhaps that God was not on his side. (*Laughter*)

PURANI: The Allies have laid extensive mine-fields. Hitler has not much chance of success in Norway.

SRI AUROBINDO: I don't know what made him take this step.

PURANI: His inner voice, perhaps.

SRI AUROBINDO: His inner voice must have been wild then.

NIRODBARAN: Is there any chance of his attacking the Balkans?

SRI AUROBINDO: Yes, when he gets wild he can do anything.

NIRODBARAN: But that would be very hazardous. He would have to lose his head to do that.

SRI AUROBINDO: He has already lost it. The Allies are waiting for him to fall into that trap. They want nothing better.

PURANI: Italy seems to be intending to take sides.

SRI AUROBINDO: With whom? She says she won't allow herself to be found like Norway.

PURANI: She may join the Germans.

SRI AUROBINDO: She can do anything. Today she will declare you her friend and tomorrow join your enemy. But if she intends to join Hitler, she should have done that at the beginning when the Allies were unprepared. Now if she joins she will have to keep her control of the Mediterranean or she will be put into a worse position than Germany. And in the navy the English and French will be stronger than Mussolini. Moreover the Italians are not good fighters; they will open themselves to attack by land. In Abyssinia they did not achieve any great success. Only after using mustard gas could they get victory. On the other hand, if they joined the Allies, they could confirm their position, though Mussolini would have to give up his idea of a Roman empire.

PURANI: Here is a letter from Sundaram on his meeting with H, who tried to explain why he went away from here. He could not understand why the Mother granted an interview to the mill owner Hukumchand who had had a monkey-gland operation, while she refused to see several poor people. The Mother replied that he should not think by the mind and judge her motives like that. On another occasion there was some dispute about a servant. That time, he said, you replied that according to French law a master has rights over a servant.

SRI AUROBINDO: I never said that and it is not true. In French law the servant has as many rights as his master.

PURANI: Then H spoke of consciousness in the heart and the force, the tranquillity, he gained here.

SRI AUROBINDO: Why does he object to the monkey-gland operation?

PURANI: He objects to the Mother seeing rich men and refusing poor men.

SRI AUROBINDO: But the Mother has refused to see rich men also. That is why she asked him not to think or reason by the mind.

PURANI: Why doesn't he say plainly that he left the Ashram because he found the path difficult, instead of trying to justify himself? He also says that you made so many interpretations of his poems that a book could be made out of them.

SRI AUROBINDO: Interpretations? I simply said "Very beautiful" and so on.

18 APRIL 1940

NIRODBARAN: Somebody, in reviewing Promode Sen's book on you, says that you are saying new things which are not according to the Shastra.

SRI AUROBINDO: The sin of having new ideas? One must speak only of things already said and otiose?

NIRODBARAN: He says the outer world is like a dog's tail.

SRI AUROBINDO: That is the old idea. So one has to cut off the tail?

PURANI: Vivekananda himself has done many new things.

SRI AUROBINDO: One can do new things but can't have new ideas, I suppose!

NIRODBARAN: In the same issue Girija Shankar has started writing your biography.

SRI AUROBINDO: Good Lord! What does he know about my life?

Sri Aurobindo cast a glance here and there at the article and read in the last portion: "It was his mother who played a great part in moulding the temperament and character of Sri Aurobindo."

NIRODBARAN: He writes also that as soon as you heard of your grandfather's death you cried out, "What a calamity!" (*Laughter*)

SRI AUROBINDO: Not a very original interjection.

SATYENDRA: The biographers will force you to write your own biography, Sir.

SRI AUROBINDO: I shall have to write it just in order to contradict the biographers. I shall have to entitle the book, *What I Did Not Do in My Life.* (*Laughter*)

EVENING

SRI AUROBINDO: What is the condition of Narvik? It seems to be a mystery.

PURANI: They say it is in British hands.

SRI AUROBINDO: Who are they? The British Government? The Germans say it is in their hands. The British have occupied some islands north of Narvik. In that case they will take a long time to come to the South.

NIRODBARAN: Chamberlain says they were not at all prepared. All preparations were made at the last moment.

SRI AUROBINDO: Yes, so they have sent a small army and the rest is to follow. But in the meantime what will be the condition of the Norwegians?

SATYENDRA: The Norwegians were so dumbfounded by the sudden invasion that they began to stare at the invaders. It seems some Norwegians have crossed over to Sweden.

SRI AUROBINDO: The Swedes have a contempt for them as fighters.

SATYENDRA: The Germans are trying to divide Norway from the North.

SRI AUROBINDO: Yes, at Trondjheim, where Norway is narrow.

PURANI: The Germans were ahead of the British at most by twenty-four hours.

SRI AUROBINDO: No, they were preparing for two months. The Germans have foresight and organisational power. (*After some time*) The Theosophical Society's prophecy about world war in May might come true. The Russians have given an ultimatum to Rumania on fourteen points, of which thirteen are non-existent, Rumania says, and one is unimportant.

PURANI: If war breaks out there, I hope Britain will strike the first blow.

SRI AUROBINDO: That will depend on Turkey. She has a pact with Russia not to go to war against her. If Germany attacks, then, of course.

NIRODBARAN: Hasn't Turkey an agreement with the Balkan powers?

SRI AUROBINDO: If she has, we don't know of it. The Balkan powers have an *entente*, and that is with Bulgaria.

NIRODBARAN: These two countries, Russia and Germany, seem to have a sinister scheme between themselves. When one takes Finland, the other keeps quiet. And after Germany takes Norway, Russia goes against Rumania.

SRI AUROBINDO: Yes.

5 MAY 1940

PURANI: I don't think England has withdrawn from Trondjheim because of the Italian threat.

SATYENDRA: The debate comes on Tuesday. The Labour Party is going to heckle Chamberlain. Simon says, "Be cheerful and we will win in the end." (*Laughter*)

SRI AUROBINDO: He means, "Be cheerful and we will muddle through." Hore-Belisha will now say, "I told you so."

NIRODBARAN: Almost all the papers have supported the Government except The *Mail*, The *Herald* and The *News*.

SATYENDRA: The papers say the Ministers have all agreed on their policy.

SRI AUROBINDO: Yes, Hore-Belisha also, I suppose! Chamberlain said, "We are perfectly agreed on policy." At the end it was seen that they had disagreed all along.

NIRODBARAN: Labour also is supporting Chamberlain.

SRI AUROBINDO: During war they stick together.

NIRODBARAN: In the last war there was a change of ministry.

SRI AUROBINDO: That was because of general discontent. The Conservatives have to become dissatisfied with Chamberlain before they change him. The question is: whom will they put in his place? Among Labour and the Liberals there is no one except Lloyd George, but he is too old. Among the Conservatives, all except Churchill and Hore-Belisha are imbecile.

SATYENDRA: Chamberlain won't easily give up.

SRI AUROBINDO: No, he will stick on with his hands, feet and teeth unless forcibly dislodged. It is because there is not a single real statesman in Europe that Hitler and Mussolini are getting their own way.

SATYENDRA: The Neutrals will lose their fear under the British strength and protection.

SRI AUROBINDO: Yes, but Sweden is very bitter.

SATYENDRA: It is their neutrality that the British are critical of.

SRI AUROBINDO: That is true. If Sweden had joined them, it would have been a great help.

PURANI: The Allies could have attacked Germany from the rear.

SRI AUROBINDO: These countries think that their neutrality will save them.

NIRODBARAN: Now Sweden is at Germany's mercy and the British can't help them as effectively.

SRI AUROBINDO: Quite so. If they want to help, they will have to do it in another way. They will have to land 300,000 troops in Narvik.

NIRODBARAN: One American paper says, "Licking rouses the British to a great impetus."

SRI AUROBINDO: That is true. They have a great tenacity.

NIRODBARAN: A few reverses for the British will be good for India.

SATYENDRA: I don't think so. They won't let us go so easily.

SRI AUROBINDO: No, unless they are beaten.

PURANI: N. N. Sircar is asking the Congress to accept the Ministry.

SRI AUROBINDO: They say that because they are officials themselves.

NIRODBARAN: Gandhi has now agreed to a smaller body, provided it is elected.

SRI AUROBINDO: Elected by whom?

NIRODBARAN: I mean not nominated by the Government.

SRI AUROBINDO: Yes, but elected by whom?

NIRODBARAN: By the people.

SRI AUROBINDO: Then it comes to the same thing as the Constituent Assembly. It has to be elected by the Assembly.

NIRODBARAN: But will the Muslims agree? They will be in a minority.

SRI AUROBINDO: They can have their own elected representatives. Either the Assembly has to elect the member or each party has to give its own schemes and have them thrashed out by discussion. Only one or the other of these two prospects seems possible. The idea of the Constituent Assembly is not likely to be practicable. It will be a large body and won't be able to reach any agreement.

NIRODBARAN: But the Muslims will still put forward their Pakistan scheme which can't be accepted.

SRI AUROBINDO: There each party, as I said, will give its own scheme. If the Punjab Muslims, Sikhs, N.W.F., Baluchistan and other Muslims, such as the Arhars and Momins, stand against Pakistan, then the League will have to drop it. Now the League leaders say that they are the sole representatives of the Muslims and the Government strongly supports them. The Congress is also half-hearted against Pakistan. But once it is shown that the League leaders are not the sole representatives, the Government will have to accept the fact. At the same time the League will be a consultative body discussing all problems and putting them before the Constituent Assembly and the Government to be approved or accepted as the case may be.

NIRODBARAN: But the Congress is making a demand that the Government must accept whatever agreement they come to.

SRI AUROBINDO: That is absurd. They can't bind themselves in advance to whatever agreement is reached. They have their own interests. You can't say that they can't have any voice in the matter. That is not practical. If you say that, you are declaring independence and asking them to go away bag and baggage; they can't agree to it. They will do so only if they are forced to, or if they are beaten badly in the war.

PURANI: You can't say that you will accept the Pakistan scheme, for instance, and ask them to accept it.

SRI AUROBINDO: That is, as Zetland said, all tall talk and phrase-making. It is not practical. The Congress is wrong in laying down such conditions. The Government is not going to submit to it. What they really intend to give is some form of Dominion Status as in Ireland, where India will be linked to Great Britain and not go over to any foreign power against her, as she can if she is independent. The British want to keep India with them and slowly and gradually release power from their hands, expecting that in time we shall become accustomed to having a connection with them. The Congress and others are shouting old slogans in changed conditions. At one time the Independence cry was all right, but now Dominion Status is almost equivalent to that and in time you will be virtually independent. Besides, it is the best option under the present conditions in contrast to charkha and non-violence. Hitler won't give it, neither will Mussolini nor Japan. Stalin may give autonomy but controlled from Moscow. Moreover, the first thing he will do will be to cut off the industrialists and middle class and establish a peasant proletariat.

NIRODBARAN: The British have no interest in the Indian problem, as was shown by the poor attendance on the India debate.

SRI AUROBINDO: That doesn't mean they won't stick to India.

PURANI: If Hitler invades India, Gandhi will declare we are all non-violent.

SRI AUROBINDO: Hitler will be delighted at it.

PURANI: Yes, he will sweep off everybody with machine guns. Gandhi believes he can be converted.

SRI AUROBINDO: It is a beautiful idea but not credible. Does anybody really believe in his non-violence?

PURANI: I don't think so, except perhaps a few of his lieutenants. Others take it as a policy. Patel does not believe in it.

SRI AUROBINDO: Will he face an army with his charkha?

SATYENDRA: Gandhi is so shrewd in so many respects; I wonder why he doesn't see this absurd side of his programme. He seems reactionary in many ways. He is against armaments because they are so ruinous.

SRI AUROBINDO: I dare say they are, but how can you avoid them?

SATYENDRA: He is against all machinery and the use of mechanical things such as fountain-pens, though he is forced to use them. It would be ludicrous to carry inkpot and pen wherever he went. Besides, it would be so inconvenient as he writes whenever he gets time – and he writes with both hands.

EVENING

The radio said that Lloyd George had severely condemned Chamberlain.

SRI AUROBINDO (*opening the talk*): So L. G. has hit Chamberlain on the head? He says he is both inefficient and ineffective.

SATYENDRA: There will be a lively debate. We shall be able to learn more about it.

PURANI: Chamberlain may have to go.

SRI AUROBINDO: If he makes another blunder he will have to. The Conservatives also are dissatisfied.

NIRODBARAN: An American paper proposes Sinclair's name. He does not seem a prominent figure.

SRI AUROBINDO: Nobody knows anything about him. But in his speeches he seems to be always to the point and his criticisms are sound, but I don't know how he would be as a Cabinet Minister.

PURANI: It is really a wonder how they thought of fighting the German army with such insufficient troops.

SRI AUROBINDO: Not only insufficient but ill-equipped. They have no heavy guns, no aircraft, no mechanised units.

NIRODBARAN: They have not given out the number of men sent.

PURANI: The odds against them are three to one, says an American paper. How can they fight such a superior force with that meagre number?

NIRODBARAN: They relied on their wonderful navy perhaps.

SRI AUROBINDO: The navy is all right. It has done good work. Even then, why didn't they destroy the German fleet at Oslo?

NIRODBARAN: Churchill also will have some grievance against Chamberlain.

SATYENDRA: Chamberlain is not responsible for everything.

SRI AUROBINDO: But he is in command of both air and navy. Perhaps he will say he acted according to military advice, but the latter may have merely chimed in with his own ideas. Britain's mine-laying also was not very successful. Otherwise how could the Germans get reinforcements? The British navy could not prevent that?

PURANI: The navy could not go into the Baltic because of the German air force which would have attacked it.

SATYENDRA: What about the air force?

SRI AUROBINDO: The British had no air base in Norway.

NIRODBARAN: They could not establish an air base in Dombas?

SRI AUROBINDO: No, that is too far inside the country. Air bases are very difficult to establish. In Norway there is only one good air base, Stavanger, and that was in German hands.

PURANI: The *Hindu* says that Skagerrak and Kattegat were too narrow and shallow for the fleet to pass through.

SRI AUROBINDO: That is an excuse. The German battleships were passing in and out. In fact that route is the only way. Russians passed their big battleships through it during the Japanese war. The papers are saying that the British sent the Territorials to Norway who had been trained only a few months earlier for the war. In France they have such a big army, they could easily have spared about 200,000 men. Even England could have spared some regular forces.

SATYENDRA: They have sent Canadian forces, they say.

SRI AUROBINDO: The Canadian forces have never fought before. They are about as good as the British forces who have only read of war in books.

PURANI: It is the French who know how to fight.

SRI AUROBINDO: Yes, because they have conscription. Everybody is compelled to undergo training, and afterwards they are called up from time to time so that they won't forget.

PURANI: Even the French Fathers had contempt for the English soldiers. During the last war they used to say, "Oh, the English!"

SRI AUROBINDO: You know the jingo poem of the English?

We do not want to fight;
But, by Jingo! if we do,
We've got the men, we've got the ships,
We've got the money too!

The Continentals say that they have others to fight for them. The Germans said during the last war, "The English will fight to the last Frenchman." But the English will say, "We need not be sentimental over that. We have defeated the French, Russians and Germans."

6 MAY 1940

The Prabuddha Bharata *gave a summary of* The Life Divine, *chapter by chapter.*

SRI AUROBINDO (*after reading the summary*): It is a mess – ideas are strung together without any connection. All very scrappy and loose!

PURANI: Nolini also said something similar. How can anyone give a summary in such a short space?

SATYENDRA: There may be people who will find something in it. This headmaster's booklet is being asked for by some friends of mine. Have you read it, Nirod?

NIRODBARAN: No, thank you.

SRI AUROBINDO: Which book?

NIRODBARAN: The book on your Yoga, which is nothing but a heap of references. Radhananda also has written a book on your Yoga.

SRI AUROBINDO: Not my Yoga, but all Yogas.

NIRODBARAN: But the title is about your Yoga.

Now the talk turned on K.

SATYENDRA: He has grown very thin.

SRI AUROBINDO: By retirement one may get either Brahman or lose one's head.

SATYENDRA: But it may do good in some way.

SRI AUROBINDO: Yes, if one knows the way.

SATYENDRA: Radhananda is also in retirement.

SRI AUROBINDO: Yes, but with the Mother's sanction. Besides, he knows the way. He has done it many times.

PURANI: However, he talks with people whenever necessary and he is quite normal in his behaviour. Only when I had to take him to the French police station last time, he got a shock of surprise at everything. Looking at the French flag he remarked, "Why is that here? Why isn't it the Congress flag?"

SRI AUROBINDO: He thought the Congress has established Swaraj already? (*Laughter*)

CHAMPAKLAL: But he exaggerates things and always talks about himself.

SATYENDRA: People in retirement usually do that.

CHAMPAKLAL: He had a bunch of bananas. He said they were for you, but he ate them all.

SRI AUROBINDO: He has a strong imagination. Perhaps he meant that when he ate the bananas, I ate them and that when he eats I eat. (*Laughter*)

SATYENDRA: This K, when asked by somebody why he took to retirement last time, said, "Some Power and Will behind told me to do so and that Will is still there behind."

SRI AUROBINDO: That is the danger. No one knows where that Will will land him.

PURANI: He seems to have or have had an inferiority complex: he believes that people don't respect him and that he has no personality, etc. This led him to the resolve to pass the M.A.

SRI AUROBINDO: The M.A. will give him personality? That shows what he wants. It is because people seek personal power that retirement becomes dangerous.

EVENING

NIRODBARAN: Lloyd George has used terms like yours about the war management!

SRI AUROBINDO (*laughing*): Yes, his speech is very truculent. This Chamberlain does not seem to want anybody with individuality around him. In place of Hore-Belisha he has put a man who knows how to do only routine work.

NIRODBARAN: Our X is fighting on many fronts while the British are fighting only on two fronts.

SRI AUROBINDO: How?

NIRODBARAN: He says he has to fight Imperialism, the High Command, the Muslim Ministry, Ad Hoc committees, the Hindu Sabha and the reactionary press!

SATYENDRA: About the Hindu Sabha leaders he says, "Where were they when we were in prison? Let them come out from the high courts and fight."

SRI AUROBINDO: I don't see why they should. They haven't, like him, given an ultimatum to the British Government.

PURANI: "And where was he when Savarkar and Parmanand were in the Andamans?", the Hindu Sabha will say.

7 MAY 1940

SRI AUROBINDO (*to Purani*): Do you know if Bhedabheda and Dwaitadwaita are the same? One, I know, is the philosophy of Nimbarkar and the other of Bhaskara.

PURANI: I think they are the same philosophy and by the same person. The two names are of one man.

SRI AUROBINDO: Everybody says that what I have said is just their own philosophy. Nimbarkar's followers, the Ramanuja school, the adherents of Appaya Dikshita – all claim they have said the same thing. Somebody in Madras says my philosophy is just what Hegel has said and lastly I am told that it is the same as Shankara's philosophy!

PURANI: Yes, somebody observed, "It is very fine and exactly what Shankara has said." Nagaraja of The *Hindu* says it is pure Adwaita and there is nothing new in it. (*After a pause*) Narvik is still in German hands.

SRI AUROBINDO: Yes, and the Allies are closing in.

NIRODBARAN: It seems to me they will make a mess of this too.

SRI AUROBINDO: Quite likely. It is said there are 130,000 Norwegians in the North. With their help I don't know why the Allies can't take Narvik. The Germans have occupied Namsos and if they send reinforcements to the North it will be difficult for the Allies.

PURANI: Yes, they are already sending troops and the air force.

SATYENDRA: We shall see what Chamberlain has to say.

PURANI: Probably there will be changes in the Cabinet.

SRI AUROBINDO: That depends on the debate.

NIRODBARAN: Labour opposition may give in at last.

SRI AUROBINDO: Moreover, they have no one to form a Ministry, although there are some good organisers among them.

NIRODBARAN: Unless they form a National Government with a Conservative Prime Minister.

SRI AUROBINDO: In that case Churchill, Hore-Belisha, Eden and Lloyd George will have to come in. Morrison may be in the Ministry of Information and Greenwood for Labour while Attlee may be given some ornamental post, Chancellor of the Duchy of Lancashire.

NIRODBARAN: Why has Chamberlain been made the leader?

SRI AUROBINDO: Perhaps because he knows the tactics of debate, that's all.

NIRODBARAN: Is Halifax good?

SRI AUROBINDO: No, Halifax is good and wise and ineffective. Eden will do well as Foreign Secretary.

PURANI: The *Hindu* says that the Allies are short of bombers.

SRI AUROBINDO: But they have plenty of fighters with which they can fight the bombers. Bombers are only meant for the destruction of military objectives or ships or towns, etc. Even then it has been shown that German bombers are not so effective, while with whatever bombers the Allies have they have been quite successful at hitting military objectives.

In Narvik they have their navy with which they can bombard the coast and then with the fleet's air force they can continually bombard the German army till they surrender. I don't know why they can't.

EVENING

PURANI: It seems Bhedabheda and Dwaitadwaita are not the same. The latter is the philosophy of Nimbarkar.

SRI AUROBINDO: I don't think Bhedabheda is the philosophy of Nimbarkar; I have read so somewhere. Yes, in the *Prabuddha Bharata* it was mentioned.

Nishtha's friend, the Swami in America, has reviewed *The Life Divine*. He has spent all his energy in defending the Sannyasis and at the end says that I don't believe in the Sannyasis.

PURANI: Is that all he has found?

SRI AUROBINDO: Practically. Of course he deals with some points here and there and says that I am a remarkable man, etc. I wonder whether these people have understood the book. The other reviewer of the Ramakrishna Mission also gives the impression that they follow the old conventional ways. But Ramakrishna did not proclaim any system of thinking. They follow Vivekananda, perhaps.

PURANI: Vivekananda does not seem to have succeeded as a philosopher.

SRI AUROBINDO: His writings on Yoga are forceful. He made an attempt at writing philosophy and said that all philosophies are on the way to the Truth but only Shankara's reaches the final goal.

PURANI: The Ramakrishna Mission doesn't have any outstanding thinker.

SRI AUROBINDO: Its people are good at the exposition of old ideas. Abhedananda had some power.

PURANI: Probably the whole speech of Chamberlain will be relayed. One can hear the shouts and cheers of members.

SRI AUROBINDO: Hardly worth relaying. Lloyd George's speech will be more interesting. It seems Stanley and Hoare will reply to the debate and not Churchill.

PURANI: Churchill is said to have some disagreement with Chamberlain.

SRI AUROBINDO: That is why he does not want to reply.

PURANI: Narvik is supposed to be in mountainous country. So there is no scope for air bases.

SRI AUROBINDO: The English speak of their difficulties but don't know how to overcome them; while Hitler, in spite of difficulties, grapples with them. He does not hesitate to establish airfields even in open fields.

8 MAY 1940

SRI AUROBINDO (*to Purani*): Have you seen Chamberlain's speech?

PURANI: No.

SRI AUROBINDO: He says the help to Norway was necessary and the retreat was also necessary. (*Laughter*) They knew about

Germany's invasion of Norway and provided for it, but they couldn't foresee everything. They sent to Norway a little more than one division – about 20,000 men. They could not send more because of fear of blows in other parts, which means that whenever they have such fear they will behave in a similar manner. He says they did not want to attack Trondjheim, but because of the call for help by the Norwegians they had to go and get beaten. Now the main thing is not the change of Ministry but more drive and push. Churchill is in command of the war and everything is all right. Attlee says the retreat was a wonderful feat of arms.

PURANI: There may be a change of government.

SRI AUROBINDO: It does not look like it. From his speech it seems that they have a very insufficient army, so they could not spare more men. But what does their conscription mean then? They have forty million people. France has as many – the British can also draw forces from the colonies and India.

PURANI: They don't want to take any risks, perhaps?

SRI AUROBINDO: How are they going to win? The English people were never like that. They have always taken risks.

NIRODBARAN (*after some time*): A pupil of Sisir went to see Ramana Maharshi and asked him two questions about you.

SRI AUROBINDO: About me? How would Maharshi know about me?

NIRODBARAN: He asked Maharshi whether you had shut yourself up in passivity or were doing some active work for political uplift.

SRI AUROBINDO: Political uplift? Like Subhas Bose in the Corporation? And what did Maharshi say?

NIRODBARAN: He did not give any direct reply. He only said you are like a dynamo and doing work in your own field. The second question was whether you had any chance of going back to politics. Maharshi said the answer would be a prophecy and he does not go in for such things. This man thinks that you are doing some political work here, training people for the revolution of the country.

SRI AUROBINDO: Again, like Bose?

NIRODBARAN: No, for the uplift of the country.

SRI AUROBINDO: It comes to the same thing. Bose also prophesies that he will get freedom by means of revolution.

9 MAY 1940

NIRODBARAN: Chamberlain has a majority of 81 votes. Is it a good majority?

SRI AUROBINDO: A very narrow one, and about 150 have abstained. He has been criticised even by his own people. Amery's voice is the strongest. It shows dissatisfaction in his own party with his policy.

SATYENDRA: Hitler will perhaps consolidate his position in Norway before he makes any other venture.

SRI AUROBINDO: Perhaps. Unless there is too much economic pressure.

NIRODBARAN: The debate has shown how shabbily the whole affair has been carried out.

SRI AUROBINDO: Yes. Some admiral has said he could have taken Trondjheim if he had been given the command. He is a famous man.

(*Later, to Purani while lying in bed*) The *Prabuddha Bharata* has a remarkable article quoted from the *Amrita Bazar Patrika*. Have you seen it?

PURANI: No.

SRI AUROBINDO: See it. It is there on the table. You may find something familiar in the style.

PURANI: It seems to be from your *Defence of Indian Culture*. (*Sri Aurobindo started smiling.*) The ideas are taken from there.

SRI AUROBINDO: Only the ideas?

PURANI: Some words and expressions also.

SRI AUROBINDO: Only some? (*Laughing*) The whole thing is taken from the *Defence*.

PURANI: But who could have sent it?

SRI AUROBINDO: Perhaps M. Bagchi, but he may be in jail now. (*Addressing Nirodbaran*) You did not see this article in the *Patrika*?

NIRODBARAN: No, I didn't notice it.

PURANI: Others have also done that. I wonder why they don't mention their quotation.

SRI AUROBINDO: If they did, they wouldn't get the credit for it. Some have made their names by taking passages from me.

10 MAY 1940

PURANI: Lloyd George has said in his speech what you said before. He says, "We promised help to Poland and did nothing. In Finland the same story and now in Norway it is repeated."

SRI AUROBINDO: His is the strongest attack, asking Chamberlain to resign.

PURANI: Churchill has said that because of the fear of communications being cut off by the German air force they had to give up.

SRI AUROBINDO: What does he mean? They did not think of it before? And why did they take up the operations in southern Norway in that case?

SATYENDRA: Somebody asked him, "Can you tell us if we now have an air base in Norway?" Churchill replied, "Now that the enemy knows, we can say 'Yes.'" (*Laughter*)

SRI AUROBINDO: The enemy knows, so we need not keep it from the British public?

SATYENDRA: The British officers said that all their movements became quickly known to the Germans.

SRI AUROBINDO: Yes, but Dr. Koht said, "It was not true that the Norwegians betrayed Norway. The fact is that some of them were sympathetic to the Germans." (*Laughter*)

PURANI: Jinnah has admitted that he has no control over the Khaksars. They are quite independent and they have not authorised him to make any settlement. On this The *Hindu* comments that it is very pleasing to see Jinnah's humility, but doesn't he claim that the Muslim League is the representative of all Muslims?

NIRODBARAN: In Bengal Muslemism is coming to sports also. The Muslim Sporting Club is claiming reservation of seats in the Indian Football Association. They have organised a huge meeting and passed resolutions asking the Muslims to boycott football till their claims are conceded.

SRI AUROBINDO: Good Lord, next they will do it in cricket also?

NIRODBARAN: Why not? It seems Bose is going to take up their cause.

SRI AUROBINDO: I see.

SATYENDRA: This is the last activity where they could bring up communalism.

NIRODBARAN: No.

SRI AUROBINDO: There are plenty of other fields where it can spread.

SATYENDRA: What will Sotuda say or do?

NIRODBARAN: His duty is over on informing Sri Aurobindo.

SRI AUROBINDO: You can tell him that God helps those who help themselves. (*Laughter*)

NIRODBARAN: I think he will only lament.

SRI AUROBINDO: And want me to lament with him?

SATYENDRA: Champaklal is not satisfied with your answer to Sotuda.

SRI AUROBINDO: No? (*Beginning to smile*)

NIRODBARAN: Champaklal believes only in Grace. Therefore your answer cannot satisfy him.

EVENING

At about 6.15 p.m. the news came that Germany had invaded Belgium, Holland and Luxembourg.

SRI AUROBINDO: I expected it. (*After a pause*) We will see.

NIRODBARAN: Perhaps Hitler has taken advantage of England's ministerial confusion.

SRI AUROBINDO: Yes, and Churchill's disclosure about their air power disparity. I was surprised that he gave it out. It is one thing to say that they had no aerodrome in Norway and another to let out the air power disparity.

NIGHT

SRI AUROBINDO: Now the expected blow has fallen. Chamberlain may say that England should be ready for future impending blows. Now they can send forces by land and sea and from the French frontier. The French have more foresight. They extended the Belgian Maginot Line against any future German attack.

NIRODBARAN: Could this attack be the reason for their withdrawal from Norway?

SRI AUROBINDO: In that case they will have to withdraw from everywhere because everywhere there will be impending blows. If they had attacked Trondjheim I am sure they would have been successful. The Germans would have been bogged down there.

NIRODBARAN: Churchill was for it, but the military advisers were not.

SRI AUROBINDO: Military advisers are always like that. They go by routine. It is like Napoleon against his generals. They lose in the right way!

PURANI: Now the ministerial crisis will recede.

SRI AUROBINDO: Yes, Chamberlain is a lucky beggar, but England is unlucky.

NIRODBARAN: Hitler is spreading war on many fronts which may not be very convenient for him.

SRI AUROBINDO: He wants to break through the blockade because of economic pressure. And if he gets air bases in the Netherlands he can attack England. He seems to be planning to attack Switzerland too. That will be a tough job for him as it is a mountainous country.

PURANI: If these neutrals had combined before, they would have been in a much stronger position.

SRI AUROBINDO: Of course. That shows how foolish humanity is. It does not see beyond its nose.

NIRODBARAN: Sweden is allying herself with Russia.

SRI AUROBINDO: That is the only thing to do.

SATYENDRA: I hope their idea of neutrality will go now.

SRI AUROBINDO: Let us hope so.

NIRODBARAN: Stalin does not want Sweden to fall into German hands.

SRI AUROBINDO: Obviously not. For, if Hitler gets Sweden, and if the Allies go down in the war, he is sure to attack Russia afterwards. He will promise independence to Finland and, through her, attack St. Petersburg and St. Petersburg's defences are not strong. What that Theosophist said about world war seems to be coming true.

SATYENDRA: Yes, Sir, he is only seven days behind. He predicted May 17th and today is the 10th.

SRI AUROBINDO: But it is not world war yet. It will be if Italy or Russia joins.

SATYENDRA: If not now, he says it will be next year, and the millennium, he says, will come in 1941 for a thousand years.

SRI AUROBINDO: Whose millennium? Hitler's or Stalin's? And for a thousand years only?

NIRODBARAN: X believes that something great will happen in 1944.

SRI AUROBINDO: Why?

NIRODBARAN: He says that every eighteenth year of your life has been marked by a notable incident. In 1908 the Vasudeva experience, in 1926 the Overmind descent.

SRI AUROBINDO: What about 1890? I don't know of anything except going to Cambridge.

NIRODBARAN: You got a scholarship, perhaps.

PURANI: They are fitting facts to theory, like Spengler in *The Decline of the West*.

11 MAY 1940

NIRODBARAN: So Chamberlain has been forced to resign.

SRI AUROBINDO: Not forced. He has himself resigned. That was the only thing to do. Now what is wanted is a national government.

NIRODBARAN: Does it mean that all his ministers too will have to resign?

SRI AUROBINDO: Of course. The King asks the new Prime Minister to make his Cabinet.

NIRODBARAN: I don't understand why those small countries could not make secret treaties.

SRI AUROBINDO: Perhaps for fear of discovery. But they could at least send some deputies to make some secret arrangements, deputies who could act on their own responsibility.

NIRODBARAN: Lloyd George has given a complimentary epithet to Hitler by calling him extraordinary.

SRI AUROBINDO: Yes, he has an admiration for Hitler.

SATYENDRA: Others have called him a mad dog.

NIRODBARAN: In the Ashram the feeling is divided. Some are for the British and some for Hitler.

SRI AUROBINDO: For Hitler?

SATYENDRA: Not exactly, but they are anti-British.

SRI AUROBINDO: Not a rational feeling. How can India, who wants freedom, take sides with somebody who takes away freedom from other nations?

SATYENDRA: Feelings are not rational.

SRI AUROBINDO: Then the subjection of India will be justified in other countries' eyes?

PURANI: This parachute-dropping seems to be a new method of warfare.

SRI AUROBINDO: Yes, it was first devised by the Russians. But I don't think it can be very effective. It can be effective for sabotage or in places where there is no military organisation. Russia used it in Finland because the Finnish frontier was near and there too it was not so effective. The parachutists can be very easily rounded up.

EVENING

SATYENDRA: The Rotterdam aerodrome is in German hands. I wonder how they were able to take it.

PURANI: By parachute-dropping, probably.

SATYENDRA: The Germans are landing in Dutch and French uniforms, it seems.

SRI AUROBINDO: Yes, that is one of Hitler's ideas. Rauschnig, his one time confidential secretary, says that Hitler's plan seems to be that many such uniformed Germans will land in Paris one day and capture it. People will be so amazed that they will forget to put up any resistance. This Hitler seems to have a romantic head.

SATYENDRA: Why is England landing troops in Iceland? What danger could there be?

SRI AUROBINDO: They could as well do it at the North Pole.

SATYENDRA: After all they have taken an initiative. Since they could not do it anywhere else, why not in Iceland?

SRI AUROBINDO: Hitler may be mad, but not so mad as to attack Iceland.

12 MAY 1940

NIRODBARAN: Churchill seems to have formed an able and effective ministry.

SRI AUROBINDO: Yes.

NIRODBARAN: Attlee has been made Lord Privy Seal. What is that?

SRI AUROBINDO: Saying "Yes" or "No."

NIRODBARAN: Like being given, as you said, the Duchy of Lancashire? Chamberlain is President of the Council.

SRI AUROBINDO: That is also something like that.

SATYENDRA: He could have been left out.

SRI AUROBINDO: He still has a great influence among the Conservatives. Halifax could have been Secretary for India and Eden, Foreign Secretary. In that case the India policy would have been less stiff in combination with Linlithgow.

DR. RAO: Hore-Belisha and Simon seem to have been promoted to the Lords.

SRI AUROBINDO: Kicked upstairs?

PURANI: In India the British Government does not seem to be inclined to make any further move.

SRI AUROBINDO: No. It can't. It has said that compromise with the Muslims has to be effected. It has given the veto to Jinnah, and Gandhi also has done the same by saying that the Hindu-Muslim problem has to be solved before dealing with the question of joining the Ministry. In that case Jinnah will see his advantage and will hold out for the best terms.

SATYENDRA: The Congress seems to be irrational in saying that. The Congress people resigned from the Ministry because of the Imperial policy, not because of the Hindu-Muslim question.

SRI AUROBINDO: Now the Muslims will say that their allegation about the Congress injustice is true.

PURANI: Y considers Hitler a Kshatriya emanation.

SATYENDRA: Oh, he is furious against the British and is in sympathy with Hitler. He says the British have become old now by their long domination.

SRI AUROBINDO: German domination will be young and new?

SATYENDRA: Both are equally old.

SRI AUROBINDO: No, Germany is older than the English people. The latter are an Anglo-Saxon mixture.

NIRODBARAN: Germany is racially purer.

SRI AUROBINDO: That's humbug. The Germans are as much a mixture of Slavs, Nordic Alpines and Celts. Nietzsche was a Slav. Kant was born in Pomerania and was a Slav.

SATYENDRA: Goebbels says that the Allies attacked the Ruhr. So the Germans had to protect the Netherlands' neutrality.

SRI AUROBINDO: Does he think anybody will believe such stories? They are probably meant for home consumption. If the French had wanted to attack Germany they would have done that before the completion of the Siegfried Line.

NIRODBARAN: Y does not believe the British news.

SRI AUROBINDO: What one devil says is true and what another devil says is a lie? (*Laughter*) The British air force and navy give correct news. It is the army that doesn't.

NIRODBARAN: Are the Dutch good fighters?

SRI AUROBINDO: I don't know. They have not fought since the time of Napoleon.

SATYENDRA: That is a long time.

PURANI: If they had made some treaty or pact with the Allies –

SRI AUROBINDO: The neutrals wanted to have the best of both worlds. If Germany does not attack, they remain neutral. If it attacks, they know that the Allies will come to their help. Still, it would have made a great difference if plans had been made beforehand so that they could at once have taken up their positions.

SATYENDRA: I told Y what you had said – namely, that it is dangerous for us to support Hitler. For some days he keeps quiet and then goes off again. But he does not say anything outside.

SRI AUROBINDO: That does not make any difference. Somebody else may speak to an outsider and thus it goes out.

13 MAY 1940

EVENING

SATYENDRA: Germany is not finding any resistance in northeast Holland.

SRI AUROBINDO: The important part is the east. In the northeast they have no defence. The defence comes after the canals. It seems that Hitler did not expect any resistance from Holland. It was reported to him that the Dutch were bad soldiers and would soon give up the fight.

PURANI: He has been disillusioned. In Belgium the Germans are trying to outflank the Maginot Line.

SRI AUROBINDO: Yes. If the Belgians had foresight like the French, they would have erected defences along their Dutch frontier.

NIRODBARAN: Italy is trying to be belligerent.

SRI AUROBINDO: Yes. But then I don't understand why she has sent all her ships abroad. They will all be caught if she joins the war.

NIRODBARAN: No revolution is likely in Poland and Czechoslovakia?

SRI AUROBINDO: Now it would be foolish. If they revolt, they will be massacred. Only after some Allied victory they may have a chance.

NIRODBARAN: We don't hear of Allied air attacks. Only Germany is taking a toll.

SRI AUROBINDO: The Allies are attacking behind the German lines and bombing troops also, only they don't speak of it. Essen was bombed. (*Addressing Purani*) It appears that Germany has worked out by some mathematical calculation that if they sacrifice 90,000 men they can then make a breach in the Maginot Line, while France will have to make a sacrifice of about one million to break through the Siegfried Line. I don't understand how they calculate.

14 MAY 1940

SRI AUROBINDO: The Germans seem to have discovered some new methods of capturing forts.

SATYENDRA: They have made a considerable advance in Belgium.

SRI AUROBINDO: Yes. In the last war also it was like that. They made rapid progress at the beginning and that, the French say, was because the British soldiers were running away at the approach of the Germans.

NIRODBARAN: If that is true, they will do the same now too.

SRI AUROBINDO: One English correspondent said that the Germans were rushing like wolves.

PURANI: From Cologne, any Belgian town, it seems, is only thirty minutes' flight by air. So they can attack very easily by air.

SRI AUROBINDO: Yes, but air flights can't decide a battle. It is the land army on which victory depends. In France the Germans proved inferior to the French, but elsewhere they proved super-ior.

NIRODBARAN: Is Amery better than Zetland?

SRI AUROBINDO: No, he is a die-hard, I think.

PURANI: In the *Kalyan*, one of Bejoy Goswami's disciples has written that in his last days Goswami was at Puri during Dana-yajna and because of that he ran into heavy debts. When he fell ill he was advised to go to Calcutta, but because of his debts he could not leave Puri. His disciples managed to pay off the debts. I don't know if he died at Calcutta.

SRI AUROBINDO: No, he died at Puri. It is said he was poisoned. By Sthambhan he stayed the effects but was ultimately overcome.

PURANI: He used to feed and take care of many people. He seems to have said that poor people without food can't accept the message of spirituality. So they must be fed first. It was done in so extensive a way that his disciples ran into debts and became poor themselves.

SRI AUROBINDO: Then their spirituality must have deterior-ated when they became poor!

PURANI: Goswami said they should not think of the morrow. Whatever they had they must distribute to the poor.

SRI AUROBINDO: Not thinking of food and distributing food to others are two different ideas without any connection between them. Spirituality does not depend upon that.

PURANI: Their idea of God is that He is all love and compassion. So we must also try to be so and relieve other people's misery.

SRI AUROBINDO: That is all sentiment and nobody will believe that God is all compassion. Feeding other people does not cure poverty, it only relieves it. That is the fallacy of philanthropy. To cure poverty one has to find the cause. And it is not true that poor people can't accept spirituality. All ascetics are poor.

EVENING

The radio news said that Germany had occupied Rotterdam and sep-arated Holland from Belgium.

SRI AUROBINDO: What are the Allies doing? After sending an advance army they seem to be trying to sit comfortably in the rear. And the Germans won't let them have any comfort.

PURANI: They don't seem to have any plan of action.

NIRODBARAN: The only plan seems to be to fall back according to plan.

SRI AUROBINDO: Yes, they are sitting behind fortifications. And if they have any plan it is quite inadequate. The war news is very obscure nowadays.

15 MAY 1940

The radio news announced that the Commander-in-Chief of Holland had asked the soldiers to cease fire because of the sacrifice of lives.

SRI AUROBINDO: What sort of idea is that? Do they think they can win without any sacrifice? Hitler seems to be right in his opinion of their power of resistance.

PURANI: There seems to be some treason among them.

SRI AUROBINDO: Probably, but the Commander-in-Chief is not supposed to be a Nazi.

PURANI: France is fighting hard, especially her air force. British pilots seem better than German.

SRI AUROBINDO: Individually they are superior to the Germans. The paper said that three Hurricanes fought with twenty German planes and brought down some. The Germans act by mass and drive.

EVENING

SRI AUROBINDO: It seems Amery is not a die-hard. He has said in an interview that India will soon have to be considered as independent and he has stood against Churchill's attack on India policy. So with his appointment as Secretary of State India may have a chance. Of course Halifax would have been best. It is a remarkable Ministry. Most of the ablest men of England are there except Hore-Belisha and Lloyd George. As I expected, Morrison and Evans are taken. Morrison is one of the best organisers. Their coming in will help to prevent any quarrel with Labour.

The Belgian position seems to be better today.

PURANI: There is talk of an attack on Switzerland. In that case Italy may take her slice.

SATYENDRA: Then it will be a European war.

SRI AUROBINDO: The Moscow radio does not approve of Germany's attack on the Netherlands, Udar was saying. It seems to be some special information.

SATYENDRA (*gravely*): It is in today's paper.

SRI AUROBINDO: Which paper?

SATYENDRA: The *Indian Express.* (*Bursts of laughter*)

PURANI: If true, Russia may go against Germany.

SRI AUROBINDO: Russia has counted on both sides being exhausted by the war and then Stalin will have his chance. But if Germany wins it will be too powerful.

PURANI: America seems to be changing her tone now and thinking in terms of war.

SRI AUROBINDO: She thinks she will be able to keep out of the war if the Allies win. But if they go down she will have to come to their help.

16 MAY 1940

NIRODBARAN: Dilip has received a letter from Sir Francis Younghusband asking him to be a member of the Fellowship of Faiths. It is an irony since he has lost all faith in fellowship.

SRI AUROBINDO: Hitler is uniting all into a fellowship of nations. (*Laughter*)

NIRODBARAN: Dilip says the Mother will have to put forth more force to save France.

SRI AUROBINDO: What an idea! He thinks that the Mother has a special concern for France?

SATYENDRA: Many people say that she does not care what happens to Britain but France she will save.

SRI AUROBINDO (*laughing*): How can it be possible to do that without saving Britain also? They are allies.

SATYENDRA: Yes, but Hitler is trying to divide them. His wrath is against England. He is likely to attack England directly.

SRI AUROBINDO: What about their fleet? Do they think that the Italians will come and destroy it?

NIRODBARAN: The Mother will save France and Sri Aurobindo India.

SATYENDRA: People think that Sri Aurobindo is not interested in India.

NIRODBARAN: He is a world citizen now.

SATYENDRA: He is too great to be busy over India. He is busy with the problem of life.

SRI AUROBINDO: Who says that?

NIRODBARAN: X. He is still very much upset over the Indian problem.

SRI AUROBINDO: The Pakistan scheme is not of much interest.

NIRODBARAN: Not Pakistan. He speaks of Indian freedom.

SRI AUROBINDO: Indian freedom? India will inevitably be free if Hitler and Stalin are removed. Otherwise I can't give a guarantee.

NIRODBARAN: They will be removed when the Supermind descends. (*Laughter*)

SRI AUROBINDO: What did you say? They will be removed when the Supermind descends or it will descend when they are removed?

NIRODBARAN: It is the same thing.

SRI AUROBINDO (*after a while*): The Dutch seem to be good fighters but they don't seem to have brains. They have lost about a quarter of their army without holding any position.

SATYENDRA: Their Commander-in-Chief has asked them to cease fire.

SRI AUROBINDO: That is in the central part. In Zeeland they are still fighting. He has asked them to cease fire because the army was being attacked from the rear. Instead of ceasing fire they could draw back to the Belgian line.

SATYENDRA: They may do that.

SRI AUROBINDO: They are only thinking about it. That's why I say that they don't seem to have brains.

NIRODBARAN: The Allies could not send any help to Holland.

SRI AUROBINDO: No, there was no time. They have taken the strategic line from Antwerp to Namur and sent an advance army in front. If there had been a previous arrangement they could have gone to their help in time.

NIRODBARAN: The Assistant Secretary of Viswa Bharati has written to Sisir that the Committee has decided to present Tagore's works to the Ashram.

SRI AUROBINDO: What is his name?

NIRODBARAN: Kishori Mohan Santara.

SRI AUROBINDO: Santara? Where is he swimming?[1]

NIRODBARAN: In his atheism. He is a staunch Brahmo and at the same time an atheist.

SRI AUROBINDO: How is that? Brahmoism is supposed to be theism or rather Deism – no, more than Deism because Brahmos pray to God for help.

NIRODBARAN: He writes that after reading your books he finds a new light.

Jatin Bal has written a letter, putting some questions to you:

1. Do you think physics and chemistry will ever be able to know the truth of the phenomenon of life?

2. There is a passage in *The Life Divine*: "Science cannot dictate . . ." Do you mean to say that there will never be any conciliation between science and metaphysics?

3. Will science do well to take into consideration the spiritual view of things or keep strictly on its own lines?

4. Einstein does not decry metaphysics but asserts that science will show him the truth. How far is he right?

5. To a friend Einstein said: "It is my inner conviction that the development of science itself seeks in the main to satisfy the longing for knowledge which psychologically asserts itself as religious feeling." Is he not right?

6. He also says that for the misapplication of science human nature is to blame and not science which is a search after pure knowledge and truth. Can it be said that science is solely responsible for all the evils of the world and religion alone stands for our good? Can we even say that religion is superior to science or vice versa? Is not each great in its own sphere?

SRI AUROBINDO: 1. Physics can know the truth of the phenomenon of life and that also when combined with biology, but not the essential truth of life. Such truth means consciousness, basic reality, and how can scientists know it by their science? Science is concerned with the process of things. If science wants to know the fundamental truth, it has to go beyond process. That is why the continental scientists do not agree with Jeans and Eddington. They say that it is not within the scope of science to be busy with the metaphysical aspect of things. It is concerned, as I said, with process; if it goes beyond that, it is no longer science. Do you understand? I have dealt with all that in *The Life Divine*, Part II.

[1] *In* Bengali *"santar"* means "swimming".

2. Conciliation? There is no opposition between science and metaphysics. Each is concerned with its own sphere and the connection between the two may be established.

3. How can science take the spiritual view? That is not its business and, if it takes that view, it will no longer be science.

4. Truth? Which truth? If he means ultimate truth, how can science show him that? If it is the truth of things, that is another matter.

5. What is meant by religious feeling and pure knowledge? Ultimate knowledge?

6. That science is concerned with discovery is true, though only partially. For application science is also responsible. Just see how scientists are engaged in devising various methods of destruction in Europe. So how can it be said that science is not responsible for application?

Science and religion are both great in their own respective spheres, but in a sense religion is superior in that its appeal is wider and deeper than that of science. If it is admitted that man has a soul, an inner consciousness, then religion is the best means for this consciousness to develop into a higher state of being.

Even scientists in Europe don't make the statement that religion is the root of all evil. Such a statement would invite the opposite view that science is the root of all evil. Science has made humanity materialistic in attitude and put tremendous powers in its hands, which it abuses. You may say that science is not responsible for the misuse, that its business is discovery. Then it can be argued that it has given humanity these instruments without making it ready for their use.

EVENING

CHAMPAKLAL: It seems Dr. R says that Hitler is winning because Sri Aurobindo is helping him with his force. (*Laughter*)

SRI AUROBINDO: What? Does he believe that I want to be a subject of Hitler's?

SATYENDRA: He must be pulling somebody's leg. America is warning all Americans to leave Italy.

SRI AUROBINDO: They expect perhaps that Italy will come into the war.

SATYENDRA: Yes. If there are any American casualties, they fear their country might be dragged into the war. They want to avoid the war.

SRI AUROBINDO: They seem to be able only to talk like their Kellogg Pact.

PURANI: Or they may come in when it is too late.

SRI AUROBINDO: Yes, everybody is too late except Hitler. Narvik is coming in again. The Allies seem to have taken a town (*laughing and pointing a finger*) – and that too because of the French troops that have landed.

17 MAY 1940

EVENING

SRI AUROBINDO: It seems it is not merely five or six of our people but more than half that are in sympathy with Hitler and want him to win.[1]

PURANI (*laughing*): Half?

SRI AUROBINDO: No, it is not a matter to laugh at. It is a very serious matter. The Government can dissolve the Ashram at any moment. In Indo-China all religious bodies have been dissolved. And here the whole of Pondicherry is against us. They cannot do anything only because Governor Bonvin is friendly towards us. But even he, if he hears that people in the Ashram are pro-Hitler, will be compelled to take steps, at least to expel those who are so. If these people want the Ashram to be dissolved, they can come and tell me and I will dissolve it instead of the police doing it. They have no idea about the world, and talk like children. Hitlerism is the greatest menace that the world has ever met. If Hitler wins, do they think India has any chance of being free? It is a well-known fact that Hitler has an eye on India. He is openly talking of world-empire. He will turn towards the Balkans, crushing Italy on the way, which would

[1] It may be mentioned that the pro-Hitler bias was due not to perversity but to ignorance. Most regrettably, the true nature of Hitlerism was not realised in the midst of the animosity against England and the other so-called imperialist powers, the possessors of colonies in Asia and Africa, who happened to be Hitler's enemies. This dangerous ignorance was a widespread phenomenon in the East.

be a matter of three weeks, then Turkey and then Asia Minor. Asia Minor ultimately means India. If there he meets Stalin, then it is only a question as to who wins and comes to India.

I hear K says that Russia can come now and conquer India. It is this kind of slave mentality that keeps India in bondage. He pretends to spirituality. Doesn't he know that the first thing that Stalin will do is to wipe out spirituality from India, apart from the fact that his own class will be crushed out?[1]

They say Hitler is applying his Poland-method on the Western Front – leading with armoured tanks and following up with infantry. (*Addressing Purani*) The Americans are waiting and comfortably thinking that the Allies will win.

PURANI: It doesn't look as if they will join the war now.

SRI AUROBINDO: No, it is very difficult for them unless they are compelled to – later on.

PURANI: The American group that came here was talking bitterly against the war and said, "No more of it." They have sacrificed heavily in the past and spent a lot of money. They want peace now.

SRI AUROBINDO: If they want peace they have to help in keeping it. They fled away after leaving Wilson in the lurch.

PURANI: Their loans also have not been paid back and they are bitter.

SRI AUROBINDO: That, of course.

PURANI: Sir Akbar Hydari has got a full set of the *Arya*.

SRI AUROBINDO: How?

PURANI: It seems his own bookseller from whom he has bought many books had a set. As soon as he knew that Sir Akbar wanted it, he gave the whole set *gratis*. Naturally Sir Akbar was very pleased.

SRI AUROBINDO: Yes, having it *gratis* would be an added pleasure. (*Laughter*)

---

[1] The same morning, it seems, the Mother also spoke to Nolini to the following effect: "It is treachery against Sri Aurobindo to wish for Hitler's victory. Sri Aurobindo's cause is closely connected with that of the Allies and he is working night and day for it. It is because my nationality is French that the Ashram is allowed to exist. Otherwise it would have been dissolved long ago. There were many attempts to do so. If Hitler or Stalin wins, spirituality is doomed. Stalin will come to India and there will be no chance for freedom for a century."

18 MAY 1940

SRI AUROBINDO: The Allies seem to have retreated not because of German pressure but for geographical configuration with the French. If they go on retreating in this way, I don't see how they can win. But have the Germans penetrated the Maginot Line?

NIRODBARAN: That is not said, but the Maginot Line on the Belgian side seems a scattered fortification.

SRI AUROBINDO: Scattered? Then it may be possible to penetrate it.

PURANI: The Allies also should attack somewhere.

SRI AUROBINDO: The French have been trained for long to be on the defensive. Now that Hitler has changed his plan, they have to take up a new position. The French are very good in attack; they are good also in defence.

NIRODBARAN: Amery says that he believes in self-government and wants to keep an open mind as regards India.

SRI AUROBINDO: Yes, he says that he won't make any pre-judgment. If he does that, it will be very good. Zetland stuck to his ideas like a leech – just like Congress to its principles.

NIRODBARAN: Dilip was very glad to learn what you had said about pro-Hitler sympathy. It has come at the right time, he says. He was being jeered at for being pro-Ally. When he said he was sad at Holland's defeat, they remarked, "You are pro-Ally?"

SRI AUROBINDO: They are glad that Holland was occupied? Very strange, and yet they want freedom for India! That is one thing I can't swallow. How can they have sympathy for Hitler who is destroying other nations, taking away their liberty? It is not only pro-Ally sympathy but sympathy for humanity that they are jeering at.

NIRODBARAN: Y was there. He remained all the time glum. He doesn't believe that England will give freedom to India.

SRI AUROBINDO: If England gave freedom to Egypt and Iraq, why not to India?

EVENING

SRI AUROBINDO: It is not such bad news. Germany hasn't entered Brussels yet; the morning radio said it had.

PURANI: No. The Allies' aeroplanes seem to be very active. They have ordered 4000 new aeroplanes costing 650 million dollars.

SRI AUROBINDO: That means one plane costs eight lakhs of rupees, and it can be destroyed in one minute?

SATYENDRA: India can't hope to build any armaments. America is putting a huge sum aside for armaments.

SRI AUROBINDO: Yes, they say they must have 50,000 aeroplanes and a standing army one million strong.

NIRODBARAN: Only one million?

SRI AUROBINDO: One million is a very large number in peace time. Except in countries with conscription there are no such large armies during peace.

PURANI: England has asked all British subjects to evacuate from Gibraltar, owing to Italy's threat, perhaps.

SRI AUROBINDO: But somebody says that Italy will have to wait at least a fortnight before joining the war because a big liner of hers is in the Atlantic, which can at once be seized. But nobody knows what Mussolini will do. He is a great bluffer and may keep on bluffing as bluffing is very pleasant to him. (*Laughter*)

PURANI: Italy has contempt for Germany.

SRI AUROBINDO: Not contempt, but hatred. (*Laughter*)

PURANI: Spengler supports this instinct of barbarism.

SRI AUROBINDO: Does he?

PURANI: Yes, he says that when a race goes down, it is by this instinct that it rises up again. By this instinct, he says, the race tills the soil, ploughs the land and builds houses and slowly builds up a culture, but when it progresses from there towards a city-life and towards civilisation its downfall begins. This has been the curve of civilisation throughout. For instance, a farmer never thinks of how many children he has, he goes on producing and producing. But a civilised man, after having two or three children, begins to think and as soon as he thinks his decadence begins. So, according to Spengler, culture exists only when man is bound to the primitive conditions of life by his instinct and ploughs land and cultivates it.

SRI AUROBINDO: That is not culture; that is survival of the force of life. And it is from this animal stage of existence that man has progressed into a higher one. What according to him would be progress then?

PURANI: He maintains that humanity will always follow this curve from the primitive stage to the height of civilisation and then to decadence. This has always been so.

SRI AUROBINDO: It may have been but need not be. Such repetition would be the failure of the human race. The human race has risen from the animal and it must push farther. If it does not, it will have to make room for some other species.

PURANI: Hitler's power seems to have started even from Hindenburg's time?

SRI AUROBINDO: Yes. The German army had already made preparations but they were afraid of what the Allies would say. Hitler gave them the first start. Of course the British are responsible for all this. They thought that France would become very powerful, so in order to keep the French in check they helped Germany to power. After this war the same trouble will occur again. Some people predict that after the war there will be a socialistic State, which means that instead of individualistic capitalism, the State will be capitalistic.

PURANI: Yes, like, "Give us your cows. We will give you milk."

SRI AUROBINDO: No, "Give us your cows and buy the milk." (*Laughter*) In Russia one has to earn one's very life.

PURANI: There they have now also made a discrimination in wages. And if anyone has more money, he can deposit it with the State and get interest on it. It is that which makes Trotsky wild and say that Stalin is for capitalism.

SRI AUROBINDO: There nobody can be rich and buy luxuries, because then he will be suspected. It seems only the authors are rich in Russia because the masses are being educated to read more. But what will the authors do with their money? Of course they can make a wise gift of it to the State.

PURANI: The Russian Government also gives more wages to the people if their output is more.

SRI AUROBINDO: That again is against Communism.

PURANI: One thing in favour of Socialism is that it promises to give bread and work to people.

SRI AUROBINDO: That is easy; it only requires a different arrangement. Under the capitalistic system people also got work. Only because circumstances have changed they have been thrown out of it. And the two things that are responsible are machinery and war.

PURANI: Machinery has made the problem of unemployment so acute.

SATYENDRA: The problem of the world remains the same.

SRI AUROBINDO: Under Socialism there will be universal poverty. Only the State will be rich. Socialism can become successful only when people have got rid of the egoistic impulse in their actions and movements.

19 MAY 1940

PURANI: Instead of always being on the defensive, if the Allies also attacked it would be good.

SRI AUROBINDO: For that one must have superior strength of the army as well as armaments. Otherwise it is dangerous. The Allies are superior in the air. It seems that their machines are better than the German ones, and the American ones are still better. If so it would be an advantage.

NIRODBARAN: The Allies are trying to cut off the German petrol supply by destroying their communications and depots.

PURANI: They may still get it from Rumania through old contracts.

SRI AUROBINDO: No, Rumania has stopped all supply. By supplying oil she would invite her own invasion.

PURANI: Even without receiving oil, Germany may attack.

SATYENDRA: Then better to be attacked without supplying.

NIRODBARAN: X has found from your own writings what happened to you in your eighteenth year. You have written in *Aurobinder Patra*: "At fourteen the seed sprouted and at eighteen it established itself firmly."

SRI AUROBINDO (*laughing*): That is a psychological event, not an outside action.

NIRODBARAN: Maybe, but it led to action.

SRI AUROBINDO: At eighteen, I think we started in London the secret Lotus and Dagger Society.

NIRODBARAN: Then it is an event!

SRI AUROBINDO: It lasted only for a day. (*Laughter*)

NIRODBARAN: X also says that your eighteen year cycle has a close link with his. In 1890 he was born, in 1908 he joined the

Swadeshi Movement and in 1926 he came here. Nolini's cycle also seems to coincide with it. He joined the Movement in 1908.

SRI AUROBINDO: But what happened to him in 1926?

NIRODBARAN: I don't know.

SRI AUROBINDO (*addressing Purani*): When was the Ashram started?

PURANI: In 1926.

SRI AUROBINDO (*laughing*): There you are!

PURANI: It is like Spengler's fitting facts to theories.

I had again a talk with Doraiswamy. He heard from Nolini that the Mother has said that at present the freedom of India would be catastrophic for the country. You have said that the demon of slavery is sucking the life-blood of India. These two statements he does not know how to reconcile. I said that there was no antagonism between the two.

SRI AUROBINDO: The Mother says that two conditions must be satisfied before India gets her freedom. One is unity; the other, defence. If there is no unity, then India will be prey to another power. We can't afford to have a civil war in India, for that would surely invite another power to occupy her. Even C. R. Das told me that this Hindu-Muslim question must be solved before the British leave and he was no less a patriot than anyone else.

EVENING

SATYENDRA: What is this flame-throwing business the Germans have started?

SRI AUROBINDO: That is a real sign of the Asura. Hitler has many devilish things in store, it seems – works of devilish ingenuity.

NIRODBARAN (*addressing Satyendra*): Your *Indian Express* prints in headlines that the Germans are only seventy miles from Paris.

SATYENDRA: It is from your American correspondent.

SRI AUROBINDO: The French frontier is about one hundred to one hundred thirty miles from Paris. So seventy miles is nothing alarming. We are accustomed to distances. Madras is more than one hundred miles from here, yet considered pretty close. But seventy miles in Europe is quite a good distance. I thought this extension of the Maginot Line had been completed before the war began. They say it was done only during the eight months of the war.

PURANI: Yes.

SRI AUROBINDO: That was during Daladier's time. That is just like Daladier. He talks more than he does. So he has been politely pushed out.

PURANI: He did not perhaps calculate an attack through Belgium.

SRI AUROBINDO: Calculations always go wrong. It is said that Russia is panicky and Stalin upset over Hitler's success.

PURANI: Yes, before also there was such news. There may be some truth there.

SATYENDRA: Stalin thought the Allies would win.

SRI AUROBINDO: That is another calculation. No, he thought that both powers would be exhausted and then he would have his chance.

PURANI: Then Dr. Andre's prophecy that he would be the dictator of Europe would come true.

NIRODBARAN: After the Finnish war, it does not seem possible. That has been a pointer to the limits of his army's capacity and strength.

SRI AUROBINDO: Yes, he has been moderate after that. What happened is no wonder after he has killed all his generals. I suppose he has no such military knowledge as Trotsky had.

PURANI: No.

SRI AUROBINDO: The Finnish war has been reassuring to Hitler. He has seen Stalin's limited strength and thinks, "Let Stalin do now whatever he likes. After the war I will handle him."

20 MAY 1940

PURANI: Hitler's declaration that before August 15 the war has to be finished and peace agreed upon seems significant.

SRI AUROBINDO: That is the sign that he is the enemy of our work. And from the values concerned in the conflict it should be quite clear that what is behind him is the Asuric, the Titanic power.

PURANI: It is strange how he takes his decisions.

SRI AUROBINDO: It is not he who takes the decisions. The Being behind him decides.

PURANI: It knows perhaps that, August 15 being your birthday, there is going to be some descent of the Divine on that date.

SRI AUROBINDO: I don't think it believes in any such descent. It would say, "I must make some decisive movement before anything decisive happens on that date." This Being comes here from time to time and sees what kind of work is going on.

NIRODBARAN: It doesn't believe in any descent of the Divine?

SRI AUROBINDO: It believes in its own descent and is too self-confident about it.

NIRODBARAN: But surely it knows that the work here is against its own interests?

SRI AUROBINDO (*laughing*): Of course.

PURANI: Is it only one Being or a troop?

SRI AUROBINDO: There are more than one, but this is a very powerful Being. Have you read Paul Richard's *Lord of the Nations?*

PURANI: No.

SRI AUROBINDO: I believe it was not published. He was in communion with this Being and the plans and methods he has written of in the book are the same as those carried out now. He said there that the present civilisation was to be destroyed, but really it is the destruction of the whole human civilisation that is aimed at, and already in Germany Hitler has done it: there is no civilisation left there. What reigns there is barbarism supported by science – science meaning physical science. And Hitler has destroyed human civilisation wherever he has gone – as in Poland.

PURANI: Christianity and all religion seem to be his targets.

SRI AUROBINDO: Yes. What he may want is Ludendorf's religion – the Norse religion of a primitive type where primitive instincts are worshipped.

PURANI: Do these Beings recognise that there are higher divine powers?

SRI AUROBINDO: It depends on the type of Being. For example, some know that there are Gods but they won't admit that they are greater than themselves.

PURANI: The fight between the Devas and the Asuras is graphically described in the Puranas. Just as the Asuras are against the human race, there must be other Beings who help the human race.

SRI AUROBINDO: Yes. Human beings by themselves are no match for the Asuras. If it is only an influence from the Asuras or other Beings, the result may depend on that influence. Here in Hitler's case it is not merely an influence but a possession, even perhaps an incarnation. The case of Stalin is similar. The vital world has descended upon the physical. That is why the intellectuals are perplexed at the destruction of their civilisation, of all the values they had made and stood for. They deny the existence of the worlds beyond the physical and so they are bound to be perplexed.

France is calling back her past to defend her present. Weygand and Pétain have been called, haven't they?

PURANI: Yes. It seems there are other military geniuses who are not getting an opportunity because of a religious bar or some such factor.

SRI AUROBINDO: Religious bar?

PURANI: They may happen to be Roman Catholics.

SRI AUROBINDO: But Weygand and Pétain are Catholics. Foch was an ardent Catholic. Nevinson, during the last war, wrote strongly against a general who was a freethinker and who had made a mess. If there were any genius about today, Weygand should know.

SATYENDRA: The Germans have made a great advance in the last twenty-four hours.

SRI AUROBINDO: Yes, a rapid advance.

PURANI: They have brought in a new kind of armoured tank which seems very formidable.

SRI AUROBINDO: The French anti-tank guns were not effective. So now they have brought up heavy seventy-five milli-meter guns. It is because of these tanks that the French were thrown off balance. Naturally, if thousands of tanks push forward, the infantry can't do anything unless they are supported by strong mechanical weapons. The British Army seems to rely on their air force, but the air force can't decide a war. It can only harass the enemy. The Mother says that the R.A.F. bombers can only act at night while the German bombers operate only during the day.

21 MAY 1940

SRI AUROBINDO: In the present war it seems there is only one line of defence. That makes it possible to attack from the rear. In previous wars there were several lines. In the last war there was a wide front.

NIRODBARAN: There may be more exposure to air attack.

SRI AUROBINDO: But there are the anti-aircraft weapons.

NIRODBARAN: It is good that the French have, after all, started counter-attacking.

SRI AUROBINDO: Defensive warfare is all right if there are strong fortifications like the Maginot Line or like Namur and Liege. Otherwise, in an extensive front it is very difficult to be always on the defensive. By standing around and waiting all the time, one is likely to lose and gets all the beating without being able to give anything in return. I thought that the Siegfried Line could be broken if the French were courageous enough. Of course it would involve loss of men. It is not a continuous fortification. There are gaps supported by troops. The gaps depend on the strength of the troops.

SATYENDRA: If the English could also launch an offensive –

SRI AUROBINDO: For an offensive you must have a sufficiently big army. In the beginning Chamberlain was violently against conscription and when he started it he didn't call everybody. He did not want to paralyse the industries and export by calling them. Only before resigning did he call the last reservists, three million, and they will take about three months to be ready.

PURANI: It seems K was in favour of Hitler. When he told Counouma about it, Counouma said, "If it is so, better not speak about it. You know it is very dangerous to talk like that." And then he kept quiet.

SRI AUROBINDO: It is strange that it required Counouma to say that. And yet it is said that people do not speak about it to outsiders.

NIRODBARAN: Counouma is not considered an outsider, perhaps.

PURANI: If he had spoken to a friend of Baron for instance, he would have at once reported it. They can't tolerate such views when their relations are fighting and dying at the front.

EVENING

SRI AUROBINDO: What is the great strategic retreat the British speak of?

NIRODBARAN: They have fallen back in Belgium to keep in communication with the main army.

SATYENDRA: They have taken up their line of resistance, they say. Between Narvik and Trondjheim they are again fighting.

SRI AUROBINDO: Yes, and the British are in difficulty. Perhaps another strategic retreat may be expected. Now they are expecting a blow on England. So they may withdraw and prepare for that.

SATYENDRA: The *Indian Express* says that India has seventy aeroplanes to defend herself against 7000 German planes.

SRI AUROBINDO: And how many tanks?

SATYENDRA: None perhaps.

PURANI: There are some tanks – more than a hundred.

SRI AUROBINDO: A very big number indeed!

SATYENDRA: Gandhi writes in the *Harijan* that there is not much to choose between Imperialism and Fascism. He finds very little difference.

SRI AUROBINDO: There is a big difference. Under Fascism he wouldn't be able to write such things or say anything against the State. He would be shot.

SATYENDRA: And he still believes that by non-violence we can defend our country.

SRI AUROBINDO: Non-violence can't defend one. One can only die by it.

SATYENDRA: He believes that by such a death a change of heart can take place in the enemy.

SRI AUROBINDO: If it does, it will be after two or three centuries. Some reaction may take place and then somebody else may turn up. (*Laughter*)

SATYENDRA: He does not seem to make much distinction between moral and spiritual force.

SRI AUROBINDO: None at all.

SATYENDRA: Nirod will bring down the Supermind to solve all the problems.

SRI AUROBINDO: What is the prospect, Nirod? Is it near?

NIRODBARAN: I will bring it down for Satyendra.

SRI AUROBINDO (*laughing*): Instead of bringing down the Supermind it will be better at the moment to enter Narvik and do something there. Churchill is speaking of an assault. He has to show that he means it by doing something practical.

SATYENDRA: They are still two miles from Narvik.

SRI AUROBINDO: And still as far away as possible.

NIRODBARAN: The *Hindu* says Gamelin recoils at the horror of the sacrifice of lives that will be entailed in an attack on the Siegfried Line.

SRI AUROBINDO: Yes, he does not want to sacrifice life as was done in the last war. No such repetition this time, he says. It will be a defensive war with as little loss as possible. But his tone is already changing.

SATYENDRA: These people didn't prepare themselves well because they thought Hitler was bluffing. They didn't take him seriously.

SRI AUROBINDO: Hitler does not bluff. He has done everything he has said he would do – only, in his own time. Mussolini bluffs, but when he acts, he does it thoroughly.

PURANI: He seems to intend to come in at the end and get a share.

SRI AUROBINDO: Yes, but that share won't be for long. Hitler will finish him in no time. Italy is vulnerable on all sides. So Mussolini can't take any action suddenly.

22 MAY 1940

PURANI: Nehru is against Satyagraha at present in view of the condition of the Allies.

SRI AUROBINDO: Why don't the leaders come to an agreement?

NIRODBARAN: They are all still thinking and thinking.

SATYENDRA: Yes, they are doing constructive work.

NIRODBARAN: Charkha? Perhaps they are now waiting for Amery to make some move.

SRI AUROBINDO: He will be busy with the defence of England.

SATYENDRA: The German drive seems to be to encircle the Allies after they have reached the sea and then to attack the Maginot Line from the rear.

SRI AUROBINDO: Yes.

PURANI: The Allies' position here seems to be the same as in Norway and Denmark with a narrow strip of sea between. The English Channel is only twenty or thirty miles wide. The Allies would be able to bring big navies there in case of a German attack on England.

SATYENDRA: Why not? And how will the Germans take their troops across?

SRI AUROBINDO: Their position is not the same. In Norway they had no aerodromes. Here they have plenty of them.

NIRODBARAN: At present the thrust towards Paris seems to have been suspended.

SRI AUROBINDO: They are driving towards the sea. After capturing the ports they will begin to attack England and continue their thrust to Paris from St. Quentin or other places.

NIRODBARAN: After capturing the ports their aim is to prevent the British from sending reinforcements to France.

SRI AUROBINDO: No, they can't do that. There will still be plenty of ports in the west and north-west.

NIRODBARAN: The French can't launch an attack against the Siegfried Line today.

SRI AUROBINDO: It is impossible now.

NIRODBARAN: Reynaud says that they have committed mistakes.

SRI AUROBINDO: A lot of them. They assume things. With Hitler one can't assume anything. He does what is unexpected. All these people go by scientific principles. Hore-Belisha is the only man who can do something new. Eden is good but not for this. He would be better as Foreign Secretary, and Irwin in the India Office where he could go on with his peace plan and appeasement. Pétain has something but he is too old.

SATYENDRA: Weygand?

SRI AUROBINDO: I don't know anything about him.

NIRODBARAN: Is there an occult influence behind the Allies as there is behind Hitler?

SRI AUROBINDO: No, they are all ordinary persons without any such influence pushing them.

NIRODBARAN: Ordinary persons against an Asura? A bad look-out!

SRI AUROBINDO: There is nobody among them who can receive the Divine Force to counteract the Asuras. The Mother has not found anyone.

EVENING

PURANI: Weygand seems to be hopeful of victory if the Allies can resist for one month.

SRI AUROBINDO: Yes. Z says she has found that the French are going to war with reluctance and with a defeatist mentality. In that case, I don't see how they can beat Hitler.

NIRODBARAN: But why is it so?

SRI AUROBINDO: I don't know. Perhaps they want to lead a comfortable life. They have given good resistance in other parts – only in the centre the main army has given way. In the battle of the Meuse they forgot even to blow up the bridges during the retreat.

PURANI: Herbert says that Hitler will get what he wants.

SRI AUROBINDO: France also? If that is the mentality, they will be defeated. It is a stupid and tamasically sattwic quality. It appears the Germans intend to occupy Ireland and make it a base to attack England and cut off supplies to her from America and other places. That is behind their plan to get to the coast. Ireland has only an army of 30,000. These plans were discovered in the custody of some Germans. And then along with Italy they will attack through Switzerland and crush France.

NIRODBARAN: But how will they carry troops there?

SRI AUROBINDO: I can't say.

PURANI: Jwalanti was telling me Neville Henderson says that in Germany even before Hitler the atmosphere of life had so much pressure that one felt constantly suffocated.

SRI AUROBINDO: Yes, practically all of Germany was like that. Boys and young men were being trained to be devilish. When there was some complaint against harsh treatment meted out by the German army, people said, "Wait till the Nazis come to power. Then you will realise what harsh treatment is."

23 MAY 1940

SRI AUROBINDO: The German generals say that they are still not in contact with the main body of the French troops. Where are the troops? What are they doing?

SATYENDRA: They may come in at the end.

PURANI: The British Government has taken very strong measures.

NIRODBARAN: They say it has turned Socialist and Communist.

PURANI: This is due to the Labour influence, probably.

SRI AUROBINDO: Yes. From individual liberty to totalitarian Socialism must be a great change, because it is against the grain of the British. Their whole history is a fight for individual liberty. In the last war also, they took such steps but they went back to their natural condition.

SATYENDRA: Lindbergh says that countries at war are bound to be dictatorial at one time or another. So he is against America joining in.

SRI AUROBINDO: That is all very well, but Hitler's next attack will be on America.

NIRODBARAN: The Allies don't seem to be able to resist the German advance anywhere.

PURANI: It was the same in the last war. About two years afterwards they recovered their position.

SRI AUROBINDO: Not so long. It was at the battle of the Marne that the tide turned. At the beginning the English were running away before the German attack. There used to be wonderful stories by the correspondents. One war correspondent wrote that when the British army was running away, Sir John French was looking on and coolly smoking a cigarette. Then suddenly he started the counter-attack and the Germans were repulsed. What actually happened was that the German commander had outrun his support. Somebody saw this and the Allies, turning the flank, drove the Germans towards the Marne where the battle took place. The German commander had found the pursuit so attractive that he had forgotten about his over-advanced position.

SATYENDRA: The war will continue till 1942, according to astrology.

SRI AUROBINDO: That is the prophecy by the Theosophists. According to astrology, there is to be some set-back for Hitler in May. There is no sign of it yet.

NIRODBARAN: Still eight days to go. If they take Narvik, then —

SRI AUROBINDO: Yes, then we can begin to think that the Allies will win. They want to take Narvik without the loss of a single man!

NIRODBARAN: But they have again changed their position against the Germans, it is said. What does it mean?

SRI AUROBINDO: Obviously it means retreat. They want to fight non-violently like Gandhi – without killing a single man to capture Narvik.

SATYENDRA: When Vidyarthi was murdered by a Muslim, Gandhi said that he would have considered it a great fortune if he could himself have given his life.

SRI AUROBINDO: Yes, he would have expressed his love and gratitude to Vidyarthi for having given him such an opportunity. He would have said, "My dear fellow, how good you are to give me a chance to get murdered."

EVENING

SRI AUROBINDO (*addressing Purani*): The Ashram has been declared a nest of pro-Nazis and pro-Communists by your friend the consul. He says he can even produce documents.

NIRODBARAN: Schomberg?

PURANI: Yes.

NIRODBARAN: A nice friend you have.

PURANI: He is quite capable of this. I haven't seen him for a long time. Most probably the talk in the Ashram has reached his ears.

SRI AUROBINDO: That undoubtedly. But if he has any written proof it will be serious. If some people have written from here to their friends and the letters have been intercepted and sent to him, he will have documents.

PURANI: Has the matter gone to the French Government?

SRI AUROBINDO: No, not yet. But he must have sent his report to the British authorities. And they can be nasty, especially if they go down in the war. They may write to the French Governor who then won't be able to defend us and, next, to the Minister of Colonies. The movement against the Ashram is growing, some reliable friends have told us. Of course, we will try to counteract it but I don't see how it can be done. The danger is not only to the Allies but to us also. (*Looking at Nirodbaran*) I hear that H's place is a club for these discussions. Y and K go there, I am told.

NIRODBARAN: I don't know but it is quite possible. The other day H and Y were present when I repeated what you had said – and H agreed.

SRI AUROBINDO: Then he shouldn't allow these talks.

NIRODBARAN: Y, I think, is still unconvinced. He says he doesn't want Hitler to come to India but he does want him to win. It is difficult to rid him of his absurd idea.

SRI AUROBINDO: Hitler will act according to what Y wants or doesn't want? It is a very simple thing to see that Hitler wants world-domination and his next move will be towards India. But if Y goes on with such talk, evidently he doesn't care whether the Ashram should continue to exist.

PURANI: D also has such ideas and finds it difficult to dislodge them.

SRI AUROBINDO: You reported the Mother as saying something to Nolini. What was it?

PURANI: She said that if India were to get her freedom now, it would be catastrophic for her.

SRI AUROBINDO: The Mother didn't exactly say that. When Nolini said that it was because of the rancour against the British that people were talking in Hitler's favour, the Mother remarked that freedom at present would be dangerous to India, because India would play into the hands of Stalin. I am perfectly sure that if the Socialists and Communists don't get their way, they will call in Russia. SB may say Stalin is almost Asiatic.

PURANI: D says, "Let the Hindus and Muslims fight it out and see what happens. Some result will come."

SRI AUROBINDO: Yes. The Muslims will call in somebody and the Socialists somebody else. The Muslims may call in Mussolini because he proclaims himself defender of Islam. But he has removed half the Arabs from Tripoli and replaced them by Italians. India must get into the habit of freedom for about twenty or thirty years and then prepare for independence. To my mind the best thing is to have Dominion Status at present and then later on get ready for complete independence. India is a poor country, has no army, can't afford to have modern armaments. So long as she has no defence, she has to rely on others, unless the Socialists have a Kemal Pasha up their sleeves or a diplomat like Ismet Pasha who kept the enemy off till the country was prepared. Very difficult work. SB won't be able to do that.

PURANI: One Kemal Pasha won't do for India. There must be at least ten. If the Hindus and Muslims go on fighting with each other, other powers are sure to come in and a fresh subjugation is inevitable.

SRI AUROBINDO: Certainly. That is from the national point of view. Spiritually Stalin and Hitler will never tolerate any kind of work like ours. Spirituality and liberty of conscience are impossible in their regime. The Socialists or perhaps the Communists may think that Stalin will give some autonomy as in Georgia or the Ukraine – but it is all humbug. Even in the Ukraine, their President was shot because he was too pro-Ukraine.

I have been reading that book of astrology. But there is not much of astrology there. It is a political and psychological treatment of persons and events, astrology coming in as a third factor only, where the stars regulate things. The author says that Hitler is playing into the hands of the army. The people will rise in revolt and kill him. His prophecies are obviously wrong. He says Chamberlain will bring in the reign of peace. Churchill won't be the Prime Minister. It is more or less propaganda for Chamberlain.

NIRODBARAN: R is also speaking in favour of the Germans. When Bansidhar told him the Mother did not wish that we should take sides with Hitler, he replied, "Sri Aurobindo says different things to different persons as Sri Krishna did to Arjuna, Vidura, etc. You don't know."

SRI AUROBINDO: R knows?

24 MAY 1940

PURANI: The British Expeditionary Force seems to be surrounded by two German contingents now. They have either to push through them or re-embark.

SRI AUROBINDO: They may try to dislodge them from their occupied positions.

NIRODBARAN: It is surprising how in two weeks the Germans have marched across Belgium. It reminds me of Genghis Khan.

SRI AUROBINDO: Not marched but driven back the Allies.

PURANI: Duff Cooper has written an article on the likelihood of America joining the war if the Allies are defeated. Otherwise, he says, America will be the next victim.

SRI AUROBINDO: Of course. But Hitler won't turn so soon towards America. He will turn first towards the Balkans and, if Stalin comes in the way, march into Russia. After gaining Asia and Africa he will turn towards America. You know Washington's three dreams: First, war with England, Second, the American Civil War, third, the destruction of America by all mixed races, coloured and white. I suppose Hitler will pick out an American gaulieter as he has done in Austria.

NIRODBARAN: What is a gaulieter?

SRI AUROBINDO: Gau is province; gaulieter is province-protector. Austria has been divided into various provinces and each put under a gaulieter. The same has been done in Norway, Denmark and Belgium. I hope he won't succeed in America. As I said, his aim is clearly a world-empire.

NIRODBARAN: If Hitler is defeated what will happen to the Being guiding him?

SRI AUROBINDO: He will try to possess somebody else, for instance, Stalin. But I should say Stalin is himself a devil. He is cold and calculating, not suitable for the action of such Beings.

NIRODBARAN: The Mother said that Stalin is an incarnation of the Devil.

SRI AUROBINDO: Yes.

NIRODBARAN: In that case, Dilip says, he is worse than a case of possession. How does he allow dancing, music, etc. in Russia?

SRI AUROBINDO: That he can do. He is an intellectual Asura. All such things are a device to keep the people contented. But if they do go against the State they are shot. And what sort of music? Folk songs? Communism is a means for keeping power in his hands. Hitler's Being is a Rakshasa.[1]

NIRODBARAN: Are these Beings immortal?

SRI AUROBINDO: No, they can be destroyed but they may be born again.

NIRODBARAN: In the physical world?

SRI AUROBINDO: No, in their own world. (*After some time*) Gamelin is said to have shot himself.

PURANI: No, that is the German news.

SRI AUROBINDO: He should have. I saw his latest picture. It is the face of a man already defeated, extremely weak. His chin is catastrophic.

NIRODBARAN: Pétain has something.

SRI AUROBINDO: Yes, he is a man with a massive force but he is too old.

NIRODBARAN: He may be able to use the force.

[1] A vital, not an intellectual, demon.

SRI AUROBINDO: But, as I said, he is too old. Still he seems to have kept his intellectual powers intact, considering that he has turned Spain from an enemy into an ally.

PURANI: Yes, he has great influence over Franco.

NIRODBARAN: Dilip has become a convert to the Supermind. (*Sri Aurobindo made an expression of pretended surprise.*) Yes, he says only the Supermind can save humanity. If he has mocked at the Supermind, it was all in jest. (*Sri Aurobindo began to laugh.*) But he is in despair and wants to leave this sorrowful world.

SRI AUROBINDO: He will have to come back into a still more sorrowful world.

PURANI: When this war is over, there may again be a recrudescence of war after twenty-five years or so, unless some solution is arrived at.

SRI AUROBINDO: Yes, we have developed the system of nations and now we have to develop the unity of nations; unless they do that there will be always these recrudescences, till Nature forces us to come to a solution of the problem.

PURANI: In *The Psychology of Social Development*,[1] you have said the same thing. The nations and tribes that resisted had to perish.

SRI AUROBINDO: It was the same condition in France before the restoration of monarchy. On one side humanity is locked together; on the other side the national egos remain. The unity has of course to be a living unity, not like that of the Roman Empire in which the same old organisations and institutions remained.

PURANI: Now that the Allies and the Belgians have been forced to pool their economies, they may form such an alliance even after the war.

SRI AUROBINDO: Unless they do, there is no solution. The big Powers must form some sort of a system; it need not be a rigid system. If the small neutrals find that it is workable they may join. It has to be some sort of a federation but not the bungle and mess of the League of Nations.

EVENING

The radio reported that the Germans have advanced through a gap in the British position.

---

[1] Now published as *The Human Cycle*.

PURANI: So they left a gap for the Germans.

SRI AUROBINDO (*laughing*): Yes, what on earth did they leave this gap for?

PURANI: Perhaps in their retreat they couldn't keep up their line.

SATYENDRA: Now the British say that they are in the town of Narvik.

PURANI: First seven miles, then five, then two miles away!

SRI AUROBINDO: Yes, they will explain that Narvik is in hilly, mountainous country, covered with snow, no roads and communications. They are slowly closing round without the loss of a single man. They began in a gentlemanly way.

SATYENDRA: Yes, by dropping leaflets and making reconnaissance.

SRI AUROBINDO: Not in what they would call the savage way of the French who took Arras in one night? Only when the Germans dive-bombed did they become wild – that too only in their navy and air force.

SATYENDRA: Because on land they couldn't do anything.

PURANI: Gandhi seems to be in a conciliatory mood now – he will leave no stone unturned, he says. He will try to come to a compromise, perhaps.

SRI AUROBINDO: He ought to, unless Jawaharlal prevents him.

PURANI: Jawaharlal is not satisfied.

SRI AUROBINDO: He will never be satisfied. That is why I say unless he stands in the way. Gandhi is now under his influence.

PURANI: But C. R. and Patel may exert some influence too.

SRI AUROBINDO: England is trying to make up with Russia, it seems. They say that Russia has asked Germany and Italy to keep out of the Balkans. That would explain Russia's massing of troops on the German frontier. Italy of course will plunge towards the Balkans if she can pluck up courage.

This book of prophecy says things which are now obviously wrong. He says Fritch, who died in Poland, would reorganise Germany after Hitler's death. I can understand now what the astrologers do. They see the position, give a general impression of things which may come true. But when they particularise, they make mistakes and try to wriggle out of them. This man says that the annexation of Poland was the last successful result of Hitler's ambition. Then he goes on to say that after Hitler and Stalin have gone, Russia and Germany will make a military alliance and create a new type of State. And then he pays high tributes to Chamberlain.

PURANI: Yes, he makes him out a saint.

SRI AUROBINDO: Yes, saint, apostle, everything.

25 MAY 1940

SRI AUROBINDO (*addressing Satyendra*): Have you read of the retreat of the Allies?

SATYENDRA (*smiling*): No!

SRI AUROBINDO: Yes, they have got away safely from Boulogne. The Allies means, of course, the British. (*Laughter*)

SATYENDRA: What do they lack? Why are they giving way like that?

SRI AUROBINDO: I don't understand. The German advance-troops are not numerous and still the Allies can't tackle them. They can only hold out for a while and then retreat. For two or three days the French have been saying that they are in the suburb of Amiens, as at Narvik – closing round.

SATYENDRA: They don't say now "according to plan". (*Laughter*)

SRI AUROBINDO: They go according to their old order and schedule while Churchill speaks of assault and attack.

SATYENDRA: Order and schedule don't come to much.

SRI AUROBINDO: It is a new method of warfare now. If they stick to their old method, then they can't hold on. It is like the football game. When one party makes a rush, the other can't say, "Let us wait to put the field in order." They can't go and occupy an unassigned place because it is unassigned. (*Laughter*) It is the famous story of Government House being on fire. They wrote to the headquarters, asking what they should do. The headquarters after some time, wrote back, "Put out the fire." (*Laughter*)

NIRODBARAN: The Germans intend to attack England, they say.

SRI AUROBINDO: That is why they are capturing the ports. Otherwise they would have turned towards Paris.

PURANI: In the course of a talk, Schomberg was telling me that volunteers are not of much use now as it is a mechanised warfare for which much training is needed.

SRI AUROBINDO: Yes, but it is not that the Allies have no mechanised troops. Besides, mechanised troops operate in open fields. In cities like Amiens they can't. There it is the infantry that has to lead the attack. France has a big army and England has a British Expeditionary Force and is now calling up reservists.

SATYENDRA: America is proposing to send all her planes for the defence of the Allies.

SRI AUROBINDO: Not all – only as many as she can spare. One senator has said that America's frontier is the Rhine. But even that limited proposal has been turned down.

SATYENDRA: The frontier is shifting. Now it is Boulogne.

SRI AUROBINDO: Still the Rhine is also there.

SATYENDRA: The new English law has not come into force yet, against private property.

SRI AUROBINDO: Private property? That would be the last thing to be touched.

PURANI: At present their aim is control of labour and industries to prevent profiteering.

SATYENDRA: And facilitate manufacture of armament.

SRI AUROBINDO: The English have never gone so far before. They are arresting M.P.'s even. In France it is quite traditional to arrest suspects in times of stress and revolution. Liberty is in a bad state everywhere in spite of Chamberlain and Roosevelt.

EVENING

SRI AUROBINDO: The Germans have passed through that convenient gap of thirty miles.

SATYENDRA: Not thirty, but twenty-five.

SRI AUROBINDO: Now they have narrowed it to twenty-five.

PURANI: The B.B.C. says it won't give news any more. The public gets scared. But they will be still more scared by the German news.

SRI AUROBINDO: They will give news of Norway, perhaps. (*Laughter*)

SATYENDRA: It seems the two contingents of Germans have separated the B.E.F. from the French. In that case they will be sandwiched by the Germans. One will come from the north and the other from the south.

SRI AUROBINDO: From the north? The Germans are in Antwerp; that is north-east. They can't make a flanking movement from there. They can only attack from the front. And it is only the advance troops of the Germans that have passed through the gap. The main body is behind. If they bring up the main body, there will be a great strategical danger of the French making an attack on their flank. This gap must have been left by the B.E.F. during their wonderful "strategical retreat" from Namur. It could not have been there at the beginning. If it had been, the Germans would have rushed forward at that time.

NIRODBARAN: If it is only the advance troops occupying, they can't be numerous. And how could they occupy the ports?

SRI AUROBINDO: There was no defence in the ports.

NIRODBARAN: Churchill says that the Germans rushed through the breach in the French army and attacked the B.E.F. from behind.

SRI AUROBINDO: That was earlier. Later it was through the gap left by the British army.

PURANI: Udar says that there is much anti-British feeling outside.

SRI AUROBINDO: Dara writes from Hyderabad that except for himself and Sir Akbar everybody is anti-British.

NIRODBARAN: Why are the Muslims anti-British?

SRI AUROBINDO: Why not? They don't want British Raj, they want Muslim Raj. I would not mind that if it were not for Hitler. Even Mussolini would not matter if he defeated the Allies, because he is not a man to conquer the world. Stalin is serious not because of himself but because of his Communism. Huque says he wants to forget that he is a Muslim Leaguer and asks the Congress and Mahasabha to forget their own parties and merge for a common object. The trouble is: as soon as the danger is over, they will start again. You have seen what the Raja of Mahmudabad has said?

NIRODBARAN: No.

SRI AUROBINDO: He wants to have separate Muslim provinces and to impose Muslim laws on all. He says there are very good laws in Islam. No usury, prohibition, and so on.

NIRODBARAN: That shows what they will do if they have their way, and they blame the Congress!

SRI AUROBINDO: They will start civil war at once. But I don't see how their Pakistan scheme can be successful if the Frontier,

Baluchistan and Sind don't want it. In that case only Punjab and Bengal remain. In Punjab the Sikhs and Hindus won't stand being Muslimised, I suppose.

NIRODBARAN: The Sikhs won't.

SRI AUROBINDO: The Hindus will, you mean? And in Bengal, I don't know what they will do. Perhaps they will wail like Sotuda.

26 MAY 1940

SRI AUROBINDO: The British have made another strategic retreat. (*Laughter*)

PURANI: Yes, they got safely away without losing a single man.

SRI AUROBINDO: The Germans allowed them to run away, perhaps.

PURANI: Fifteen generals have been relieved of their command in France.

SRI AUROBINDO: That is quite a big number.

PURANI: They were said to be indifferent and negligent.

SRI AUROBINDO: That is why Reynaud said that if the French could stand for a month, there would be a better chance. They will have to look for new men to take the place of the old generals.

NIRODBARAN: Was there sabotage in the army?

PURANI: The generals were just indifferent.

SRI AUROBINDO: Not sabotage exactly. Some officer here said that along with the first French refugees some two thousand Germans came in and produced a demoralising effect. And yet the authorities took no action against them. Daladier exhibits himself as a strong man but he is really very weak.

PURANI: A French counterpart of Chamberlain?

SRI AUROBINDO: Quite so.

PURANI: The Germans praise Lord Gort and General Ironside, saying they are quiet and don't show what they are going to do.

SRI AUROBINDO: But they haven't done anything so far, except make strategic retreats. They do what the Germans want them to and hence the praise. They haven't shown any very brilliant capacity till now.

NIRODBARAN: The British rely much on Weygand.

SRI AUROBINDO: They know that they themselves have no capable persons.

NIRODBARAN: I wonder if there is any sabotage in the British Army. Or is it the inherent weakness of the army itself? But the situation seems to have improved a little.

SRI AUROBINDO: On the French side. The British are always retreating. If they go on in that way, the Germans will reach the ports and the British will have to retreat into their ships. That will be good in one way. The French will have a more easily defensible line – not too long. At present they have four lines along four rivers – the Somme, the Oise, the Meuse and the Scheldt. They can defend themselves without difficulty against mechanised units, but they haven't yet found anything against dive-bombers.

NIRODBARAN: Dilip had a letter from Niren R. Chowdhury. It seems Dilip sent Huxley's book to Charu Dutt and asked him to forward it to Niren. Niren, after reading it, says, "It is all right, but Marx's Dialectical Materialism is the last word."

PURANI: Marx's own followers are now differing among themselves about his Dialectical Materialism. What exactly is it?

SATYENDRA: Huxley hasn't developed any philosophy in his book. He has only described his experience. It is *neti, neti* ("Not this, not that").

SRI AUROBINDO: No, it is not all *neti, neti*. So far as I have gathered from the extracts I have read, it is not that alone.

SATYENDRA: But he has not given any philosophy.

PURANI: He is a moralist.

SRI AUROBINDO: He has said, as I have done, that there is no solution to the problem of the world except by spirituality and the spiritual way.

SATYENDRA: Can spiritual experience solve the problem?

SRI AUROBINDO: It is the basis. What people try to make out of Huxley and Gerald Heard is that theirs is a confession of defeat and that they on their part want to escape from the world. It is not really this, as Isherwood has pointed out in the *New Statesman*. He says that what he understands from Huxley and Heard is that they want to discover a way to change the present human consciousness by which alone the social and political problems will be solved. Somebody also said that Heard advocates Buddhist fatalism. To which Heard replied that he didn't advocate fatalism at all. Nor is there any fatalism in Buddhism. All human history has been a question of change of consciousness, and Huxley says that the change can come only by spirituality. Hitherto people have worked on the principle of opposition and indifference. That can only make a patchwork solution. Behind the multiplicity and division one has to see the identity and oneness. Of course, if you say spirituality is not a solution, then you have to fall into Mayavada (World-Illusionism).

SATYENDRA (*after some time*): Do you envisage the gnostic being as living and acting in the world in a group formation?

SRI AUROBINDO: Yes. If the individual has to remain in society, the gnostic being has to do this too and the individual must merge in the group.

SATYENDRA: In place of individual isolation, it will then be group isolation?

SRI AUROBINDO: From the group the gnostic being will act on the world. Since the Supermind wants to change the world, the group will have to take up the outer life of the society and the individual has to throw himself into the outer life. I am not speaking of the inner life. Either the individual has to live secluded and isolated from the life of the society or take up its own outer life in order to change it. Without group action the individual will have to give way to the life of the society and be like one of the group.

SATYENDRA: There has been plenty of spiritual life lived in the world.

SRI AUROBINDO: Is that why it had no effect on the world?

PURANI (*after Satyendra's exit*): What I understand Satyendra to say is: Why should one be compelled to lead a group life?

NIRODBARAN: There is no compulsion and, if at all, it is an inner one.

SRI AUROBINDO: Why should there be any compulsion? One can go, if he likes, to the mountains and live there, but if one is impelled from within to lead a group life he can follow the impulsion. If the Supramental Truth commends itself to one, one can live according to it.

PURANI: I told Satyendra that the very fact that he talks of compulsion and of keeping one's individuality, shows that he is talking from his mental imagination. For, if one attains to the Sachchidananda consciousness, one is no longer bound by such ideas, one is led to accord oneself to that higher consciousness.

SRI AUROBINDO: And if he wants to keep his individuality, for that he has to accept the Supramental Truth; for in the Supermind alone there is diversity and difference but without division – diversity there is based on unity and difference is a play of the One.

EVENING

PURANI: That book of astrology is hard on Sir Oswald Mosley, and what the writer has said has come true. Mosley has been imprisoned.

SRI AUROBINDO: Yes, but Mosley may comfort himself by thinking that Hitler too was once imprisoned.

PURANI: As regards particulars, the book is not correct at all.

SRI AUROBINDO: Only about general influences does he make some right guesses.

27 MAY 1940

NIRODBARAN: Nolini Sen writes that Meghnad Saha wants to come here.

SRI AUROBINDO: To embrace X? (*Laughter*)

NIRODBARAN: Sen has a deep respect for Saha. He says he is very sincere, honest, open-minded, generous.

SRI AUROBINDO: Perhaps not open-minded.

PURANI (*giving a letter to Sri Aurobindo*): Sundaram has written to you, asking what his duty is in connection with the war. He is much puzzled.

SRI AUROBINDO: You may tell him that God's Front is the Spiritual Front, which is still lagging much behind. Hitler's Germany is not God's Front. It is the Asuric Front, through which the Asura aims at world-domination. It is the descent of the Asuric world upon the human to establish its own power on the earth.

NIRODBARAN: It seems Hitler says that by the end of June he will proclaim a New Order from a city in France.

SRI AUROBINDO: A New Order for what? And from which city? Vervains?

NIRODBARAN: Or Amiens?

SRI AUROBINDO: Amiens will be made unsuitable for him by the R.A.F., if they know he is there.

NIRODBARAN: He will dictate the terms of peace also.

SRI AUROBINDO: Dictate by the end of June?

NIRODBARAN: Yes.

PURANI: And everything will be over by August 15.

SRI AUROBINDO: He expects everything to go according to schedule.

EVENING

PURANI: Ramakrishna's new temple at Belur is supposed to be the biggest on the eastern side.

SRI AUROBINDO: What does the eastern side mean?

PURANI: On this side of the temple of Jagannath.

SRI AUROBINDO: Hindu temples are usually not big. Whom do they worship at Ramakrishna's temple?

PURANI: I think there is a life-size photograph of Ramakrishna and the sign OM somewhere.

SRI AUROBINDO: That is Vivekananda's creed.

PURANI: Yes, but I am not sure of the details.

SRI AUROBINDO: In Ramakrishna's temple there ought to be at least an image of Kali.

28 MAY 1940

PURANI: The morning paper says that two German generals are advancing with their infantry. And French and British units are trying to join and make a line of defence before they arrive.

SRI AUROBINDO: It doesn't look as if those units will be able to do it. (*After a time*) This extension of the Maginot Line seems to be a myth. There are no fortifications anywhere.

PURANI: After the last war, if they had strengthened the fortifications, things would have been better.

SRI AUROBINDO: But where are the fortifications? They do not exist. That is why the Germans have walked over easily to Amiens and other places.

PURANI: The Allies seem to have stemmed the tide now.

NIRODBARAN: In one sector they are badly placed, where the Germans are attacking from the rear.

SRI AUROBINDO: I don't know why they didn't provide for it.

PURANI: The R.A.F. have done very good work. They are destroying all communications, tanks, depots, etc.

SRI AUROBINDO: In the air and on the sea the British as well as the French are superior.

NIRODBARAN: Daladier wanted to bluff the Germans.

SRI AUROBINDO: Bluff? They have all the necessary information. A Deputy said to Daladier, "If France is destroyed, it will be your fault." Daladier said, "No, we have been good. But in infantry we have been outclassed."

NIRODBARAN (*after a while, giving Sri Aurobindo* Udbodhan *to read*): Here is a review of Nishikanto's *Alakananda*, written by one Debabrata Roy Chowdhury, who says, "Nishikanto's poetic life grew up in the shadow of Tagore's poetry; so his poems of those days are colourless like a shadow-grown tree.... Today he has found the direction towards the Beyond in the shelter of Sri Aurobindo."

SRI AUROBINDO: Tagore won't like that.

NIRODBARAN: In this same issue has come the second instalment of your life by Girija S. R. Chowdhury. This man has brought out the whole history and origin of Brahmo Samaj to show its influence on your birth and your connection with it.

SRI AUROBINDO: What have I got to do with that? My father was an atheist.

NIRODBARAN: Your grandfather, Rajnarayan, was a Brahmo. The writer links that up with your life.

SRI AUROBINDO (*addressing Nirodbaran after taking up the copy and reading*): Look here! He says that the people of Khulna have designated the town of Khulna the playground of Aurobindo's adolescence – because my father was a civil surgeon in Khulna. It is not true. Up to the age of five I was in Rangpur, as my father was in Rangpur, not in Khulna. I went to Khulna long after returning from England.

NIRODBARAN: From five to seven, you were in Darjeeling Loretto School, he says.

SRI AUROBINDO: He may have got that right. He says, "The place where Sri Aurobindo was born in Calcutta has not been fixed yet. Nobody has tried to fix it, and it should be done." I was born in the lawyer Manmohan Ghose's house on Theatre Road. (*Then Sri Aurobindo began to read and put marks in various places. He stopped at one place.*) Have I said anything against immolation of the Satis anywhere?

PURANI: Not that I know of.

EVENING

News came that Belgium had surrendered. It was a surprise to us all.

PURANI: King Leopold has not consulted even his commander-in-chief Blanchard. The Belgian Government says that it won't accept the King's order and will raise another army in France.

NIRODBARAN: Yes, but how will it reach Belgium? It is really very extraordinary.

SRI AUROBINDO: The commander-in-chief is not bound to obey the king's order. The king is not the nation. The surrender means that Dunkirk – and also Calais – will fall to Germany.

PURANI: I wonder if he has been bribed.

SRI AUROBINDO: He has always been an unreliable person, used to taking many steps on his own account. The Mother said that he killed his own wife, and now he kills his country. His wife was better than he, and she would not have allowed this.

NIRODBARAN: Did he kill his wife?

SRI AUROBINDO: Yes, he was to blame for the accident.

The lieutenant here, who is the son of a French general, has said that Belgium's Albert Canal is almost as impregnable as the Maginot Line. There must have been some act of treason for Belgium to give way so spectacularly.

PURANI: It didn't hold out even for two weeks.

NIRODBARAN: It didn't hold out at all. We've heard so much about Holland's dams and the Albert Canal!

SRI AUROBINDO: The great defect of advanced democracy is that it listens to anything – to slogans, as they say – without being able to think or judge for itself. In the French army also at the beginning there was disaffection: "What are we fighting for? These generals will kill us in the war." All the slogans were in the air owing to German propaganda. That is the result of mass education. All that such education gives is information, and people don't know what use to make of it, how to apply it in the right and not the wrong way. It is already a difficult problem for educated people; what then about the masses? Hitler has openly said in his book that to carry the public, one has only to lie, to give false promises, and they will be with you. It shows now that what he has said is quite true.

PURANI (*after some time*): Jinnah seems to be seriously ill.

SRI AUROBINDO: About two days ago he gave out a statement on the Pakistan scheme.

PURANI: This Gujarati paper says he is ill. If he goes, then –

SRI AUROBINDO (*smiling*): Have you read what Gandhi has said in answer to a correspondent? He says that if eight crores of Muslims demand a separate State, what else are the twenty-five crores of Hindus to do but surrender? Otherwise there will be civil war.

NIRODBARAN: I hope that is not the type of conciliation he is thinking of.

SRI AUROBINDO: Not thinking of it, you say? He has actually said that and almost yielded. If you yield to the opposite party beforehand, naturally they will stick strongly to their claims. It means that the minority will rule and the majority must submit. The minority is allowed its say: "We shall be the rulers and you our servants. Our *harf* (word) will be law; you will have to obey." This shows a peculiar mind. I think this kind of people are a little cracked. (*Looking at Purani*) Don't you agree?

PURANI (*after a pause*): Rajkot seems to have some reforms now.

SRI AUROBINDO: Yes, what has happened there? This Thakur must have done something very wrong.

PURANI: Probably. It may be he is in debt and spending State money. He is an idiot. Virawalla also is now dead.

NIRODBARAN: After all, Gandhi's fast is bearing fruit. (*Laughter*)

SRI AUROBINDO: You mean Virawalla died as a result of his fast?

NIRODBARAN: People will take it in that way.

SRI AUROBINDO: That is what I have written in the *Arya* – that "soul-force" sometimes creates forces which are much more violent. Gandhi may agree to the change of constitution as a result of his fast but not Virawalla's death. (*Laughter*)

PURANI: But the whole public feeling against him must have weighed on him.

SRI AUROBINDO: Who is this new Dewan of Rajkot? I seem to have heard his name. Was he in any legislature?

PURANI: He is a Parsi, one of the Anklesarias. He is a barrister from Bombay.

29 MAY 1940

PURANI: It is said that there were 300,000 Belgian troops. Their surrender has made the position of the British Expeditionary Force extremely grave.

SRI AUROBINDO: Yes. There is no way out for them unless Dunkirk can hold on or they can rush through the gap from the French line.

SATYENDRA: I don't understand why King Leopold has ordered the surrender.

SRI AUROBINDO: He has always been unreliable and taken independent decisions. It was he who prevented alliance with France just before the war and he kept his wonderful neutrality. Now he has been given a castle and a pension for his service to Hitler.

SATYENDRA: The surrender came as a surprise even to the German commander.

NIRODBARAN: If the Army rises in revolt –

SRI AUROBINDO: That would be something.

PURANI: The Belgian Cabinet is trying to raise a new Belgian army.

NIRODBARAN: Yes, but it's not much use. They can't go to Belgium and fight there.

SRI AUROBINDO: Still, it shows the rebellion of the people.

PURANI: It will be like the Czech and Polish armies – with only small numbers of men.

SRI AUROBINDO: With our Sammer we can start a Czech army (*laughter*), so that they may realise the situation and learn a lesson.

NIRODBARAN: Dilip is passing through ups and downs. Now he is trying to take a philosophical view of the Allied reverses and set himself in the right position.

SRI AUROBINDO: What is that?

NIRODBARAN: He says that perhaps it is necessary that the Allies should go through hardships and sufferings at the beginning. He got strength from the Mother's message in which she has said that the Asuras can't be victorious eternally against the Divine. The hour of Hitler's downfall must come.

SRI AUROBINDO: That doesn't mean it will come by the Allies. (*Laughter*)

SATYENDRA: No, but don't tell him that or he will be depressed.

SRI AUROBINDO: Yes.

SATYENDRA: It seems that everything touches him badly.

SRI AUROBINDO: How do you mean?

SATYENDRA: I mean that if anything goes wrong anywhere, it affects him. Perhaps he has become depressed about Subhas Bose too.

NIRODBARAN: No, not now. He has seen through him.

SRI AUROBINDO: Subhas Bose is starting another revolution.

SATYENDRA: Yes, Narendra Deo calls his Forward Bloc "Backward Bloc".

SRI AUROBINDO: "Forward and Backward Bloc" would be better still. (*Laughter*)

SATYENDRA: In the *Chandi* there are descriptions of these fights of the Asuras – I am telling Nirod as he may not have read it. So many times the Asuras attack the Mother. At the last moment, they are defeated.

SRI AUROBINDO: That is the Indian tradition: up to the last moment the Asuras are victorious; and that is the general tradition as well. At the last moment, some miracle happens.

SATYENDRA: They also say that Shiva supports the Asuras, gives them boons.

SRI AUROBINDO: He makes many blunders.

SATYENDRA: And Vishnu comes to the rescue.

NIRODBARAN: Sometimes it seems that Shiva favours one side and Parvati the opposite one. Madhusudan has depicted it in *Meghnad*, his epic poem.

SRI AUROBINDO: Madhusudan had a sympathy for Ravana.

Then Purani read out from a Hindi paper an article by some Arya Samajist attacking Ramana Maharshi, and also Agarwal – that is, one of our group – who had held a joint meditation in Gurukul. The Arya Samajist who went to Ramana Maharshi said that the Maharshi observes the caste system. When asked why this was so, the Maharshi replied, "Should all horses, donkeys and pigs eat from a common plate?" (Laughter)

SATYENDRA: But he doesn't believe in caste – he eats with non-Brahmins.

SRI AUROBINDO: He must have said that deliberately to the Arya Samajist.

PURANI: Yes, I know of an Arya Samajist who had an altercation with Ramana Maharshi some time ago. This is probably the same man. It was said that Ramana Maharshi got excited and angry and began to shout. This man also says he became angry.

SRI AUROBINDO: Angry?

PURANI: Yes, Brunton too has said that he gets angry.

SRI AUROBINDO: Ramakrishna also used to get angry, for that matter.

PURANI: He says that in Gandhi's Ashram there is no caste.

SRI AUROBINDO: And why does he say that the Maharshi was jealous because he criticised him? Does one criticise out of jealousy? Gandhi doesn't believe in the caste system?

PURANI: Oh yes, he does.

SATYENDRA: Varnashram. The Maharshi has a very good relationship with Gandhiji. He sent him blessings.

SRI AUROBINDO: The Sannyasins don't observe caste?

PURANI: Oh yes, they do.

SRI AUROBINDO: Then what strikes him as so very strange?

SATYENDRA: If the Maharshi observes the caste system, it is because he doesn't want to disturb the established order of society.

SRI AUROBINDO: Why should he disturb it? It is not his business.

PURANI: Besides, he himself takes his meals with non-Brahmins. What more can he do?

EVENING

The radio news said that King Leopold had surrendered because of a military stress.

SRI AUROBINDO: What is this military stress under which he had to surrender and had no time even to inform the Allies or consult the Cabinet?

PURANI: Roger Keyes seems to have sent some confidential message to Churchill about it, which may have been that the army was refusing to fight.

SRI AUROBINDO: Even so, did they have no time to inform the Allies? That is more than I can swallow. And if the army refuses to fight, it is a dishonour to the whole nation; in the other case, it is a dishonour only to the king.

NIRODBARAN: They say the Germans launched a heavy attack against the Belgian army.

SRI AUROBINDO: Just two or three days ago it was said that the Belgians were fighting gallantly.

NIRODBARAN: The *Hindu* seems to support the king.

SRI AUROBINDO: It shows sympathy for the Belgian king's army.

SATYENDRA: It seems also to be generous.

SRI AUROBINDO: Generous? When the whole army is going to be destroyed, it is difficult to be generous. No, Roger Keyes doesn't clear the mystery. It seems the whole world of humanity has lost all sense of honour and truth. For the sake of self-interest one is capable of doing anything.

PURANI: Street fighting is going on in Dunkirk.

SRI AUROBINDO: That means it will fall into the hands of the Germans.

SATYENDRA: The Maharaja of Travancore has placed his whole army at the disposal of the British (*laughter*) – an army of a hundred or so.

SRI AUROBINDO: A little more, perhaps.

SATYENDRA: Sometimes the Maharaja of Nepal also does the same – a few thousand people.

NIRODBARAN: At any rate they wouldn't surrender.

SATYENDRA: I don't know. Against mechanised warfare, what can they do?

SRI AUROBINDO: They would do very well. They have initiative, dash and daring, and they can easily adapt themselves. They would start some sort of guerilla warfare in which they excel.

SATYENDRA: Yes.

PURANI: The R.A.F. are doing very good work.

SRI AUROBINDO: I don't see how they can do much. The soldiers are pressed from east and west and if the supplies from Dunkirk are cut off, then without food and ammunition how are they to hold on? If the Belgian army has capitulated for lack of supplies, one can understand, but even then, they would have had time to inform.

NIRODBARAN: Perhaps escape through the ports is the only way open to the British Expeditionary Force.

SRI AUROBINDO: Which ports? Ostend was in the hands of the Belgian army. By their surrender Dunkirk will be vulnerable unless they have sufficient troops there to defend it. Now escape also is difficult. They may try to dash through the gap and line up with the French on the Somme. Otherwise I don't see any way. Where is the main body of the French army they speak of? Why don't they employ it now to disengage the trapped soldiers? I don't understand this warfare.

PURANI: Weygand is organising in other parts. He is hoping to dislodge the Germans and occupy the bridges. He will take a month to consolidate. Perhaps he thinks that if he brings in the main army at this weak moment, it may also lose.

SRI AUROBINDO: Even then this will be a tremendous loss – 300,000 people! (*After a pause*) The whole thing is absurd. Why did England send this Expeditionary Force against an army highly mechanised? Perhaps we shouldn't criticise them. India would have made a bigger mess, "a Himalayan blunder" as Gandhi would call it. The whole history of India has been a running away of armies from battlefields as soon as their king or their leader was killed. For instance, in the battle of Calicut after the king had fallen, the soldiers – they were of the finest type – could not stand it for a moment; they simply ran away. In England I read a book by some

Englishman about the Battle of Assaye. He said that when the French king fell, the soldiers didn't know what to do. They simply stood at their posts and were mopped up by the British.

PURANI: The Indian people also had no unity among themselves. They didn't think in terms of their country as a whole. Someone, in writing about the Mahrattas, said that they had tremendous national egoism but no unity, and that their system of Jagirdars[1] was the cause of their ruin. Very often these Jagirs were given as hereditary posts without any consideration of the individual's fitness. Khare, ex-chief minister, also said to the Mahrattas, "You don't know what Swaraj is, you never had it."

SRI AUROBINDO: They had it during Shivaji's time; at that time they were all united. Among the Sikhs too there was unity, though later on it broke down. The Rajputs, of course, didn't know what unity was. Europe is now inheriting. The ancient peoples also didn't know how to achieve the malady unity. Porus, after being defeated, allied himself with Alexander and fought against his own countrymen.

In Europe also the same thing happened during the Middle Ages, and continued even up to the early part of the reign of Louis XIV. Some provinces of France were at one time fighting for France, and at another time against her.

PURANI: Yes, a part of France was sometimes calling England to come and rule her.

SRI AUROBINDO: Which part?

PURANI: Normandy.

SRI AUROBINDO: Oh, Normandy. At that time there was a Norman king in England, so they thought themselves to be allies. Besides, it was the period following the feudal kings and lords, so the people thought it their duty to serve their feudal lords. They had no sense of country at that time. In spite of all that, it is remarkable that France became so united.

PURANI: Some contemporary has written the whole of French history in two pages. He says the whole question amongst them is: Who is the best leader?

SRI AUROBINDO: That is at least something. In India, it was: Who is the most powerful?

1. Those holding land without paying tax on it.

30 MAY 1940

SRI AUROBINDO (*addressing Purani and smiling*): Have you heard of the great and glorious British victory?

PURANI: Conquest óf Narvik? Yes. The Germans also admit it now.

NIRODBARAN: We can say now that Hitler's decline has begun. (*Laughter*)

PURANI: Dunkirk is still in the Allies' hands. There is a great concentration of navy. Perhaps the B.E.F. will be able to escape.

SRI AUROBINDO: They seem to be very clever in retreat (*laughter*) – the French are not.

SATYENDRA: It will be a great feat if they can escape.

SRI AUROBINDO: Yes, it can be called a great military feat.

PURANI: The Germans are leaving a great number of dead in this campaign.

SRI AUROBINDO: Yes, they are always reckless.

PURANI: Shaw says that what Russia has not been able to do in twenty-three years England has done in two-and-a-half years.

SRI AUROBINDO: What?

NIRODBARAN: State Socialism.

SRI AUROBINDO: Russia has not done it.

PURANI: No – only according to Shaw. And then he says that when the British people are frightened they flare up. The Kaiser frightened them and he was defeated. Hitler also will have the same fate.

SRI AUROBINDO: Is he defending the war now?

PURANI: Yes.

SRI AUROBINDO: He has been frightened himself then? (*Laughter*)

PURANI: He asks Ireland to join with the Allies; otherwise they will have the same fate as Poland in German hands.

31 MAY 1940

Sri Aurobindo opened the talk by referring to the evacuation of Allied troops from Dunkirk.

SRI AUROBINDO: So they are getting away from Dunkirk!

PURANI: Yes. It seems the fog helped the evacuation.

SRI AUROBINDO: Yes. Fog is rather unusual at this time. *(By saying this, it seemed that Sri Aurobindo wanted to hint that the Mother and he had made this fog to help the Allies.)* Now they have let out King Leopold who has been in sympathy with Germany for a long time. The Belgian ambassador in Spain said that he has always had sympathy with totalitarianism.

SATYENDRA: This fight has given some confidence to the British Expeditionary Force.

SRI AUROBINDO: Yes, the British were becoming used to quiet and comfort.

Purani *(after some time, when the others had gone)*: Adwaitanand *(a visitor)* says that wherever he has travelled in India he has found a living current of spirituality and he is very glad. Even people who have been atheists and materialists are now turning to spirituality or having a regard for it.

SRI AUROBINDO *(laughing)*: Even Subhas Bose when depressed talks of spirituality. *(Laughter)*

PURANI: He has met the Congress leaders and they are also changing, he says. Rajendra Prasad he found to be a very good man. About Nehru he is silent.

SRI AUROBINDO: I thought he was against any spirituality.

Purani *(after a while)*: This Muslim delegation to the All India Muslim Education Conference has arrived.

SRI AUROBINDO: Delegation? It is not a delegation.

PURANI: Hasn't it been sent by Calcutta University? The Vice-Chancellor of the University is the President.

SRI AUROBINDO: Calcutta University? I thought he had done it in his own capacity. Does he want to Mahommedanise Calcutta University?

NIRODBARAN: Dilip says he is not impressed by them. Almost all look "stolid", he says.

PURANI: I don't see why they have come to Pondicherry. *(After a while)* Wells considers that the German threat to invade is a myth to keep British forces in England instead of letting them come to France.

SRI AUROBINDO: I don't think an invasion is likely or possible.

SATYENDRA: They can only make air raids.

SRI AUROBINDO: Yes. The British are preparing their defences now.

K12

Nirodbaran (*addressing Purani*): Jinnah has come out. So he is not ill.

SRI AUROBINDO: He practically says to the Government, "You side with us and we will see."

PURANI: What can the Congress do?

SRI AUROBINDO: Yes.

NIRODBARAN: If the Government concedes to the Congress, can the Muslim League do anything effective against it?

SATYENDRA: What can they do?

NIRODBARAN: Non-violent non-cooperation?

PURANI: Non-violent? By the Muslims?

SRI AUROBINDO: They can start some Khaksar agitation.

EVENING

PURANI: The Germans claim to have sunk three warships and many troopships of the Allies.

SRI AUROBINDO: Three warships?

PURANI: Two battleships and one cruiser.

SRI AUROBINDO: Two sloops probably. Difficult to believe German claims even when they say what is true.

After some time Sri Aurobindo lay in bed.

SRI AUROBINDO (*to Purani*): I was reading this book of Amiya Chakravarty, The *Dynasts and Post-War Poetry*. Most of the quotations he gives from Hardy, Auden, etc. are what I said of Ramesh Dutt's poetry: execrable. (*Laughter*) Give me the book, I shall read out some. (*After reading out from the book here and there*) Each one is worse than the other. Compared to the modern ones, Hardy's are better, though he does not hesitate to write flat prose. (*Laughter*)

PURANI: The *Dynasts* is about Napoleonic times.

SRI AUROBINDO: Yes, it is a caricature of Napoleon. It makes him a tyrant – it is pacifist poetry.

1 JUNE 1940

PURANI: The Muslim delegation was very pleased with Dilip's music last night – especially so when Dilip said that the Muslims have made a great contribution to music. (*Laughter*) That pleases them very much but they are not so pleased when any Hindu contribution is spoken of. It is quite apparent. It was Aurangzeb who banned music among the Muslims. The Koran also forbids it.

SRI AUROBINDO: The Koran also?

PURANI: Yes, that is why other Muslim countries like Persia have no music. In India, after Akbar music dwindled among the Muslims; by Aurangzeb's order all court musicians were thrown out of employment.

SRI AUROBINDO: What about painting?

PURANI: Painting also.

SRI AUROBINDO: Do they think that birds and animals can be representative of God?

PURANI: Perhaps they consider it a luxury.

SRI AUROBINDO: But that is inconsistent. They can have many concubines. Is that not a luxury?

PURANI: Yes, four are sanctioned and that only in Arabistan. It may be due to a disproportionate number of men and women.

SRI AUROBINDO: That has not been recorded.

PURANI: In this visiting Muslim group only one or two are open to spiritual things and interested in them. One is a professor of mathematics in Aligarh and another from Murshidabad is Secretary of the Assembly. The others are all closed. But the vice-chancellor took pride in the Ashram because it was started by a Bengali.

SRI AUROBINDO (*laughing*): The Bengali Muslims have some such feelings. Nazimuddin said that the Congress has done injustice to Bose and it was an insult to Bengal.

SATYENDRA: Italy is coming into the war.

PURANI: Demanding Corsica!

SRI AUROBINDO: France can as well claim Sicily saying that France conquered it at one time, and Sardinia because it is near her.

PURANI: It seems Roosevelt is standing for the third time.

SRI AUROBINDO: Is he? Is it decided?

PURANI: Almost. Somebody whom Roosevelt was to back for President has given a hint that Roosevelt will stand. Absence of precedence is no reason, he says. Some American admiral has said that instead of waiting to deliver four thousand airplanes after some years, America should send one thousand planes straightaway to the Allies.

SRI AUROBINDO: Roosevelt would have done that except for this election affair. Wilson took his stand because he had already been elected.

PURANI: The President has unlimited powers.

SRI AUROBINDO: Oh yes, he can do practically anything except get money from the Congress.

EVENING

SRI AUROBINDO (*starting the talk*): The French are not clever at retreat. The Germans seem to have separated the French army from the B.E.F., the main part of which is now evacuating. The French were covering the B.E.F. By this separation two divisions seem to have been lost. The Germans claim that they have captured General Prioux. The paper says that the Germans have divided the line from Lille and Dunkirk and that there are some hills in Belgium which afford natural defence lines. The Germans were trying to occupy these hills, one of which, Mount Cassel, they have captured. By that move they have been able to separate the French army. (*After a time*) I was wondering why the Allies were not erecting something like trenches around Dunkirk to defend it more effectively against mechanised tanks, and I now find that they have done exactly that.

SATYENDRA: Yes, they have dug moats and flooded the area. What news about Narvik? (*Laughter*)

SRI AUROBINDO: Yes, now we find that Narvik was taken by the French, Poles and Norwegians. The British helped only with their navy.

PURANI: Sisir told me to ask Azizul Huque for the Calcutta University publications for our Ashram. Huque consented to give them. It seems he was only an ordinary pleader at Krishnanagar. It was because he was somehow connected with Fazlul Huque that he got a lift.

SRI AUROBINDO: Oh, he belongs to the Huque dynasty?

EVENING

PURANI: The Allies did not seem to have correct information about the strength of the German air force. Their espionage system wasn't very efficient. Neither did they know the strength of the German mechanised units.

SRI AUROBINDO: No.

PURANI: What a tremendous number of planes they have brought forth! They must have about 20,000, I suppose.

NIRODBARAN: But not very efficient.

SRI AUROBINDO: Even as regards their tanks they are inferior to the French ones, it seems.

PURANI: Yes, one French tank is almost equal to two or three German ones.

SRI AUROBINDO: You saw the story of two Frenchmen attacking, like the Abyssinians, a German tank with revolvers. As soon as the German tank driver saw the revolvers, he cried out, "Kamarad" and surrendered. (*Laughter*) The Germans act by sheer mass drive and daring. But individually the soldiers were better in the Kaiser's time. They had more initiative.

SATYENDRA: If Italy joins in, the French will be in a difficult position. They will attack France from the south.

SRI AUROBINDO: Yes, but the observers say that France has kept a big army there.

SATYENDRA: Yes.

NIRODBARAN: It seems Italy is going to attack Egypt, Tunis and Corsica first. The Russians call it all bluff.

PURANI: Their breaking off of trade negotiations with England is significant.

SRI AUROBINDO: Still England hopes for an agreement!

NIRODBARAN: The *Amrita Bazar* says that due to the influence of a certain general, Leopold surrendered.

SRI AUROBINDO: The *Amrita Bazar?*

NIRODBARAN: It is a special cable news. And Leopold's sister and mother also, who were in Rome, exercised their influence on him. This general had been to Rome and returned just three days before the surrender. It seems Hitler exerted his influence through Mussolini and has promised Leopold the kingship of Holland. (*The paper was shown to Sri Aurobindo and after reading it he asked us to give it to Pavitra for the Mother to see.*)

SRI AUROBINDO: Then what the Mother said comes true. She said that it might be due to some pro-Nazi general and the influence of his mother that he surrendered. (*Looking at Nirodbaran*) Have you seen what Rukmini Devi says?

NIRODBARAN: No.

SRI AUROBINDO: She says that it is not fair to blame the King and to demonstrate before the statue of King Albert in that way. She was in sympathy with Belgium.

3 JUNE 1940

PURANI: Franco's representative seems to have met Mussolini and then gone to meet Hitler.

SRI AUROBINDO: Who is he?

PURANI: I forget his name – some general. Military circles say that after seeing the Dunkirk operation they are convinced that the navy is still superior to the air force. The German air force could not cause much damage to their soldiers or to the navy.

NIRODBARAN: That is because of the R.A.F. resistance and because the German air force is not so efficient.

SRI AUROBINDO: An air force is effective only on land. On sea it is not so effective.

PURANI: They say that tons and tons of bombs have been lost without causing any proportionate damage.

SRI AUROBINDO: That, of course. Still it is not as bad as the old bombardment. You know the story of the bombing of Smyrna?

SATYENDRA: No.

SRI AUROBINDO: After a whole day's bombardment they killed only a goat and a donkey! (*Laughter*)

SATYENDRA: These had perhaps come there on hearing the noise!

PURANI: General Prioux is said to have reached Dunkirk – the morning radio news says.

SRI AUROBINDO: No, it is not correct. It seems only a part of Prioux's troops has reached there. Looks as if they were lost. Almost the whole of the B.E.F. has escaped. The French were farther away from the coast.

PURANI: King Leopold's mother is said to be a German.

SRI AUROBINDO: German? I see. Who said so?

PURANI: Jwalanti.[1] Nishtha[2] also says that she is an enigma. During the last war's peace negotiations, her face used to be like a

1. The mother of Gabriel Monod-Herzen.
2. Margaret Woodrow Wilson.

mask. Nobody knew whether she sided with Germany or with the Allies. Nishtha has met her.

SRI AUROBINDO: But it was said that she strongly supported the king against the Germans. Just because she is a German does not mean that she should side with Germany. The English king also was German; so was the Rumanian king.

SATYENDRA: Maeterlinck says that the German blood is alive.

SRI AUROBINDO (*laughing*): Yes.

NIRODBARAN: I thought Maeterlinck was long dead.

SATYENDRA: So did I.

SRI AUROBINDO: Very much alive!

SATYENDRA: This Hapsburg dynasty seems a very long one; that is what Gunther says.

SRI AUROBINDO: No, most European royal families married into small German states which are now extinct and the rest in Scandinavian countries.

NIRODBARAN: It is said that the Germans will now make a drive towards Paris instead of England.

SRI AUROBINDO: That is one of the possibilities. Otherwise if the French consolidate their position in the north, it will be difficult for the Germans to penetrate. So they may think of striking.

SATYENDRA: And if Italy comes in, it will be difficult for France.

NIRODBARAN: Italy's coming in means the extension of the war to the Balkans too.

SRI AUROBINDO: That depends on Mussolini. He may do it later on after winning the war, provided Hitler does not come in the way.

SATYENDRA: If Spain also comes in, it will make it still worse for France.

SRI AUROBINDO: Yes, attack on three sides.

NIRODBARAN: But Spain has not yet recovered.

PURANI: Still, it can attack Gibraltar. The French, of course, can attack through the Pyrenees.

SRI AUROBINDO: France would have enough to face before attacking Spain. No, Italy can take possession of Majorca and Minorca and separate France from her colonies with its navy.

PURANI: Also she can establish an air base. Spain's change of attitude may have been helped by Pétain's departure too.

SRI AUROBINDO: Yes. France has had such dangers before, as Reynaud says. She has been invaded a hundred times. But England is in a dangerous position only now. Even during Napoleon's time she had her allies in Europe. Now she has only France to rely upon.

NIRODBARAN: We do not hear of Gamelin now.

SRI AUROBINDO (*laughing*): No.

NIRODBARAN: Has he committed suicide then?

SRI AUROBINDO: No, he has been relieved of his duty.

NIRODBARAN: The *Amrita Bazar* says that the failure to blow up a bridge on the Meuse was responsible for the German penetration.

SRI AUROBINDO: That is one reason, but Gamelin's disposition and his placing of troops under X, was weak.

NIRODBARAN: India is increasing her defence measures now, by three or four times.

SATYENDRA: From seventy to eighty aeroplanes, perhaps. (*Laughter*)

SRI AUROBINDO: The Indian Navy is said to be having a portentous force. (*Laughter*)

NIRODBARAN: The chance of Gandhi's starting his civil disobedience is getting more and more remote.

SATYENDRA: He does not want to embarrass the British now.

SRI AUROBINDO: Also he says that the Congress and the country are not non-violent enough. If he waits for everybody to become non-violent, he will never be able to start it.

NIRODBARAN: I think he just says it in order to prepare the people. In fact he does not want to start it now.

SRI AUROBINDO: He would have come to a compromise but for Bose with his Forward Bloc and Nehru.

PURANI: He wants England to be in a better position before he starts the civil disobedience. But with Italy and Spain coming in –

SRI AUROBINDO: It will be much worse. By the way, have you seen that Nehru is prepared to shed his blood for the country against Hitler?

SATYENDRA: He wants to be recruited.

EVENING

SRI AUROBINDO (*addressing Purani*): Have you seen that history repeats itself? Germany dropped two bombs on England and killed only a chicken! (*Laughter*)

PURANI: Yes, yes. It must be a joke.

CHAMPAKLAL: In the morning it was a donkey and a goat and now a chicken!

PURANI: Bombing from the air does not seem to be as effective as they think it to be. There is a lot of waste, for many bombs miss the target.

SRI AUROBINDO: To hit properly the plane has to come down very low, but then it exposes itself to the anti-aircraft guns, while from a height it can't aim correctly.

SATYENDRA: What is the news about the British Expeditionary Force evacuation?

SRI AUROBINDO: It is very confused. They say that four-fifths have been removed. Since Lord Gort is in England, it may be true. But there is no news of the unfortunate Prioux.

PURANI: Italy seems to be preparing to enter the war. France will have to face another menace.

SATYENDRA: We thought that if Italy joined it would be advantageous for the Allies. It will enable them to make an offensive.

SRI AUROBINDO: Yes, but just after this great struggle in Flanders the Allies have become weak. If at this moment Italy gives a blow, it may be serious.

PURANI: If Spain also joins then there will be a double menace.

SRI AUROBINDO: Spain has sent a military mission – not any general. That does not necessarily mean anything; of course it may, but it need not. If Spain joins, it will be at the mercy of Germany and Italy if they win. And besides there are many discontented elements in Spain who are waiting for an opportunity to revolt. If Spain joins, they will at once seize the opportunity.

PURANI: Spain can take possession of Majorca and Minorca at once.

SRI AUROBINDO: Perhaps it will wait for Italy to take them. The Spanish are a virtuous people and think that virtue will win in the end. (*After some time*) You have seen that in India everybody is prepared to shed his blood. (*Laughter*) Asaf Ali is not satisfied with the defence measures.

NIRODBARAN: The commander-in-chief says that we have everything except technicians.

PURANI: All the tanks and mechanised units of the Germans have people who are skilled technicians as well, so that they may repair at once anything that goes wrong.

SRI AUROBINDO: Not only that but there are highly trained soldiers in the mechanised units. It is because the British were raw in Norway that they could not cope with the Germans. In Flanders, though the B.E.F. were territorials, they have been trained for a long number of years. When Napoleon was thinking of attacking England and was preparing the navy, a general said to him, "It is very well to talk like that. To train a sailor requires many years, while a soldier can be trained in just six months." Napoleon said, "Don't talk like that. A soldier requires at least two years' training."

PURANI: Gandhi said the same thing as you do. He said it would require at least twenty-five years for India to prepare herself for defence.

SRI AUROBINDO: That is obvious to everybody.

Purani (*after a while*): Somebody in Gujarat has prophesied that Hitler's decline will begin in June – that is, now.

SRI AUROBINDO (*laughing*): That fulfils my prophecy – which I myself never made! Some Anglo-French woman said that the sage of the Ashram had prophesied that Hitler's decline would come in May. The decline will really depend on the strength of the French line. They have now built it up.

PURANI: In the last war, they threw in a large number of men against the Germans coming to Paris. It was an immense sacrifice against all military codes. "Not to Paris at any cost," was their resolve. And the German attack slowed down.

SRI AUROBINDO: The credit for it went to (*name missed*).

Krishnalal's picture of a terrified monkey clasping her young one in protection was shown to Sri Aurobindo.

SRI AUROBINDO: Have you seen the photo of two refugees cowering from the explosion of bombs? (*Laughter*) These monkeys look very much like those refugees.

5 JUNE 1940

EVENING

The radio said that Germany had resumed her attack along the Somme.

PURANI: It means her drive towards Paris.

SRI AUROBINDO: Yes.

PURANI: I hope Weygand has been able to reconstruct the line. He has a heavy work to do.

SRI AUROBINDO: Oh yes, a tremendous work.

PURANI: If he can drive back the Germans –

SRI AUROBINDO: Then he will go down in history as the greatest military leader. If only he can resist them for some months till the French are ready for an offensive, that would be something.

NIRODBARAN: Germany has started war against Switzerland also.

SRI AUROBINDO: Just the preparation for it.

PURANI: I suppose Hitler wants to bring in Italy then and it will be very advantageous to him.

SRI AUROBINDO: Yes.

PURANI: Italy seems to be vacillating because of the strong American pressure.

SRI AUROBINDO: You saw how Bullitt escaped? It is lucky for Hitler. I was wondering what America would have done if Bullitt had been bulletted. He had a double escape, it seems. The bomb did not burst in the restaurant but in the courtyard and it did not hit him.

NIRODBARAN: He said that God was with him.

SRI AUROBINDO (*laughing*): I had said he would feel the presence of God. The French have awarded Prioux the Légion d'Honneur. In that case he must have been in Dunkirk. The papers said that it was due to his organisation that the British Army was able to evacuate. Then the German statement that he was taken prisoner long ago must be a myth. The British Government was wise in asking the French Government to escape by aeroplane, while Prioux could not. Such men are worth more than soldiers.

PURANI: Duff Cooper was also in Paris during the raid.

SRI AUROBINDO: Yes, he was also in a restaurant.

NIRODBARAN: Munching bread and butter! (*Laughter*)

SRI AUROBINDO: As the waiters were forbidden to serve the meal during the air raid. Are the waiters not allowed to go and take shelter during the raid?

6 JUNE 1940

The radio said that the Germans had penetrated through the French lines in some places.

SRI AUROBINDO: The Germans' technique is to accumulate all their strength at one point and then make a drive. The French don't seem to be able to prevent the thrust.

PURANI: No, though their air force is attacking the rear.

SRI AUROBINDO: That cannot prevent the advance, it can only hamper it.

PURANI: The French also could gather their mass against the Germans.

SRI AUROBINDO: That is what they should do. I don't know why they don't. I suspect they have dispersed their forces too much. In the east, of course, if Italy comes into the war, it would be helpful. In the last war they found some counter-measures against German attacks. This time they don't seem to have found anything yet.

EVENING

SRI AUROBINDO: Have you seen that India is going to be a great military country? The Viceroy is forming civil guards for defence. (*Laughter*)

PURANI: If they were trained to handle machine-guns and tanks, that would be something.

Nirodbaran (*smiling*): They will be given only batons!

SRI AUROBINDO: Batons?

NIRODBARAN: Yes.

PURANI: Gandhi will object even to that. It is against non-violence.

SATYENDRA: Why? He doesn't object to the nation using violence, if it wants to. His ideal is only for himself.

PURANI: Yes, the nation can have its army for defence.

SRI AUROBINDO: But he changed his principle with regard to monkeys.

PURANI: Monkeys?

SRI AUROBINDO: Monkeys in his Ashram!

PURANI: Oh, yes. You mean he may change with regard to Hitler-monkeys also? (*Laughter*) He is quite capable of that.

SRI AUROBINDO: Hitler was born to prove the inapplicability of Ahimsa.

NIRODBARAN: The small neutrals seemed to have followed Gandhi's method in submitting to Hitler so easily.

SATYENDRA: In Holland and Belgium he met some resistance.

NIRODBARAN: In Holland? There was no fight there, I think.

SRI AUROBINDO: There was a fight there but they allowed themselves to be killed more than kill. Perhaps Gandhi's non-violence? They did not go the whole hog in the Gandhi way.

SATYENDRA: The Poles also surrendered very quickly in spite of their being good soldiers.

SRI AUROBINDO: That was because of their generals and leaders. If they had had somebody like Mannerheim, then Germany would have been foiled.

7 JUNE 1940

PURANI: Churchill's speech has come as a revelation to Italy.

SRI AUROBINDO: Yes, Italy thought the Allied Army had been annihilated.

PURANI: Ironside is now forming mobile units to guard against a German invasion. Doing it too late.

SRI AUROBINDO: Why too late?

PURANI: When the attack is imminent.

SRI AUROBINDO: I don't think any attack is likely now except by small armies which will be crushed by overwhelming numbers. There is no more chance of surprise attacks. Besides, the Allies have destroyed all the ports and without ports the Germans can't launch an attack. It will take time to put them in order, and by that time England will be still more ready. Even now she has a strong army ready. No, Hitler won't attack; he has not intuition but intimation. That is why he is driving against Paris. He knows that if he sets out to repair the ports and attack England, by the time he is ready the Allies will be quite prepared and afterwards attacks on Paris won't be possible.

EVENING

SRI AUROBINDO: The French have destroyed four hundred tanks they say. It is a very good number – one-fifth of the whole.

PURANI: Yes, the Germans have brought in two thousand tanks.

SRI AUROBINDO: It seems Hitler brought two-and-a-half million men to Belgium and only fifty thousand were lost. Still he has two million while the Allies did not use even a million there; no wonder they were defeated. Have you read that the Belgian consul has become furious with the *Amrita Bazar* and calls it a gossip-monger? He praises Churchill and The *Hindu*. But now Churchill says that one can form one's own opinion about the conduct of Leopold. (*Laughter*)

Nishtha met him in America. She says that he is a man of under-handed dealings. When she heard of his defection, the first thing she said was, "Oh, it must be his mother."

8 JUNE 1940

PURANI: Daladier has been ousted altogether from the Cabinet.

SRI AUROBINDO: Yes, the man whom Reynaud has taken in his place is said to be a specialist, and non-political.

PURANI: There are already plenty of political people. It seems it was Daladier who relieved Weygand and put Gamelin in his place. And when there was apprehension of trouble he sent him to the Middle East. Weygand is a Catholic.

SRI AUROBINDO: I see. Pétain also is a Catholic.

PURANI: Yes.

NIRODBARAN: Daladier is anti-Catholic?

SRI AUROBINDO: He is a radical.

Nirodbaran (*after a while*): Italy is between two fires.

SRI AUROBINDO: Yes, Russia has warned her against any move in the Balkans and America against extending the field of war while Hitler is pressing Mussolini.

PURANI: Even in today's paper there is something about American pressure on Italy. America has already sent some dive-bombers, it seems, lending them to the Allies.

SRI AUROBINDO: Not lending but sending to some company which will forward them. (*Laughter*)

NIRODBARAN: Hitler is quietly swallowing all that. He does not utter a single word of threat against America.

SRI AUROBINDO: Yes, he is very cautious. He does not want her to join the Allies.

SRI AUROBINDO (*after a while, laughing*): J has written to the Mother denouncing her action in supporting the French who are killing the communists. (*Laughter*)

PURANI: Still he has his sympathy for the communists? But he didn't write about his approaching marriage?

SRI AUROBINDO: Marriage?

PURANI: Yes, as soon as his B.A. result is out he will get married.

NIRODBARAN: How can he write about it? It will bring denunciation on him.

PURANI: He is going to marry in his caste.

SRI AUROBINDO: Communists have castes?

PURANI: He has seen in Bombay, perhaps, that educated girls are more forward and won't tolerate any subjection.

NIRODBARAN: Has his health improved?

PURANI: Yes. He says he is much better now. He wrote to the Mother about his health.

SRI AUROBINDO: Marriage might do him good – make him sober. Because much of his trouble was due to sexual imbalance.

NIRODBARAN: Yes, but who will be the unfortunate bride, I wonder!

SRI AUROBINDO: Yes, she may be unfortunate.

PURANI: He is going about giving lectures on Yoga, the Ashram and you. His communist comrades don't understand how he, being a communist, praises you. They think, "Is he a black sheep in the fold or what?"

SRI AUROBINDO: A bi-striped animal. (*Laughter*)

PURANI: The socialists in Bombay are not in the forefront now.

SRI AUROBINDO: Why?

PURANI: After the seceding of Masani, they have lost ground.

SRI AUROBINDO: Why has Masani seceded?

PURANI: He does not seem to have found anybody sincere among them. He now lives a retired life.

SRI AUROBINDO: The socialists generally have not stood the test. In the beginning there were sincere people, but later on they became respectable. The communists are more idealistic than the socialists. They have to live and work in obloquy and that requires sincerity. It is like religion. When a religion is new and fresh, plenty of people come in, but as it gets older it is no longer so; people become respectable and it becomes a church. (*After a pause*) Why does J say that the French are killing the communists? They are only imprisoning them.

PURANI: Because of the death penalty hanging over them.

SRI AUROBINDO: That, only if they do any subversive activity like interfering with the soldiers. They were trying to make a pact with Hitler.

PURANI: The French seemed to have destroyed seven hundred tanks.

SRI AUROBINDO: Yesterday it was four hundred – a very good number.

PURANI: Today's paper says seven hundred.

SRI AUROBINDO: Which paper? The *Hindu*?

PURANI: No, *The Indian Express.* (*Laughter*) Hitler is not using dive-bombers in the attack this time.

SRI AUROBINDO: He did at first, but it was not effective due to the measure adopted on the direction of Weygand – that the troops should disperse as soon as a bomber arrives, and close in after it has left. Bombers are very costly.

SATYENDRA: If they can hold on for a month, it will create a very good effect; it will give confidence to the soldiers.

SRI AUROBINDO: Oh, if they can hold on for a month, then they will be able to hold on as long as they like. (*Addressing Nirodbaran*) Have you read Krishnaprem's review of *The Life Divine*?

NIRODBARAN: Yes.

SRI AUROBINDO: How do you find it? (*Nirodbaran gave a laugh.*)

SATYENDRA: He says that the two denials are the same as in Buddhism – their avoidance points to the middle path.

PURANI: And Mahayana's equation of Nirvana and Samsara also is the same teaching as in *The Life Divine* – about the acceptance of life.

SRI AUROBINDO: Did Buddha say that? I thought he preached renunciation.

PURANI: It is the Mahayana school, which came into existence after Buddha, that holds this view of the acceptance of life. The Hinayana school does not.

SATYENDRA: Everybody finds things in *The Life Divine* according to their own predilection. Somebody found Tantra and Krishnaprem finds Buddhism.

SRI AUROBINDO: Especially as he is in a Buddhistic phase now.

NIRODBARAN: Sisir says that the reviewers should give quotations from the writers. That is the modern trend now.

SRI AUROBINDO: I don't find that in the *New Statesman and Nation*. On the other hand, sometimes their quotations are irritating, especially in poetry. But they should give quotations in poetry.

EVENING

The newspaper and radio said that the British Army in the west had retreated in the face of the German attack.

SRI AUROBINDO: So the British troops are getting mastery in retreat? They have withdrawn to Brussels leaving their former position. They say that their division consists of the Highlanders. The Highlanders are better fighters. It is the territorial force, I think, without any sufficient training, that has been pushed to the front. Even if it had been the Expeditionary Force it would have been something.

NIRODBARAN: They could not hold on even for a day! It is said that the German pressure was heavy in that sector.

SRI AUROBINDO: So was it in the French sector. They should be withdrawn to the rear and first given some training in fighting or removed to the Maginot Line.

NIRODBARAN: They could be set to deal with the tanks in the rear.

SRI AUROBINDO: Oh, they will be no good for that!

PURANI: Hitler must be getting wild with America.

SRI AUROBINDO: Why? Has he said so anywhere?

PURANI: No, they are sending naval planes, dive-bombers and all possible help short of sending an army.

SRI AUROBINDO: Yes, the isolationists are quiet now.

NIRODBARAN: Gayda is trying a little outburst.

SRI AUROBINDO: Yes, if America intervenes in Europe, why shouldn't we intervene in America? Roosevelt knows that the Nazis will do it in any case; so there is nothing much to lose. (*After a while*) We are getting more anti-imperialistic letters denouncing our help to the imperialistic Allies. Jatin Sen Gupta, also, it seems, has written to the Mother.

PURANI: That contractor?

SRI AUROBINDO: Yes.

PURANI: It is, as Satyendra says, due to the big figure of 10,000 francs. They don't know that it is equivalent to only a few hundred rupees. (*Laughter*)

K13

SATYENDRA: About seven or eight hundred.

PURANI: They also don't know about the political movement here against us.

SRI AUROBINDO: This contribution should stop it. They should know that I have been living here under the protection of the French Government. Were it not for that, I would now be in an English prison. And apart from that, after India, France has most of our disciples and some have gone to the front in Belgium. The Mother's nephew is there – he was in Belgium – we don't know if he is still alive. And France has the best sale of our books. Though it was spreading to Czechoslovakia and then through Switzerland to Italy, even to Chile where somebody wanted to translate *Thoughts and Glimpses*. Now all that is stopped due to this war.

If Hitler achieves domination of the world there won't be any national independence left anywhere and spiritual work will be doomed. England and France are bad enough but still some liberty of thought and spirituality are left under them. Besides, as I don't hold the principles of the objectors, why should I act according to them?

Purani (*after a pause*): *The Modern Review* has brought out an article on the Khaksar movement. I haven't read it as yet.

SRI AUROBINDO: The Sunday Express says that the Khaksar movement was being fed from Germany.

PURANI: It is quite true. That came out in the secret police investigation. That is why the Indian Government came down on them and Sikandar Hyat could not protect them any more.

NIRODBARAN: Hitler has duped them with Muslim Raj?

SRI AUROBINDO: No, maybe independence of India. This Mushriki has been to England?

PURANI: Yes, he is an I.C.S. Independence by Hitler? He says that Indians are a primitive race.

SRI AUROBINDO: Yes, even the other day when he was trying to be friendly with England and to divide France, he said that the white races should keep the black races under subjection.

9 JUNE 1940

NIRODBARAN: I find Dilip in my company regarding Krishna-prem's review of *The Life Divine*. He is not much impressed by it.

SRI AUROBINDO: Why?

NIRODBARAN: He says that there is nothing characteristic about it, and it doesn't go far enough. And Krishnaprem does not seem to have understood the Supermind.

SRI AUROBINDO: No, that he hasn't.

NIRODBARAN: When Dilip saw that Krishnaprem makes Nirvana and Samsara equal according to Buddha, he revolted. That was too much because Buddha has always been against Samsara.

SRI AUROBINDO: Of course, Buddha never said that. Krishnaprem speaks according to the Mahayana. Mahayana went much further. Buddha didn't say what Nirvana is and he did not say that Nirvana and Samsara are equal.

PURANI: As an authority on Buddhism, Mrs. Rhys Davies seems to be the best person.

SRI AUROBINDO: No, she is not very reliable. The Mahayana conception of Nirvana seems to be something like Laotse's Tao. Tao, according to him, is a condition of nothingness that is beyond all present construction, and that is the nothingness which contains everything. (*Addressing Purani*) Do you know anything about the *Nous*, the Divine Mind, of Plotinus? Krishnaprem appears to make the Supermind and the *Nous* the same. *Nous* seems to be Intelligence.

PURANI: I do not know if Divine Mind would be the same as Supermind.

SRI AUROBINDO: When they consider Shankara the greatest of realists and my philosophy the same as his . . .

PURANI: What can you say about others? (*Laughter*)

SRI AUROBINDO: Is it the supramental urge for unification? (*Laughter*)

PURANI: Italy has ordered her ships to neutral ports.

SRI AUROBINDO: It means war then.

PURANI: And it seems the German generals are to go to Italian Africa.

NIRODBARAN: What a huge mass Hitler has thrown into the north!

SRI AUROBINDO: Yes, if Weygand can hold on, it's all right; otherwise a dark lookout. Germany has the advantage of concentrating all its strength at one point, while the Allies have to keep their forces scattered.

NIRODBARAN: Germany seems to be making for the ports – first, Dieppe.

SRI AUROBINDO: Dieppe is a minor port. Le Havre, Cherbourg, Boulogne and Calais are the major ones.

NIRODBARAN: Why are the British not sending their army? They have a big force.

SRI AUROBINDO: Their army is still in training. They have adopted conscription too late. Somebody from Switzerland informed France that if Germany attacks her through Basle, Switzerland will be able to hold on for forty-eight hours and has warned France to make arrangements beforehand. Basle is flat forestland. From the end of France to Basle there is what is called a *trou* – a hole, that is – there is no Maginot Line there. Of course Switzerland can fight by retreating into the mountains. Hitler may not think of attacking there now because of his concentration in the north.

PURANI: Perhaps he is waiting for Italy to join and then make a combined attack there.

SRI AUROBINDO: Probably.

NIRODBARAN: It is very strange that France did not build any Maginot Line on the Belgian frontier.

SRI AUROBINDO: There were only scattered fortifications.

PURANI: Even during these eight months they did not do anything.

SRI AUROBINDO: That is not enough. France counted on the Belgian fortifications which were supposed to be very strong. Liege held up the enemy for a long time. They also thought that the forest of Ardennes would form a natural barrier and the Germans would find it difficult to cross it. Of course, it is all Daladier's work – the most indefensible War Minister. He seems to have done nothing. It is like the story of the general of Napoleon III. When Napoleon asked him, "Is everything prepared?" he replied, "Yes, up to the last button," and when the attack began everything broke down at once! As for Gamelin, he seems to know only the names of officers and nothing more and is quite helpless when in difficulty. That shows that it is easy to build up a reputation during peace.

PURANI: In the secret session they will try to throw out Chamberlain and other previous ministers who were responsible for this bad preparation.

SRI AUROBINDO: I see.

PURANI: And it is the Conservatives who will lead the attack, it seems.

SRI AUROBINDO: Of course they made a tremendous blunder.

NIRODBARAN: Tom Paine says in the *New Statesman and Nation* that Chamberlain wanted to make an alliance with Germany.

SRI AUROBINDO: Not so far as that but it was Baldwin and Chamberlain's policy to make a four Power alliance: Italy, Germany, England and France to settle all European affairs. Of course England is responsible for all this, for it is England that raised Germany so that France might not be too powerful. It is the old policy of balance of power. She did not think that her own weapon might strike against her.

10 JUNE 1940

SATYENDRA: Will there be any hierarchy among the supramental beings?

SRI AUROBINDO: Supramental beings? In the Overhead, there is a hierarchy: Higher Mind, Illumined Mind, Intuition and so on.

PURANI: That includes the Overmind.

SRI AUROBINDO: Yes, among the supramental beings too there is a hierarchy, in the sense of a gradation of consciousness towards the Sachchidananda.

NIRODBARAN: Sisir was saying you have written in the last volume of *The Life Divine* that the supramental beings will retire into islets.

SRI AUROBINDO (*laughing*): I meant by islets, living in collective groups.

NIRODBARAN: I also said the same thing to him.

SATYENDRA: Like individual isolation, it will be a collective isolation. That is still my difficulty – why should there be any collective group? One can exercise one's influence individually as well.

SRI AUROBINDO: Yes, but collective influence will be of a different kind — so that it may exercise its influence on the whole world. Individual isolation is for those who want Mukti. But this will be an ideal collective group along with the change of the outer mould to serve as an ideal life to others.

NIRODBARAN: Will there be missions to other countries?

SRI AUROBINDO: Good Lord, missions for preaching? No! Groups will develop and will have different expressions according to different conditions. Whatever is necessary, and in whichever way needed, will grow up of itself.

SATYENDRA: I do not know how Pondicherry could have been selected.

SRI AUROBINDO (*laughing*): When I came it was very quiet, there was no life. Of course there was a lot of beating and fighting, if you mean by that life.

Then the talk changed to the topic of war.

NIRODBARAN: Germany has thrown in a huge army.

SRI AUROBINDO: A tremendous number. They have lost about half a million, and as many in Belgium, and still they are putting in fresh numbers. Can France stand against it all?

NIRODBARAN: Why does not England send her Expeditionary Force?

SRI AUROBINDO: Good Lord! You must give them at least seven days' rest.

NIRODBARAN: But she is supposed to have a big army.

SATYENDRA: It is under training now and it will take some time. The English have no conscription and so are as raw as ourselves.

NIRODBARAN: What about America? There is a big army there.

SRI AUROBINDO: Not so big — only fifty thousand, and they want to make it a million. They are also not properly trained. Of course they can call up their volunteers. Even they will have to be trained till August. The question is whether France will be able to stand so long.

NIRODBARAN: If Paris falls, will the French be able to continue the fight?

SRI AUROBINDO: They can, but it will mean a decentralisation of their whole life. And, besides, a great moral shock. It is not like India shifting the capital to several places.

PURANI: In the last war they shifted the Government to Bordeaux.

SRI AUROBINDO: Besides, north France is the most important part because of the industries and commerce there. If Paris goes, Normandy also will go, that is, France virtually will go. In the south, Bordeaux and Rhone are the few important places. That has always been the difficulty of France – that Paris is too near the frontier. If Paris is taken, Hitler will have some breathing time before he attacks other countries.

SATYENDRA: England will continue to fight, Churchill says, even after England is gone.

SRI AUROBINDO: Yes, that is something new. The English people are very tough, they will go on till they are directly touched. (*After a while*) These huge migrations are quite unprecedented in history. Two million Belgians have gone to Paris.

NIRODBARAN: They can be put in the army.

SRI AUROBINDO: That is what is being done.

NIRODBARAN: If the British Government had started training in India, India would have played a great part at present. The commander-in-chief speaks of one hundred thousand soldiers.

SRI AUROBINDO: That is nothing.

SATYENDRA: Now everybody is speaking of India's defence. *The Statesman* of Calcutta is pleading for a compromise and settlement and starting the defence preparation. The European Association in Calcutta is also urging it.

SRI AUROBINDO: Because they have seen things with their own eyes and know and are practical people. The Statesman has always been for some self-government for India. Englishmen have got a correct vital instinct. They know that it is a time of necessity, while the ruling class is shut up in its traditions and runs in grooves. The Labour Party can now exert its pressure on the Government.

SATYENDRA: When they are out of the Government they can press, but when in the Government practical difficulties come in the way.

SRI AUROBINDO: Yes, but necessity now demands self-government. Of course if the Congress had been conciliatory it would have been easy for the British Government. They can't accept whatever the Constituent Assembly decides.

SATYENDRA: Englishmen here have their own vital interest at stake.

SRI AUROBINDO: Yes, but that interest is also connected with England and if England goes, they also go.

11 JUNE 1940

The radio news: Italy has joined the war.

SRI AUROBINDO (*looking at Purani*): So Mussolini has butted in? When he sees that Germany is winning he comes to share the spoils.

PURANI: Yes. It's a jackal policy. But he says it is according to his understanding with Hitler.

NIRODBARAN: Understanding? No, he says pledge.

SATYENDRA: Pledge or no pledge, why say all that? Why not say plainly that he wants to join?

SRI AUROBINDO: Then what becomes of diplomacy?

PURANI: He has only declared war, not started any attack.

NIRODBARAN: Why don't the Allies take the initiative?

SATYENDRA: Their hands are full with the defence.

SRI AUROBINDO: Quite so.

PURANI: He may perhaps invade Corsica with aeroplanes or land parachutes.

SRI AUROBINDO: I don't think so. That requires dash and daring.

PURANI: Hitler may have kept off Russia by guaranteeing that Italy wouldn't go to the Balkans.

SRI AUROBINDO: Quite possible. But for how long? It will come later on. If the Allies could attack Germany through Greece, then some pressure would be relieved. That is the only way.

NIRODBARAN: But it is not possible at present.

SRI AUROBINDO: No, this neutrality stands in the way.

PURANI: Turkey will be for the Allies now since Russia is not involved.

SRI AUROBINDO: Yes, but when war spreads to the Mediterranean?

NIRODBARAN: Roosevelt's important speech is not so important after all. He speaks of all possible material help to the Allies.

SRI AUROBINDO: He has already said that before. But he asks the people to be ready. That may be a hint.

SATYENDRA: If he could he would have declared in favour of the Allies.

PURANI: He seems to have said to Italy that Italy's coming into the war would bring in a series of interventions.

SRI AUROBINDO: I see.

NIRODBARAN: America may come in when it is too late.

SRI AUROBINDO: They are all too late in everything.

NIRODBARAN: It is a pity that France is paying heavily for England's misdeeds.   •

SRI AUROBINDO (*laughing*): France is also to blame because of Daladier's betrayal of Czechoslovakia.

NIRODBARAN: That was partly due to Chamberlain's pressure. France alone couldn't fight Germany.

PURANI: There was Russia. Both France and Russia could have combined and England would have had to come in later.

SRI AUROBINDO: Yes.

NIRODBARAN: Natesan was saying that Daladier has been driven out because he was pleading for surrender – that is the rumour.

SRI AUROBINDO: Rumour? May be. You have seen that Britain has left Norway?

PURANI: Yes.

NIRODBARAN: From Narvik too?

SRI AUROBINDO: Yes.

SATYENDRA: From Norway altogether.

NIRODBARAN: And she lost three destroyers.

SRI AUROBINDO: Yes, I don't know how. But it is nothing to her. She has many destroyers.

EVENING

Italy has declared war on the Allies and said that she will carry out war according to the international and humanitarian law.

SRI AUROBINDO (*sarcastically*): So Italy will fight according to the international law?

Purani (*laughing*): Yes. She says so.

SRI AUROBINDO: That means, "Don't strike me." Mussolini knows that if he hits he will be hit back. Italy has never been humanitarian anywhere.

PURANI: Italy may attack Marseilles by sea or she can invade the frontier overland.

SRI AUROBINDO: Yes, but France is quite prepared for the defence. Italy's main strength is in her fleet, strength not on paper but in organisation and fighting power. But it hasn't been proved yet.

PURANI: Her aeroplanes also seem to be very strong.

SRI AUROBINDO: That also has to be proved.

12 JUNE 1940

SRI AUROBINDO: What has happened to the Italian flotilla? (*Addressing Purani*) The news was that the Italian flotilla has started for Africa. It requires so many days to reach Africa?

There was very little talk today. The Germans are approaching nearer and nearer to Paris.

13 JUNE 1940

The German army is less than twenty miles from Paris.

PURANI: André Maurois, the writer, has flown to England to ask for more men to be sent to France – raw recruits don't matter. They are badly in need of men.

SRI AUROBINDO: Men who know how to shoot? (*Laughter*) You said the number of Germans is ten to one against the French?

PURANI: Yes, in certain sectors.

SRI AUROBINDO: How can France fight against such odds? It seems it is by sheer mass that Germany is carrying on. The mechanised units are not so effective now.

NIRODBARAN: Hitler also must have had tremendous losses.

SRI AUROBINDO: For that he is prepared. He has said already that he is prepared to sacrifice one million men against the Maginot Line. (*After a while*) Paris has been the centre of human civilisation for three centuries. Now he will destroy it. That is the sign of the Asura. History is repeating itself. The Graeco-Roman civilisation was also destroyed by Germany.

NIRODBARAN: But if France does not defend Paris?

SRI AUROBINDO: Then he will not destroy it immediately. The unfortunate thing is that all are tied to modern civilisation – even China and Japan.

NIRODBARAN: If Americans had come in!

PURANI: They ought to have come in four months ago.

SRI AUROBINDO: Everybody has realised what German rule will be like. You have seen what an Irish minister has said? He says, "If Ireland dies we do not want to live." They know what life will be like under Hitler. Ireland has no feeling for England. Left alone it would not mind if England went down.

NIRODBARAN: England is responsible for this bitterness.

SRI AUROBINDO: In the past, yes. Ireland has undergone more repression than India. Everybody but India realises this. You have heard what picture Roosevelt has drawn of the future under Hitler?

Purani (*after some time*): The Khaksars have been rounded up; three hundred people have been arrested. Sikander Hyat Khan has said that the Government has found the link between Khaksars and the enemy countries.

SRI AUROBINDO: Oh, has he? Where has he said that?

PURANI: I do not know, but he has said so and therefore he has no sympathy for them.

SRI AUROBINDO: At last he has woken up. The Khaksars were a terrible danger to the Hindus too.

PURANI: It seems the Thakore of Rajkot died as the result of tiger hunting.

SATYENDRA: Not heart-failure?

PURANI: Heart-failure as a consequence probably. Virawalla is also dead. Our people will surely link up these two deaths with Gandhi's fast. They will say, "It is a punishment for their behaviour with the saint."

SATYENDRA: Oh yes!

SRI AUROBINDO: That proves what I have written in the *Essays on the Gita* about soul-force.

SATYENDRA: There may be some subtle way in which the moral force will work. But Gandhi did not change his heart.

SRI AUROBINDO: He may have changed the Thakore and his Dewan – but not the heart, maybe the head. (*Laughter*)

EVENING

PURANI: Some officer's wife has written that the Germans dropped about 160 bombs in the village she lives in but not a single one exploded. The village is in the lower region of Paris.

SRI AUROBINDO: Mother's brother's family is also in the lower region. They thought it would be quite safe.

PURANI: The French claim to have pushed the Germans back five miles. Something!

SRI AUROBINDO (*smiling*): That is only in one sector. There are thirty others. This time the British could not be masterly in their retreat. Some six thousand troops have been caught.

PURANI: No, they seem to have been cut off.

SATYENDRA: England can easily send half a million troops. What France needs now is men.

NIRODBARAN: Perhaps they fear an invasion by Germany.

SRI AUROBINDO: That is not likely now. After France is occupied, Hitler may turn his attention there. But the English Army is still in training.

PURANI: Neither are they good soldiers. They can of course be sent to the south.

SRI AUROBINDO: Yes, they may be good for the Italians. (*Laughter*)

SATYENDRA: How is that? At one time they were considered good soldiers. In India they fought us well.

SRI AUROBINDO: That was only groups of people. Now the whole nation has to be prepared to fight. Besides, they have all become comfortable and ease-loving. Even the French are not as good as in the last war. The French peasants and farmers have become rich and used to comforts and they don't like to be disturbed.

SATYENDRA: The Germans, of course, have always the will to power but when will they settle in peace?

SRI AUROBINDO: Militarism is in their blood. They were at one time hired as mercenaries.

14 JUNE 1940

PURANI: Jaswant has been arrested under the Defence Act. As the president of All-India Students' Federation or something of the sort he gave lectures for which he has been arrested. He is not careful about what he says.

SRI AUROBINDO: He never was.

PURANI: I am wondering what will become of his marriage.

SRI AUROBINDO: God allows marriages but the Government prevents them! Marriages are made in heaven, they say.

SATYENDRA: That is difficult to swallow. Marie Corelli writes of such things in her novels, bringing in Christianity – Electric Christianity, etc. She was very popular at one time, at least in India.

SRI AUROBINDO: I used to see her novels everywhere. In England also she was a best-seller. Only the critics were hard on her.

SATYENDRA: The poor *Indian Express* is not allowed up here now.

SRI AUROBINDO (*laughing*): Why?

SATYENDRA: Premanand says that the Mother has asked him to send only The *Hindu* and the *Patrika*. The others spoil the atmosphere. The thing is that it gives all the news though not the views.

PURANI: Paris is not going to be defended, no street fighting.

SRI AUROBINDO: That is to prevent the destruction of Paris. Hitler is getting remarkable inspiration from his Asura. He doesn't go by reason but only by the voice. He considers all possibilities and when he fixes on something he goes ahead. Only, he did not foresee the British and French intervention on behalf of Poland.

SATYENDRA: Ordinary people won't believe that it is the Asura guiding him.

SRI AUROBINDO: No, they won't.

NIRODBARAN: Already he is being hailed as greater than Napoleon.

SRI AUROBINDO: That he is not. Napoleon did not have Hitler's resources. If he had had them, he would have conquered England.

SATYENDRA: Ludwig writes in his biography of Napoleon that Napoleon was the first to conceive of a federation of Europe under France.

SRI AUROBINDO: No, Henry IV and his minister were the first to conceive of federated European states.

SATYENDRA: Napoleon of course wanted the federation to be under France.

SRI AUROBINDO: Under himself.

SATYENDRA: He was France.

PURANI: Even the Germans favoured the idea. Goethe welcomed it.

SRI AUROBINDO: Goethe was not a patriot. He said that the Germans were barbarians and would always be barbarians.

PURANI: Kant also did not have much sympathy with Prussia. He was a professor in Prussia, at Konigsberg, I think, but he was not allowed to publish his books there. He had them sent to Weimar and published from there. The authorities were wild at him.

SRI AUROBINDO: The Duke of Weimar was a liberal.

PURANI: The Christians tried to make out that Kant disproved the existence of God.

SRI AUROBINDO: No, on the contrary, he tried to prove the possibility of the existence of God. Goethe was a cosmopolitan. When he was asked to express hatred against France, he said that he owed most of his culture to France.

PURANI: Frederick the Great had a deep respect for France. He tried to establish a friendship with Voltaire and frequently invited him to his court. Voltaire used to get disgusted with the company of all the German generals sitting so upright and very often he refused the invitation.

SRI AUROBINDO: Naturally. English generals are no better, perhaps. Frederick tried to write poetry in French and once sent some to Voltaire. Someone seeing the bundle asked him what it was. Voltaire said, "Frederick has sent some of his dirty linen to wash." (*Laughter*)

PURANI: He was very bad-tempered and nobody dared to take any liberty with him, except Voltaire.

SRI AUROBINDO: Both were bad-tempered and they were difficult for anybody to live with. Frederick was an egotist too.

PURANI: He was very charitable, it seems.

SRI AUROBINDO: Yes, that was one good side of his character.

NIRODBARAN: Has Paris been taken any time before?

SRI AUROBINDO: Oh yes, during Napoleon's time and then during the Franco-Prussian war.

PURANI: The difficulty is that Paris is very near the frontier, just as Madras to Pondicherry.

SRI AUROBINDO: Yes, but each yard of fighting costs a tremendous loss. This war is not so bad as the last one, as that was trench warfare. Besides, in the defence the loss is less than in the attack.

SATYENDRA: Even in the open field?

SRI AUROBINDO: Yes, because in the defence the army remains behind the guns.

Purani (*after some time*): They are all calculating Italy's strength, economy, materials, and military power.

SRI AUROBINDO: Calculations are always wrong.

PURANI: Reynaud has appealed to Roosevelt for materials.

SRI AUROBINDO: Yes, everything short of an expeditionary force.

NIRODBARAN: Why does he stop there?

SRI AUROBINDO: He doesn't want to offend the American people, so he repeats himself in the same language.

PURANI: If the French had more materials, guns, bombs, then they could stand.

NIRODBARAN: If America sends an army at all, it may be too late, as Reynaud says.

SRI AUROBINDO: Quite so.

PURANI: If Roosevelt had been secure in his presidential seat, then –

SRI AUROBINDO: Then he would have declared war at once. He is too clever a politician to do it now. After he is renominated by the Democratic Party at the end of June, he may declare war. If Washington had been destroyed by the Germans, then –

PURANI: Then of course on that pretext he would have done it.

SRI AUROBINDO: Constitutionally he has the power to declare war.

PURANI: Oh yes, he can do anything, like a dictator. In that way the President has immense power.

NIRODBARAN: Reynaud says that the French will fight from Africa.

SRI AUROBINDO: And even from America. They have taken that example from King Albert. In the last war he carried on the war from France, and Wilhelmina is also doing that.

NIRODBARAN: The French can bring their African Army to Paris – perhaps the Africans are not good fighters.

SRI AUROBINDO: No, they are excellent fighters.

PURANI: Some French military officer said that the French knew all about the German dive-bombers, tanks, etc.

SRI AUROBINDO: That is said to protect the Government. If they had known, they would have done something to counter the heavy tanks.

NIRODBARAN: What are these secret bomb-sights of America?

PURANI: With them they can see clearly at night, even from a distance of ten thousand feet, and thus strike accurately.

NIRODBARAN: But seeing, is not enough; they may miss.

PURANI: No, what about the *Graf Spee* fight? Both parties were ten miles apart and yet they could hit accurately. The bombs are mechanised in an accurate way.

SRI AUROBINDO: It is as with guns – you see and shoot. That is not the difficulty.

EVENING

The Germans have entered Paris as it was proclaimed to be undefended. There was very little talk; all seemed to be sad and stunned by the news, though it was not quite unexpected as the French had been fighting against heavy odds.

PURANI: The French troops must have been thoroughly exhausted by so many days' consecutive fighting. They seem to have no reserve force.

SRI AUROBINDO: Yes, no reserve force. But such a force was the first thing they saw to in the last war. (*After a pause*) They have not defended Paris to prevent destruction, I suppose. But I don't think it has been a wise decision. They would have done well if they had defended it, because it is not likely that Germany will preserve it. Destruction of Paris means the destruction of modern European civilisation.

NIRODBARAN: Especially if the tide of war turns against them, they are certain to destroy it.

SRI AUROBINDO: The French first decided to defend; what made them change their minds?

PURANI: Maybe England advised them so.

SRI AUROBINDO: It is not England's business.

PURANI: Dara has written from Hyderabad how he is faring and how everybody is kind to him. Then he says, "It doesn't matter

much to the world whether I remain here or go elsewhere."
(*Laughter*)

SRI AUROBINDO: Why "much"? It doesn't matter at all!
(*Laughter*)

15 JUNE 1940

PURANI: Haradhan is convinced that France will win.

NIRODBARAN: Is he sending spiritual force?

PURANI: Of course he is!

SRI AUROBINDO: France might win after great suffering but she is likely to be overrun before that.

NIRODBARAN: Already they are being chased by Germany. The Germans have bombed the new centre of government.

SRI AUROBINDO: They must have got the information from the communists. It is like Norway.

PURANI: Yes, there the Germans knew the exact place where the Government had shifted.

NIRODBARAN: What has happened to the communist prisoners now? Have they been released?

SRI AUROBINDO: Why? They are in Britanny. I hope they will be sent to French Guiana before anything happens. (*Laughter. Looking at Purani*) By the way, Hitler has said that he will enter Paris on the 15th. He may have meant the army.

NIRODBARAN: By Jove, how remarkably precise!

SRI AUROBINDO: Yes, he is getting remarkable guidance from his Asura. Sometimes the Asuras have an extraordinary foresight that comes true with perfect precision both on the vital and subtle-physical planes, just like that which is possible on the spiritual planes. Of course they are not always infallible. But Hitler committed only one mistake: when attacking Poland he thought that the Allies wouldn't intervene. (*Smiling*) Napoleon did not have such guidance.

NIRODBARAN: Had Hitler's Asura anything to do with your accident?

SRI AUROBINDO: I don't think so.

NIRODBARAN: Do the Asuras know about their own destruction?

SRI AUROBINDO: No.

NIRODBARAN: That's like the astrologers who know of others' death but not their own.

SRI AUROBINDO: No, some know of their own death also. Kasherao's father knew the exact day to the minute. He was an astrologer. Did I tell you the story of Louis XI and his astrologer? He received an invitation from Charles of Burgundy. Louis consulted his astrologer whether he should go or not. The astrologer said, "It is quite safe, you can go." And Louis was imprisoned! From the prison Louis arranged to have his astrologer murdered. But the astrologer came to know of the plot from the hangman. The plot was that when the astrologer was about to leave after seeing the king in the prison, the king would say, "Peace be with you, peace be with you," which would be the signal to kill him. So when the astrologer came the king asked him, "By the way, do you know the hour of your death?" He replied, "Exactly twenty-four hours before your death." The king got the fright of his life and accompanied him all along the way to see that he might be quite safe. (*Laughter*) This story is told by Scott in *Quentin Durward*. But it turned out later on that the king actually died twenty-four hours after the astrologer. Many other stories are there where the hour of death was precisely known.

NIRODBARAN: Turkey is on the point of taking grave decisions. Is it about joining the war?

SRI AUROBINDO: Probably. She is bound by a treaty with the Allies to do so when war breaks out in the Mediterranean.

NIRODBARAN: That means the involvement of the Balkan powers.

SRI AUROBINDO: She is consulting them.

NIRODBARAN: Russia seems to be frightened by Germany's success and is taking many precautions in the Balkans and the Baltic.

SRI AUROBINDO: Precautions won't help if Hitler is triumphant. (*After a while to Purani*) Do you know if there are still any people with political tendencies in the Maharshi's Ashram? Once it had revolutionaries like Ganapati Shastri.

PURANI: I don't know but I don't think there are any such people now. Somebody in the Maharshi's Ashram holds the view that knowledge and power are quite separate aspects of the Divine. The one is dissociated and quite distinct from the other. That is, knowledge won't have power; they don't go together.

SRI AUROBINDO: Won't have?

PURANI: Or need not have.

SRI AUROBINDO: That is another matter.

SATYENDRA: We have seen this in so many people who have knowledge but no power. One who may have experience or knowledge of Sat need not know of Chit and thus have no power, unless it is of Chit-rupa.

SRI AUROBINDO: If knowledge gave power all intellectuals would have power, and really they have none. (*Laughter*)

PURANI: I am not talking of –

SRI AUROBINDO: I know, I know. (*Laughing*) I am talking of principles. Even the knowledge of Chit does not necessarily give power. The power may be there but it may not manifest; it may remain quiescent. The Spirit is not impotent but it may remain static and quiescent. It depends on the line one follows, whether one leans on the witness side or the dynamic side. On the other hand there are many spiritual people who have little knowledge but much power.

PURANI: Olaf is angry with Nolini because Nolini did not tell him at first that he had to accept the Mother.

SRI AUROBINDO: He did not come here as a disciple but only as a visitor. Even then he has said that if he had known about the discipline of the Ashram, he would have left it at once. Anyway, I would like to see him go as soon as possible.

PURANI: In the Maharshi he has found his right Guru, he says. I hope he will be able to stay half the time there. Premanand was waiting for Sarojini Naidu's visit to the Library. Pujalal remarked, "Keep both parts of the door open!" Premanand did not understand the joke, so I said, "She may not be able to pass through only one open part of the door!" (*Laughter*)

SRI AUROBINDO: It would have been awkward if she came and got stuck and then the other part of the door had to be opened. In the photographs she looks hardly human. How has she become so fat? Eats much? Of course, some people have the tendency to grow fat in spite of sparse meals. (*Looking at Nirodbaran*) Is it due to glands?

NIRODBARAN: In women sometimes the change of life brings it in, because of the action of the glands.

SATYENDRA: Yes, women get fat after menopause.

PURANI: Not all women.

SRI AUROBINDO: Otherwise the world would be full of fat women. Suvrata[1] is tolerable compared to Sarojini Naidu.

1. Madame Yvonne R. Gaebele.

PURANI: Oh yes, because she is taller too.

NIRODBARAN: Sisir had a vision of the Mahakali aspect of the Mother in meditation as a sort of reply to his sorrow over the fall of Paris and he heard a voice saying, "Don't worry, don't worry."

PURANI: I had the perception of an angel praying to the Mother for Paris and the descent of peace over Paris.

EVENING

PURANI: I don't know how to interpret Suvrata's report to me that she heard on the radio that you have appealed to Roosevelt to intervene on behalf of the Allies. She heard your name clearly. (*Laughter*) I don't see what the relation between you and Roosevelt is.

SRI AUROBINDO: Oh, I know. It may be because of Nishtha.[1] That may be the relation. (*Laughter*)

PURANI: Later on it struck me that it may be Sailen Ghose who might have appealed.

SRI AUROBINDO: I see!

16 JUNE 1940

PURANI: It was Tagore and not Sailen Ghose who appealed to Roosevelt yesterday. (*Laughter*) I don't know how Suvrata could confuse your name and Tagore's.

SRI AUROBINDO (*laughing*): Perhaps because my name also has bin as in Rabindranath and the second syllable of Tagore has a similar sound to Ghose. (*Laughter*)

NIRODBARAN: Dilip says that the Americans won't come into the war; he is quite definite about it.

SRI AUROBINDO: They are hesitating and they may not unless they are frightened of conquest by Hitler.

PURANI: Americans are now willing to enlist for the Allies but their law doesn't allow them.

NIRODBARAN: Can't the law be changed?

SRI AUROBINDO: It can be but the Congress has to do it. It is not sufficiently war-minded, perhaps.

1. An American disciple, the daughter of Woodrow Wilson.

NIRODBARAN: Dilip says, "If the Americans don't come now, why should they come later to board a sinking ship?"

SRI AUROBINDO: Quite so.

NIRODBARAN: I lay a bet that America will come. But the point is, if she comes too late it won't be very effective, specially if France is already overrun.

SRI AUROBINDO: Exactly.

NIRODBARAN: He says that the Americans haven't much sympathy for Paris, but they have for London. If London falls then they may come, for after all they belong to the same stock.

SRI AUROBINDO: That is not true. They have more sympathy for Paris than for London. As a matter of fact they don't trust Englishmen.

PURANI: So many Americans visit Paris all round the year!

NIRODBARAN: Somebody told Dilip that now that the Germans are pushing southwards and to the rear of the Maginot Line, the French run the risk of being annihilated.

SRI AUROBINDO: Annihilated? How? They can withdraw towards the south. They still have their fleet.

NIRODBARAN: They can go to Africa and fight from there, as they say.

SRI AUROBINDO: If they can defend the Maginot Line and provided they have the supplies and the ammunition, they can stand for a long time.

NIRODBARAN: But does it operate both ways?

PURANI: Yes, that is the arrangement.

SRI AUROBINDO: The French made the mistake of not concentrating all their troops against Hitler.

NIRODBARAN: Dilip says if America is attacked by Hitler, it will only be after a long time.

SRI AUROBINDO: Yes, he will settle first with Asia and Africa.

NIRODBARAN: England?

SRI AUROBINDO: An attack on England is not likely unless her navy is first destroyed.

NIRODBARAN: England won't give the fight up even if France is conquered.

SRI AUROBINDO: No; so long as she has her fleet, she will carry on.

NIRODBARAN: And Russia is there.

SRI AUROBINDO: Yes, Hitler is the great danger to Russia.

NIRODBARAN: Stalin is already taking measures to protect himself in the Baltic.

SRI AUROBINDO (*addressing Purani*): Yes, what is this pact of non-aggression with Lithuania that Russia speaks of? Non-aggression against whom? Sending troops can only mean landing in Germany.

PURANI: Yes, there was some non-aggression pact. Of course these are all excuses.

SRI AUROBINDO: Stalin wants to fortify his position while Hitler is engaged elsewhere. He is fortifying it in Galicia too.

SATYENDRA: These governments are all a nuisance. Perhaps what Sisir said may come true that we may have to seek refuge on some islets. (*Laughter*)

SRI AUROBINDO: Yes, if islets are available. (*Laughter*) We shall have to if Hitler or Stalin comes in. Stalin will at the very outset liquidate – this is the Russian term – all Sannyasins and religious institutions. As for Hitler, he will ask us to accept him as the head; and factories and industries will be run by the Germans. There will be thorough Nazism. Doraiswamy will have a hard time. As for Y, he will be beaten to death. (*Laughter*)

PURANI: Astrologers say that after the 20th of this month Hitler's decline will begin.

SRI AUROBINDO: Which astrologers?

PURANI: The Parsi one and somebody else also. Pavitra too knows astrology, but he did not try to see Hitler's horoscope.

SRI AUROBINDO: He is not good at events. He studies the character, and there he has made remarkable readings. About Hitler he has found that he will cause terrible bloodshed and that he runs a great danger to his own life.

NIRODBARAN: Amery has repeated the old formula about India's internal differences.

SRI AUROBINDO: Yes, these Labour leaders seem to be useless as regards India. In their own affairs they can exert pressure on the Government. Even the *Manchester Guardian* defends Jinnah. It doesn't know enough about India, it seems.

NIRODBARAN: That paper sometimes takes this side and sometimes that side.

SRI AUROBINDO: If the Congress had agreed to the scheme of a few people coming together for discussions, then they could have tried for a compromise. The English people are a practical people.

They don't understand the principles the Congress stands for. And for them to agree to whatever the Constituent Assembly decides is out of the question. Stafford Cripps may do that but he is not the Premier.

About Lady Hydari who died one or two days ago, Sri Aurobindo said that she would not have lasted long, but her death was hastened. Doctors said that she should have lived eighteen months more. She was much better here. In order to live longer she would have had to make an inner effort. She was open to various influences, even to those who are hostile towards the Ashram.

EVENING

SRI AUROBINDO: Fazlul Huque has come down again on Bose's paper by demanding more security. By the way, this agitation against the Holwell monument seems to be a pre-arranged affair. The *Forward* says that Fazlul Huque has already said that it will be removed.

NIRODBARAN: Yes, there was an attempt on the part of the Muslims to remove the monument and Bose has taken up that cry. In the Corporation, a European member proposed to withdraw all advertisements from the *Star of India* because of its attack on Sri Krishna, and the Hindu Sabha supported him. But Bose opposed it. His party, himself and other Muslims voted against it.

SRI AUROBINDO (*laughing*): You mean he is also a Muslim? (*Laughter*)

NIRODBARAN: Going to be!

PURANI: The Germans claim to have taken Verdun which means they have crossed the Maginot Line.

SRI AUROBINDO: The Mother says that the Maginot Line is a farce because from the point where the Rhine divides France and Germany, there is no proper Maginot, only scattered fortifications. Only in the north from Montmedy the Maginot proper begins. I don't know why they have done that. Have they thought that the Rhine will be a natural barrier? It is absurd. If such is the case they ought to remove their troops from there in time.

17 JUNE 1940

Reynaud has resigned, Pétain has become the Premier and other members of the Cabinet have been picked from the military.

NIRODBARAN: Was there any difference in policy among the members of the Cabinet?

SRI AUROBINDO: Probably. Reynaud is unpopular. Now it is practically a military dictatorship.

PURANI: Even after the war it may remain. Most of them seem to be Catholics and from the right wing.

NIRODBARAN: Weygand hasn't shown any remarkable qualities till now.

SATYENDRA: Pétain has no time, and besides the supplies and equipment are too poor. What can he do? At present what is most necessary is men; equipment doesn't matter so much.

SRI AUROBINDO: Oh, it does matter. They say that because their ammunition was exhausted they couldn't use the seventy-five-mm gun. On the first day they were able to destroy four hundred tanks. Afterwards we didn't hear any more about this. This was due to lack of ammunition.

NIRODBARAN: The Germans have now reached the south end of the Maginot Line.

SRI AUROBINDO: That means all industrial areas have fallen into their hands. The British have opened disused coal mines in Wales to supply coal to France.

SATYENDRA: The situation is very grave now.

SRI AUROBINDO: Yes, one of the tactics Germany applied was to capture the generals by means of tanks so that the troops might get disorganised.

NIRODBARAN: And at this late hour England is calling up the twenty-nine-year-old age-group. People who are twenty-nine years old are quite strong and able-bodied; they could have been called up long ago.

SRI AUROBINDO: Quite so. I suppose they wanted to keep men for commerce, agriculture, industry, etc., so that export would go on leisurely as in 1914.

PURANI: And they could rely on the blockade.

SRI AUROBINDO: Yes, but except for war materials the blockade can't be so effective if Hitler becomes master of Europe.

EVENING

News arrived at about 6.20 p.m. that Pétain has decided to stop fighting and negotiate with Hitler for honourable peace terms. The Mother gave the news to Sri Aurobindo and went away.

SRI AUROBINDO (*after reading the news*): France has stopped the fight. This is Pétain's doing. He is too old!

Naturally it came as a great surprise and we were all thrown into a gloom.

Purani (*later in the evening*): No terms have been given yet?
SRI AUROBINDO: No.
NIRODBARAN: It seems to me France has acted more dishonourably than the Belgian king.
SRI AUROBINDO: Oh, yes. Besides, Hitler now becomes the master of Europe.
NIRODBARAN: But why has France done this? She still has a huge army and navy intact. She could have withdrawn somewhere else, as Reynaud said, instead of surrendering like that.
PURANI: France has become decadent now.
NIRODBARAN: Hope England won't give up.
SATYENDRA: I don't think she will.
SRI AUROBINDO: The English don't give up. But it has to be seen if England also has become decadent or not. After all Poland fought much better than France. It was only the Polish generals who were incompetent, the people went on fighting. Finland also fought very well.
SATYENDRA: In Belgium it was the king, not the Government who surrendered; but here it was the Government that has surrendered. The navy could perhaps disobey and revolt?
SRI AUROBINDO: Not possible. Pétain has put Admiral Darlan in the Ministry. The Navy is not likely to disobey him.
PURANI: Now the Mediterranean situation will be critical. If Hitler gets the French fleet, then with Italy on his side he will be very powerful.
SRI AUROBINDO: Yes, and Turkey's position will be dangerous. Now only Hitler's death can save the situation.
NIRODBARAN: Everybody is astounded, for Russia is already preparing for future attacks.

Talks with Sri Aurobindo

SRI AUROBINDO: Yes, the Russian Army has marched into Lithuania and Latvia, hasn't it?

NIRODBARAN: Japan is threatening Indo-China and may capture it, any time now. She won't allow Germany there.

PURANI: Yes, it must have shaken the whole political structure of the world and I think everybody realises the danger if Hitler occupies France.

SRI AUROBINDO: Does India realise it? Everybody seems to be busy with his own interest and none considers anything in the light of the world situation. The Congress Committee is now in session. Will it realise the danger?

NIRODBARAN: I think it will.

SRI AUROBINDO: Let us hope so. Nehru seems to shut his eyes and calls all these fears of foreign invasion a bogey. I am wondering what our Ashram's fate will now be. Like the others we are also considering our own self-interest! (*Laughter*) Shall we be under Stalin or under Hitler? Stalin will be the more serious risk.

NIRODBARAN: Why Stalin? He will first have to conquer India.

SRI AUROBINDO: That won't take him a long time and he won't allow our existence at all.

NIRODBARAN: The British will grab Pondicherry if France capitulates.

SRI AUROBINDO: If England gives in to Germany, Japan may come and drop some bombs on India.

PURANI: Could it be the result of Karma that France is being defeated and overrun?

SRI AUROBINDO: Of course there is past Karma, but it is not fixed. It can be counter-balanced by the right Karma at present or it can exhaust itself through suffering. Even if France is conquered now, she can rise again through the exhaustion of her Karma by suffering. New forces can come into play.

NIRODBARAN: In that case England also has a heavy Karma to pay for.

SRI AUROBINDO: Oh yes. It has to be seen what she does.

NIRODBARAN: If England had given India freedom, wouldn't that have counted morally?

SRI AUROBINDO: Certainly, it would have had a great moral value for her.

PURANI: Apart from that it would have been a great benefit from the practical point of view.

NIRODBARAN: That, of course, but I am talking of moral and spiritual values.

PURANI: It seems Suryakumari or somebody else brought some French coins to the Mother; on seeing them the Mother said, "What coins are these? I don't know them. They seem to be the coins of a ruined country." It was after the Munich pact.

SRI AUROBINDO: I didn't know about it. But when France betrayed Czechoslovakia the Mother said that France was condemned.

NIRODBARAN: Do you foresee all possibilities?

SRI AUROBINDO: The possibilities can be foreseen but we don't accept them as fixed or inevitable. They can be changed.

PURANI: Reynaud should not have resigned.

SRI AUROBINDO: What could he do? He is unpopular in France. And he is not a military man. He could have made a coup d'état and arrested all these people, but he must have felt that the nation would not be behind him.

Now two things can save the world: one is Hitler's death and the other is if Hitler exhausts himself so much that he has to wait before farther adventures. In that case time will be gained.

NIRODBARAN: If America and Russia joined with England, the three of them would make a formidable combination.

SRI AUROBINDO: That is common sense. But nobody listens to common sense. Even if Hitler dies, there is Stalin. And if Stalin invades India, Subhas Bose and Nehru will oppose him, perhaps.

NIRODBARAN: I wonder what Hitler's next move will be.

SRI AUROBINDO: Yes, it will be interesting to see what he does next.

NIRODBARAN: Not likely that he will go to the Balkans, as it will involve him with Russia. He will now avoid friction with Russia and America.

PURANI: America, of course, and America won't come in unless a variety of odd incidents happen: for instance, the sinking of an American ship.

SRI AUROBINDO: Hitler will never do that. The Asura who guides him knows very well what would happen then.

18 JUNE 1940

PURANI: The people in Pondicherry have become very panicky. They are thinking about what their fate will be now.

SRI AUROBINDO: I see.

SATYENDRA: The Working Committee of the Congress is sitting now. With the coming of the war it has set up a radio and trunk line. It must have got the bad news. But I don't know how much it will influence its decisions. People are talking about a National Government now.

SRI AUROBINDO: But for Nehru's influence, Gandhi would have come to a compromise.

PURANI: Rajagopalachari also seems to be in favour of some settlement.

SRI AUROBINDO: He is a practical man.

PURANI: I don't know how Churchill's offer to France of one nationality will work. Two nations temperamentally so different!

SRI AUROBINDO (*laughing*): Yes, the French will say one thing, and the English will nod their heads to quite the opposite.

PURANI: And France won't accept the king!

SRI AUROBINDO: No!

SATYENDRA: But it is a brilliant offer of an economic combination.

SRI AUROBINDO: Not only economic but much more than that. Practically one nation. It is a tremendous step for the English, beyond all tradition, prejudice and character of the nation.

PURANI: Yes, and after the war it might form the nucleus of a European federation.

SRI AUROBINDO: Yes, if they combine, the small nations may enter and the British dominions come in and, along with them, India may be asked to join. In that case it may turn into a world federation. The English do not seem to have lost their elasticity which is shown by two steps they have taken. The first is the socialisation of their government in two hours and the second is their offer to the French. The English lead a practical life; they don't live in ideas. That is why they are so successful in life. In times of crisis or necessity they are driven to take practical steps as the situation demands.

NIRODBARAN: Only, they are not applying their practicality to India.

PURANI: They may not yet have felt the necessity.

SRI AUROBINDO: Pétain and Weygand are inelastic and too old. Hitler is neither practical nor a man of ideas. Still he is very successful because of his remarkable inspirations.

NIRODBARAN: Hitler has not yet sent any reply to France's peace offer.

PURANI: He will be more cunning now in the face of the British proposal.

SRI AUROBINDO: Yes, as in the case of Czechoslovakia. He struck later at the most opportune moment. He knows that he can't conquer England without the support of France. Hitler's first idea was to get hold of the north of France so as to control the Channel ports.

NIRODBARAN: The 20th of June is not very far away; today is the 18th.

SRI AUROBINDO: Yesterday was Paul Richard's birthday. You know what he used to say?

PURANI: No.

SRI AUROBINDO: That his ideas would be fulfilled on his birthdays.

NIRODBARAN: France can still retrieve her honour if she accepts England's offer.

SRI AUROBINDO: Quite so. But, as I said, Pétain and Weygand are too old and inelastic.

SATYENDRA: It is perhaps too late.

SRI AUROBINDO: If it had been offered earlier they would not have accepted it.

SATYENDRA: That is true.

NIRODBARAN: It seems to me that the capitulation of Paris has demoralised the army. Otherwise how could the Germans advance so fast?

SRI AUROBINDO: Yes. Besides, I don't understand Weygand's strategy of ceding territory to the enemy with the idea of exhausting him. That only lengthens the line of defence which is very difficult to keep together. It is only by a short line that the forces can be concentrated. It is the Champagne Line that is broken. The fall of Paris has, of course, divided the army into three sectors. The other two sectors are still fighting well.

NIRODBARAN: Some people in India defend France's peace offer. They say, "What can the French do? Their army was being annihilated. As they were defeated they had no other course."

SRI AUROBINDO: That is the typical Indian mentality. That is why India is under subjection. Just because an army has been defeated, must it surrender? Will a subject nation then always be a subject nation? Won't it fight for freedom? See what the Poles have done. They have resisted in spite of their severe defeat. The Belgian and the Dutch Governments have not surrendered, they have withdrawn.

PURANI: Besides, the French still have a big army intact. The navy and the air force are theirs. Why should they surrender?

SRI AUROBINDO: Quite so. Moreover, as you go on fighting, moral and spiritual forces may rise up and assert themselves. No, France has become inferior now.

NIRODBARAN: France does not believe in moral forces.

SRI AUROBINDO: But ancient France did believe.

NIRODBARAN: Dilip believes that England also will give up the fight. How can she fight alone?

SRI AUROBINDO: She has always fought alone. That again is the Indian subject mentality. No great things can be done unless one sticks on in the face of defeat and failure. Hitler had himself been imprisoned but he stuck on like a bulldog even after defeat. Now he is the master of Europe.

EVENING

PURANI: It seems Reynaud has resigned on the issue of the appeal of Churchill, which he wanted to accept while Pétain and others didn't. And Pétain has started communication with Hitler.

SRI AUROBINDO: Yes, they want military nationalism, that is why Pétain speaks of believing in the destiny of France.

NIRODBARAN: I hope Hitler's terms will be unacceptable and that they will be forced to accept England's offer.

SRI AUROBINDO: I hope they will accept this offer. To do so would be much better than the surrender of France to Hitler.

SATYENDRA: If the Navy could get away –

SRI AUROBINDO: Pétain has put two naval officers in his Cabinet to stop that. Unless there is a revolt in the Cabinet the outlook is bad. These people ought to be shot for the betrayal of France.

PURANI: In Africa the Italians are not faring very well.

SRI AUROBINDO: No, the Africans don't seem to be willing to give their lives for the Italians.

PURANI: Sammer still holds that if France declared herself communist, the Russians would attack Hitler and come to help France. And people here in Pondy believe that Hitler doesn't want the British Empire. He only wants hegemony among his colonies.

SRI AUROBINDO: Are they so idiotic as to believe that he will be satisfied with that? He has said plainly in *Mein Kampf* that his aim is to destroy France and Russia. Now he is speaking of colonies which means that England also must be destroyed. These people know nothing about war. It is better for us to learn German now or both German and Russian – as a precaution! (*Laughter*)

19 JUNE 1940

PURANI: The Berlin paper says that when Germany asked for peace in the last war, the Allies did not reply for six weeks. Why should they now expect a reply in two days? Let them remember Versailles.

SRI AUROBINDO: Then what the Mother says may be true, that the Germans will keep silent so that the French Army may be crushed in the meantime.

PURANI: Churchill says in his speech that almost all the British troops – , about three-and-a-half lakhs – have been removed from Dunkirk in a few days.

SRI AUROBINDO: Three-and-a-half lakhs? Then he must be referring to the Flanders troops. For if they had sent such a big army the French people would not have quarrelled over insufficient British help.

NIRODBARAN: But it has been said, "three-and-a-half lakhs during these few days".

SRI AUROBINDO: There must be some confusion. Pavitra may have made some mistake. Churchill is usually very clear in his statements.

NIRODBARAN: In some papers there was a complaint against inadequate supplies to France.

PURANI: That can't be true after Churchill's speech.

SRI AUROBINDO: No. They sent three-and-a-half lakhs to Flanders and their best troops. After the Battle of Flanders, they sent only three divisions and Churchill has already said that it would take a long time to recover from the Flanders disaster. He asked that they should be properly equipped. Without the proper equipment it is sheer foolishness to send troops to fight against Germany. He promised Reynaud that he would send fifty thousand men and all available help.

PURANI: Besides, the British have to keep a sufficient number to protect their own land.

SRI AUROBINDO: Of course. Otherwise there would be a great danger. No, no, it is all French over-sensitiveness and suspiciousness. This is exactly what happened during the reign of Napoleon III – different political parties playing at governing the country and that is how he was defeated.

PURANI: There is still a notion among people that England will fight to the last Frenchman.

SATYENDRA: If that is so why are they calling France to unite with them?

SRI AUROBINDO: They may be saying that to make France another dominion.

SATYENDRA: But England sent her best troops and equipment to Flanders.

SRI AUROBINDO: Quite so; besides, if France falls, England knows that it will be difficult for her to survive.

PURANI: Some eye-witness describes that there is no organisation, no equipment in the French Army. They do not know what is happening. They think that a truce has been declared; so fighting has stopped and Germany is marching rapidly to take advantage of the situation.

NIRODBARAN: And the troops have also become demoralised after the truce proclamation.

SRI AUROBINDO: Yes, the loss at Flanders, the capitulation of Paris and the truce have demoralised them. They may be thinking, "What is the use of being killed when we are going to surrender tomorrow?" Of course as soldiers they will fight, but not with heart.

England has not shown any military genius but she has shown power of organisation while France has shown neither military nor organisational power. Gamelin is a fraud and Weygand and Pétain too old. Weygand has done nothing remarkable. Neither has any other military genius shown himself.

PURANI: England is now preparing vigorously.

SRI AUROBINDO: Yes, if Hitler gives them one more year, they will become tremendously powerful. Both Daladier and Chamberlain seem to be impotent. They have done nothing at all. The Mother says that Hitler has asked for all French colonies contiguous to the British. That means we go to Germany. (*Laughter*)

NIRODBARAN: I do not think Hitler has heard the name of Pondicherry.

SRI AUROBINDO: Oh yes. He knows every detail. In Germany they have schools for giving people such training and they know every town, every street in France and England. In the Kaiser's time, it is said, he knew even the location of trees in some places. Now it is more thorough. Japan and Germany are the most thoroughly organised countries.

EVENING

SATYENDRA: Some people here say that nothing happens without the sanction of the Divine Will and that nothing happens against Sri Aurobindo's will. I want to know if that is so. Germany's taking Czechoslovakia, Poland and other countries and bringing about the war – was all this sanctioned by your will? You said at that time you did not want war.

SRI AUROBINDO: The will was that there must be no war. But I didn't want this will to be effected at the cost of betraying Czechoslovakia. Is the fighting going on in France due to my will? It is due to her own Karma.

SATYENDRA: That is what I thought but you seem to have written to somebody that no major event happens against your will.

SRI AUROBINDO: To whom and when have I written that?

PURANI: Oh, I know. I think he is referring to Dilip's letter. You once wrote to him during the Abyssinian war that you have seen that whenever you have willed something, invariably it has been fulfilled.

SRI AUROBINDO: That is a different matter. I willed in my boyhood that Ireland and Alsace-Lorraine should be free. Then I willed things which I forgot and afterwards they were fulfilled. Again, other things I willed, which I now don't want to be fulfilled, but they have been and in a way which I don't want. I wanted the British Empire to be crushed and Hitler is now doing it in such a thorough fashion that I don't want it any more because Hitler has become a greater danger. (*Laughter*) Does it mean I willed that my leg should be broken? Or that France should be defeated?

SATYENDRA: That is what I said to them.

SRI AUROBINDO: Yes, but that does not mean the absence of consent. The Divine may consent to things and events happening, whose results may not be favourable for the present, but may lead to some utility in the future. The Divine doesn't see things from the human mental point of view or only from the present and immediate results. Perhaps people think that the Divine is like a super-Mussolini according to whose Will everything must turn. When a person descends to do some particular work for the Divine, he accepts the play of forces and works through that play so that ultimately the Divine Will may prevail and fulfil itself; for a time the opposing forces may conquer and the Divine Will withdraw, as is said in the Bhagavad Gita. Did not Sri Krishna have to leave the battle? The Divine foresees and provides for everything in the original plan but that plan is carried out through the play of forces whatever the ultimate purpose is. The Divine does not take up each particular thing and say that it must be done, that it must happen and so on — unless there is some Supreme Vision to be imperatively carried out.

SATYENDRA: Besides, when he comes down into limited matter he himself becomes limited to some extent.

SRI AUROBINDO: That limitation is a self-imposed limitation. Christ knew that he would be crucified and yet it was not the whole of him that wanted crucifixion. Some human part didn't want it and he prayed, "O God, let this cup be passed to somebody else." Everything that happens can be said to happen according to the Divine Will.

SATYENDRA: That is a religious idea.

SRI AUROBINDO: Only people who have reached a certain stage of consciousness can say that. For they see and know what is behind the play of things. For others it is only faith. And faith is sometimes very ignorant.

NIRODBARAN: Have you read Arthur Moore's article? He has pleaded very strongly for Dominion Status.

SATYENDRA: Many Europeans are now supporting it.

SRI AUROBINDO: Yes, it is only the bureaucracy, tied up in its old tradition and routine, that doesn't see things that way.

20 JUNE 1940

NIRODBARAN: Japan is talking of sending an expeditionary force to Indo-China.

SRI AUROBINDO: Yes. The Governor there has intimated that he will resist.

PURANI: There are plenty of Pondicherry people in the army there.

NIRODBARAN: They have no chance against the Japanese Army.

SRI AUROBINDO: Bulloch has said that the Indians can very quickly learn the technical side of warfare. Provided they get proper leadership, with sympathy and understanding, they can make very good soldiers.

NIRODBARAN: Will England help – if the Governor asks – against Japan?

SRI AUROBINDO: Can't say. England can help only with her navy. She has no troops there. Japan will attack overland. But if Japan attacks Indo-China, it will be the last straw on America's back. America won't tolerate Japan in the Pacific, just as during the Dutch East Indies question.

NIRODBARAN: Japan may have a shot at Pondicherry too.

SRI AUROBINDO: Yes, but the navy will have to pass through Singapore, Malacca, etc. India will then be between Japan, Germany and Russia.

SATYENDRA: Russia? Russia is far away and doesn't show any intention.

SRI AUROBINDO: Russia is always silent before she acts. Nobody knows what is in Russia's mind until the last moment. The same with Japan. It is only now that Japan talks about her aims and objects.

NIRODBARAN: Hitler is repeating his old game of asking for plenipotentiaries. In the meantime he intends to crush France.

SRI AUROBINDO: Yes, she must withdraw her army in time. There is a rumour that even if this Government submits, another Government will be started in London. Algeria will declare independence. The commander of the Middle East will not submit and neither will the navy.

PURANI: That will be very good. Hitler can't stop the navy. Except for the Italian Navy, he has no sea power.

SRI AUROBINDO: Three things are important: French gold, her air force and her navy. If the navy falls to Hitler, it will be a difficult time for England.

PURANI: Oil reserves also; it is not known what the French have done with them – whether they have destroyed them or if they have fallen into enemy hands. It seems the Pétain Government is Fascist in tendency and wants to make an alliance with Germany and rule over France.

SRI AUROBINDO: If Hitler allows. Even then, after taking England he will turn to them and destroy them completely. These people are idiots, not politicians. Hitler has clearly said in his *Mein Kampf* that France must be crushed. So long as France exists, Germany will be in danger. Hitler first wanted to make friends with England. When that failed, he said he had no enmity with France; his grudge is only against the English. His tactics are very familiar now.

Nirodbaran (*after a while*): Another indictment against Bose by Bipin Ganguli. It seems that because Bose let out news about the talks of the Working Committee regarding acceptance or non-acceptance of the federation – talks which were confidential – Gandhi and the High Command strongly objected to the federation. It means Gandhi and the others were at one time in favour of accepting the federation.

SRI AUROBINDO: Of course. Gandhi and Bulabhai Desai and Satyamurti were discussing it. It is Bose who spoiled it by his untimely disclosure. What Amery has said is true – that if the internal differences were resolved then Dominion Status would be easily granted.

NIRODBARAN: But what can Congress do?

SRI AUROBINDO: Why? They can take the four Muslim Premiers together – what Azad is doing now – and come to a solution and settle the Dominion Status. Once you get that, it is practically independence, even if that independence is precarious nowadays. It would be the next practical step.

NIRODBARAN: Rajagopalachari, I think, would accept it.

PURANI: Yes.

SRI AUROBINDO: It is only Nehru who would object. He lives in his ideas.

PURANI: He may say, for example: "What interest has Japan in Indo-China?" (*Laughter*)

SRI AUROBINDO: What interest had she in China? What interest had Hitler in Uruguay? They have unearthed a plot there which is evidently of Nazi origin.

SATYENDRA: My paper – The *Indian Express* (*laughter*) – writes in its editorial that Nehru says, "Come to terms with the Muslims anyhow."

NIRODBARAN: He may do quite the opposite the next day.

SATYENDRA: Yes, as the conditions change.

SRI AUROBINDO: That is supramental.

PURANI: Rajagopalachari will be willing to accept Dominion Status, I think.

SRI AUROBINDO: He is a practical man. Now they are neither doing civil disobedience nor going to the Ministry. Gandhi knows only his Charkha. The Charkha is going to give Swaraj, non-violence, everything – his wonderful "co-ordination" of ideas.

NIRODBARAN: Won't it give realisation of God?

SRI AUROBINDO: He has not come to that yet. But he has found the Charkha in the Gita.

If India accepts Dominion Status, that will remove one of the difficulties of America's joining the war.

NIRODBARAN: Is that really true? Some papers, of course, mention it.

SRI AUROBINDO: Quite true. Even the British people have said that there is a strong sympathy for India in America. The Americans say, "England is fighting for her imperialism. Why should we fight for her?"

NIRODBARAN: Of course, Duff Cooper also admits that there is a strong pro-India sentiment there.

SRI AUROBINDO: Then? He is an imperialist. He doesn't want India to be free. Why should he say that if it were not true?

(*After some time*) If England goes down, there won't be any free country left except Russia, Japan, Germany and Italy. I am speaking of the old world. I think the next war will be between Russia and Germany. If Russia finds that England is in a difficult position, then Stalin will put pressure on Turkey and Rumania for control of the Black Sea, as he has done with the Baltic states; of course, not without difficulty, for they may resist. Hitler is not likely to keep quiet over the trouble in the Balkans. With Italy's help he may settle the Balkan problem and that of Asia Minor. Or he may allow Russia a free hand now, knowing that he can settle with her afterwards.

NIRODBARAN: Will Pétain hand over France to Hitler?

SRI AUROBINDO: These people – (*Sri Aurobindo left his sentence incomplete.*)

EVENING

PURANI: The Governor-General of Madagascar has wired the Pondicherry Government that he is not going to accept peace and will fight on. Our Governor also has decided not to accept. And they are going to wire to Pétain not to make peace.

SRI AUROBINDO: That will be a great thing. All these telegrams may put some shame into the heart of Pétain. I am afraid the news about the French fleet leaving for an unknown destination is not very reliable. It is American news.

PURANI: Some part of the fleet is under the British command. They can prevent it from falling into German hands.

SRI AUROBINDO: They can't force the navy. It is for the navy to decide.

NIRODBARAN: They have not given out the names of the envoys.

SRI AUROBINDO: No, one of them seems to be Bondain. He is pro-British. It is he who stands for an honourable peace. He is supposed to be a very capable man. It was due to him that the Indo-China bank flourished.

PURANI: The envoys may be shouted down by Hitler like Hacha.

SRI AUROBINDO: Yes, or they may be starved till they agree to sign the terms imposed.

PURANI: They can have some food brought to them by parachutists.

SRI AUROBINDO: Yes, some chemical food to eat surreptitiously. (*Laughter*)

NIRODBARAN: Churchill's statement is not clear about how many divisions of British troops were sent after the fight in Flanders.

SRI AUROBINDO: No, he says three – while he says again that twelve divisions were equipped and that was what France was led to expect. There may be nine divisions fighting in France and these three, making twelve in all.

PURANI: Rajagopalachari is speaking of non-cooperation in France. He says the occupied countries may offer non-cooperation to Hitler.

NIRODBARAN: He can be sent to preach and practise it.

SRI AUROBINDO: He won't preach very long. He will be given a passport to heaven. (*After some time*) Japan is not marching to Indo-China yet. She has appealed to the Axis powers to preserve the status quo there.

PURANI: Yes, but if France accepts peace, then Japan may grab it.

SRI AUROBINDO: Yes, of course. It has been a long-standing aim of Japan to drive out the Europeans from the Far East. If she can do that and come to the Far East, the Near East also won't last very long.

PURANI: The Japanese seem to be getting displaced from Chungking.

SRI AUROBINDO: That means they don't have their old strength. In former times, once Japan occupied a place, it was impossible to dislodge her. That shows what happens if one gives up one's Swadharma. According to the German advice, to grow tall the Japanese are taking raw meat, wearing shoes and adopting other European customs. In former days, eating grains and with bare feet, they used to fight splendidly, as in the Russo-Japanese war. They may have improved their stature by eating meat but they have lost in other ways.

NIRODBARAN: If the Italian colonies in Africa could be seized, which does not seem difficult considering the wonderful fighting quality of the Italians, it would be something.

SRI AUROBINDO: And if, in addition, the Italian fleet can be smashed, then it would be bad for Germany too. If England can hold on for one year at least, or two winters, there is a chance.

21 JUNE 1940

SRI AUROBINDO (*addressing Purani*): The armistice seems to have failed; the envoys came back almost immediately yesterday. Hitler must have pressed for complete acceptance or complete refusal and didn't give any chance for discussion. The

French Government seems to have gone to Morocco from Bordeaux.

PURANI: Then it is all right; no more chance of peace.

SRI AUROBINDO: Can't say. Pétain is dangerous so long as he is in the Government.

NIRODBARAN: If the army could now be withdrawn!

SRI AUROBINDO: Yes, that is the first thing to do now. If Hitler had got the French fleet, he would have attacked Africa and taken possession of her colonies. Have you seen the other news? That Roosevelt has taken two Republicans into the Government?

PURANI: Yes.

SRI AUROBINDO: This is unprecedented in history.

PURANI: They have been made secretaries of Navy and War. If he plunges into war, he wants to have the Republican party with him perhaps.

SRI AUROBINDO: Yes. Another unprecedented step is his standing for a third term.

PURANI: The Democrats will nominate him, I hope.

SRI AUROBINDO: Oh yes, and then he may decide about the war. If Roosevelt declares war now and somebody else becomes the President, he may disown the policy and it will be very awkward.

NIRODBARAN: Italy is not showing herself anywhere – neither on land nor in the air. It seems the Italians could easily be driven out of Africa. Then Mussolini and Hitler can quarrel over France.

SRI AUROBINDO: Not so soon. As long as Hitler has England to fight, he will keep Italy with him.

EVENING

According to Bhaskar's radio, peace terms have been placed before Pétain. Laval and fifty other Government officials pledge to support Pétain and all the deputies place their confidence in him. But this report seems to contradict what Gabriel said. He said that it was all untrue. Plenipotentiaries have not returned. Protests are coming to Pétain from all sides against peace and the Government has been removed from Bordeaux. All communications are to be sent to Casablanca in Morocco.

SRI AUROBINDO: Probably the plenipotentiaries have refused to sign the terms and Hitler has himself communicated the terms to

Pétain. That is how the two news reports can be reconciled. Bhaskar's news is sometimes very confusing.

NIRODBARAN: What is the next news item about Gandhi being absolved of responsibility by the Working Committee?

SRI AUROBINDO: Perhaps they want to start civil disobedience and Gandhi is against it. He has always stood against it. So they may want to go ahead on their own initiative.

NIRODBARAN: The *Patrika* gave the news that British papers had published a message from Wardha that Gandhi and others were trying to start a provisional government with the Hindus, Muslims and the untouchables.

SRI AUROBINDO: That must come then from Abul Kalam Azad and the Muslim Premier's conference.

PURANI: The American Republican party has disowned the two Republicans Roosevelt has appointed.

SRI AUROBINDO: What a pity! Why?

PURANI: Because they are strongly pro-English. Not that the Republican party is itself anti-Allies. Spain perhaps will enter the war on Germany's side.

NIRODBARAN: She already took the first step by declaring non-belligerency.

SATYENDRA: Everybody is taking Hitler's side.

SRI AUROBINDO: Yes, and those who have not are afraid of him. Unless America declares war, England will be alone. Egypt is also trying to back out. With Gibraltar on one side and the Suez on the other, England will be in a difficult position, unless she can create some revolution in Egypt and bring in Nahash Pasha. Russia is trying to keep out Turkey.

NIRODBARAN: Keep out of what?

SRI AUROBINDO: Out of the war on the side of the Allies, as a possible troublemaker in the Balkans. Is it true that Italy is bringing down her own planes? (*Laughter*)

It seems, in a raid over some Italian town by English planes, not a single plane was brought down by the Italians and much of their ammunition was wasted for which the commander reprimanded the anti-aircraft personnel and asked them to be more careful next time. In the next English raid the Italians fired accurately and carefully and brought down two out of three planes. But those two turned out to be Italian planes.

SATYENDRA: Who is this Sir Patro of Madras? He is also clamouring for India's defence.

SRI AUROBINDO: Oh, everybody is doing that now.

NIRODBARAN: The Congress Working Committee has asked Congressmen to take precautionary measures for defence. What precautionary measures can they take?

SRI AUROBINDO: They can make a battle cry with their Charkhas and shoot down the parachutists with them. Gandhi may have disagreed with the Working Committee on this point of defence. Being non-violent, how can he support any defence measures?

SATYENDRA: I don't think he will object to others taking them for the sake of the country.

SRI AUROBINDO: But on principle he can't allow them.

NIRODBARAN: I don't understand how without Gandhi they can launch civil disobedience. It will end in a fiasco.

PURANI: Quite so. (*Sri Aurobindo smiled.*)

SRI AUROBINDO (*after some time*): Russia is following a dangerous policy for herself. Does she think that Hitler will be so damaged by his fight with England that Stalin will be able to destroy him by an attack? When Hitler gets the whole of France he will build up his position very strongly; then he might try to blockade England, since a direct invasion of England is out of the question. If the French Navy falls into his hands, he will become tremendously strong. But when England is conquered, he will have all the French colonies and most of the British ones. His next step will naturally be to move towards the Balkans and then a clash with Russia is inevitable unless Hitler has given up his project of becoming master of Europe. The Balkan powers are foolish enough not to see that their turn will come later on.

PURANI: England is not going to have Mediterranean engagements with Italy.

SRI AUROBINDO: Too much occupied with Africa probably.

PURANI: If the English can take the whole of Africa from Italy and crush her navy then Italy will be crippled. Her long sea coast will be open to attack everywhere. I don't understand why Egypt is backing out.

SRI AUROBINDO: This king can't be trusted; he is a man of the dictator type. He can do anything.

NIRODBARAN: Laski has written to America that he expects Labour to make an early agreement with England.

SRI AUROBINDO: He expects many things that don't come off. He expects that every Frenchman will fight till the last Frenchman falls.

NIRODBARAN: The Congress Working Committee admits that some useful purpose has been served by Abul Kalam Azad's talks with the Muslim Premiers and says the talks may continue.

PURANI: This Iyengar of Madras is supporting the fifty-percent demands by Muslims.

SRI AUROBINDO: Who is he?

PURANI: He is a crank, giving opinions when nobody wants them.

NIRODBARAN: Oh, somebody was saying that Sir Akbar also demands fifty percent for Muslims.

SRI AUROBINDO: That is for Hyderabad where the Muslims have had a monopoly till now. He can't suddenly bring it down to twenty or thirty percent, the same as in Kashmir. There the Hindus had all the monopoly. Now if the Muslim demands are acceded to, the Hindus will be wiped out.

PURANI: People here are defending the French Government. They say that the people on the spot know best what the situation is and they have to act accordingly.

SRI AUROBINDO: Who are the people? Indians?

PURANI: Yes, they say that Hitler has allowed Holland to keep her own Dutch Government.

NIRODBARAN: Government is all right. What about the policy? The Dutch will have to follow Hitler's policy.

SRI AUROBINDO: Why won't he allow them their own Government? Hitler can bring in his own men to rule everywhere, but I don't think he wants to attach all his conquered countries to Germany. He will make them all vassal states and have them all ruled by their own people. How can he govern all the colonies with his own people? For that matter England can't govern India without the help of Indian officials.

22 JUNE 1940

SRI AUROBINDO: The French Government is still at Bordeaux and negotiations have only started now! The Pondicherry

Government news was that the French Governor had left for Casablanca.

PURANI: The Germans speak of the heroic resistance of the French Army and say that their terms will not be unjust or dishonourable.

SRI AUROBINDO: No, they say they won't be shameful but severe.

SATYENDRA: The Italian news says that they won't be as bad as Versailles.

SRI AUROBINDO: They may not be as bad but still bad enough. If, as is reported, Hitler wants all the colonies contiguous with British colonies, then our position becomes unsafe.

NIRODBARAN: But the colonies may refuse to accept such terms.

SRI AUROBINDO: Yes, in that case Pétain may find an excuse and break out. But if he surrenders the navy and the colonies nothing can be more shameful and more disastrous.

SATYENDRA: Hitler may not be so severe now and may be content at present with only the occupation of France.

SRI AUROBINDO: France in any case is gone now. Resistance is out of the question but Hitler may give such terms as to make them so powerless that he can later get the colonies and the navy.

SATYENDRA: Many soldiers are passing to Switzerland, they say, and are being interned. They must have been tired.

SRI AUROBINDO: No, not tired. They don't want to surrender, perhaps. From Gamelin's photo which I saw the other day it seems to me he has no brains. He has been under the notion that defence is stronger than attack and he prepared everything only according to that principle. Being fortress-minded himself, he made the soldiers also fortress-minded. It is said that when he met the German mechanised troops he didn't know what to do; he was so unprepared for such things as open attacks. And the wonderful Maginot Line is not a complete line. Some areas have only scattered fortifications. This Daladier, who was supposed to be an indispensable War Minister as Briand was an indispensable Foreign Minister, has done nothing. He and Chamberlain were saying all the time, "We are preparing and preparing", but they have prepared nothing at all. That is what surprised me most, that Daladier was considered the strong man of France, while he was so evidently weak. In their meeting with Hitler, Hitler was clearly the most cunning, strong and powerful as if he could break them into bits; Daladier was of course the weakest and Chamberlain was a crafty fool thinking that he was dealing most diplomatically with Hitler while he didn't see the reality of what he was doing. I wonder how Chamberlain had such a tremendous influence on the Conservatives.

SATYENDRA: Perhaps because of his laissez-faire policy and his policy of appeasement.

SRI AUROBINDO: How can a laissez-faire policy build up a reputation as a politican?

SATYENDRA: Except for the war, he would have gone down in history as a big politician.

SRI AUROBINDO: Quite so.

PURANI: A certain military officer has written that France had no idea about Germany's strength, the tremendous number of her tanks, mechanised units, etc.

SRI AUROBINDO: The French had some idea but not much. The fact is that they didn't expect such an overwhelming onrush. As I said, they have been made fortress-minded, not prepared for an open attack on such a huge scale. What is England doing to meet these tanks? They are talking only of their air force.

PURANI: Yes, they are providing for it by building tanks themselves.

NIRODBARAN: But how will the Germans carry the tanks to England? Besides, Churchill doesn't expect an invasion.

SATYENDRA: No, not a big invasion. Because of their navy they will be able to crush much of the German Army. Churchill says that as the fighting will be on their own ground they will be at an advantage.

SRI AUROBINDO: What Hitler may do is that he may choose a point and strike with his aeroplanes, destroy the ports and carry troops inland. That is the only possible way, it seems to me. But to maintain a regular supply line will be difficult.

PURANI: There is Nazi activity in Uruguay. If America takes up Uruguay's cause, perhaps Berlin will stop threatening her.

SRI AUROBINDO: Oh, if Berlin intervenes, then America will certainly intervene and it may serve as an excuse for Roosevelt to join the war.

EVENING

This evening there was very little talk.

SRI AUROBINDO: The radio first says the plenipotentiaries are communicating with Pétain. Then it says they are not plenipotentiaries.

NIRODBARAN: So all the previous news was rumour?

SRI AUROBINDO: It comes to that.

PURANI: It seems the meeting is being held in the same old cabin as at the end of World War I. The terms are about thirty typed pages.

SRI AUROBINDO: Then there can't be any discussion?

PURANI: Not likely. If in the meantime the Italian navy could be destroyed it would be a great gain.

SRI AUROBINDO: Yes, but the navy is not wandering about. It must be hiding in ports behind mines.

PURANI: Alexandria has been bombed again.

NIRODBARAN: Egypt was once on the point of declaring war. She said that she would do it if her ports and country were attacked.

SRI AUROBINDO: Yes, she has changed now. She considers what has happened as simply incidents. She removed her troops from the Italian frontier when, in an engagement, some were killed. She didn't want to get involved.

23 JUNE 1940

According to B.B.C. radio the armistice between France and Germany has been signed. Navy, air force and colonies are supposed to be handed over to Hitler. But French radio from Saigon said nothing.

PURANI: If the navy and air force revolt and join the British? (*Sri Aurobindo simply shook his hands meaning "I don't know what they will do."*) Rumania also has declared itself totally in line with the Axis Powers.

SRI AUROBINDO: Oh! The whole world seems to have been taken up by self-interest, cowardice and treachery.

NIRODBARAN: It makes the situation very complicated.

SRI AUROBINDO: Yes.

NIRODBARAN: But Russia may intervene if Rumania goes over. She has her claims in Bessarabia.

SRI AUROBINDO: She has been assured and so may not press them now. If Turkey also backs out and Gibraltar goes, then England will be in a precarious condition.

NIRODBARAN: Still there are people in the Ashram who think that Hitler wants only his old colonies and nothing more.

SRI AUROBINDO: He may not till he has consolidated his position in France. Didn't the American consul say that Germany wants France's colonies and a little more?

PURANI: France may establish a Fascist dictatorship. This present Government is all right-wing people.

SRI AUROBINDO: Fascist dictatorship under a dictator?

SATYENDRA: Has it been in the paper?

PURANI: That is not necessary. One can surmise because they are right-wingers.

SRI AUROBINDO: Yes, in the extreme right wing there are two sections. One wants Fascist dictatorship and the other wants to bring back monarchy.

PURANI: Hitler may try a blockade on England.

SRI AUROBINDO: Yes, if he has control of the Mediterranean then it will be dangerous.

NIRODBARAN: But before that the English navy has to be crushed – unless the French navy surrenders to Hitler.

PURANI: The French navy and Italian submarines will be powerful enough – if America joins the war!

SRI AUROBINDO: If Roosevelt can conquer the anti-intervention feeling –

NIRODBARAN: By the inclusion of two Republicans into his administration, the situation seems a little worse.

SRI AUROBINDO: How?

PURANI: Has it been confirmed that they have been disowned by the party?

SRI AUROBINDO: No, they have said that they owe allegiance to the President.

NIRODBARAN: But the Republican Party has said that it is strongly pro-Allies and wants to lead America to war. The appointment of two of its members speaks for itself.

SATYENDRA: How is England going to fight alone?

SRI AUROBINDO: If she can win against the Germans, it would mean that she is specially protected.

NIRODBARAN: But why should there be a special treaty with Italy?

SRI AUROBINDO: Perhaps Italy has special demands.

NIRODBARAN: Hitler is protecting Italy's interests. (*Laughter*)

PURANI: Gandhi writes in the *Harijan* that violence hasn't improved the moral stature of man. Non-violence can do that.

SRI AUROBINDO: But he is putting the cart before the horse. The moral stature has to be improved before man becomes non-violent.

SATYENDRA: Sarojini Naidu seems to have visited Ramana Maharshi. She writes that she has seen two Mahans. One is Maharshi and the other Gandhi. Maharshi gives peace.

SRI AUROBINDO: And Gandhi gives Charkha? (*Laughter*)

NIRODBARAN: There seems to be a Khaksar movement in Bengal also.

SRI AUROBINDO: I see; I didn't know that. In Bihar it exists, so it may also be in Bengal.

NIRODBARAN: The *Hindustan Standard* says that the Government is not taking any measures against it while it talks of communists and other people.

SRI AUROBINDO: The *Hindustan Standard* is Bose's paper, isn't it?

NIRODBARAN: Yes.

SRI AUROBINDO: Then why doesn't it object? They are half Mohammedans themselves!

EVENING

PURANI: It seems to me that very soon there will be a revolution in France. There will be dissatisfaction in the army and among various parties. Already with the peace-terms many sections are dissatisfied.

SRI AUROBINDO: Oh yes, within a year of Hitler's going.

PURANI: I don't know if they will wait even for that. The French are such people.

SATYENDRA: Revolution is in their blood and tradition.

SRI AUROBINDO: Yes, but there won't be much chance of success in Hitler's time. There are very few Monarchists and

Fascists. Most are Republicans It seems many Leftist leaders have reached London along with rich Jews and others.

NIRODBARAN: In that case it will fulfil the prophecy that France will become communist!

SRI AUROBINDO: All the prophecies have proved wrong. Those from Pondicherry said that from the 23rd June Hitler's fall will begin, and those from Bombay chose the 20th. Prophecies can't be relied on. A French astrologer says that as regards world events European prophecies have always proved wrong while Hindu astrologers were right. Who are these Hindu astrologers? Kapali Shastri also couldn't say anything about the Year of the Gods.

PURANI: No.

SRI AUROBINDO: They have spoken about past events.

SATYENDRA: In the Bhavishya Purana there are some prophecies.

PURANI: They are more historical.

SRI AUROBINDO: Apart from historical ones, there are others too. Isn't it so?

PURANI: Yes, but they are more individual than general. The writer speaks there of the return of the House of Delhi.

SRI AUROBINDO: The House of Delhi? Mogul? That is finished.

PURANI: He means Rajput. As regards historical events, the Bhavishya Purana deals with them up to the advent and establishment of British rule in India.

SRI AUROBINDO: Yes. I remember how during the Swadeshi movement the Bengal revolutionaries used to quote passages from it to show the downfall of the British.

NIRODBARAN: Have you seen that Bose is trying to make a pact with Jinnah?

SRI AUROBINDO: Yes. What about Pakistan then?

NIRODBARAN: He will agree to it.

SRI AUROBINDO: Does he want to Mohammedanise Bengal?

NIRODBARAN: Have you read Gandhi's statement today? He supports the French surrender, saying they did well by bowing to the inevitable.

SRI AUROBINDO: It was not inevitable.

PURANI: He adds: provided the terms are honourable.

NIRODBARAN: And provided they refuse to be a party to mutual destruction.

SRI AUROBINDO: Does that mean that you go on being defeated till you are destroyed? If according to him peace is the aim of life, why fight at all, violently or non-violently? You can simply go on peacefully with love for – what is that fellow's name?

PURANI: Virawalla?

SRI AUROBINDO: Yes, with love in your heart for Virawalla.

PURANI: He says fighting Hitlerism will produce super-Hitlerism, and that is no solution. Now regarding the gospel of Charkha, he says its purpose is not only economic but it is a great instrument of training in discipline and other moral qualities.

SRI AUROBINDO: I see. Why Charkha then? Why not cricket? You can play cricket with love in your heart for the bowler? (*Laughter*) I suppose it is because Charkha is a weary and monotonous business that it helps more to discipline. Is that it? (*Laughter*)

(*After a while*) If Bhaskar's new version of radio news is true it means that the Germans will occupy all the ports and frontiers and coasts and the French will be interned in Paris and places around it.

PURANI: Yes.

24 JUNE 1940

The armistice terms were announced on the radio.

PURANI: I took Dilip to the British Consul today. He expressed his sympathy for the British and wished their victory, to which the Consul replied, "It is not like the old times now, just throwing in a huge number of people. The warfare is quite different now, everything is mechanised and highly technical." Then Dilip said, "India also will fight alongside the British if only she is given the opportunity. We have no arms, no ammunitions, no training. How can we help? If the Government made some gesture, then everybody would willingly help. Sarojini Naidu has said that nobody in India wants Hitler's victory. If the British gave some self-government – for instance, Dominion Status – all would help the Allies."

SRI AUROBINDO: Is what she says true? I thought that India was anti-British. Mitran has told the Mother that Madras is pro-Hitler.

SATYENDRA: That must be the bazaar gossip. Mitran can't have the opportunity of mixing with various people. Natesan also expressed some sarcasm at the cost of Britain. I suppose some pleaders may be of that sentiment, but the rest of the public won't side with them.

NIRODBARAN: I think most of the young people are anti-British. Only elderly people and leaders are not.

SRI AUROBINDO: The young people have no sense then and don't seem to understand anything.

SATYENDRA: They have no political sense.

SRI AUROBINDO: But in Europe it is the youth who are alive and active.

SATYENDRA: Yes, but we are not entrusted with any responsibility or any opportunity to take part in active political life.

PURANI: These armistice terms mean practically the end of France.

SRI AUROBINDO: Oh! I wonder whether it was treachery or cowardice that made them accept these terms. This fool of a Marshal Pétain has sold France.

SATYENDRA: If at least a part of the navy could be saved!

SRI AUROBINDO: Don't know. Pétain has put three admirals in his cabinet to prevent that.

SATYENDRA: Yes, they go by rules and traditions and authority. The navy is not likely to revolt, perhaps.

NIRODBARAN: All this talk about soldier to soldier must be a hoax. How can one think it to be true after seeing the acceptance of such terms? How could they accept such a peace?

SRI AUROBINDO: They will accept anything. If they are asked to give Morocco to Spain or Indo-China to Japan they will agree.

NIRODBARAN: There is no mention of colonies in the terms.

SRI AUROBINDO: That will come in the final peace terms. It is only an armistice now – unless it is left to Italy to demand it. Their original plan was that Germany would take the north of France and Italy the south, now it comes almost to that and the French Government is interned with no communication with the outside world.

NIRODBARAN: If the navy and the air force don't come back?

SRI AUROBINDO: They can't be brought back. Hitler may then say that the armistice terms have been broken and he will occupy the whole of France.

PURANI: And how will Hitler subjugate the colonies that don't accept the French Government? In the Middle East the authorities have said they will fight on. Pétain will have to send the French fleet against them.

SRI AUROBINDO: The navy won't do; he will have to send land troops.

PURANI: Then he can transport them by the French navy.

SRI AUROBINDO: That will be too obvious an alliance with Hitler and will make people still more furious. The Mother said that the bazaar people were so frightened that when they heard of England's promise of assistance and of a National Committee in London, they were relieved. You have seen in Saigon how the people crowded round the British embassy and expressed their allegiance to the Allies. But the public alone is not enough. The soldiers and the officers must also accept them.

NIRODBARAN: Now that Laval is appointed a minister it is clear that he was acting from behind.

SRI AUROBINDO: Yes, now what will be the plight of the refugees who have taken shelter in France – Czechs, Belgians, Italians and Poles? They will have to be surrendered to Hitler and will undergo severe trials.

NIRODBARAN: Some people here still believe that Hitler has no eye on India as he does not want colonies.

SRI AUROBINDO: He is talking of colonies now.

NIRODBARAN: I don't see what can prevent him from coming to India if Britain goes down. And they say that Hitlerism after all may not be much worse than imperialism.

SRI AUROBINDO: Good Lord!

PURANI: Y says that. I told him that under Hitlerism he won't be allowed even to talk of freedom.

SRI AUROBINDO: Not only that, nobody will be allowed to think or speak anything worthwhile. Of course one can think, but most people are fed by others' thoughts and writings. Very few can think for themselves. Under Italy it would be the same except perhaps with a little less thorough suppression. Under Russia too the same. Japan might allow thought and speech so long as you don't say anything offensive against the police and the State.

PURANI: If France is not allowed commerce, the people will be in an awful plight.

SRI AUROBINDO: In winter there is likely to be starvation in all the occupied areas. Without crops and exports how will they survive? There is failure of crops this year, they say. In all the countries occupied by Hitler, the same fate will visit them. Denmark was a prosperous country, its prosperity has gone; so too with Belgium. The Scandinavian countries were some of the most advanced economically. They tried to solve the problem of poverty. Now all that is gone. The German invasion has come as a cataclysm. It is on the way to destroying all civilisation.

PURANI: Subscriptions raised here for the war won't be sent to France, they say.

SATYENDRA: What will be the state of the French currency if the colonies recognise the Bordeaux Government?

SRI AUROBINDO: Then we will lose all our money and the Ashram will have to be dissolved. But if they decide to side with Britain, there won't be any trouble. If Pondicherry recognises the Bordeaux Government the British will at once take possession of it.

SATYENDRA: Again it is given in the paper that the Americans will keep off.

NIRODBARAN: Dilip's prophecy will be true then? They don't want to board a sinking ship.

SRI AUROBINDO: They will have their own ship sinking.

NIRODBARAN: That will be ten or twenty years later.

SRI AUROBINDO: Not so long. Hitler won't wait so long.

NIRODBARAN: The *Patrika* says Germany has built many flat-bottomed boats which will sail from the Scheldt on a calm day and, strongly supported by warships, etc., invade England.

SRI AUROBINDO: Every day won't be calm, and what will they do then? How will they maintain their supplies?

EVENING

According to the radio news the Viceroy will be meeting Gandhi and Jinnah during the week.

SATYENDRA: This Viceroy Linlithgow is a good man.

SRI AUROBINDO: Yes.

PURANI: Better than Willingdon at any rate.

NIRODBARAN: It was Mrs. Willingdon who was worse.

SRI AUROBINDO: So Linlithgow is better than Lady Willingdon. (*Laughter*)

PURANI: The French officers, members of the Cercle, are going to send a wire to De Gaulle in England that they will also fight along with the British.

SRI AUROBINDO: It will have a moral value but if the Governor sent such a declaration, it would have a political value. De Gaulle should declare at once the names of the members of the National Committee. A single person won't command confidence.

SATYENDRA: But the French colonies have appealed already.

PURANI: Appealing is not enough. They must repudiate the Government. That is more important.

SRI AUROBINDO: Mombrant on hearing the armistice terms said, "It is not armistice, it is treason." The *Patrika* says that Laval and Flandin have engineered the whole thing, Laval being friendly with Italy and Flandin with Germany.

PURANI: Very soon after the war began, there came the news that there was sabotage in France. The shells that were supplied were too big for the cannons; the ammunition and gunpowder wouldn't ignite.

SRI AUROBINDO: That means that it was in the factories that this happened. Work of the communists?

PURANI: Perhaps.

Nirodbaran (*after a while*): The Viceroy's and Gandhi's meeting is Amery's work.

SRI AUROBINDO: Yes. We have to see what comes of it. If the British grant what Amery calls Dominion Independence, there is some chance. Or if they agree to what the Indian leaders decide about the nature and formation of their own Government, subject to some conditions, there is also some chance.

NIRODBARAN: In Bengal the Governor has formed a war committee representative of all the parties except the Congress. Shyama Prasad and M. N. Mukherji are there.

SRI AUROBINDO: The Muslim League also?

NIRODBARAN: Yes.

SRI AUROBINDO: N. R. Sircar?

NIRODBARAN: I didn't see his name. Oh, he is said to be indisposed.

SRI AUROBINDO: Really or conveniently? (*Laughter*)

25 JUNE 1940

François Baron, presiding over a meeting of French people at Calcutta, passed a resolution that they would side with Britain.

SRI AUROBINDO: Baron has taken a position.

PURANI: Yes.

SATYENDRA: Did he give any speech?

SRI AUROBINDO: No, he was the President. They passed a resolution.

PURANI: X is going to write a book on Charkha, showing the virtues of Charkha and warning that unless Europe adopts it there is no salvation for Europe. The machine has played tremendous havoc and destroyed life. It is the Charkha alone that can save it, he says.

SRI AUROBINDO: When the Charkha was in full swing, was there no destruction?

PURANI: Not such as caused by the machine.

SRI AUROBINDO: There was a tremendous and widespread destruction, of course not caused by modern weapons but by the crude ones proper to those times. People were massacred on a large scale.

PURANI: Yes, Baghdad, for example, was destroyed completely. Timur and others caused no less destruction. In Baghdad he erected a minaret of skulls.

The British have invented some air raid shelters called Anderson shelters, about the size of a policeman's watch cabin. They are supposed to be bombproof against any explosion, even one occurring nearby. Though other buildings might fall, these shelters would remain standing erect, it is claimed.

SRI AUROBINDO: The greatest preoccupation of modern man seems to be to find means of destruction as well as to find means of protection. Human ingenuity! – but after all it is an extension of the animal ingenuity. Man is supposed to be a reasoning animal. In early days destruction was intelligible – it was necessary for self-protection.

EVENING

The radio news: clash between the Russian and Rumanian soldiers on the frontier. Gathering of the Japanese navy near Indo-China.

PURANI: It doesn't look as if Russia will wait till the end of the war. A clash has started on the Rumanian frontier.

SRI AUROBINDO: It may be a rumour which will be denied later. But if true, it must be because Rumania has declared herself Nazi.

NIRODBARAN: But if war starts between them Hitler will have to look on at present.

SRI AUROBINDO: Perhaps.

PURANI: In that case Italy will jump in and that will bring Hitler in.

SRI AUROBINDO: Yes, but it doesn't look as if Russia and Italy will involve themselves at present in the Balkans.

NIRODBARAN: Turkey is not likely to join Rumania, especially as she has fallen in line with the Axis Powers.

SRI AUROBINDO: In a war with Rumania, Turkey will certainly side with Russia.

PURANI: Oh yes. It is easy for her. They are in one line.

SRI AUROBINDO: Hitler will then have to postpone the invasion of England.

NIRODBARAN: If England and Russia combine, will the result of such a combination of human and Asuric forces be good?

SRI AUROBINDO: Not a true combination. They may win but the result won't be good for us.

PURANI: Japan is also bringing her navy near Indo-China.

SRI AUROBINDO: That is to see that no supply of goods passes through to China.

NIRODBARAN: No arms are likely to pass now as France is preoccupied.

SRI AUROBINDO: Yes, but other goods that may help China to continue the struggle may go through if Japan is not watchful.

NIRODBARAN: Have you read what Jawaharlal says?

SRI AUROBINDO: Yes, that he doesn't think there is the slightest likelihood of a major invasion of India. Only a minor invasion from Afghanistan and such places perhaps?

NIRODBARAN: No, he says there may be some internal disturbance during the transitional period.

SRI AUROBINDO: In the meantime there may be a transition of his head from his shoulders. (*Laughter*)

NIRODBARAN: If Nehru says that, how can we blame Y? Nehru who is supposed to have international politics at his fingertips!

SRI AUROBINDO: All the knowledge most Indian politicians have of the international situation is some illusions about extreme political ideas, which have been shattered everywhere.

PURANI: During the Munich crisis X was in Czechoslovakia. Even being on the spot, he could not foresee what others did from far away as to what would become of Czechoslovakia, as a result of the separation of Sudetenland. He said it would be all right.

SRI AUROBINDO: Didn't he go to Barcelona during the Spanish War?

PURANI: Yes, and he said that the Republicans would win.

SRI AUROBINDO: Prophecy didn't come true.

PURANI: No. Amery is bringing in an Emergency Bill.

SRI AUROBINDO: Yes, I hope the Viceroy will have some sense in giving good terms to Gandhi when they meet.

26 JUNE 1940

PURANI: Hitler has presented a plan for the federation of continental Europe from which England and Russia will be barred. This man is full of ideas.

SRI AUROBINDO: His New World Order?

PURANI: Yes, Europe will be divided into three blocks: they will have no armies.

SRI AUROBINDO: Wait a minute. How will the blocks be formed?

PURANI: One block in the Balkans, one in Belgium, Holland, France, etc., and another in Spain, Portugal and other countries, I suppose. They won't have any armies. Hitler alone will have an army.

SRI AUROBINDO: Of course, small nations won't be able to resist, except Franco's Spain, and she can have some weight and Turkey too can resist.

NIRODBARAN: Italy's claims, as we see from the published terms of the armistice signed with her, seem to be mild. No territorial claims, only the French Mediterranean ports to be demilitarised.

SRI AUROBINDO: After which she can easily seize them whenever she wants to. She may reserve territorial claims for the peace treaty.

NIRODBARAN: There has been a warning that Hitler may ask Italy to be mild now in order to lull the French people into a false sense of security.

SATYENDRA: The French fleet has been demobilised already, Churchill says, and is under German control.

SRI AUROBINDO: Oh, he has said that?

NIRODBARAN: Yes, in the morning news it was announced. Of course one doesn't know if it is the whole fleet or only a part. This is Pétain's free Government!

SRI AUROBINDO: Pétain means that the French are not ruled by Germany as are the people of Poland and Czechoslovakia.

SATYENDRA: And they may expect good terms during the peace talks.

SRI AUROBINDO: Even if good terms are given, Hitler will see to it that France has no power to rise again.

SATYENDRA: The newspaper seems to say that Britain has recognised the Pétain Government. After all there is no gain whether they do or do not. France can't help England even if she wants to.

NIRODBARAN: Even if she could, would she?

SRI AUROBINDO: She would; she could send goods, but no commerce seems to be allowed by Hitler. France will be terribly impoverished.

PURANI: She can trade with Italy and Germany.

SRI AUROBINDO: That is across land but if any trade is allowed by sea, it will only be under German control.

SATYENDRA: Why don't the colonies come to any decision? They must do it quickly, when the enthusiasm prevails.

SRI AUROBINDO: Yes, they may be waiting for the full ratification of the truce. If they recognise the Government, they will be demilitarised and Japan will easily walk into Indo-China.

PURANI: In the paper there is a scheme of how the German parachutists will land in England, how they will be equipped, etc.

NIRODBARAN: Parachutes have not been very successful in France.

SRI AUROBINDO: No, most of the parachutists have been killed. In England they won't be successful at all. Parachutists are of no use unless they are followed up by the army.

PURANI: It seems some French officers have approached the British consul with their offer of fighting along with the British.

The customs regulations have become tighter. The pass that was allowed to French officers is no longer valid.

SRI AUROBINDO: Of course they are justified now. If the Government had sided with the British, many of the regulations would have been relaxed.

SATYENDRA: The British Government has consented to buy one lakh tons of Indian sugar subject to the approval of the International Sugar Committee.

SRI AUROBINDO: Good Lord!

SATYENDRA: But where is the International Committee now? (*Laughter*)

SRI AUROBINDO: Quite so.

SATYENDRA: At such a time they are quibbling over law!

SRI AUROBINDO: The English people are legal-minded. If they want to break a law they must do it legally. So also with their morality. If they do anything immoral, they do it in a moral-seeming way so as to preserve their righteousness. (*Laughter*)

PURANI: Dr. Rao has retired.

SRI AUROBINDO: Oh, now the P.A. will dance with joy.

NIRODBARAN: But will the Congress Ministry come to power?

SRI AUROBINDO: Don't see any chance now.

EVENING

PURANI: Japan says she recognises only the Bordeaux Government.

SRI AUROBINDO (*laughing*): Of course!

PURANI: There is unconfirmed news that Japan has either entered twenty miles inside Indo-China or spread along the frontier.

SRI AUROBINDO: Inside means she is going to occupy the country.

NIRODBARAN: But it was said that all frontiers had been closed.

SATYENDRA: The colonies are still undecided. Are they going to recognise Bordeaux too?

SRI AUROBINDO: Then they will have to be demilitarised and Japan will easily walk in. The colonies say that they are all willing to fight.

NIRODBARAN: Not a very determined attitude. They seem to be hesitating.

SRI AUROBINDO: Yes, and Churchill's speech also is more hesitating than it ought to be. They will go on fighting till they are demilitarised, I suppose.

NIRODBARAN: They are hesitating because of the National Committee. They ought to declare the personnel.

SATYENDRA: They should do it soon.

SRI AUROBINDO: Yes, if they don't, they will let the psychological moment pass.

SATYENDRA: There is no news of Mandel or Reynaud.

SRI AUROBINDO: Some say that Reynaud is in America. I don't see why they can't come together. There may be some reason for their hiding.

Have you seen Hoover's statement? He says that America must prepare for her defence and only help the Allies to a certain limit so that her own resources may be kept intact for her own defence. Besides, he says, helping the Allies will be bad for the Allies. (*Laughter*) He is using this as a political stunt against Roosevelt and is trying to preach his isolationism. The world is getting queer. No wonder the British consul says it is Kaliyuga. (*Laughter*)

NIRODBARAN: The other day, while talking about the Divine Will, you said that Christ knew that he was to be put on the cross and yet one part of him didn't want it. Did you mean that the crucifixion had been divinely willed?

SRI AUROBINDO: That is what the Bible says. It says that Christ came to take the sins of humanity upon himself and deliver humanity from suffering. Even then some parts of his lower vital didn't want it because of the suffering, the desertion of his disciples and the humiliation. But he felt the suffering on the cross. Otherwise there is no use in suffering. If the suffering is not real there is no meaning in it.

PURANI: In our Puranas there are many stories of the Divine's intervention, not by His omnipotent power but according to the rules of the game.

SRI AUROBINDO: Of course, if it were to be by omnipotent power it could be done from above. Why should the Divine come down into a body for it?

Champaklal (*after some time*): Just a while ago I heard distinctly the Mother's voice saying, "Hitler will die on the 26th."

SRI AUROBINDO (*laughing*): That is too good to hope for.

CHAMPAKLAL: I am not very sure about the date, whether it is the 26th or some other date.

SRI AUROBINDO: I don't care about the date. If he dies it is enough. (*Laughter*)

27 JUNE 1940

PURANI: If Russia demands Bessarabia it might be through an understanding with Hitler.

SRI AUROBINDO: If Rumania accedes then Russia will next enter Bucharest. Hitler has demanded all the German refugees from the French Government which means that he will harass them now.

PURANI: Our people in Calcutta have asked whether, in the proof of *The Life Divine*, it shouldn't be "founded on" instead of "founded in". Not only that but in anticipation they have already put "founded on" in the final proof.

SRI AUROBINDO: In the context concerned it must be "founded in" and not "on".

PURANI: It makes a big difference: "in" or "on".

SRI AUROBINDO: A big difference and quite a different meaning.

PURANI: I came to know afterwards that they had already changed it.

SATYENDRA: Perhaps some Calcutta persons have pointed it out thinking it unusual.

SRI AUROBINDO: What idiots some people can become.

PURANI: They are familiar only with "founded on", it seems.

SRI AUROBINDO: All these people think that they know better English than I do.

NIRODBARAN: They perhaps think that it may be an oversight or some mistake in typing or printing.

SRI AUROBINDO: I have used the same expression in the previous pages and there I said it must be "in" and again they change it! Indians, when they write English, use stock phrases and conventional usages while a good writer will never do that. That is why their English is so flat and lifeless and gives the impression that they have learned English. A good writer will always avoid stock expressions and vary the usages. (*Smiling*) Stephen Phillips, the poet, said that the English language is like a woman who will only love if you take liberties with her. (*Laughter. After a pause*) Sir Dinshaw Wacha sent a book here he had written. I found on every page almost forty stock phrases – what are called clichés – and all the papers were praising it, saying, "What a wonderful style!" To an Englishman it would seem horrible.

EVENING

The evening radio news said that the Pétain Government had asked the Governors of Indo-China and Africa to resign and that new men would be appointed in their places.

SATYENDRA: They haven't yet repudiated the Pétain Government. Now they will be forced to decide what they should do, whether to recognise it or revolt against it.

SRI AUROBINDO: Nogues of Africa has said that he won't give an inch of French territory to Italy without a fight.

PURANI: Will the Pétain Government send warships then to make them obey?

SRI AUROBINDO: They may do anything. When they have recalled the Governors, it means that the colonies haven't obeyed. What about Syria? The Pétain Government hasn't recalled its Governor. Perhaps they know that he will send them to the devil.

SATYENDRA: Will Indo-China be able to resist Japan?

PURANI: At least the French there will be able to give a good account of themselves.

SRI AUROBINDO: It won't be a promenade for Japan.

NIRODBARAN: Besides, if Indo-China makes an alliance with Britain, Britain will have to go to her help. That means war with Japan.

SRI AUROBINDO: Yes. Will Japan undertake all that with Russia and China at her back?

PURANI: The Pétain Government may ask Japan to occupy Indo-China.

SRI AUROBINDO: That will be too much. They will be shot in that case or bound.

NIRODBARAN: But if Hitler presses?

SRI AUROBINDO: Even so they can't. They have been able to save face by saying that they have saved France from destruction by the armistice with Hitler, but to allow foreigners to kill the French people, that would be –

PURANI: Germany has begun regular air raids on England.

SRI AUROBINDO: But that is not an attack yet. After settling with France Hitler may start. He may also have to attack Africa. The situation won't be safe if the French fleet falls into his hands.

NIRODBARAN: According to Churchill's speech some units of the fleet seem to have escaped. He is asking them to come to British or go to neutral ports.

SRI AUROBINDO: Yes, but not to Spain, I hope. The understanding was that the full fleet would make for the British ports.

28 JUNE 1940

PURANI: Russia's occupation of Bessarabia seems to be the result of an understanding with Hitler and the proper time was also fixed beforehand.

SRI AUROBINDO: Probably.

NIRODBARAN: But the question is: Will Russia stop here?

SRI AUROBINDO: No.

NIRODBARAN: In that case Hitler will have to look on, thinking how he can deal with her later on.

SRI AUROBINDO: He can't afford to quarrel with Russia at present when he is fighting England, so Russia may try to acquire Africa also, unless, of course, Italy jumps in in a rage.

PURANI: Yes, then Hitler will be dragged in. Russia will come too near Italy then.

NIRODBARAN: Isn't Russia a danger to Turkey?

SRI AUROBINDO: Of course.

NIRODBARAN: Some Englishman wrote in The *Indian Express* that the idea of a Russian invasion of India is a bogey.

SATYENDRA: That is an old article and all old views.

SRI AUROBINDO: What does the writer say?

SATYENDRA: He says that India has mechanised units, aeroplanes and good defences. What mechanised units have we got? Perhaps the British have sent a few more aeroplanes now. Russia, he says, will have first to conquer Turkey, Persia and Afghanistan.

SRI AUROBINDO: What are Turkey and Persia to Russia?

NIRODBARAN: He speaks of natural defences.

SRI AUROBINDO (*laughing*): Natural defences! Natural defences are no defence nowadays. One can't sit comfortably behind natural defences in modern warfare.

SATYENDRA: He says even Napoleon couldn't take up such adventures.

SRI AUROBINDO: Napoleon existed long before the advent of modern warfare.

SATYENDRA: Even Finland with her strong army and equipment stood only a few days against Russia.

SRI AUROBINDO: Yes, with her very strong artificial defence of the Mannerheim Line she still couldn't hold on.

NIRODBARAN: My impression is that when Hitler gets involved with Britain, Stalin may march towards India.

SRI AUROBINDO: Before that he will have to take Asia Minor and then Hitler will get nervous.

PURANI: Daladier seems to have been arrested in Casablanca.

SRI AUROBINDO: Why in Casablanca? They are not giving sufficient news. They say the French admirals have arrived in London but don't give the names.

NIRODBARAN: The American Republican Party in its manifesto accuses Roosevelt of ineffective defence preparation during his term.

SRI AUROBINDO: That is a political stunt. He has almost doubled the defence.

SATYENDRA: What has happened to the public declaration of the Pondicherry Governor?

SRI AUROBINDO: He hasn't brought it out yet. It seems he went to see the British Consul who told him: "Don't fear, your successor will never arrive here. I can assure you."

NIRODBARAN: How will a new Governor ever go to Indo-China, then?

SATYENDRA: He may go in disguise.

SRI AUROBINDO: As an American? But it will be too humiliating.

SATYENDRA: Yes.

SRI AUROBINDO: Syria will resist. She has about one-and-a-half million troops, along with the British.

NIRODBARAN: In North Africa, there are about fifty thousand, it appears.

SRI AUROBINDO: Fifty thousand? Can't be. Italy alone has ninety thousand. How can they hold out against Italy with that number and at the same time put down any insurgence of the native people, which is always likely?

PURANI: No, no. It must be at least half a million.

EVENING

SRI AUROBINDO: So Bonvain has declared himself? And Pavitra has to take up mobilisation under the order of the Foreign Minister!

PURANI: Who is the Foreign Minister?

SRI AUROBINDO: That is what I would like to ask.

PURANI: It can't be the Minister of the Pétain Government.

SRI AUROBINDO: No, Bonvain has allied himself with the British.

SATYENDRA: But he has not repudiated the French Government.

SRI AUROBINDO: No, but it comes to that.

NIRODBARAN: Pavitra can be sent anywhere now.

SRI AUROBINDO: Yes, wherever he is called. But only after training, which will require eight months.

SATYENDRA: They must have an army to protect Pondicherry also.

SRI AUROBINDO: Of course.

PURANI: After training, the troops will be sent to Saigon, they say.

SRI AUROBINDO: Added to these fifty thousand they can raise another fifty thousand in Africa, and the same from the Senegalese and about one million from the Arabs. The difficulty will be getting equipment. It is as in India. India has man-power but that is all. Mittelhauser said to America that what is required are aeroplanes and other machines.

NIRODBARAN: It was half a million, not fifty thousand troops in Africa.

SRI AUROBINDO: I was wondering how it could be fifty thousand for such a vast country. (*Looking at Satyendra*) Have you seen in today's map what a vast colony it is?

SATYENDRA: Yes, compared to it France looks very small.

SRI AUROBINDO: This news about Daladier's arrest is from Gibraltar. It must be Gibraltar gossip.

SATYENDRA: Otherwise I don't understand why he should be arrested in Casablanca.

SRI AUROBINDO: Quite so.

PURANI: We may soon hear that he has reached London.

SRI AUROBINDO: Yes, like Blum. The only important man who has reached London is Blum.

SATYENDRA: Where is Reynaud?

NIRODBARAN: Could he have been arrested?

SRI AUROBINDO: No.

SATYENDRA: America is becoming queer. Ford has refused to build aeroplanes for the British, but will build them only for U.S.A.

SRI AUROBINDO: Yes.

NIRODBARAN: But they can sell them to England.

SRI AUROBINDO: No, the new machines can't be sold according to their law unless they declare war.

PURANI: This Republican candidate Wilky is an anti-isolationalist: he favours all the help to the Allies.

SRI AUROBINDO: Isolationalists are all those who don't want to go to war. All the rest want to help with their ammunitions and arms.

NIRODBARAN: Rumania doesn't seem to have gained by her Axis sympathy and declaration.

SRI AUROBINDO: No, this king is a fool. He sways from this side to that.

NIRODBARAN: Hitler has rewarded the king by sacrificing him.

SRI AUROBINDO: He will sacrifice anybody.

PURANI: He can't afford war with Russia now.

SRI AUROBINDO: No, that will be too much for him. He has started his game in England.

Radio news that Chamberlain and his party wanted peace with Hitler was strongly denied.

SRI AUROBINDO: That must be German propaganda. Chamberlain can't open his umbrella now.

NIRODBARAN: As soon as he declared his Axis policy, Stalin got his chance.

SRI AUROBINDO: Quite so.

NIRODBARAN: The other neutrals, Hungary, Bulgaria and Yugoslavia, are repeating the same policy — closely watching the situation.

SRI AUROBINDO (*laughing*): Yes, watching to see whose turn comes next!

NIRODBARAN: And Turkey also is getting nervous. Sent her fleet to the Black Sea.

SRI AUROBINDO: That is nothing. Unless she wants Dobruja, where there are plenty of Turks.

PURANI: Hungary wants Transylvania?

SRI AUROBINDO: Yes. Bulgaria wants Dobruja and Yugoslavia — while Italy wants to swallow Yugoslavia.

NIRODBARAN: How is Turkey going to gain by alliance with Russia?

SRI AUROBINDO: Don't know.

NIRODBARAN: Unless she fears an attack by Russia.

SRI AUROBINDO: Yes, they have always been friendly. Russia helped to build Turkey after the last war.

29 JUNE 1940

Radio news had it that Mittelhauser under Weygand's persuasion had given up resistance and accepted the armistice.

PURANI: There is unconfirmed news that General Nogues is also doing the same.

SRI AUROBINDO: It must be true then.

PURANI: The Belgian Minister also seems to be nego-tiating with Hitler about terms on which they can return to Belgium.

SRI AUROBINDO: The general is out then!

After his walk Sri Aurobindo took up the discussion again.

SRI AUROBINDO: Rajagopalachari is getting uneasy. He says that India is like a pet cat kept in the jungle by the British. (*Laughter*)

SATYENDRA: He wants to support the war effort.

SRI AUROBINDO: Yes, he wants to go to war.

SATYENDRA: He wants to go back to the Ministry also. It seems about thirteen people voted against him in the Working Committee.

SRI AUROBINDO: He is a practical politician. If the colonies surrender, England remains all alone. If she gets India with her, then she can get India's man-power and resources and in that case America also may join. That is the only way left to meet Hitler. In America the two parties are pro-Allies. I hope she will have the grace to do what is necessary.

SATYENDRA: I don't think the British are likely to concede anything to India yet. They will say, "If we go down, let them go also", and if they want to retain authority after the war, they won't want to arm India. Besides, it is very difficult to part with power.

SRI AUROBINDO: Oh yes!

NIRODBARAN: The English psychology is to give in when they are forced to and no other way is left. Otherwise they don't act.

SRI AUROBINDO: If they want to act, they can do so provided they have the right man. For instance after the Boer War, Sir Campbell Bannerman gave self-government to South Africa. Self-government has also been granted to Iraq and to Egypt. In Egypt they have kept control of the Suez only. That is the advantage of England over Germany, that you can deal with England, while with Germany – (*Sri Aurobindo began to shake his head.*)

NIRODBARAN: I suppose Britain has a fear that we may not help her in the war if Dominion Status is given.

SRI AUROBINDO: There can be an understanding. I hope the Viceroy will come to an agreement with Gandhi. If the Government does not want to make any advancement on previous terms why do they call these people?

SATYENDRA: What is the Congress' stand now?

SRI AUROBINDO: Constituent Assembly, I suppose, Ramgarh Resolution.

NIRODBARAN: The Congress' stand is to sit, till their demand of Constituent Assembly is acceded to.

SRI AUROBINDO: I suppose it is Nehru who leads now.

NIRODBARAN: Now that the Viceroy has four Muslim Ministers on his side he can easily make some compromise between the Congress and the League.

SRI AUROBINDO: Quite so.

PURANI: The best way is for the Viceroy to tell Jinnah that he is going to give self-government to India in spite of the League's refusal and resistance and if Jinnah goes against it, he will be brought under the Defence Act. One thing Jinnah is afraid of is jail. He will never go to jail. That is the only way. (*Sri Aurobindo began to smile.*)

SATYENDRA: It seems Hertzog is also clamouring in Africa for peace with Germany.

NIRODBARAN: That he has been doing since the beginning of the war.

SRI AUROBINDO: Yes, that means there will be a split there, Natal and Cape Town are mostly English and they will form a separate state. The others want white domination in Africa over Indians and natives. The old race superiority under German rule – they can safely carry it through.

This Mittelhauser has been brandishing his sword all the time and now he quietly puts it down.

PURANI: Now German and French troops will kiss and embrace as in Bessarabia.

SATYENDRA: But why did he brandish it at all? He could as well have kept it inside.

SRI AUROBINDO: Quite so. If Africa also accepts, then it will be difficult for Indo-China and Madagascar to hold out.

PURANI: The Belgian Minister also is speaking of submitting.

SRI AUROBINDO: Like Norway?

SATYENDRA: Only Poland remains.

SRI AUROBINDO: Yes, Poland has the best record so far.

SATYENDRA: The Poles won't submit, I hope.

SRI AUROBINDO: No, they are not politicians.

PURANI: Besides, they have nothing to gain. Their whole country is now under Nazi rule.

SRI AUROBINDO: They have had long training in resistance to subjection and they have never yielded.

SATYENDRA: When the world becomes free from Nazi domination, France should be kept in subjection.

SRI AUROBINDO (*laughing*): Yes, she doesn't deserve freedom.

EVENING

SRI AUROBINDO: Pétain seems to have adopted the Fascist method. He has arrested Mandel and said it was by mistake. When

Mandel demanded that, in that case, he should make a public apology or keep him in custody, he kept him in custody. Then this motor accident of Reynaud looks a suspicious affair, nobody knows where he is. If it is an accident everybody ought to know where he is. Either they have tried to assassinate him or Reynaud has used it as a cover to escape.

SATYENDRA: Why has Mittelhauser given up resistance?

SRI AUROBINDO: Weygand, it seems, flew to Syria and persuaded him.

PURANI: I think he must have said that the colonies wouldn't be touched and that they would remain with France after the peace.

SRI AUROBINDO: Are they such fools as to believe in Hitler's words?

NIRODBARAN: It would be surprising indeed if even now they were taken in by him.

SRI AUROBINDO: That is the Asuric influence cast all over the world. The Mother says that in *Apocalypse* there is a prophecy that before the millennium when the anti-Christ will come everybody will believe in his sweet words and be deceived and no one will judge him by his acts.

SATYENDRA: Japan also is turning Fascist.

SRI AUROBINDO: Yes, she has asked for "hands off the East" and is trying to adopt an Eastern Monroe Doctrine. But that has been her well-established policy for thirty or forty years, to drive out the Europeans from the East. Now is the best opportunity for her.

NIRODBARAN: I won't be surprised if France uses her army against England.

SATYENDRA: That will be the last step.

SRI AUROBINDO: That is what Weygand must have told Mittelhauser – that the French should get whatever they can. Japan is not like Hitler. She can wait patiently, but she never gives up her policy. When the right time comes she will strike.

SATYENDRA: She has recognised the Bordeaux Government.

SRI AUROBINDO: Of course. The Bordeaux Government has accepted Japan's demand not to send arms to China through Indo-China.

NIRODBARAN: But Japan intends to occupy it, it seems, unless America comes in.

SRI AUROBINDO: America can't do anything because Japan will come by land. In the Dutch Indies America could have intervened with her fleet. That is why Japan kept quiet.

NIRODBARAN: Britain is now all alone; she hasn't replied to the Japanese note yet.

SRI AUROBINDO: All my life I have wanted the downfall of the British Empire, but the way it is being done is beyond all expectation and makes me wish for British victory. And if I want England to win, it is not for the Empire's own sake but because the world under Hitler will be much worse.

NIRODBARAN: The world is already getting darker and darker.

SRI AUROBINDO: Yes, but that has been foreseen.

SATYENDRA: Foreseen by whom?

SRI AUROBINDO: Foreseen since the age of the Bible that the Asura will dominate the world for a time. (*After a while*) Gandhi's interview with the Viceroy seems to be the same old story. There is likely to be no change in Simla's attitude. Poor Gandhi, he was in such high spirits! Simla's atmosphere has spoiled Linlithgow, it seems.

NIRODBARAN: Roosevelt has invited Wilkie, the Republican candidate, for a talk.

SRI AUROBINDO: Yes, to discuss the defence policy – to ask whether he will follow the same policy. He is also pro-Allies.

PURANI: Nishtha says nobody knew him in America and he is a big businessman.

SRI AUROBINDO: Because he is from the West? Perhaps.

SATYENDRA: Dr. Kher has given a lecture in favour of a war committee and asked everybody to sink all differences now. He has tried to imitate Rajagopalachari by using metaphors and examples. He says that India and England are two goats; the Indian goat must allow the English one to pass over her.

SRI AUROBINDO: Rajagopalachari's examples are more apt and come more easily. The example of the pet cat is a very fine phrase and it describes the situation exactly.

30 JUNE 1940

PURANI: Russia has penetrated thirty miles further into Rumanian territory.

SRI AUROBINDO: Thirty miles beyond Bessarabia? Or thirty miles into Bessarabia? She had said she would cover the first zone; it may be that. If she occupies more than Bessarabia, then it becomes interesting.

PURANI: Hungary and Bulgaria are also pushing their claims.

SRI AUROBINDO: Hitler and Mussolini have asked them to wait for the present.

SATYENDRA: Why are the English people being evacuated from Hongkong?

SRI AUROBINDO: Because Japan is going to blockade the coast; in that case it will be very distressing for them.

NIRODBARAN: China will be put in a very difficult position then.

SRI AUROBINDO: There is Russia. She helps China with all that is necessary.

NIRODBARAN: Why is Russia against Japan?

SRI AUROBINDO: Because she doesn't want Japanese supremacy in China and, besides, Japan is her traditional enemy.

Nirodbaran (*after a while*): The Gandhi-Viceroy meeting is another failure.

SRI AUROBINDO (*laughing*): Yes.

SATYENDRA: Is any proclamation issued?

NIRODBARAN: No; since Gandhi is talking of leaving Delhi, one infers that the meeting is a failure.

SRI AUROBINDO: If the Viceroy is willing to give only three more seats in his Council, he can't expect anybody to agree.

EVENING

Radio news: Gandhi telephoned Azad to come to Delhi and the Working Committee meeting is called on Wednesday, 3rd July. This was the last item in the news written down from the radio.

SRI AUROBINDO (*as Purani was reading out the news*): The last item is interesting. Seems to be encouraging. I hope both the parties will have some common sense.

PURANI: Yes.

SRI AUROBINDO (*when Satyendra arrived*): Gandhi is staying on. He has called Azad and the Working Committee. There may be some hope. Something more than three seats, perhaps. (*Laughter*)

SATYENDRA: Better to end this stalemate now. They have been sitting idle for so many months.

PURANI: Gandhi also may now pressure the Working Committee. Since they have given up non-violence for defence, they have a good opportunity for training.

SRI AUROBINDO: Gandhi after thirty years doesn't find a single Satyagrahi as his follower.

NIRODBARAN: Azad seems to be more moderate and would like some compromise.

SRI AUROBINDO: Yes. But Nehru is stiff. (*After some time*) The Pétain Government is adopting the Fascist method of giving news – ambiguous and insufficient. They say that Reynaud had a motor accident but the doctors are not able to decide what is wrong. Motorcaritis? He was himself driving the car and for some unknown reason dashed against a tree. They don't say who was with him and where he is.

NIRODBARAN: Why don't the doctors know whether it is a fracture or not? If it were a matter of some disease, I could understand the uncertainty.

SRI AUROBINDO: That is why I say motorcaritis! (*Laughter*) You remember Daladier also had some accident. It was an attempt at assassination by some communists. The news was not given out but kept as official.

1 JULY 1940

SRI AUROBINDO: The Governor has stopped mobilisation because of the general confusion everywhere. Nogue's army does not want to surrender and in Syria the army is dissatisfied. They want to continue the fight and an invasion of Indo-China by Japan is imminent.

PURANI: Applying the Monroe Doctrine?

SRI AUROBINDO: But you can't dispossess them of their colonies by that Doctrine. America too has her colonies.

PURANI: America may not like it.

SRI AUROBINDO: That is another matter. It is apparent that the Pétain Government is breaking up the French Empire.

NIRODBARAN: Why have they stopped mobilisation?

SRI AUROBINDO: Because of the general confusion. Moreover, they have no money – they have to depend on Indo-China.

PURANI: It seems the Indo-China Bank is refusing the money from the Bank of France.

SRI AUROBINDO: Because nobody knows what the state of France will be.

NIRODBARAN: I hope Bonvain won't join the Pétain Government.

SRI AUROBINDO: Even if he does, he will be removed and the British will occupy Pondy and he knows that.

PURANI: Some astrologer from Gujarat says that by the end of August the war will be over and England will win.

CHAMPAKLAL: This August?

PURANI: Yes.

SATYENDRA: Not likely. If the invasion of England begins it is not going to be over so soon, or if Hitler is defeated England will still have to conquer back the European territories.

SRI AUROBINDO: It is only possible if apart from the repulsion of Germany by England, the Italian fleet is destroyed so that a complete blockade of the whole continent can be effected and, as a result of general starvation, Hitler may be assassinated.

NIRODBARAN: Meher Baba has gone again into one year's silence. No communication at all except regarding urgent telegrams.

SATYENDRA: He has asked all his followers to fast for one day a week or to take only water and milk and to abstain from lust and greed and to inculcate love. He says that chaos is necessary for the uplifting of humanity and the higher manifestation. He has a big role to play. He is always charged with a mission. His philosophy is difficult to understand. Some say that he believes in one Atman everywhere.

SRI AUROBINDO: Then why does he want the higher manifestation?

SATYENDRA: Then again he says the world is Maya, illusion.

SRI AUROBINDO: Then it is an illusory higher manifestation he wants?

SATYENDRA: No, it is an illusion only from the phenomenal point of view.

SRI AUROBINDO: Why doesn't he say so then?

EVENING

SRI AUROBINDO: The Viceroy hasn't given any new proposal, it seems. Still Gandhi is calling Azad and the Working Committee to meet at Delhi. How is that? Has he been in telephonic communication with Azad or does Azad take a different view and want the Working Committee to meet?

PURANI: Maybe the Viceroy wants a quick reply. (*After a while*) Gabriel Monod-Herzen says that Mandel has been freed by Pétain. Perhaps he has threatened him with imprisonment if he continues any subversive activity in the future.

SRI AUROBINDO: Mandel is not a man to be frightened by his threats. He himself told Pétain either to make a public apology or to detain him.

2 JULY 1940

SRI AUROBINDO (*looking at Purani*): We are in a queer position about money.

PURANI: How?

SRI AUROBINDO: The British Government has stopped the British notes from coming here and the French notes are not accepted by this Government.

PURANI: Why have they done that?

SRI AUROBINDO: Don't know. The Consul seems to have written to the Government to make an exception for Pondy, but no reply has come as yet. Swiss money also is not accepted. Jwalanti says that she is ruined. All her money is in Switzerland.

PURANI: Perhaps because people here are converting all their money into British money. M has been doing that for the last six months. The Chamber of Commerce also saw the Governor about these banks refusing to accept French money.

SRI AUROBINDO: That is about the Bank of France. Naturally the banks here can't accept French money because the value of the franc has fallen.

PURANI: It is similar to the last war. The mark had fallen so low that people began to buy it in large numbers. Perhaps Germany may introduce the mark now in France.

SRI AUROBINDO: Amrita went to see some businessman here and during the talk the businessman said, "Oh, I am ruined!"

PURANI: Oh yes, plenty of people will have the same fate.

SATYENDRA: In the market there is panic.

SRI AUROBINDO: Panic? People are desperate.

NIRODBARAN: Is it all caused by the Indian Government?

SRI AUROBINDO: No. The Indian Government has no jurisdiction over the colonies. Must be the British Government.

NIRODBARAN: Is it done to exert pressure on the colonies?

SRI AUROBINDO: No, in that case it would also have operated in Africa and Madagascar. They have nothing to do with British money.

PURANI: Gabriel says that he approached the French Government through the Governor to allow his wife to come here, and the reply was that the wives of the functionaries would not be allowed to leave France.

SRI AUROBINDO: Then others' wives can? (*Laughter*) No, nobody is allowed to leave France now.

PURANI: Perhaps they fear that the internal condition of France will be revealed by these people. But the tourists will be doing that. Have you seen De Gaulle's statement about the French Army? He says that France has been defeated without any fight. Only sixty thousand people have been killed and nearly a million imprisoned – where was the fight? This is most absurd! One million imprisoned!

SRI AUROBINDO: Worse than the fall of the Third Empire. There was mismanagement at that time. But they fought before they lost.

PURANI: What Dr. André says may be partly true, that the French Army didn't really fight. Otherwise it couldn't have collapsed like that. The French air force perhaps didn't fly over Germany at all and so dropped no bombs, saying, "Who is going to risk being killed?"

SRI AUROBINDO: We didn't hear much of the French air force, except at the beginning and that was only in the rear of the French line.

PURANI: De Gaulle's accusation may be true. All these huge fortifications of the Maginot Line built at such a cost have come to nothing.

SRI AUROBINDO: He has the right to speak. He was the one man who was in favour of mobile warfare and urged having tanks and mechanised units. He became so troublesome that they had to remove him. Reynaud made him the Chief of Staff and from him he must have gathered all this news.

SATYENDRA: He has now been degraded and has retired.

SRI AUROBINDO: Yes, he speaks now in his own right and appoints vice-admirals.

SATYENDRA: The colonies are still undecided. They don't seem to have made up their minds.

SRI AUROBINDO: No, except the Jibouti Governor who has said clearly that he won't surrender. Others are still hesitating. After tomorrow it will be seen what happens. Tomorrow the tenth day of the armistice will expire and five more days will remain for the African and Mediterranean coasts.

SATYENDRA: They are hoping Micawber-like that something will turn up.

SRI AUROBINDO: Yes, waiting for that and to see who does what.

PURANI: Russia has already come into the Balkans.

SRI AUROBINDO: No, not quite. Still in central Europe. Her claims on Hungary are understandable. It will be the completion of her Polish campaign. But she has no claim on Bulgarian ports in the Black Sea. It has to be seen now what attitude they take.

PURANI: If something happens in the Balkans it will be interesting.

SRI AUROBINDO: Yes, that is the only way to save the situation. Hungary and Bulgaria are relying on Germany and Italy to protect them. Now it has to be seen what Hitler and Mussolini will do against Russia. If something happens Turkey and other powers will also pluck up courage.

PURANI: What will happen to Hitler's pact with Stalin?

SRI AUROBINDO: "Pact of brotherhood sealed in blood." That's what he said. Hitler has cloven-hoofed everybody. Now it is his turn to be cloven-hoofed. Carol says the British and the Jews dislike Russia having taken this step. Molotov will laugh at the idea.

PURANI: In the recent naval engagement it seems that the Italian fleet ran away from the British.

SRI AUROBINDO: Italy may not want any engagement now unless the odds are in its favour. It might be waiting until the armistice and if the French fleet is removed it may start something.

EVENING

SRI AUROBINDO: There is no confirmation of Russia's ultimatum to Hungary.

PURANI: No, it may be just a rumour.

SRI AUROBINDO: Yes, the news is too good to be true. (*Laughter*)

PURANI: The communists in Bessarabia are very happy and the Rumanians are fleeing. Trainloads seem to be crossing each other carrying refugees.

SRI AUROBINDO: And the Jews are running away to the Russian territory. (*Laughter*)

PURANI: The clashes, they say, are due to the overflow of the Russians.

SRI AUROBINDO: Yes, they outpaced the scheduled time!

PURANI: The clashes on the Hungarian frontier have stopped.

SRI AUROBINDO: Italy and Germany have asked the Hungarians to suspend their claims for now.

SATYENDRA: De Gaulle wrote a book before the war which has been translated into German. It seems he foresaw modern warfare in the form of mass employment of tanks at selected points, as Hitler has done, as well as, mechanised units, armoured cars, surprise attacks in the Ardennes and on the Meuse and the defection of Belgium. He says, "This mechanical system of fire, shock, speed and camouflage will reveal itself when first let loose by bringing into action at least two thousand tanks."

SRI AUROBINDO: I see! That is prophetic! Where is that news?

SATYENDRA: In the *Indian Express*. (*Laughter*) But it quotes a French paper.

SRI AUROBINDO: Of course, it can't write that itself. It seems France invents these plans and Germany accepts them. It was the same as the plan of depth-defence in the last war. Some soldier invented it but the French refused to accept it. One of the copies of the plan was seized by the Germans and they put it into operation; it gave a lot of trouble to the British at the end of the war. The Siegfried Line is modelled on that system for about thirty miles!

PURANI: Spain's attitude seems to be doubtful. Hitler has massed an army on the Franco-Spanish frontier.

SRI AUROBINDO: Why?

PURANI: Perhaps he wants to take Gibraltar with Franco's help.

SRI AUROBINDO: Then it will be very difficult for the British to hold it. Gibraltar is only a rock and, besides, Spain has got Tangier on the other side.

NIRODBARAN: They shouldn't have allowed Spain to get that.

SRI AUROBINDO: Then they shouldn't have allowed Franco to win at all. If they had helped the Republican party, Franco would have been defeated. All this has been due to Chamberlain.

PURANI: Lloyd George also asked for help to the Republicans at that time.

NIRODBARAN: And they would have had Russia as their ally and she would have been more trustful of them. Now to take Gibralter may well be Hitler's next move.

SRI AUROBINDO: Most probably.

PURANI: Subhas Bose has been arrested.

SRI AUROBINDO: Yes, by a friend of his. (*Laughter*)

PURANI: It may be a prelude to the arrest of Congressmen. It seems there has been no change in the Government policy as a result of the Gandhi-Viceroy meeting. Repetition only.

SRI AUROBINDO: Looks like that. Otherwise Rajagopalachari wouldn't have said what he did in his speech. It must be due to these officials at Simla. They are all fossilised people. Once they have a fixed idea, they won't give it up.

SATYENDRA: The I.C.S. mentality.

SRI AUROBINDO: Yes. Englishmen in England are quite different. Many of them, even conservatives, are speaking of a change in India.

SATYENDRA: Though Amery seems to be a strong man, he doesn't have any idea about the Indian situation and the official mind.

SRI AUROBINDO: He knows what is going on behind the scene.

3 JULY 1940

SATYENDRA: People here have become panicky about the currency. I hear that many people are coming to the Ashram to have their British notes changed into French money.

SRI AUROBINDO (*laughing*): Yes, but there is not yet any official order. The post office is still giving out British money.

SATYENDRA: Shopkeepers refuse to give any change.

Chamberlain has said that England would rather go down than make peace with Hitler.

SRI AUROBINDO: No more appeasement?

SATYENDRA: No. He says England is fighting for the liberty of the world's peoples.

NIRODBARAN: The trouble is that the British people's own liberty is so endangered that no one will believe him.

SRI AUROBINDO: But what he says is true. Why did the British fight for Poland?

NIRODBARAN: Hore-Belisha is supporting India's case.

SRI AUROBINDO: Yes, and also working for an understanding with Ireland. They say that Germany may try to occupy Ireland, from where it will be easier to attack England. Ireland has a long coast which is quite undefended. An army can land anywhere. And the British will have to prepare the defence of the whole west coast of England.

SATYENDRA: They have an army only thirty thousand strong.

NIRODBARAN: But how will the Germans land there?

SRI AUROBINDO: Why can't they? The British Navy is not always keeping watch over all that area.

NIRODBARAN: If Ireland doesn't want to join the British, they have no chance.

SRI AUROBINDO: The Irish people are strongly against joining the British because of the Ulster question.

NIRODBARAN: Craigayon has said to De Valera that he won't make common cause with him unless he takes sides with the British.

SRI AUROBINDO: De Valera can't do that because the Irish people are strongly against it unless the Ulster question is solved.

NIRODBARAN: But it is the Ulster people who want to keep separate like our Muslim brothers.

SRI AUROBINDO: Yes.

SATYENDRA: They want their Pakistan.

NIRODBARAN: Ireland has as difficult a problem as India. But don't they realise the danger of invasion?

SRI AUROBINDO: They are like the Americans.

NIRODBARAN: But Ireland's danger is more imminent and the Americans may not believe in the possibility of an invasion of their land, at least at a near date.

SRI AUROBINDO: No, everybody now is realising the danger.

PURANI: The next step of Hitler after England will be America.

SRI AUROBINDO: Not quite the next, because he may have to square with Russia first.

NIRODBARAN: Burma has given unconditional help to Britain while the English response to it is that they "will be very willing to discuss".

SRI AUROBINDO: Burma's policy is comprehensible while I don't understand the Congress position at all. They are neither helping nor going to offer resistance so long as Britain is at war. If they started some movement for their objective, it could be understood. But now they lose both the advantages of helping and those of resistance.

EVENING

SRI AUROBINDO (*suddenly to Nirodbaran*): Do you know Savitri Devi? She is a Greek married to a Bengali.

NIRODBARAN: I seem to have read about her in the papers.

SATYENDRA: Yes, there was some mention of her.

SRI AUROBINDO: She is a militant Hindu-Sabhaite.

SATYENDRA: Converts are sometimes more enthusiastic. But she may have become Hindu out of genuine regard.

PURANI: The Viceroy's proposals seem to fall far short of a National Government.

SRI AUROBINDO: Yes, it is a short extension of his Executive Council. How many Congress members did the Viceroy propose last time?

PURANI: Two, perhaps.

SRI AUROBINDO: Now he may make it four and, if they refuse, he may take in the League, the Liberals and probably Savarkar and Ambedkar.

PURANI: The Working Committee is giving counter-proposals, it appears.

SRI AUROBINDO: Yes, many are in favour of the National Government. So Rajagopalachari prevails.

PURANI: If the Executive Council with its defence powers were handed over to the Indians?

SRI AUROBINDO: The Viceroy is not likely to agree. The British won't like to abdicate, leaving all defence measures in inexperienced hands.

PURANI: Chamberlain is being attacked by Lloyd George and asked to go.

SRI AUROBINDO: That can't be done. It will create a dissension by offending the Conservative Party.

4 JULY 1940

NIRODBARAN: Today is the date of expiry of the armistice terms.

SRI AUROBINDO: No, two days more are there, except for two ports.

NIRODBARAN: The Pondicherry Governor seems to be backing out from his previous stand.

SRI AUROBINDO: Looks like that; the stand is becoming a "seat" now.

SATYENDRA: He made a diplomatic statement ending with "Long live Britain and France" and saying that he would align himself with the British – but without repudiating the Pétain Government.

NIRODBARAN: Why is he backing out now?

SRI AUROBINDO: Frightened, I suppose. Except Jibouti and Caledonia, both tiny places, all the other colonies are undecided.

NIRODBARAN: Perhaps the British will capture Pondicherry.

SRI AUROBINDO: For that they will have to have an excuse; for example, Nazi agitation here.

SATYENDRA: Even the British Government is hesitating about the Pétain Government.

SRI AUROBINDO: Yes, if they had formed an alternative Government then it would have been easier.

SATYENDRA: All the leaders seem to have been unable to leave France.

SRI AUROBINDO: Except Blum; he must have brought away some money with him.

SATYENDRA: Gandhi has offered his help, through the Viceroy, to the British Government and has asked them to lay down their arms and practise non-violence.

SRI AUROBINDO: He must be a little cracked.

SATYENDRA: While asking them to lay down their arms, he wants them to keep up their spirit.

SRI AUROBINDO: And be subjugated in practice!

NIRODBARAN: The French papers are being governed by Goebbels, it seems, and *Le Matin* has already started its campaign against the British.

SRI AUROBINDO: Le Matin is a government-aided paper. Most of the French papers are aided. During the Abyssinian campaign Italy bought up almost all the papers in her favour.

SATYENDRA: After a long time the judgment on the Bombay prohibition case has come out.

SRI AUROBINDO: Yes, the judges seem to be fond of drink. Are they going by the amendment of the Abkari law? It seems clear that if the Congress Government came back, it would have no control over the import of foreign liquor.

PURANI: No, because export and import become a reserved subject.

EVENING

Radio news: Most of the French fleet has fallen into British hands. Only at Oran in North Africa has the French fleet resisted and a naval fight is going on between the British and the French.

SRI AUROBINDO: This is what is called "*coup de tonnerre*".

SATYENDRA: The British move is quite logical in pursuance of their blockade. They said all French ports are under blockade.

PURANI: The French could have simply said they had been over-powered and so surrendered to the British fleet.

NIRODBARAN: Fleet means what?

PURANI: Some naval units.

SRI AUROBINDO: Oran is a big port in North Africa.

NIRODBARAN: Now the colonies may buck up.

SATYENDRA: Yes.

SRI AUROBINDO: The Pondicherry Governor is sliding towards the Pétain Government. But the British have now shown they won't stand any nonsense.

NIRODBARAN: The only thing now, perhaps, is that French soldiers will be used against the British because of the naval fight between them.

SATYENDRA: What can be done? It has to be done sooner or later.

SRI AUROBINDO: But will the French fight for Germany? There won't be any later as they are already in German hands.

PURANI: Moreover, after demilitarisation it has to be seen how much vim is left in them.

SRI AUROBINDO: Why is this fleet trying to go to France to be demobilised instead of having it done by England?

PURANI: Perhaps they are Fascist.

SATYENDRA: No reply to Gandhi's offer? (*Laughter*)

SRI AUROBINDO: But the British are now demobilising the French fleet. The French can lay down their arms and go home.

PURANI: Grazziani is being sent to Libya.

SRI AUROBINDO: Yes. It was he who established peace in Libya by killing all the people who resisted. Do you know about the will?

PURANI: What will?

SRI AUROBINDO: The will that has been found in Balbao's plane. People are asking how the will could have remained intact when everything else was burnt and why Balbao would have carried a will with him. If it is a suicide, why would he have committed suicide with ten people?

5 JULY 1940

News has come today about the details of the naval fight between the English and the French fleets in Oran. But Sri Aurobindo did not seem to be in a mood to talk. Almost all the time he listened to us.

PURANI: Pétain is being called the Führer of France.

SRI AUROBINDO: Yes, he has realised the dream of his life at eighty-four.

NIRODBARAN: They say that a major part of the French navy has fallen to the British.

SRI AUROBINDO: A large part.

EVENING

PURANI: The German radio says that the Pétain Government has cut off all diplomatic relations with England.

SRI AUROBINDO (*laughing*): There is not much relation to cut off. They have only a *chargé d'affaires* at London. On this side things are getting tighter.

PURANI: In the Balkans?

SRI AUROBINDO: No, in Pondicherry. The Consul has left for the North, nobody knows where. The Vice-Consul also left for the North with the director of the Bank, perhaps to arrange for the currency directly without passing through the Governor. The Viceroy is coming to Madras. The French Governor is now frightened because the Pétain Government has issued orders to carry out government orders as it is the duty of the *fonctionnaire* to obey the superior authority. Moreover, Hitler has threatened the admirals, officials and others that if they don't obey their wives and children will be taken to the concentration camps.

SATYENDRA: Then what remains for them to resist for?

PURANI: The British also are taking strong measures, I hear. They have forbidden all British ships to touch Pondicherry. That means a blockade.

SRI AUROBINDO: Yes, they must have done that after learning of the Governor's attitude.

NIRODBARAN: And now if diplomatic relations go, the British will take possession of Pondicherry.

SRI AUROBINDO: Not necessarily. Even if diplomatic relations go, Pondicherry may simply remain hostile without being at war.

NIRODBARAN: It seems that the Pétain Government will very soon take up a hostile attitude towards England and even go to war with her, especially now after the naval intervention.

SRI AUROBINDO: Looks like that. Their policies are lining up more and more with Germany. (*To Nirodbaran*) Have you seen the new constitution of France that Pétain has proposed?

NIRODBARAN: No, I haven't seen it yet.

SRI AUROBINDO: It is all authoritarianism and dictatorship. Pétain is the dictator and Weygand is the vice-dictator, I suppose the successor. Weygand, Mother says, is tremendously rich. He is one of the chief shareholders of the Suez Company.

PURANI: Dr. André seems to have been correct in his estimation of the French officials here. He said, "You will see all of them back out when the Government order comes from France. They only say big things but they don't actually want to go to war. I know about two doctors in our hospital."

SRI AUROBINDO: Yes, all those who were shouting have become tame. I mean the military officers who wanted to fight with the British. One of them even wanted to commit suicide. (*Laughter*)

PURANI: I told Dr. André about Bulloch who has been earnest and sincere and gone to war willingly. He said that because he was a technician he had to go.

SRI AUROBINDO: That is not correct. He has gone because he wants to fight, wants to get a promotion.

PURANI: Some people say that conditions in France must be all right. The peasants must be getting enough food, otherwise they would have revolted.

SRI AUROBINDO: Who are these people?

PURANI: Some townspeople.

SRI AUROBINDO: Then the peasants in India must be very prosperous because they don't revolt. (*Laughter*)

PURANI: I told them that in Germany people had to be on war rations for seven years.

NIRODBARAN: Due to this blockade we shall also suffer.

SRI AUROBINDO: Of course, especially as our wheat is detained at Madras. If we had our own wheat we could go on till the millennium.

NIRODBARAN: Then instead of wheat we shall have rice. (*After a while*) Have you read Harin's poems?

SRI AUROBINDO: Yes, they are good but nothing wonderful. I have read part of Anilbaran's conversations[1] too. I don't see that all of them are worth publishing. There are plenty of trivial things. A selection has to be made and even then it may not be worthwhile publishing it.

NIRODBARAN: Besides, the style is very poor. He hasn't taken any care to present things in an elegant way.

SRI AUROBINDO: Of course I didn't speak to him in Bengali.

PURANI: It seems to me that such things require a bit of rounding off to be presentable and to have a literary value.

SRI AUROBINDO: But he may fear that it will be too much rounded off like Charu Dutt's stories! (*Laughter*) It is all about his

---

1. The conversations Anilbaran Roy had with Sri Aurobindo on his first arrival were sent to Sri Aurobindo for revision with a view to publishing them.

sadhana. There is nothing literary there. Things like, keep your mind quiet and aspire.

PURANI: That reminds me of Noren. He says, "Charubabu says, 'Keep your mind quiet and aspire'; Sri Aurobindo also has said this. What is new in that?"

SATYENDRA: Easy to say but difficult to do.

SRI AUROBINDO: But Anilbaran seems to have done it all right. When he was asked to do it, he said he tried and his mind became quiet but nothing descended. (*Laughter*)

PURANI: At that time everybody used to feel something very concretely after having a talk with you.

At this point Satyendra began to smile, looking at Nirodbaran.

SRI AUROBINDO: That was the golden period of the Ashram. And now (*looking at Nirodbaran significantly*) it is the age of the "physical crust". (*Laughter*) The scientists have a special term for it.

SATYENDRA: But a most momentous period for us.

After a while Purani read out a poem by B. K. Thakore on Hitler. In it Thakore says, "We will gather all our might to crush you."

SRI AUROBINDO (*laughing*): Not so easy as in poetry. (*Laughter*)

6 JULY 1940

PURANI: There is a German order that ships must keep twelve to twenty miles off the French coast. I suppose it may apply to colonies too.

SRI AUROBINDO: Even if the ships come nearer, what can Pondicherry do? It has no guns.

PURANI: Mohanlal says he saw three sepoys with guns on the pier.

SRI AUROBINDO: To shoot British warships? It seems all communications, trains, etc. are going to be stopped between Madras and Pondicherry. The people are in a panic. Hitler has declared that the French fleet is not to be demobilised, (*laughter*) because he can't get at it and he has threatened Turkey and Yugoslavia. It depends now on what Russia will do because it will be dangerous for Russia to allow Hitler to get control of Turkey which means control of the Dardanelles also, an entry into Asia Minor. The position will then be that except for Russia and Britain everybody will be under Hitler. Spain is practically under his thumb. That is the New World Order, I suppose. Only North Africa will be out of it, since it is being guarded by the British navy.

PURANI: I suppose Turkey will consult Russia before yielding.

SRI AUROBINDO: Yes. Everybody is climbing down. Have you noted that Cordell Hull said that America won't participate in European politics? America will only concern itself with trade!

NIRODBARAN: For some time America has been following that policy.

SRI AUROBINDO: Yes.

NIRODBARAN: I wonder if it is because of the impending election. On the other hand Knox and other Republicans have said that Britain's defence is their own defence. Are there only two parties in America?

SRI AUROBINDO: Yes, but there is a split in the parties. The Democratic Party is solidly behind Roosevelt, I think, while in the Republican Party there are isolationists, interventionists, etc.

PURANI: France has cut off all diplomatic relations with England, Germany says. In that case the Indian Government will naturally take stern measures and they won't hesitate to take possession of Pondicherry.

SRI AUROBINDO: Diplomatic relations are already cut off here. It seems the Consul has gone to the North with the Vice-Consul. When the British Consul asked the Governor why he was hesitating, he replied, "Your own Government has not decided what to do." That is practically a refusal.

NIRODBARAN: But he could have acted like Indo-China and the British status quo.

SRI AUROBINDO: Yes, but what if he wants to go back to France? The Pétain Government will be there.

NIRODBARAN: Is Hitler trying to checkmate Russia in Turkey or working in league with Russia?

SRI AUROBINDO: Don't know. But Stalin and Molotov would be off their heads to allow Hitler to get Turkey. Hitler would next occupy Asia Minor and then Asia. Then Jawaharlal might think that the invasion of India has become real.

NIRODBARAN: Can't say. He still might not believe it.

SRI AUROBINDO: He might say that there are mountains, deserts, etc!

NIRODBARAN: But Turkey is in a better position. She has the Allies on her side.

SRI AUROBINDO: Yes, but there is Syria in between. The British will have to occupy it first.

SATYENDRA: Hitler has made a calculated move. He has first alienated Syria, then he will impose himself on Turkey. He and Italy have warned Turkey and Yugoslavia against an independent policy.

SRI AUROBINDO: If Kemal were there, he would never submit. I don't know about these other people.

NIRODBARAN: Italy calls Churchill a criminal gangster because of his action against the French fleet.

SRI AUROBINDO: Italy? Of course. A gangster like Mussolini?

SATYENDRA: Where was the Italian fleet at that time?

SRI AUROBINDO: Italy said that it couldn't arrive in time.

NIRODBARAN: Italy has thrown a challenge to the British navy to come to the Italian naval base.

SRI AUROBINDO: The fact is that the Italian fleet is hiding in the Adriatic. (*Laughter*)

EVENING

PURANI: There was a great rush at the bank to exchange French notes for British money.

NIRODBARAN: So Pondicherry is becoming a British colony? And diplomatic relations also seem to have been cut off.

SRI AUROBINDO: The French chargé d'affaires in London has resigned. But why "resigned"? They are called back in such cases. Is it a new term?

PURANI: Perhaps he is in sympathy with the British and so has sent his resignation to Pétain. The French fleet has been asked to scuttle itself.

SRI AUROBINDO: The British also have made a similar offer to sink it.

DR. RAO: What do you think of Gandhi's offer to the British?

SRI AUROBINDO: The result of the offer here has been that those officers who wanted to fight don't want to any more. They say, "If submission is heroic, why fight?" The French forces stopped fighting not because they were non-violent but because there was no hope. If there had been any hope they would have fought on.

PURANI: Any news of the Congress Working Committee?

SRI AUROBINDO: No, they are still holding sessions. Something important seems to be going on there, otherwise they wouldn't have taken so many days.

DR. RAO: There is a rumour of a mysterious letter sent by the Viceroy through Aney to Gandhi.

SRI AUROBINDO: Rumour from where?

DR. RAO: The *Indian Express*. (*Laughter*)

As Dr. Rao didn't get the joke about The Indian Express, *he looked from one person to another.*

SRI AUROBINDO: The paper comments that the Simla office circle is hard in its attitude.

PURANI: It seems Grig is against any wide reforms.

SRI AUROBINDO: It is the resistance of Simla that stands in the way, I am sure the English people would give larger terms. The *Manchester Guardian* describes the Viceroy as rigid and asks Amery to visit India.

7 JULY 1940

PURANI: Baudoin is furious with the British.

SRI AUROBINDO: Yes. He says that this aggressive action of the navy is a blot on English honour – people who are entitled to honour!

Have you heard that the banker and the Vice-Consul of Pondicherry are back?

PURANI: No.

SRI AUROBINDO: They are back and now the blockade will be withdrawn. Trains won't be stopped; the currency will be all right.

PURANI: They must have settled with the Madras Governor.

SRI AUROBINDO: Maybe. But nothing is known on this side. I mean, what the Pondy Governor has decided.

DR. RAO: Weygand, in a statement appearing in today's paper, has laid the blame on the British. He says that he asked them to fight in the southwest, but instead of that they went to the north so that they could escape, and by sacrificing the majority of the French army their Expeditionary Force was able to get away.

SRI AUROBINDO: To fight in the southwest would have been the maddest thing to do. They would have been completely destroyed – both the French and the English.

PURANI: Yes, by this move at least the English Army has been saved.

SRI AUROBINDO: Yes, that was the only course open. The French also should have withdrawn.

DR. RAO: They say that France is their own homeland; they can't leave it and get away.

SRI AUROBINDO: It is not a question of homeland. The question is one of military strategy and the only strategy was to withdraw as quickly as possible. If the French had done that, they could have come back to France again and fought. And it was not only the British who escaped. They rescued more than a lakh of French people too. The fact is that after the breakdown at Sedan and the Meuse, the French, British and Belgian forces were encircled, and then no other course was left but to withdraw. Weygand has done nothing and is now trying to justify himself.

NIRODBARAN: There is a notion among our people that the British played tricks and were treacherous.

DR. RAO: Yes.

SRI AUROBINDO: These people know nothing about war. Why would the British do that? Don't they know that if France falls England will be in the greatest danger? Besides, Churchill has proved that he sent more soldiers than he had promised to Reynaud.

PURANI: The British lost fifty thousand lorries.

SRI AUROBINDO: One thousand guns and other material.

Satyendra (*after a while*): Is there no news about the invasion of Portugal?

SRI AUROBINDO: No. It must have been a false rumour. Franco doesn't seem to intend to claim Gibraltar. He won't as long as the English navy is supreme. The Spaniards are only taking a promenade with one aeroplane and leaving a few bombs as mementos.

NIRODBARAN: The important news was vague today – about the Alexandrian fleet.

SRI AUROBINDO: Yes, they couldn't catch the keyword.

NIRODBARAN: The Italians can send their navy to help the French.

SRI AUROBINDO: They will take good care not to.

PURANI: Alexandria is too far away, they might say.

SRI AUROBINDO: They have their fleet in the Dodecanese; they could have sent it from there.

DR. RAO: The Italians are said to be bad fighters.

SRI AUROBINDO: Till now they haven't proven themselves very good. Of course there have only been raids and skirmishes till now. One can't judge from that.

PURANI: Malta is such a small place and so near. The Italians have not been able to do anything till now. (*After a while*) Savarkar is not enthusiastic over the Viceroy's extension of the Executive Council, it seems.

SRI AUROBINDO: Nobody would be enthusiastic. It is like the old reforms, giving one or two seats.

PURANI: Since the Hindu Maha Sabha's and the Liberals' defence policy is the same as that of the Congress, it is asked why the Government should take the minorities instead of the Congress majority with them and win the confidence of the masses.

SRI AUROBINDO: Yes, but the minorities like the Maha Sabha and the Liberals merely advocate their policy and don't insist on it like the Congress. The Liberals say that they should have this and that. If nothing is conceded, they say, "All right, we shall wait till the next time." They are a peaceful lot like the Pétain Government. Gandhi ought to like them.

EVENING

Due to the war there has been a Government rule that all arrivals and departures, even for only two hours, must be reported to the police. Dr. Rao had not been reported yet. As soon as Purani entered the room, Sri Aurobindo commented on it.

SRI AUROBINDO: Purani, have you reported this dangerous character?

Purani (*smiling*): No, I will do it tomorrow. Under cover of Sunday I was taking rest. Tomorrow I will go. (*After a while*) Is there any proposal by the Committee? Sikander Hyat Khan, it seems, has met the Working Committee and Gandhi, and is trying to come to a settlement. Fazlul Huque also was there.

SRI AUROBINDO: Yes, but there is no proposal. They are still discussing. But Gandhi is making the Congress position as difficult as possible.

PURANI: How?

SRI AUROBINDO: Haven't you read his article today?

PURANI: No.

SATYENDRA: He is asking the Congress to keep aloof from the irresistible temptation of going back to office, to stick to non-violence and to declare independence as the immediate goal.

SRI AUROBINDO: And yet it was he who asked the Congress to accept Dominion Status and even made a proclamation about it.

PURANI: Yes. The French fleet has been demolished in Alexandria.

SRI AUROBINDO: Yes, and the British and French sailors are drinking together in the port. The French Senate met with only 450 members out of 932, a bare majority. The socialists, communists and radicals must have kept aloof because they knew the price of opposition. De Gaulle has been sentenced to four years' imprisonment and fined one hundred francs by Pétain.

PURANI: For fighting against Germany.

SRI AUROBINDO: Oh no, for that the punishment is penal servitude for life or death. I suppose it is for their lack of fidelity to their promise to Hitler. I have read about that statement of Baudoin. After Weygand took command in the southwest, the French, British and Belgian armies were encircled by the Germans. The Belgians were asked to take up a new position which they refused to do and then defected. As a result the British were exposed from the north, while the French were encircled. If the British Expeditionary Force had not retreated, all would have been encircled and escape would have been impossible.

After some had left, Nirodbaran brought up the topic of Gandhi again.

NIRODBARAN: Gandhi seems to have been in a hurry to bring out his article before the report of the Working Committee.

SRI AUROBINDO: Yes, he would have been too late otherwise.

NIRODBARAN: If Gandhi takes up this attitude there is no chance of a compromise.

SRI AUROBINDO: It is impossible.

NIRODBARAN: His hasty departure for Wardha, his short meeting with Sikander Hyat Khan and everything else show he is in no mood for any compromise.

SRI AUROBINDO: Yes.

NIRODBARAN: And yet it was such a fine opportunity when Hyat Khan, Fazlul Huque and the Liberals were on the point of coming to a settlement with the Congress!

SRI AUROBINDO: Yes, it was a unique opportunity thrown away. With Bose on one side and Gandhi on the other, future unity will be difficult. And if Hindus and Muslims had now made a united demand the Government would have had to submit.

NIRODBARAN: C. R. and Azad are for a compromise.

SRI AUROBINDO: Yes.

NIRODBARAN: But I don't think they will dare to make a break with Gandhi.

SRI AUROBINDO: No. Gandhi would make a big row. Of course he is right in one respect. He says private armies will be of no use if you go in for defence. They will be like the Khaksars. Then you have to join with the British Government. I didn't see any reference to the mysterious letter to Gandhi sent through Aney. I thought it was impossible.

8 JULY 1940

PURANI: Gandhi has said that as the other party's programme is the same as that of the Congress they can form ministries and carry out the administration together. If that is so, why did the Congress seek an election at all?

SRI AUROBINDO: Where has he said that?

PURANI: In yesterday's *Hindu.*

SRI AUROBINDO: Does he mean that except for his point about non-violence the others agree? How can it be? The Muslims want Pakistan and if they are allowed to take up administration they will establish Muslim Raj.

SATYENDRA: No, no. Gandhi has said that only about the defence policy. Otherwise why should the Congress seek any election at all? He says also that if you follow his programme, India will get Swaraj even before the war is over, provided you are non-violent.

SRI AUROBINDO: But what is his programme? His programme is to sit and wait as he doesn't want to embarrass the Government during the war. If he had started some movement for the goal, I could have understood.

SATYENDRA: He doesn't want to start civil disobedience as the country is not prepared.

SRI AUROBINDO: And the country will never be prepared according to the conditions laid down by him.

NIRODBARAN: How to explain this shift in him from Dominion Status to independence?

SRI AUROBINDO: Don't know. He doesn't know himself, probably. Caught by forces.

SATYENDRA: Or is it his principle of non-violence that is the difficulty with him?

SRI AUROBINDO: In that case why did they resign the Ministry? They shouldn't have resigned at all. Reforms of whatever kind would have come as a natural step.

Purani (*after some time*): Huque has started his tirade against Jinnah.

SRI AUROBINDO: How? He says that he wants a settlement with the Congress and the League.

PURANI: Yes, but he doesn't like Jinnah's asking the League members not to take part in the war committee. He wants, if he can, to come to a settlement with the Congress behind Jinnah's back.

SATYENDRA: What about the arrests connected with the Holwell monument?

NIRODBARAN: Still going on.

SATYENDRA: Bose has started the agitation, after all.

SRI AUROBINDO: What a thing to fight over!

NIRODBARAN: He has taken it up as a common measure between Hindus and Muslims, thinking they will also join.

SRI AUROBINDO: All joined against the monument? But his friend Huque arrested him.

NIRODBARAN: I thought it was the Central Government.

SRI AUROBINDO: The Central Government doesn't care about the monument. When Bose said that he would start Satyagraha, he was arrested by Huque. Huque says he is not going to be compelled by anything or any movement.

PURANI: Yes, he says he will do what is right and just, but not under any compulsion.

SRI AUROBINDO: That is the advantage of popular government. It can do anything it likes because of its majority and say the country is behind it. C. R. has done the same. The Muslim League is exasperated with the Congress not because of any oppression by the Congress but because they are nowhere in the Government.

SATYENDRA: The Bombay Congress Committee observed silence on the arrest of Bose.

SRI AUROBINDO: In honour of his arrest?

EVENING

SATYENDRA: Just now, is the stress of the Yoga laid mostly on Karma, Sir?

SRI AUROBINDO: No stress is put on anything. If you mean that the sadhaks have to do more work now as the Mother had to dispense with many servants because of the war, it is true.

DR RAO: Your patella should be moved by somebody to give it a greater range of flexion.

SRI AUROBINDO: I know. You have said that before.

RAO: By passive movement the adhesions will break.

SRI AUROBINDO: Do you think so?

DR RAO: Yes, Sir. You can guide Nirod to do it, if you can't do it yourself. It can be done for five minutes to start with, when the leg is in an extended position.

SRI AUROBINDO: Explain all that to Nirod.

NIRODBARAN: It is not the explanation but the sanction that is required.

RAO: Yes, you are right.

SRI AUROBINDO (*after a pause*): The Purusha is a Drashta and merely observes all that is done.

PURANI: That means permission is given. You can do the flexing.

9 JULY 1940

PURANI: The German troops are being concentrated on the Franco-Spanish frontier. Hitler wants to march through Spain to Gibraltar.

SRI AUROBINDO: Yes, that may be his intention. I don't see then how the British can hold out against him.

NIRODBARAN: Is Hitler working in collaboration with Franco?

SRI AUROBINDO: Of course.

NIRODBARAN: Then Portugal also would be left out.

SRI AUROBINDO: No.

PURANI: Hitler is trying to cut off supplies.

NIRODBARAN: Not only that. If he gets Gibraltar, he can block the Mediterranean gate.

SRI AUROBINDO: That must be his intention, as he can't invade England directly. With Spanish Morocco and Tangier on the other side, the route will be closed.

NIRODBARAN: Won't that put the British in a bad plight?

SRI AUROBINDO: Not in a bad plight, but certainly in some difficulty.

PURANI: Rumania has lined up with the Axis.

SRI AUROBINDO: It had already done that before.

PURANI: Yes, but now it has openly declared it and cut off oil supplies to England. Some Englishmen have left Rumania. The Nazis seem to say, "Oh, it is too friendly!" (*Laughter*) Obviously Germany is afraid of Russia. To turn to Indian affairs: the Congress has asked for a declaration of complete independence in the future.

SATYENDRA: Yes, and a provisional National Government at the Centre.

SRI AUROBINDO: On what lines? What about the defence?

SATYENDRA: Nothing about it, perhaps. The details aren't out yet.

SRI AUROBINDO: In that case what remains of independence?

NIRODBARAN: They say that only when everything is in their hands can they throw their full weight behind the defence of the country.

SRI AUROBINDO: Defence against whom?

PURANI: Pétain has become a Führer.

SRI AUROBINDO: Not yet, going to be.

PURANI: He says that now is the last phase of the third Republic and the motto will be not Liberty, Equality and Fraternity, but Work, Family and *Patrie*.

SRI AUROBINDO: That is the Fascist motto.

PURANI: The priests are happy because Pétain is a Catholic.

K19

SRI AUROBINDO: Oh yes, but our position will be bad. If a Catholic government takes control, then our Ashram won't be allowed to exist.

NIRODBARAN: All moves seem to fall on us in some way or other.

SRI AUROBINDO: Of course. The Asura is more concerned with us than anything else. He is inventing new situations so that we may fall into difficulty. Nazis, Fascists and communists are all against us and we are safe under none of them. Mussolini perhaps may allow us to continue.

SATYENDRA: He has read some of your books.

SRI AUROBINDO: Yes.

NIRODBARAN: He will allow us so long as he is not criticised.

PURANI: It seems Bonvain is unable to communicate with the Pétain Government. The British office won't accept his telegrams.

SRI AUROBINDO: Then we may be safe, at least during the war, unless they send somebody by aeroplane which may be shot down by mistake by the British.

PURANI: But the aeroplane has to land at Karachi – unless they make a nonstop flight from Syria, for example.

The French are again accusing the British of having dislodged Weygand.

NIRODBARAN: The British staff officer's reply that Weygand's plan was good on paper but not in practice, makes one suspect that the allegation is true.

SATYENDRA: Yes, he should not have said that.

SRI AUROBINDO: But they don't say they disobeyed him. His plan may have been strategic at the beginning but after the German breakthrough and encirclement, things changed. And then they disagreed about the plan.

SATYENDRA: There must have been some agreement afterwards, otherwise how could the evacuation of French soldiers have taken place?

SRI AUROBINDO: Quite so.

PURANI: These are all political views put forth by the French leaders, not by the military. They are dictated by the German High Command.

SATYENDRA: If they have surrendered everything, why did they fight at all? Without their co-operation, England would have kept aloof.

SRI AUROBINDO: Yes, England could have been on the defensive. But England has learnt one lesson from the fight. She could have gone on evading Hitler and then been put to some difficulty later, but now she knows all his tactics.

NIRODBARAN: Has Gandhi himself proclaimed independence for India or has the Working Committee forced it on him?

SRI AUROBINDO: It must be his own move. He is warning the Congress against accepting Dominion Status.

NIRODBARAN: Our fate seems to be changing. Before we were under the French and now perhaps we will be under the British.

SATYENDRA: Can't say; everything is in a flux.

SRI AUROBINDO: The British, at least, won't give in so easily to the Government in France.

SATYENDRA: No.

Purani (*after reading a letter from X stating that a court judgment had been in her favour by the grace of Sri Aurobindo and Sri Krishna*): Setalvad's son, who is the Advocate General and related to the lady, may have spoken to and influenced the judges against her husband who is a drunkard.

SRI AUROBINDO: But do the judges discuss a case with anyone when it is *sub judice*? If he is defending the case it is different.

PURANI: No, he is not defending it.

NIRODBARAN: In Calcutta the judges are said to take bribes.

SRI AUROBINDO: In Calcutta?

NIRODBARAN: Yes.

SRI AUROBINDO: High Court judges?

NIRODBARAN: People say so.

SRI AUROBINDO: People say all sorts of things. One can't believe what people say. Mofussil judges may sometimes take bribes, but I don't think High Court judges do. The British judges have so far kept a very high standard.

EVENING

SRI AUROBINDO: The Mother said that the 10th of last month seemed to have been significant.

10 JULY 1940

PURANI: The *Hindu* says that Mittelhauser has resigned.

SRI AUROBINDO: Resigned? He was relieved, they said.

PURANI: No, the paper says he has resigned and that many French officers have joined the British.

NIRODBARAN: Yes, mainly those of a high rank. There seems to be unrest in Syria. The Syrians want independence and are being supported by Turkey and Iraq.

SRI AUROBINDO: Syria is a mandated territory like Iraq.

NIRODBARAN: What exactly is a "mandated territory"?

SRI AUROBINDO: It means that the French hold the country in trust and when the people are fit they will be given independence. The French have been going back and forth for some time in this matter – they have been vacillating.

PURANI: De Gaulle is bitter because the British have destroyed the French fleet. He says they cannot claim it as a naval success as there was really no fight and that every Frenchman is in grief and pain over the tragic episode.

Gandhi has appealed to Britain to accept the Working Committee's resolution.

NIRODBARAN: Yes, it seems to be a resolution brought by C. R. It was carried by a majority against Gandhi's. Gandhi has given a statement to explain the background of the resolution. C. R. gave a bit of the hard truth to Gandhi saying that Gandhi has become obsessed with the idea of Ahimsa by constantly brooding over it. Gandhi says, "He went on to say that my vision is blurred."

SRI AUROBINDO (*smiling*): He said that?

NIRODBARAN: Yes, Gandhi pays a tribute to C. R. for the patience and skill by which he carried the members with him. As an individual, he has placed his services at England's disposal, he says.

SRI AUROBINDO: Spirit of non-violence?

NIRODBARAN: Yes. But the demand of complete independence remains.

SRI AUROBINDO: That is difficult for the British to accept.

NIRODBARAN: And the National Government will include defence. Will the Viceroy give it?

SRI AUROBINDO: It depends on how they work it out. But as for defence and war, they are all inexperienced. In England a minister can carry on with the help of the Civil Service, the Admiralty, etc.

Jinnah is already speaking against the National Government. He wants Pakistan. I suppose that if a Muslim majority is granted, he will accept such a government.

PURANI: In Pondicherry the officials are laughing over Gandhi's appeal of non-violence to the British. Of course it is beyond their conception. They are saying, "Is he mad?" (*Laughter*)

SATYENDRA: But by non-violence he does not mean what the officials have done in France.

SRI AUROBINDO: What then?

SATYENDRA: He says the British should refuse to carry out Hitler's orders, not cooperate. They may be killed for that. Still.

SRI AUROBINDO (*laughing*): Still?

PURANI: Even the Congress regime has adopted the police system.

SRI AUROBINDO: I don't see how non-violence can work in the administration.

SATYENDRA: The Americans are praising Churchill, comparing him to Pitt.

NIRODBARAN: I wonder what Chamberlain would have done if he had been the Premier.

SRI AUROBINDO: He would have committed twenty mistakes.

SATYENDRA: He may also be compared in the future to somebody and given praise.

SRI AUROBINDO: Praise in the sense that nobody has ever committed so many mistakes? (*Laughter*)

PURANI: No, people may say he worked for peace and reconciliation. During the Munich Agreement they were going to name streets after him.

SRI AUROBINDO: Chamberlain Street and Umbrella Square? (*Laughter*) Peace? Yes, it was meant to be peace for our time, but a short peace. This is how people like Pétain and Chamberlain, who make mistakes, get a following.

PURANI: The Italian navy is withdrawing under a smoke screen from contact with the British navy.

SRI AUROBINDO (*laughing*): Yes, the meeting with the British navy was an unexpected surprise for them. If the British can destroy the Italian navy, then it will be a big gain in their favour.

SATYENDRA: On land too, the Italians are not shining. Perhaps Hitler will employ them to guard the French territories?

PURANI: If he can trust them.

SRI AUROBINDO: Trust? Hitler can drive them out and conquer Italy at any time.

NIRODBARAN: Nolini, in his translation of a chapter of *The Life Divine*, is finding some difficulty about the word "defy" in "defy matter". He has used the word *abajna*.

SRI AUROBINDO: *Abajna* implies "contempt" which isn't the case here. It should be something like "challenge".

NIRODBARAN: But we couldn't find the Bengali for "challenge", either. *Asvikar, amanya, agrahya*, etc. – none gives the sense of "defy".

PURANI: Bengal doesn't challenge anybody, so no word exists for it. (*Laughter*)

NIRODBARAN: Bose's talk doesn't do anything but challenge.

SRI AUROBINDO: Perhaps you could say in Bose's language: "Give an ultimatum to matter"! But has even "ultimatum" any equivalent in Bengali?

EVENING

SRI AUROBINDO (*after some stray talk had been going on*): By the way, the Government here has given up the 14th July celebration. Since Pétain has become a dictator there is no meaning in that occasion and, for that matter, the whole of France is now one big Bastille. Pétain has killed the Revolution, the Revolution which had required three more revolutions to make it firm and established.

SATYENDRA: There is no hope of any revolution now.

SRI AUROBINDO: So long as Germany doesn't leave, no.

PURANI: Now the motto is: "Work, Family and Fatherland" – most mundane and stupid. It doesn't evoke any inner feeling at all, while "Liberty, Equality and Fraternity" acts like a mantra.

SATYENDRA: Not stupid but mundane, as you say.

SRI AUROBINDO: Work and Family will always be there.

PURANI: Yes, so there is nothing new in it.

SRI AUROBINDO: What does Counouma say about this Government?

PURANI: He is not here now. But he is against it. He said, "Armistice may be all right, but if they try to destroy the Republic, I will enlist myself. I don't know what Dr. André and others think about it. They still support Pétain in his peace move and say, 'People on the spot know better than others', and blame the British for their insufficient help."

SRI AUROBINDO: If people on the spot know better, it means Pétain and his minority know better than others. One may also suggest perhaps that Pétain is working to give bread to the people. (*After a while*) If David were to become a dictator of Pondicherry and say that he would give bread, would he know better because he would be a man on the spot?

As for the inadequate help of the British, you can blame Chamberlain for their late conscription. But instead of trained soldiers whom they could have sent if they had started conscription earlier, they sent whatever army they had and could muster. And if they had adopted conscription earlier, the Labour Party would have made a row. It is no use blaming the British people for that.

PURANI: They blame Chamberlain's Munich peace policy for all this and say England has directed the French foreign policy so far.

SRI AUROBINDO: But all the Rightists who are now against it supported the Munich policy at that time.

SATYENDRA: De Gaulle doesn't accuse the English of destroying the French fleet. He only asks that it not be claimed a naval success.

SRI AUROBINDO: One man voted against the Munich policy in the Senate. His name seems familiar. (*Turning to Purani*) Do you remember there was somebody with the same name in Italy who was shot at by Mussolini's mistress?

PURANI: Yes, I remember.

SRI AUROBINDO: Is he the same man or does he perhaps belong to the same family?

11 JULY 1940

PURANI: Italy says that the change of the French constitution has come too late. Just because of the change, they can't waive their claims on France.

SRI AUROBINDO (*laughing*): Of course not. That would be an easy way to get out.

NIRODBARAN: Ireland is getting more and more into a difficult position. What do you think of De Valera's proposal?

SRI AUROBINDO: Which proposal?

NIRODBARAN: About provincial autonomy to North Ireland?

SRI AUROBINDO: They won't consent unless De Valera joins the British in the defence of England. I don't think De Valera is so foolish as to say that by remaining strictly neutral Ireland will avoid a German attack. Hitler may or may not attack as it suits him.

NIRODBARAN: Even after so many examples before his eyes, he doesn't learn!

SRI AUROBINDO: Maurice Magre has said that one of the chief characteristics of the human race is stupidity. I think he is right.

SATYENDRA: But even England's help would not be of much use in case of attack.

SRI AUROBINDO: Why not?

NIRODBARAN: The defence will be far more effective without it.

SRI AUROBINDO: Of course. Still Germany may start aerial bombing.

EVENING

NIRODBARAN: Roosevelt has declared that America won't join the European war.

SRI AUROBINDO: Yes.

SATYENDRA: What we have been hearing about America's participation is only from the New York papers which are pro-Allies. Other papers have not mentioned it at all. The isolationist sentiment is still very strong in all other parts.

NIRODBARAN: He says in case of aggression they will attack, which goes without saying. (*Laughter*)

PURANI: There won't be any choice left then.

SRI AUROBINDO: If New York is invaded, they may take action.

NIRODBARAN: But Roosevelt's attitude was strongly pro-Allies at one time.

SRI AUROBINDO: That was before the fall of France. After the fall, things have changed and now America is not likely to join.

PURANI: Yes, but the Americans see that England can't stand alone against Germany.

SRI AUROBINDO: Besides, they can't send an expeditionary force if they joined. Where will it land?

SATYENDRA: In England there are plenty of people to fight.

NIRODBARAN: The Americans can land somewhere in England if Germany invades her.

SRI AUROBINDO: Yes, but if they can't do anything with forty million people, a few hundred thousand Americans won't help much. Of course America can help with munitions and the navy.

SATYENDRA: The American navy is not strong, either.

SRI AUROBINDO: No, but they are building fast. They have a navy for one ocean and now they will have navies for both.

SATYENDRA: England has sent the Duke of Windsor to the Bahamas, as far away as possible.

SRI AUROBINDO: Yes, he may be talking freely again, though not in public, and the Government thinks perhaps that he may be made a Fascist king if England is defeated.

SATYENDRA: Hitler has already declared that.

SRI AUROBINDO: Has he?

SATYENDRA: Yes.

PURANI: Sammer has a very nice idea. He says that all Europe will turn communist.

SRI AUROBINDO: Every communist says that. If Hitler is defeated, Germany may turn communist. In that case the whole of Europe will be communist. And after Hitler's death there may be dissensions in Germany and then communism may follow. But that is a remote possibility.

12 JULY 1940

NIRODBARAN: Dilip says he met a Turkish lady at Madras. She said England has not the ghost of a chance against Germany. "They won't fight at all, you will see," she said. "Don't live in a fool's paradise, Dilip." When Dilip asked whether Turkey would back Britain as she is her ally, she said, "That was before the fall of France. Now we have to save ourselves first."

SRI AUROBINDO: How?

NIRODBARAN: By alliance with Russia, perhaps.

SRI AUROBINDO: Then she is a fool herself. (*Laughter*)

NIRODBARAN: Russia is following a very secret method. Behind all these rumours and denials of an ultimatum to Turkey nobody knows the truth. It may be true as in Rumania's case.

SRI AUROBINDO: If Russia has demanded free passage through the Dardanelles it would be quite natural, for free passage is quite different from control, and the denial of it would be unnatural.

NIRODBARAN: H has paid back seven out of nine rupees.

SRI AUROBINDO: Oh, then his character must have changed.

PURANI: Is Satyendra still with him?

NIRODBARAN: No.

SRI AUROBINDO: She refuses to be a party to his polygamous tendency and says that so long as this dancing girl is with him, she will have nothing to do with him.

PURANI: He is trying to start a school there for training young people and wants to give it the name of this dancing girl.

SRI AUROBINDO: Training in mutual borrowing? (*Laughter*)

PURANI: In Bombay also he got some money from the public for such a national school. When they came to know him they feared all the money –

SRI AUROBINDO: Would be nationalised? (*Laughter*)

EVENING

Purani was discussing art with Sri Aurobindo, apropos of Laurence Binyon's book.

PURANI: Binyon has not adequately dealt with Indian art here.

SRI AUROBINDO: Hasn't he done that in a separate book?

PURANI: Yes, with Mogul art. Coomaraswamy says that images were found in India even in the pre-Buddhistic period, before the Greek influence.

SRI AUROBINDO: What proof is there? It may be that they have shaken off the Greek influence and taken up a new line. Greek art had Egyptian influence, so why not Indian art?

PURANI: Gandhara art may be Greek.

SRI AUROBINDO: No, it is mixed. No scholar claims it to be pure Greek art.

13 JULY 1940

PURANI: There is a rumour that Pétain may retire and Flaudin take his place. Pétain is having a disagreement with Germany.

SRI AUROBINDO: Yes, first it was Laval and then Flaudin. Flaudin is pro-German and worse than Laval. But will the name of Flaudin be enough to enthuse the people?

SATYENDRA: The 15th of August is nearing.

PURANI: Yes, Hitler said he would dictate peace terms on that date.

SATYENDRA: Not only that. He will go to England, he said.

SRI AUROBINDO: And not come back? (*Laughter*) Did he say that?

SATYENDRA: Yes, it was on the German radio.

SRI AUROBINDO: There does not seem to be any preparation for the invasion of England. But, of course, he does not do what is expected. Evidently he has no intention of going to the Balkans. Could it be Spain he has in mind? Gibraltar won't be difficult for him to take and then he may cross over to Morocco. In that case it will be difficult for the English ships to cross the strait of Gibraltar. If thus he can break the British Empire in Africa with the help of the possessions of the French whom he will oblige to hand them over, it will be a great stroke. Unless he achieves this, I don't see how he can invade England. No doubt, Ireland is a weak point. But the British are raising a ten-thousand-strong army.

SATYENDRA: That would be nothing.

SRI AUROBINDO: But combined with the air force, it can prevent Hitler's landing.

15 JULY 1940

SATYENDRA: The British Government has issued a notice that France and her African possessions will be treated as enemy countries as regards trade. All trade is forbidden with them. They don't mention Indo-China or Pondicherry perhaps because they have declared a status quo. They know that if there is no trade, they won't get anything from outside.

SRI AUROBINDO: And nothing from inside. (*Laughter*)

PURANI: Sammer must be glad over the arrest of workers in France. He says that Fascism will help towards bringing about communism in France.

SRI AUROBINDO: How? It is Germany that has arrested the workers because they refused to work.

PURANI: Oh, I see.

SATYENDRA: But that was one of the conditions of the armistice.

SRI AUROBINDO: The workers didn't make the armistice! (*Laughter*) Gandhi ought to be happy because of their passive resistance.

PURANI: I think Germany may try to push the French soldiers to war against England.

SRI AUROBINDO: Not likely, because to do that Hitler will have to arm France which he doesn't want to do. He hoped to get the navy.

NIRODBARAN: He must have made a mistake if he hoped that.

SRI AUROBINDO: Evidently he hoped. Now that he can't get it, he is getting whatever he can by plunder.

SATYENDRA: Yes. All the money and jewels in the banks. Investments are prohibited without permission.

NIRODBARAN: England has made a three-month agreement with Japan regarding the Burma route. But China may not be affected much.

SRI AUROBINDO: It will be affected considerably.

SATYENDRA: The Japanese radio has been declaring that England must concede the demands. Otherwise they will have to take the necessary steps. So England has given way.

SRI AUROBINDO: England can't deal with anything else now except Hitler. She can't deal with Japan or Russia.

SATYENDRA: Churchill saw long ago the necessity of alliance with Russia and also the need of increasing the air force.

NIRODBARAN: And Chamberlain did neither. And still he has a big influence.

SRI AUROBINDO: That is because he looks after the class interest while Churchill sees what is good for England.

16 JULY 1940

PURANI: Italy has published a long article, it seems, on the New Order in Europe and if England doesn't recognise it, she will have to pay the price.

SRI AUROBINDO: Even if she recognises it, she will have to pay. (*Laughter*)

PURANI: It says war on England is to begin in a week.

SRI AUROBINDO: A German paper says England won't enjoy another weekend. Hitler will appear in a triumphal march on 27th July for which windows are being hired.

SATYENDRA: That means hardly two weeks.

SRI AUROBINDO: Yes. I don't know how he is going to do it.

NIRODBARAN: Italy says her navy will involve the British navy in engagements in the meantime.

SRI AUROBINDO (*laughing*): Not involve it in engagements but threaten to engage it, so that it may not go elsewhere. If there were actual engagements, there wouldn't be any Italian navy left to keep the British navy engaged. Italy knows this very well.

NIRODBARAN: Britain seems to be mediating between Japan and China.

SRI AUROBINDO: That is what the Governor of Malaya says. If true, he shouldn't have said it.

After this there was an interval in which Satyendra, Champaklal and Purani were talking among themselves. There was a stain on Satyendra's shirt which brought up the following topic.

CHAMPAKLAL: Paul Richard used to say that a stain on the clothes means a stain on the soul. If he saw any stain on his clothes – a dhobi stain even – he would be very angry and consider it a stain on his soul.

SRI AUROBINDO (*laughing*): If it was a dhobi stain, it would be a stain on the washerman's soul. (*Laughter*) That was one thing Richard believed in – signs, emblems, omens, etc.

CHAMPAKLAL: Every time he saw a stain, it would make him angry.

SRI AUROBINDO: If he knew the cause of the stain, why should he be angry afterwards?

SATYENDRA: He did not like the cause to be revealed to him. (*Laughter*)

SRI AUROBINDO: He revealed it himself. If a clothes stain had been a stain on the soul, then no place would have been left on his soul. (*Laughter*) But the soul has no stain.

PURANI: No, that's how I argued with him saying that according to Hindu philosophy the soul is pure and immaculate. It can have no stain.

SRI AUROBINDO: He means the vital being, perhaps.

PURANI: Yes, he was a very self-contradictory man. At one moment he would say one thing, at the next another.

When others had gone, Purani said Hitler was not getting any inspiration to attack England.

SRI AUROBINDO: No, nobody knows what he has up his sleeve. But I don't think that he can attack. He can attack by air and destroy the industrial centres, which will be something. Britain's air force also has increased but it is still inferior in number. She is inferior in the army also. There are now about three million men in arms. They will be sufficient to deal with Hitler if he makes a land attack, for he can't first land his whole army and armoured units. Most probably he has not worked out his plan yet.

PURANI: Or he may be considering various possibilities that may come in his way.

SRI AUROBINDO: That doesn't matter to him. He never considers possibilities. If he gets the right inspiration, possibilities don't matter. That is how he goes against all the generals who show him various possibilities that may go against his ideas. All through he has been guided by inspiration and he has gone ahead depending on luck. Regarding France, Poland and all other countries he had set out a plan beforehand and carried it out. But regarding England nobody knows what he has. He has a most original mind, because it is not his own mind.

I can understand if he wanted to take Gibraltar first. That wouldn't be difficult; then he could go to Africa and destroy the British Empire there which would be a great stroke. Then he can turn towards Asia unless Russia comes in the way. The British island can then remain as it is. Of course it will still have its navy. But Germany is a land power.

EVENING

The second volume of The Life Divine *(in two parts) has come out. The two volumes are very big in size. Sri Aurobindo said they were like two elephants. We were discussing the price (Rs. 16) which seemed too high. Especially Satyendra asked how the money was to be got. He said some people (meaning himself) had deposited the money in advance and had withdrawn it.*

SRI AUROBINDO: Well, after all, the publishers try to solve all the problems of existence. (*Laughter*)

SATYENDRA: That they do both internally and externally; they are very sound in every way. I was, in fact, wishing for this book to come out. Nirod has not finished the first volume yet.

SRI AUROBINDO (*laughing*): By the time you finish the three volumes, you will become a philosopher. (*Laughter*)

NIRODBARAN: I doubt it.

SATYENDRA: It doesn't follow.

SRI AUROBINDO: No?

NIRODBARAN: Some say Part I of Volume II is the most difficult.

SRI AUROBINDO: The psychological and metaphysical chapters may be difficult.

NIRODBARAN: What has the sale been like in America?

SRI AUROBINDO: There were some orders from America, but there are no books available. Biswanath couldn't send any.

SATYENDRA: Now they are busy with something else and can't take any interest in *The Life Divine*.

SRI AUROBINDO: Yes, busy with bombs.

17 JULY 1940

SRI AUROBINDO (*smiling and addressing Purani*): Hitler's hope of a triumphal march into England is diminishing day by day.

PURANI: Yes, there is yet no sign of any preparation to attack.

SRI AUROBINDO: I see only two ways possible – either landing troops in spite of the British navy or an attack by air. No other way seems possible.

NIRODBARAN: Could it not be a bluff, for an attack somewhere else?

SRI AUROBINDO: That is another matter.

NIRODBARAN: If Gandhi's proposal to Britain to offer only passive resistance had been accepted, perhaps Hitler's hope would have been fulfilled. (*Laughter*)

SRI AUROBINDO: Yes. They appreciated his proposal but couldn't consider it.

PURANI: Churchill has made a very fine speech.

SRI AUROBINDO: Yes, he was inspired.

PURANI: Exact, precise and summing up the situation very well.

NIRODBARAN: But he takes good care not to say a word about India – all Europe, the continent, America come into it. Half of the speech was devoted to France.

SRI AUROBINDO: He has been always a lover of France.

SATYENDRA: To what a pass England has come to declare the battle at Oran a great naval success!

SRI AUROBINDO: Success? No, it was to prove the decisiveness of the British and their readiness to fight to the last. Otherwise it was no battle.

SATYENDRA: England has now found a leader. If she is defeated it will be due to her position and karma.

SRI AUROBINDO: Yes. If she had declared Dominion Status to India, then a large part of her karma would have been wiped off.

SATYENDRA: That was also what Gandhi's moral support meant.

SRI AUROBINDO: No, moral support is quite different.

PURANI: The *Statesman*, whose editor is Moore, has again written for Dominion Status, and in the *Hindu* also some Briton wrote of it yesterday.

SRI AUROBINDO: They are only individuals. If Amery were strong and firm against the Simla attitude, then he could do something. Till now he hasn't said anything against the granting of Dominion Status.

PURANI: If English opinion also turned in our favour?

SRI AUROBINDO: No, English opinion won't do. It is the opinion of the House of Commons and that of the Conservatives that matter. Some of the Conservatives are in favour of it but it must be the majority and I think the majority doesn't want any drastic change. The majority are under Chamberlain. I am almost sure they are standing in the way; otherwise, with the Labour pressure and with the Liberals also joining, something would have been done. Of course they have some trouble over Jinnah. They don't want to create any trouble among the Muslims just now.

PURANI: He has been put up by the Government.

SRI AUROBINDO: I don't think so. Wherever it suits him, he goes against the Viceroy. I think he has put up himself.

SATYENDRA: He has taken up an impossible attitude. There is no chance of any agreement.

SRI AUROBINDO: Unless on such terms as the Khilafat and whatever other demands they make.

NIRODBARAN: Or Pakistan. India's karma is also standing in the way. So many years' slavery hasn't wiped off the karma.

SRI AUROBINDO: Slavery doesn't wipe off the karma.

SATYENDRA: Slavery associated with suffering.

SRI AUROBINDO: Provided you learn from suffering. (*Laughter*)

SATYENDRA: That is a different matter.

PURANI: Jinnah is a sort of dictator. He wants to be obeyed in everything and he would discard no means for his aim.

SRI AUROBINDO: In that case it would be bad for Huque and Sikandar. (*After a while*) If the Hindus consent to accept Jinnah as their Badshah, then he may agree. He will say, "Oh the cause of the Hindus is so dear to my heart!" (*Laughter*)

SATYENDRA: And Jinnah is demanding fifty-fifty representation.

SRI AUROBINDO: Yes, soon he will say that the pressure exerted by the Hindu fifty is too much for Muslims and will claim another twenty-five out of the fifty.

SATYENDRA: How?

SRI AUROBINDO: Why not? I think Sir Akbar's son is also standing in the way. He has some influence with the Viceroy.

NIRODBARAN: Which son? The one who came here?

SRI AUROBINDO: No. This one won't come here any more than he would think of going to hell. (*Laughter*)

EVENING

SATYENDRA: America is going to follow an independent policy in the East.

SRI AUROBINDO: Yes. She has no claim to make in China.

K20

PURANI: It seems according to N.S.N. that on 27th May the Japanese Army was routed by the Chinese.

SRI AUROBINDO: Who writes that?

PURANI: Some military correspondent.

SRI AUROBINDO: With the Chinese?

PURANI: Yes.

SRI AUROBINDO: Can't be believed! The Japanese claim that only eighty thousand Japanese have been killed so far, while the Chinese make it out to be half a million. Evidently neither number is true. Even if the Chinese estimate is true, it doesn't seem to make any difference to the war, and the Chinese are nowhere near driving out the Japanese. War is still going on. The Chinese are braggarts and the Japanese follow a silent policy till the whole thing is done.

PURANI: After the resignation of the Japanese Cabinet, it is probable that Prince Konoye will be the Premier. He doesn't know what will be the policy, Fascist or otherwise. If Fascist, the Japanese may line up with the Axis.

SRI AUROBINDO: If they do that, they will be bound to the Axis and later on Italy and Germany may want to enter in the East, which the Japanese won't like and which is against their policy. Japan's aim is to turn all the Europeans out of Asia. So if she joins the Axis it will be only to suit her present position and purpose.

(*After a while*) I don't want the Japanese to go down in the fight against the Chinese because they may be needed as a counter-balance against Germany or Russia when, in case England goes down, they try to come to Asia. That is the only chance for India. While they fight each other, India can prepare herself, provided people like Jinnah and Bose are not there.

NIRODBARAN: But if England goes down, Japan may herself grab India.

SRI AUROBINDO: She may. But out of the three evils, she may be the best and I don't think she will annex India. She may start some Government as in Manchuria. The Chinese can't be relied on to fight against Russia or Germany. Everyone knows that Italy has her eye on Asia Minor and that Germany wants to get into Baghdad. Japan won't like that. She won't like the "barbarians" taking possession of Asia.

NIRODBARAN: Roosevelt is standing for election after all.

SRI AUROBINDO: Yes, of course, he was manoeuvering all the time.

18 JULY 1940

SATYENDRA: Tomorrow Germany is going to attack England.
SRI AUROBINDO: Yes, tomorrow night and finish it in a week. On the 26th the preparation and on the 27th the triumphal entry into London.
PURANI: But there is no sign yet anywhere of the attack. Nolini was saying that just as Napoleon was scratching his head at Boulogne thinking about how to invade England, Hitler also must be doing the same. (*Laughter*)
SRI AUROBINDO: During the reign of King Harold, the last invader crossed over to England.
NIRODBARAN (*after a pause*): Huque has paid a high tribute to Bose.
SRI AUROBINDO (*laughing*): Yes. With tears in his eyes he had to arrest him.
PURANI: What has he said?
NIRODBARAN: That Bose is the most lovable person in Bengal politics, reputable, admired, revered, etc.
PURANI: He is trying to humour him so as to have a smooth time when he is released.
SRI AUROBINDO: I think everything was ready for the monument to be removed when Bose started the agitation. All the parties have agreed, Europeans and others, to have it removed.
PURANI: He found an easy way of combining the Hindus and the Muslims. Now the women are also starting Satyagraha on the men.
SRI AUROBINDO: On the men? What for?
NIRODBARAN: For equal rights. (*Laughter*) Hamida Begum said this at some conference of women.
SRI AUROBINDO: No cooking, no conjugal rights and no housekeeping? Is that the programme?
SATYENDRA: That is secret yet. They don't let out their strategic moves.
NIRODBARAN: That's all they can do.
SRI AUROBINDO: All? That is a great deal.
PURANI: Men will start cooking.
SRI AUROBINDO: But they may upset the whole thing. An irruption of women suffragists may invade and upset everything. (*Laughter*) But after they get their rights, they should combine and

fight Hitler because wherever he goes, he deprives women of their rights.

PURANI: The Fascist slogan is back to the family.

SRI AUROBINDO: That is the Fascist and Nazi and now the French slogan – *Famille*. Women will have no other duties except the household one.

EVENING

SRI AUROBINDO (*in a grave tone*): We have lost eighty-seven crores of rupees due to the collapse of the Bank of France. (*Seeing us all agape*) That is why we are dismissing many servants. (*Laughter*)

PURANI: I was wondering why it was eighty-seven.

SRI AUROBINDO: And neither has the Bank of France collapsed. Today Dyuman heard people talking in the bazaar – "Ashram, Ashram!" When he enquired what it was about, he came to know that this was the news they were discussing. It is the bazaar radio!

SATYENDRA: They have very big ideas about our wealth and think we are very rich.

SRI AUROBINDO: Yes, the underground of our new Secretariat is supposed to contain an immense mass of gold, and formerly some British police thought it was a fortress we were building!

19 JULY 1940

PURANI: Hitler has called the Reichstag and is delivering a speech.

SRI AUROBINDO: Instead of a triumphal entry, a triumphal speech?

PURANI: He is going to offer peace to Britain.

SRI AUROBINDO: He knows Britain won't accept. Why then does he offer it?

SATYENDRA: To keep a historical record that he was a peace-loving man. (*Laughter*) He is creating a New World Order and becoming a protector of small nations, taking them under his protection without any loss of their honour and prestige.

SRI AUROBINDO: They are rather being kicked into the New World Order.

SATYENDRA: Anyhow our India is joining the international federation. The Women's Mission is going to China. The Nehru family will be represented.

SRI AUROBINDO: Without the Nehru family there can't be anything international. (*Laughter*)

SATYENDRA: Vijayalakshmi is the President.

SRI AUROBINDO: They can send Nehru as the head of the delegation. (*Laughter*)

SATYENDRA: No, Begum Hamida won't like a mere man being put at the head of the ladies.

SRI AUROBINDO: Which one was Hamida in yesterday's photo?

SATYENDRA: The one on the right. On the left was Amrita Kaur. She doesn't look so terrible.

SRI AUROBINDO: As in her speech? No, she looks quite matronly and amiable. Whose Begum is she? Or who is her Nawab?

PURANI: I think an I.C.S. man called Hamid.

SRI AUROBINDO: And she is Hamida? Just as Hindu names have Dev and Devi.

Then followed talk about censorship, for all our letters were now being censored.

SRI AUROBINDO: Even insured letters are being censored. It is better that it is being done by some special body instead of by the police. By the way, is Jaswant in prison now?

PURANI: Yes, in B class, very happy, gets books to read and is carefully looked after, he writes.

SRI AUROBINDO: By the Imperial Government? (*Laughter*)

PURANI: Yes.

SRI AUROBINDO: Then they haven't started killing the communists yet? It is lucky he is in prison, otherwise he would have sent all sorts of communist pamphlets here. For how long has he been sentenced?

PURANI: It is under the Defence of India Act. Simply interned.

SRI AUROBINDO: That is for the duration of the war? That means from five months to fifty years. (*Laughter*) Some people say that the war will last fifty years.

PURANI: Then Churchill and Hitler will be no more.

SRI AUROBINDO: No, it will become a normal condition of life. From this occasional bombing and no serious damage, it is not unnatural to suppose that the war will last fifty years.

PURANI: I don't think the present R. A. F. bombing of Germany will affect it materially very much.

SRI AUROBINDO: If it can destroy the industrial cities then it will.

EVENING

SRI AUROBINDO: The original date to attack England seems to have been last Monday. So they have changed the date now.

PURANI: Oh, was the talk in Turkey about that?

SRI AUROBINDO: Yes, Hitler's dates regarding France and other countries proved to be true.

PURANI: That shows they were all planned in cooperation with the people inside.

SATYENDRA: There is a Peshawar prophecy that Hitler's decline will begin from 27th July and that he will try to commit suicide on the 9th of August.

SRI AUROBINDO: For failing to enter into England in triumphal march?

SATYENDRA: But such an easy misfortune is not for him; he won't die like that.

SRI AUROBINDO: Oh!

NIRODBARAN: We will be quite satisfied with that.

SRI AUROBINDO: Yes, we are not vindictive. Is that the war contribution from Peshawar?

SATYENDRA: Yes.

NIRODBARAN: Franco has declared his rights over Gibraltar.

SRI AUROBINDO: Yes, this is the first time he has spoken about it publicly. (*Then addressing Purani*) You have seen some Japanese commercial man's proposal?

PURANI: No.

SRI AUROBINDO: He has gone to Europe, to Italy, for some mission or trade purpose. He is said to be an important man. He says Germany and Italy should make an axis with Japan. They will be exhausted after the war and lose all spring for action. Japan and these countries may help one another by trade agreements between East and West. Here the implication seems to be that Japan would represent the East and that the whole East would be left under Japanese influence.

After some time Purani brought in the subject of art.

PURANI: Sammer has a queer idea. He says that nowhere in Europe and India was there any popular art. Only in Russia has it come now. Communism has brought in popular art, he says.

SRI AUROBINDO: That is the stock-in-trade argument of all communists.

PURANI: I was staggered. He has no knowledge of Indian history. I told him that even today there is a village in Pondicherry where pottery is done and the village is known for it. These carvings on the wooden seat[1] of the Mother which is such a fine piece of art were done by an ordinary workman. The Mother was pleased with it.

20 JULY 1940

PURANI: Hitler has simply poured abuse on England in his speech and said the usual things. If England doesn't accept peace, she will be destroyed.

SRI AUROBINDO: How? He talks only of air attack. With aeroplanes he can, destroy a good deal no doubt, but the same can be done to Germany.

SATYENDRA: He didn't want to attack the British Empire, but now he will if the British don't accept peace. He is a man who wants to live in peace and has no territorial ambition!

SRI AUROBINDO: No, he didn't want anything outside Germany. Now there is no democracy left in Europe except in Yugoslavia. Only in Asia does democracy remain, Persia being the true democracy.

SATYENDRA: Turkey?

SRI AUROBINDO: Turkey doesn't claim to be democratic. If England didn't stand in the way Hitler would settle first with Russia, then proceed to Asia and then to India.

1 The carved divan now kept on the northern side of the upstairs meditation hall. On 21 February 1928, the Mother and Sri Aurobindo both sat on this seat and gave darshan.

SATYENDRA: Russia may not like Japan's collaboration with the Axis.

SRI AUROBINDO: Privately she won't. Japan wants to make a non-aggression pact with Russia as Germany did. But she has nothing to offer Russia while Germany gave Russia a free hand in the Baltic and half of Poland.

EVENING

SRI AUROBINDO: I have read Hitler's speech. In many respects this man is a mountebank and yet he has become so successful. Of course, it is not his success, but that of the force behind him.

NIRODBARAN: Some people in the Ashram find his speech full of reason, and according to them everything he has said is true.

SRI AUROBINDO: Everything true? Don't they read the papers? Don't they see his speech is full of misstatements and misrepresentations?

NIRODBARAN: It is true in the sense that whatever he has prophesied he has carried out. Look at Poland and Norway. And since he has succeeded everywhere else, he will succeed also against England. England will make peace.

SRI AUROBINDO: That is another matter. What about his lies about the British Expeditionary Force, which he claims he has destroyed?

NIRODBARAN: These people seem to believe Hitler more than others.

SRI AUROBINDO: And these people pretend to do Yoga? The French themselves have said that the B.E.F. was rescued – the majority of it – and people who have returned from Flanders have written to us about the evacuation. If this Asuric influence acting through Hitler is being cast on the Ashram too, it is dangerous.

PURANI: What about his seeking friendship with Britain or his love of peace? Are they all true? And because he has succeeded so far, will he succeed always? Is he omnipotent? Greater than the Divine?

SRI AUROBINDO: Omnipotent and omniveridical? Then, as he says himself, has Providence guided him and given him success? I have not seen any other person who has followed the Asura with such extraordinary fidelity. Three things of the Asura he adopts strictly: first, if you go on telling lies long enough with assurance, people will believe you; second, you must adopt treachery and appeal to the basest passions of the people; third, care only for success without regard for truth. There have been men who have done that with some pretence of truth. But Hitler speaks openly of his method of falsehood and yet people believe him.

NIRODBARAN: Except for the air attack, what else can Hitler do against England and how far will the air attack be successful?

SRI AUROBINDO: I don't know. Aeroplanes can be tremendously destructive and if the industrial areas are destroyed, it will be a great blow.

25 JULY 1940

For four days there was practically no talk. Then Bhaskar's radio news said that Germany was making intense preparations to attack England.

SRI AUROBINDO: Bhaskar doesn't give the source of his news. He says that such intense preparations are going on that the universe is moving towards destruction. (*Laughter*)

SATYENDRA: The universe? Nehru also speaks in terms of planets. The *Sunday Times* has given the news that somebody in America has discovered some submarines which can be made into tanks. There is a humorous story along with this news.

SRI AUROBINDO: That may be Germany's new weapon to attack England.

SATYENDRA: Is that an accomplished fact?

SRI AUROBINDO: It is an America-and-*Sunday Times*-accomplished fact.

Here Sri Aurobindo related the humorous episode of the tank which was much enjoyed by all.

Purani (*after some time, smilingly*): Have you read in the Sunday *Hindu* the article saying that there are Hindu tribes in Arabia?

SRI AUROBINDO (*laughing*): Yes. It is like the Tamil Christ and the Madrasi Virgin Mary.

SATYENDRA: What is that?

SRI AUROBINDO: Oh, you don't know? A Tamil scholar discovered that Christ was a Tamil belonging to Madras and he found all the equivalent Tamil names for Christ, Mary and even the streets.

PURANI: Here also this man says that Araba equals Arava, Saracen equals Surasen and Ansari equals Anusari. (*Laughter*)

SRI AUROBINDO: That was the fashion at one time. It was Colonel Todd, I think, who said that Krishna was Hercules who is also called Heracles. He derived the Greek name from Harikula. (*Laughter*)

EVENING

SRI AUROBINDO: It is now known what Bhaskar's source was for the report of the coming German attack on England. A detailed document was found in the pocket of an American reporter who had died in France. It told of the German plan to attack England from Belgian and French ports, supported by aeroplanes, smoke-screens, etc. The Germans will land at various places. In that case they may have some chance of success.

PURANI: Yes. Otherwise I don't see how it is possible. So they are putting Daladier and others on trial?

SRI AUROBINDO: Yes, that is Laval acting out of revenge. Poor Delvos is also to be tried. Laval was ousted from politics in all the ministries. His photo in the paper shows the face of a criminal. The paper says he began as an errand boy and ended as a millionaire.

PURANI: This action of his may also be to satisfy Hitler.

SRI AUROBINDO: Yes, and out of revenge and fear of these people as well.

26 JULY 1940

SATYENDRA: The Bengal Government is removing the Holwell monument after all.

SRI AUROBINDO: Yes. Huque didn't stand up in his dignity then.

Huque said that unless Satyagraha is stopped he won't do anything.

NIRODBARAN: This Islamia College incident has contributed to it, perhaps.

SRI AUROBINDO: Yes.

NIRODBARAN: Bose has got some success.

SRI AUROBINDO (*laughing*): Yes, it was all pre-arranged, only he hurried up the process of removal.

27 JULY 1940

PURANI: America has agreed to supply three thousand planes per month.

SRI AUROBINDO: Yes. In that case England will very soon match Germany in air-strength.

NIRODBARAN: Amery says the Indian situation is not serious.

SRI AUROBINDO: Because there is no chance of civil disobedience, perhaps. And Gandhi is now preparing the world for non-violence.

PURANI: But nobody accepts it.

NIRODBARAN: De Gaulle has advised passive resistance to the French people. C. R. says England may be thinking that if we were independent we wouldn't help her.

SRI AUROBINDO: Yes, they have a fear that we may do just as Ireland is doing.

PURANI: They say there is a difference of opinion among Hitler's generals regarding invasion.

SRI AUROBINDO: May be only a story. He may be trying to settle the Balkan problem first. But if it is true, it is remarkable that Keitel is against invasion. He has always been for attacking England. He is a general in name only; he knows nothing about war, he is only Hitler's mouthpiece.

EVENING

PURANI: Nolini was saying that he found this book of modern poetry very difficult to understand. How many people will read it?

SRI AUROBINDO (*smiling*): Not worth reading. I have read Eliot's Hippopotamus; it is amusing. Nowadays one reads poetry not to enjoy oneself or for pleasure, but as a duty or a task. All that these Moderns are doing is to take the most commonplace ideas and try to express them in poetry. Whatever is beautiful is to them romantic and whatever is grand is rhetoric. You should take only commonplace, mean things, express them in mean, dirty language, with very little or no rhythm – that is the recipe for modern poetry.

PURANI: The same thing is happening in art.

SRI AUROBINDO: It is an age of decadence like the Roman decadence, only in a different way. That took a thousand years to start. Now also it may take a thousand years. Hitler's threatened millennium of the New Order will be like this, probably.

28 JULY 1940

Mussolini, on his fifty-seventh birthday, has given an interview to the press reporters. He bared his upper body and said, "Am I sick? Am I old?" and then galloped around on a horse.

NIRODBARAN: Mussolini has been dramatic.

SRI AUROBINDO *(laughing)*: Yes.

PURANI: But what about his fleet? It doesn't seem to venture out.

SRI AUROBINDO: No, for fear of becoming sick. *(Laughter)*

According to a press report the size of the British Army in Africa is not sufficient. If true, it should be reinforced; otherwise if the Germans take Alexandria and the rest of Egypt, it will be bad for England. Alexandria is like Gibraltar. I suppose England has concentrated all her forces in England itself.

PURANI: Yes, the French collapse may have changed this plan.

SRI AUROBINDO: Yes.

Have you read about America's army strength in *New Statesman and Nation*? It is lamentable.

SATYENDRA: Yes, what has she been doing all these years?

SRI AUROBINDO: No wonder she is against sending any expeditionary force to Europe.

SATYENDRA: Now Japan is also threatening her.

SRI AUROBINDO: America has her navy to deal with Japan. If Hitler had a navy, then after defeating England he would have gone straight for America. The present state of America's army would have been a great opportunity for him.

29 JULY 1940

Germany has sunk a French refugee ship.

SRI AUROBINDO (*smiling*): You have seen how Hitler says Churchill has sunk the French ship.

PURANI: Does he say that?

SRI AUROBINDO: Yes. The *Daily Herald* has a report, perhaps true, about Germany inventing the story that England is going to invade France and Germany will come in as a saviour. (*Laughter*)

PURANI: Hitler wants all the world to believe this!

NIRODBARAN: Probably it is meant for home consumption.

PURANI: He is making Brittany an autonomous state, it appears.

SRI AUROBINDO: Yes. If reports are true, he intends to take back Alsace-Lorraine and make a kingdom of Flanders with Northern France included in it. Perhaps Italy will take Savoy, Nice and Corsica.

NIRODBARAN: Mussolini is stretching his arm to Palestine too.

SRI AUROBINDO: Yes, and he wants to drive out the Jews en masse.

SATYENDRA: Poor Jews! They have been cursed through the ages, driven out from everywhere

NIRODBARAN: Why is it so?

SRI AUROBINDO: Firstly, they have always tried to keep their individuality and, secondly, everywhere, by their cleverness, they have come to the top in all the professions and have created envy among others.

30 JULY 1940

SRI AUROBINDO (*starting the talk*): So Hitler has changed the date to September 15th.

PURANI: Yes. He doesn't know what to do and the Balkan problem is also engaging him.

SRI AUROBINDO: He must have relied on the French fleet surrendering to him. If he had attacked at once there might have been some chance of success.

PURANI: Yes, time has been on England's side. She has prepared herself and learnt her lessons. If the French had not surrendered, they could very well have carried on the war from their colonies. They still had a sufficiently big army and their navy was substantial. They could have at least taken hold of the Italian possessions in Africa.

SRI AUROBINDO: Yes, and it would have been a great gain.

EVENING

PURANI: There is a rumour in the *Cercle*[1] that Mandel is going to be shot.

SRI AUROBINDO: Ah! If they begin shooting people, how will it all end? But on what charge?

PURANI: On the charge of entering into some secret agreement with England.

SRI AUROBINDO: But England was not an enemy. If it was for overthrowing the Pétain Government I could understand. No, it must be out of revenge. During his ministership he imprisoned many Fascists.

PURANI: In this way the revolution may be quicker.

SRI AUROBINDO: Yes, but people everywhere are tame and timid now. The Socialists and Democrats have no ardour like the Nazis and Communists. The Poles seem to be the only brave people: they are still continuing a guerilla war; they have not yet caved in. The Finns were also doing well but as soon as defeat began they caved in.

SATYENDRA: Where is Colonel Beck?

SRI AUROBINDO: He is in Rumania. Rumania's Government does not allow him to go to England. It is just as well, because he would clash with the Polish Government there and make a lot of mistakes.

NIRODBARAN: Rajagopalachari says the English are a desirable lot.

SRI AUROBINDO (*laughing*): Yes, he has seen what others are like.

NIRODBARAN: And he says England gives way to public pressure.

SRI AUROBINDO: That is true.

---

1 The French club in Pondicherry.

31 JULY 1940

The Hindu *published the information that the Mother and Sri Aurobindo have given Rs. 1000 to the Allied war fund.*

SATYENDRA: It is good Jaswant is in prison. Otherwise he would have sent another letter.

SRI AUROBINDO (*laughing*): Yes.

PURANI: I had a letter from his brother. He is very happy in jail, he says. Put in B class.

SRI AUROBINDO: Like Oswald Mosley?

PURANI: They had fixed his marriage but due to his imprisonment they had to drop it.

SRI AUROBINDO: Why? They couldn't arrange it in jail?

PURANI: Russia has demanded the return of her trucks from Rumania.

SRI AUROBINDO (*smiling*): Yes. She seems to be looking for an excuse for a quarrel.

PURANI: Rumania has given no reply and is perhaps turning to Hitler.

SRI AUROBINDO: Hitler will say he is not going to fight Russia over some trucks. He will advise her to settle the affair.

NIRODBARAN: As in the case of Hungary, Bulgaria, etc.? If Rumania concedes to all of them, very little of her will remain.

SRI AUROBINDO: Yes, and she will be so light that she won't weigh on the Axis.

PURANI: Mandel, Reynaud, Gamelin, etc. are going to be tried, it seems.

SRI AUROBINDO: Gamelin for insufficient preparation. In that case Pétain is also to blame. He was Minister of Defence for so many years and he has done nothing. Mandel and others have been betrayed by Nogues. It seems he invited them to Africa to fight from there against Germany and then betrayed them to Pétain. It was very unwise of them to have gone there. This De Gaulle is a remarkable man. He foresaw all these things and knew what was in store for him and left for England beforehand.

SRI AUROBINDO (*after some time*): This book on modern poetry by F. R. Leavis is very heavy reading.

PURANI: Nolini also said that. He couldn't make anything out of it. The author says that the reading public of poetry is getting very small.

SRI AUROBINDO: Yes, and he says it is a very good thing. (*Laughter*)

PURANI: But the number of poets is increasing, he says, and many have talents. But the talent depends on what use society will make of it.

SRI AUROBINDO (*laughing*): Obviously!

PURANI: You have seen at the end of the book what he says about the sale of poetry books?

SRI AUROBINDO: No.

PURANI: He has quoted a publisher's statement – very revealing. The publisher says that out of many books published, some – about one dozen – brought twelve pounds altogether from the sale and, as for the rest, he lost almost double the sum.

SRI AUROBINDO: You know what an English publisher said when my poems were presented to him by somebody for publication? He said they were very striking but nobody would buy them, as no one read poetry now. He added, "Let the poet write some prose first and make a name and then his poetry may sell."

NIRODBARAN: No wonder people won't read poetry after what the Modernists have done with it.

PURANI: It is the same thing in painting too. I remember how François and Agnes used to cudgel their brains to find out the significance of some bizarre, grotesque pictures.

SRI AUROBINDO: Perhaps it was meant only as a joke and no meaning was there. You know the origin of Cubism? Mother used to go among the artists. One day she found that two artists as a joke had made some queer figures but people began to find great originality in them and praise them. Then they took it up seriously. There was a postman who painted a green cow grazing on red grass. People began to remark: "How original! How striking!" and now he is an outstanding painter. I forget his name. (*Laughter*)

EVENING

NIRODBARAN: This arrest of a well-known Englishman in Japan on an espionage charge looks fishy.

SRI AUROBINDO: Very fishy. The Japanese are showing themselves as masters and want others to submit. For espionage the British give regular training; they don't employ well-known people in that business.

NIRODBARAN: And the death of Knox also is not very convincing. How could he get through the resistance of the gendarmes? As Mother said, the Japanese themselves may have got rid of him to cover up some crime of their own.

SRI AUROBINDO: No, the manner of death is not convincing. The Japanese are becoming bullies now. It is the new spirit of the Nazis and Fascists they have got from the West.

NIRODBARAN: But I don't think an Englishman would have done what they say.

SRI AUROBINDO: No, not a high-class Englishman. The English and Americans are very haughty and disdainful; they haven't understood the Japanese as, for instance, people like Lafcadio Hearn did. And they are now being paid back.

NIRODBARAN: The English in India have, of course, done worse things.

SRI AUROBINDO: Oh yes, in the colonies they are quite different. All other Powers except the French treat their subject races alike.

NIRODBARAN: But just when England is involved Japan is taking these steps.

SRI AUROBINDO: People show themselves in their true colours in times of danger.

Purani (*after some time*): Have you seen the *Masnavi* by Jalaluddin Rumi? A professor from Hyderabad reviewing your *Life Divine* says that all you've said in it about evolution and descent has already been said by Rumi.

SRI AUROBINDO: I have glanced at the *Masnavi*. Yes, Rumi does speak of evolution but it is an individual evolution. Surprisingly he does not mention rebirth. If he admits individual evolution he has to admit rebirth. An individual can't evolve in one birth only.

PURANI: Sufis do admit rebirth, I think, in a way.

SRI AUROBINDO: Oh, do they? Rumi speaks of transmigration which is quite a different matter – taking different bodies, animals, birds, etc. Transmigration would bar entrance to other worlds. It would be an immediate process.

K21

1 AUGUST 1940

SRI AUROBINDO: Hitler wants peace not in Rumania only but all over the world.

Purani (*laughing*): Yes, he has already said he does not understand why the war should go on.

SRI AUROBINDO: He would say, "Now that I have won, why should it?"

NIRODBARAN: The newspaper says there is a great concentration of troops along the French Channel coast to attack England.

SRI AUROBINDO: Troops? Not ships? A concentration of ships is required.

PURANI: Perhaps they will swim across with swimming belts and allow themselves to be arrested.

SRI AUROBINDO: Swimming parties can't be arrested.

This man Leavis is less partial to Ezra Pound than to Eliot. He says Pound's earlier poems are a preparation for later ones which have rhythm, form, etc., but have no substance. Have you found any wonderful rhythm?

PURANI: None. Isn't that poem "O Apollo...tinwreath" by him? Nolini said tin-wreath is wonderful! (*Laughter*)

SRI AUROBINDO: Yes, it is in Greek tina; most idiotic it is. And he says it is a great pun; not a pun but most idiotic.

PURANI: I told you Amal's joke that Pound is not worth the penny! (*Laughter*)

SRI AUROBINDO: Among all these people only Eliot has done something.

PURANI: Yes, though he has no form, he has substance.

SRI AUROBINDO: Yes, and rhythm and energy. No wonder that old English people can't enjoy their poetry and they call it idiotic. It is a new kind of decadence. The old decadence was intellectual. The intellect was sterilised and petrified but this is dotty and crazy.

PURANI: Yes, if "You are thinking? What are you thinking?" can be called poetry!

SRI AUROBINDO: And striking rhythm! He admits that few people read poetry. That is good, he says, for then poetry becomes more precious. It is like Einstein's theory; only five or six people understand it.

PURANI: And they also differ among themselves.

Evening

PURANI: Westerners say that ancient Indian art is religious and spiritual.

SRI AUROBINDO: That is because only these types still exist. There was also secular art which has been destroyed.

PURANI: And Indian art is not so much aesthetic as expressing some religious emotion – the artists wanted more to express these emotions and feelings than to make the work a piece of art or aesthetic. And if they became art, it was in spite of themselves.

SRI AUROBINDO: Nonsense. If art is not aesthetic, it is not art. Indians have no aesthetic sense, they mean to say? What about the Indian idea of *rasa*?

PURANI: Coomaraswamy says all art must pass through the intellect in order to be real art. The Modernist conception also is like that to a certain extent.

SRI AUROBINDO: What the Modernists aim at is to make their sensations pass through the intellect, sensations in place of emotions. Sensations not only of the vital but the physical too. As they say, Hopkins's poetry must be heard not only through the ear but through the body. And it is these sensations modern poets are labouring to express through their poems.

2 AUGUST 1940

PURANI: Have you read the review of a book on Russia in the last *Manchester Guardian*? It says that some Englishmen who worked in Russia think that an alliance between Russia and England is not possible; it is possible between Russia and Germany. Between themselves they have divided their spheres. Hitler is to take the West and Stalin the East.

SRI AUROBINDO: I suspected some such thing. So India is to fall under Stalin? Only, Indians don't yet realise it. But though Hitler may allow it for now, he may turn against Stalin afterwards.

NIRODBARAN: So India will be treated with another subjugation by Russia? Communists, of course, won't call it an aggression.

SRI AUROBINDO: No, they have no national sense.

PURANI: Besides, they will have favourable positions under Stalin.

SRI AUROBINDO: Our condition will be worse, even worse than under Germany. But Russia will have to face Japan before Stalin comes to India. It is Japan's firm, agelong aim to drive out all Europeans from Asia. She considers herself as holding and guarding the destiny of Asia. This aim is stronger than her own imperialism.

NIRODBARAN: Japan has already given a hint of her aim – she wants to link China, Indo-China and the Dutch East Indies.

SRI AUROBINDO: Even before that, she had the same rooted aim. Mother's friends who were prominent people hold that idea and for that reason they have been protecting Indian refugees. The leader of the Black Dragon first developed the idea and Okakura too had it. China can't be expected to have that mission. She is more self-regarding and international.

PURANI: Yes, she won't mind taking European help for her purpose.

SRI AUROBINDO: Only the Japanese have lost their clear mind and high vision by Western contact, and their soldiers also are not what they were.

NIRODBARAN: The Western races know Japan's aim very well and they call it the yellow peril.

SRI AUROBINDO: Yes, and theirs is the white peril, which Japan knows.

NIRODBARAN: The Supermind ought to descend now; the conditions are getting very bad with Hitler and Stalin threatening everybody.

SRI AUROBINDO: The Supermind is not concerned with these things.

PURANI: Nirod is surprised to find that the Supermind goes by different values and he doesn't like it.

SATYENDRA: If it had not different values, it would not be worthwhile.

SRI AUROBINDO: Quite so.

NIRODBARAN: We are hoping the 15th will come soon so that the descent on that day will act as a check against Hitler.

SRI AUROBINDO (*smiling*): According to the rather discredited astrologers the 3rd, tomorrow, is the date of his death.

SATYENDRA: It has been estimated that about two and a half crores of rupees will be required to equip one division.

SRI AUROBINDO: Then forty such divisions will be necessary against Hitler or Stalin.

PURANI: The Pétain Government has declared that French pilots fighting for England will be shot if they land in French territory while the English will be taken prisoners.

SRI AUROBINDO: So it means France is at war with England.

PURANI: Practically.

3 AUGUST 1940

To a letter of Dilip's regarding the present world condition, Krishnaprem wrote a reply which was read by Sri Aurobindo.

SATYENDRA: Krishnaprem quotes the Gita's, "By Me these have been slain" and says, "The war has already been fought and won," by which he means action in the subtle worlds.

SRI AUROBINDO: Yes, of course, it is there that things first happen. They are decided in the higher worlds before they are projected here.

NIRODBARAN: So what happens here will be the result of the decisions and actions above?

SRI AUROBINDO: Yes, but what happens here doesn't always take place exactly in the same way. There are variations, and the decisions also can be changed. When there is a struggle of forces it is always possible to change the balance of forces and thus alter the decision. But there can be variations only in what has been decided by the Supreme Vision.

For instance, there are forces which are trying to destroy the British and their Empire – forces above and here in this world – I mean the inner forces. I myself wished for the Empire's destruction but at that time I didn't know certain other forces would arise. These forces are working for the evolution of a New World Order which is bound to come. But for this new arrangement the British Empire need not be destroyed. It can be achieved in quite a different manner by a change in the balance of different forces, more quietly and without much destruction. Were it not for Hitler I wouldn't have cared whether the British Empire remained or went down. Now the question is whether this New Order is to come after much suffering and destruction or with as little suffering as possible. The destruction of England would mean the victory of Hitler and in that case, perhaps after a great deal of suffering and through various difficult reactions on the part of men to Hitlerite oppression, the New Order will come or it may not come at all or come only after Pralaya! Of course the issue has been decided by the Divine Vision and there can be no change in that. But nobody knows what it is.

Krishnaprem puts it in a rather absolute way which I don't think is true. He doesn't give sufficient importance to the material world. If everything is fixed and whatever happens is, as he says, according to the decisions above, then this world would be only an illusion. He says that by a psychic change, the New World Order can be brought about. Psychic change is useful only for much higher spiritual purposes. Even so, it is possible only in a small number of people, and how can that alter the world? Besides, for changing the World Order the psychic change is not necessary, it can be done by a change in the balance of forces.

NIRODBARAN: That balance will follow by the psychic change?

SRI AUROBINDO: Yes, but is the psychic change possible for the whole world? By psychic I suppose he means the mental and vital changes. I don't know how even these are to come about if Hitler wins and if everybody is busy taking refuge in cowardice and trying to save their own skin.

NIRODBARAN: You said that what is decided above takes place here with a certain variation. Is that variation the process and method of working things out?

SRI AUROBINDO: No, even the whole decision may be changed, as I said.

NIRODBARAN: Can the Vision of the Supreme be different from the decision of these higher worlds?

SRI AUROBINDO: Why not? There can be a variation of the play of forces in the different planes. The play of forces may appear as if the destiny were in favour of one or another group of forces and that they were the makers of destiny. There are different layers of destiny, so to say. When one is born one comes with a physical destiny, then there is the vital and mental destiny. By bringing in vital and mental forces the physical destiny can be changed. It is the mental destiny that is difficult to change. The astrologers are usually concerned with the physical destiny. They don't see the others and hence make mistakes because they look at the physical graph of things. Only the Supreme Vision can't be changed.

NIRODBARAN: What is the Supreme Vision?

SRI AUROBINDO: Nobody knows.

NIRODBARAN: Not nobody; you must know, and as you said just now the New World Order is bound to come, that must be the Supreme Vision?

PURANI: But at present before the Supreme has a chance there are many others who are already busy with their own idea of the New World.

NIRODBARAN: To the supramental vision the Supreme Vision must be known.

SRI AUROBINDO: Yes, but I haven't yet become the Supermind and no one knows whether the Supermind will descend.[1]

NIRODBARAN: How is that? You have already said it is bound to descend.

SRI AUROBINDO (*laughing*): But I didn't fix a date – whether it will be tomorrow or not.

NIRODBARAN: The Mother seems to have said that the Divine Descent will take place when everything will be dark with not a ray of hope anywhere.

SRI AUROBINDO: That was the ancient prophecy she repeated.

PURANI: I suppose the world is sufficiently dark already. England alone stands in the way of Hitler's triumph.

SRI AUROBINDO: Have you not read the Mother's prayer this year?[2]

NIRODBARAN: I have.

SRI AUROBINDO: Those who received it in France are already realising what it means.

EVENING

NIRODBARAN: I couldn't quite follow Krishnaprem when he said that this war is not a real war. His words are: "It is the troubled wake of a ship that has passed, the trail of a snail, the dead ash of a forest fire," etc.

---

1 What is perhaps meant – as we suspect from other pronouncements of Sri Aurobindo and from the Mother's statements – is that *bodily* Sri Aurobindo had not yet become the Supermind. In other words, the final plenary stage of supra-mentalisation – the total transformation of the body by the Supermind's descending power – had still not been reached.

2 The New Year message of 1940: "A year of silence and expectation . . . Let us find, O Lord, our entire support in Thy Grace alone."

SRI AUROBINDO: He means the psychic past as he makes clear afterwards. All Karma that has been done in the past has passed into the inner worlds. What is here now is only the result of it. It is a one-sided view of the matter. Of course he takes the psychic in another sense than ours as he speaks of the world-psyche.

PURANI: He takes his stand on the Buddhistic Karma theory.

SRI AUROBINDO: Yes. His contention that everything is fixed reduces this world to Maya. Even the result of the psychic past belonged once to the material world before it passed away into the subtle. And the material can always modify the result. He himself admits that in the case of Hitler he could reject the influence. So can others. It is the same as in Yoga. If you accept the influence, it will then try to throw its formations on you and come true in the material plane. There also the manner of acceptance makes a difference. If you accept it in one way, a certain result comes; you accept it in another, then there is a different result.

NIRODBARAN: Krishnaprem says England has some soul-purpose to manifest.

SRI AUROBINDO: He puts a big *if* and says that if it is so England will win.

SATYENDRA: Yes, he says that every drop of his blood says this. His English blood!

SRI AUROBINDO: Yes, in spite of his being a Sannyasi, his blood is English. At this moment all Englishmen will feel like that. Even Arjava who cavilled at the English would have felt so. By soul-purpose Krishnaprem means perhaps some higher values. But standing for higher values doesn't make for victory. Look at Poland and Czechoslovakia. Perhaps you may say Poland made many mistakes, but wasn't Czechoslovakia absolutely blameless?

SATYENDRA: Japan has now openly declared her aim and policy toward Indo-China, the Dutch East Indies and the South Sea Islands.

SRI AUROBINDO: Yes, but let China be settled first, though there is no sign of settling.

These Russians are the most brazen-faced people. Have you seen Molotov's speech?

PURANI: No.

SRI AUROBINDO: He says America is trying to be imperialistic in the Western hemisphere. That is the move he sees behind the

Pan-American conference (*regarding the transfer of American territories to the Western Powers*). And Russia is going to take steps against America and England's illegal action in freezing the Baltic States' finance. What can she do against America?

NIRODBARAN: To these Russians everybody is imperialistic except themselves and their grabbing of the Baltic States is for self-protection! The world is not so foolish as to believe that.

SRI AUROBINDO: That is meant for the communists who will believe everything from Russia.

4 AUGUST 1940

SRI AUROBINDO (*addressing Purani*): The death-sentence has been passed on De Gaulle.

PURANI: Yes, and he has given a reply.

SRI AUROBINDO: Has he? What does he say?

PURANI: He says the Pétain Government is dictated to by Germany. At the end of the war he will appeal to the public to give their verdict.

Rumania is now turning away from the Axis – perhaps it wants to go to Russia.

NIRODBARAN: What is the use if Hitler divides and gives away Rumania to other powers?

SRI AUROBINDO: Rumania's claim on Transylvania is right because the majority of people there are Rumanians and they don't want to go to Hungary. Already their peasant leader is organising resistance against any such move.

PURANI: This is all due to their separate policy. If they had made the entente together, these things wouldn't have happened.

SRI AUROBINDO: No, then their entente would have been formidable. Turkey tried her best for it. Turkey, Bulgaria and Yugoslavia are fighting races; Armenia and Greece are not.

EVENING

Purani started a talk on art and on Coomaraswamy's criticism on art, saying that he had written very well.

PURANI: Coomaraswamy says the artist expresses his individuality in his art.

SRI AUROBINDO: Individuality? Who has done that? Does he mention any name? Michelangelo?

PURANI: No, he means the ego, perhaps.

SRI AUROBINDO: The ego! That is different. But an artist doesn't express his individuality. I don't think Coomaraswamy is right there. A poet may do that. If you speak of individual tendencies it is different. An artist may have theories and ideas about art but he does not express his individuality. In modern art, the artist figures much, while in old Indian art he didn't: he remained behind.

5 AUGUST 1940

PURANI: I was reading Okakura's book on Japan. He says that even if the Japanese have to be Westernised to protect their independence, they will go to that length.

SRI AUROBINDO: Being Westernised won't serve. As you say, the Western nations lost their independence.

EVENING

Champaklal and Purani standing at either extremity were making gestures at each other; Champaklal burst suddenly into laughter and Purani joined in. Sri Aurobindo looked at them. They continued to laugh.

SRI AUROBINDO: Unspoken jokes seem to be more successful.

PURANI: Champaklal was showing different poses of standing. The British have started arresting the Japanese.

SRI AUROBINDO (*laughing*): Yes, and they say it is not retaliation. Extraordinary coincidences, I suppose.

PURANI: Yes, many such coincidences are possible in this world.

SATYENDRA: This is better than wordy warfare.

PURANI: The Bengal Government is taking many communal measures. The Hindus should organise.

NIRODBARAN: They held a protest day on the 4th.

SRI AUROBINDO: Mere protest won't do anything.

NIRODBARAN: Shyama Prasad is the only figure now who says other measures have to be taken.

6 AUGUST 1940

PURANI: The Viceroy has issued an ordinance banning all volunteer organisations – political or communal. Only for social service can an organisation be retained, sanctioned by the provincial Government.

SRI AUROBINDO: I see. That would give an occasion for starting civil disobedience.

PURANI: Yes. One good thing is that the Khaksars will go – all the other organisations too: Hindu Sabha, Mahavir Dal, etc.

NIRODBARAN: Gandhi will issue another threatening statement. But the Government may be taking advance measures to stop any civil disobedience movement.

SATYENDRA: That won't prevent Gandhi. If he issues a call, people will join.

SRI AUROBINDO: How can that be possible without organisation?

SATYENDRA: During the Dandee march it happened automatically.

SRI AUROBINDO: But he admitted there were many mistakes. Of course he says he will start the civil disobedience in his own way. Nobody knows what that way is.

PURANI: The Viceroy says that in any such private organisation one man gets more power than he is legally entitled to, which is not desirable. The Government has enough capacity to deal with any trouble.

SRI AUROBINDO: Has it? The Government hasn't shown it recently.

PURANI: People can join the Civil Guard, the Viceroy says.

SATYENDRA: Setalvad has declared for expanding the Council and trying for independence after the war.

SRI AUROBINDO: Trying for what?

SATYENDRA: For independence.

SRI AUROBINDO: Independence? He can try for twenty thousand years, he won't get it. He has been trying already by giving speeches, writing, etc.

PURANI: Have you read the article in the Sunday *Hindu* about the collapse of France? It says that Reynaud's speech helped to break the morale of the army.

SRI AUROBINDO: How? Churchill also said that if England fell, they would go to the Empire and fight from there. That didn't break their morale.

SATYENDRA: And his appeal to America was to avert the armistice move in the cabinet.

PURANI: He says it is a mystery that when the whole nation was against it, a small number of people could make them accept the armistice.

SRI AUROBINDO: When a small number of persons is determined to do a thing, they can do it. It has been done any number of times in history. There is no mystery there. Here especially, when there was no chance of communication with the people or the Parliament, it was quite easy. He assumes that constitutional opposition would have been possible. But how when there was no proper senate? At Bordeaux there were only fifty or sixty members and they were all Laval's men. Lebrun played into the hands of these people.

PURANI: Mandel is said to be the natural son of Clemenceau. It may be true as is evidenced by his energy and vigour.

SRI AUROBINDO: And Weygand is said to be the illegitimate son of Leopold II, one of the most notorious kings in history. Weygand is also very rich, holding many shares of the Suez Canal. A lieutenant here, who used to attend the French cabinet meetings as a police officer, said that Mandel was the only clean and honest man. In Reynaud there was something excited and unsteady, but he was very intelligent. Outwardly his decisions were all right but one could see that inwardly he was liable to make many mistakes.

SATYENDRA: It is lucky that England has got a leader now. Nobody knows what the old Government would have done by now. The back numbers of the *New Statesman and Nation* make a very interesting study. They are still discussing the defection of Belgium. One doesn't know what they will do when they hear of Paris' fall and the Vichy Government. When one reads these back numbers one feels like a minor god who knows the after-events and is ahead of them while others are still occupied with the old events.

SRI AUROBINDO: They show how people commit mistakes in their judgment and calculation similar to what we are doing ourselves at the present time. (*Laughter*)

SATYENDRA: People chafe at these past mistakes. If they knew of their past lives life would become a burden.

SRI AUROBINDO: And yet they want to know their past.

EVENING

Radio news: The Germans are concentrating for an attack on the Channel ports and are embarking and disembarking in the Baltic.

PURANI: So it is true that the Germans are preparing.

SRI AUROBINDO: Yes. Perhaps they will attack from Holland and Belgium. The Baltic is too far away. If it is a quick stroke and cleverly done, then it is possible and it depends on where they land. The British Navy can't protect the whole coastline.

PURANI: But if after landing they can be checked successfully once, then it will break their morale. Hitherto they have thought themselves invincible.

SRI AUROBINDO: Not one check, but many checks.

PURANI: At any rate England knows all about their plan and preparation.

7 AUGUST 1940

SRI AUROBINDO: Hitler's invasion can't come off on the 10th.

PURANI: He still has three days' time. Otherwise it will break his sequence. He is preparing.

SRI AUROBINDO: I wish it had been fixed to come after the 15th; I don't want the Darshan to be disturbed.

NIRODBARAN: Hiren Dutt finds *The Life Divine* obscure and loose.

SRI AUROBINDO: Obscure to himself?

PURANI: I haven't much regard for his opinion and learning. I met him in Bombay.

SRI AUROBINDO: He has an ordinary mind and it runs in the traditional groove. When the *Arya* was being published, I think he said that he couldn't understand it.

NIRODBARAN: Yet he has made a name as a scholar.

SRI AUROBINDO: Not a very big name!

NIRODBARAN: Prashanta Mahalnavis seems to have said that *The Life Divine* is Ganja?

SRI AUROBINDO: He is a Brahmo, isn't he?

NIRODBARAN: Yes.

PURANI: He means he found it as intoxicating as Ganja?

NIRODBARAN: Oh no, Brahmos don't touch Ganja.

PURANI: He was the same man who came here with Tagore and was not allowed to accompany Tagore during his interview with you. He was very angry. I remember the story of a Brahmo. He was asked by somebody where some particular theatre was; he said he didn't know. He realised that he had told a lie and then called the man back and said, "I do know, but I won't tell you." (*Laughter*)

NIRODBARAN: That is Heramba Maitra.

SATYENDRA: I like this comment about Ganja. He means we have been smoking Ganja in solitude here.

NIRODBARAN: Oh, they think much worse than that.

PURANI: Some of these people are strictly ethical and moral.

SRI AUROBINDO: That is the Pharisee's "I am not a sinner" type.

Hiren Dutt was a clever solicitor. He was the solicitor in my case, in all my cases, I think, and he was one of the few who remained faithful after the collapse of our Movement. When the meetings were getting smaller and smaller, he was the one who was always present. Ramananda was another.

NIRODBARAN: Ramananda has now joined the Hindu Movement.

EVENING

SATYENDRA: China is also threatening Indo-China!

SRI AUROBINDO: Yes, in case they allow Japan to use any ports.

PURANI: It seems Italy has launched an attack against British Somaliland and Egypt.

SRI AUROBINDO: Yes, but not against Egypt. It is evident that the British have a very insufficient force there. I don't understand why Australian soldiers are being sent to England. They ought to have been out there.

Then Purani brought in the talk about Nandalal Bose's coming here and said that it must be due to consideration for Tagore that he has suspended his coming for this Darshan.

SRI AUROBINDO: Artists can't keep their resolutions!

8 AUGUST 1940

PURANI: The Viceroy has issued a declaration that the expansion of the Council can't be delayed any more. India will have the right to frame her own constitution as soon as possible after the war.

SRI AUROBINDO: Did he say that?

PURANI: Yes, and he has invited Abul Kalam to see him.

SRI AUROBINDO: But how is the constitution to be framed? What procedure?

PURANI: He doesn't say. It may not be a round table conference again.

SRI AUROBINDO: Will the Indian leaders be able to come to an agreement? If the Congress stands for the Constituent Assembly, Jinnah won't consent.

SATYENDRA: If the Viceroy has conceded our right to frame our own constitution, it is quite reasonable.

SRI AUROBINDO: Yes, only people don't listen to reason nowadays.

SATYENDRA: And it is a greater step than Dominion Status.

SRI AUROBINDO: Certainly.

SATYENDRA: And the expansion of the Council, that is also quite reasonable.

NIRODBARAN: But one must know what part they would play.

SRI AUROBINDO: Quite so. But the Government can't be expected to pass all authority to people who have no idea about war and no experience of it.

PURANI: But what will be the procedure for the constitution?

SRI AUROBINDO: It is better not to quarrel over that now. The Indians can decide that themselves afterwards and they ought to be able to do it if they can speak of a National Government.

SATYENDRA: On the whole it is a very good advance unless there is some catch. One must read the text first.

SRI AUROBINDO: Quite so. It depends also on what powers they give to the Council. The Viceroy ought to have seen Rajagopalachari too. Perhaps he was not in Madras during the Viceroy's stay.

SATYENDRA: Yes, Rajagopalachari is the leader now.

SRI AUROBINDO: No, Gandhi is the leader. But he doesn't want to lead and the others refuse to follow him. (*Laughter*)

PURANI: Perhaps there may be a conference of Premiers in which Rajagopalachari will be present. Now only Punjab and Bengal are left to decide. Sind also to some extent.

SRI AUROBINDO: Sind's stand is very near to that of the Congress.

PURANI: But the Princes may stand in the way. They ought to make a common cause.

SRI AUROBINDO: How can they when the Congress has intimated that they have no right to exist and that in a free India they may have no place? If the Congress had kept its claims moderate, then by an inner pressure of circumstances they would have come round. You have read C. P. Ramaswamy's speech the other day? It is a very telling speech. He says: You ask us to depend on you, but you have already spoken about our extinction in the future constitution of India. How can we acquiesce in that extinction?

By the way, the Viceroy has banned only drills with weapons and what they call para-military uniforms – any that may have a military-uniform semblance. Apart from that, organisations can exist.

NIRODBARAN: Somebody said to Charu Dutt, "You speak of the dominating influence of Sri Aurobindo over the sadhaks. How is it then that idiots living under his influence produce only third-rate works?"

SRI AUROBINDO: Has the "somebody" read Nishikanta's poems? If he also calls them third-rate, he must be an idiot himself.

NIRODBARAN: Dutt was speaking highly – as in fact all do, Dilip, etc. – of Jyoti's book *Sandhane (In Quest)*. According to Dutt she has taken a long stride from *Rakta Golap (Red Rose)*, her last book.

SRI AUROBINDO: I see!

NIRODBARAN: Dutt says *Rakta Golap* is an imitation of Tagore's poetic-prose novel *Char Adhyaya (Four Chapters)*. Only the style is very good. That is true to some extent. She gave most of her attention to style and tried to make it poetic. And *Sandhane* she wrote long ago. *Rakta Golap* was the latest.

Sri Aurobindo was amused to hear that the latest book was inferior to the previous one.

SRI AUROBINDO: What does the idiot say about it?

NIRODBARAN: He may not have read it.

SRI AUROBINDO: But can a novel be written in a poetic style?

NIRODBARAN: Tagore's is not a novel but a novelette, one may say.

SRI AUROBINDO: One can write a romance in such a style.

PURANI: Tagore is doing so many new things. They say he has written mystic poems about death after his recent serious illness – what death is like, one's feelings about it and so on.

SRI AUROBINDO: Anybody can write that out of imagination; one needn't have any experience.

NIRODBARAN: And everywhere he is talking of his approaching death.

SRI AUROBINDO: He has been dying for the last twenty years. When he came here, he spoke of it.

PURANI: Even his stories are not very good.

NIRODBARAN: Not true. He is considered one of the best story-writers.

PURANI: I mean like Chatterjee.

SRI AUROBINDO: Yes, but he is not a novelist.

NIRODBARAN: No.

PURANI: You have seen *Patrika*'s review of Nishikanta's book? While Tagore has praised his *chhanda* and *bhasha*, people call it halting and Sanskritised.

SRI AUROBINDO: Stupid review!

EVENING

Satyendra said something about the Commonwealth. Sri Aurobindo then spoke about the recent declaration of the Viceroy.

SRI AUROBINDO: The British have more of diplomacy but less of the right spirit. A great deal depends on the way things are put. This statement is most uninspiring and unconvincing. And there is a snag too. If the constitution is unacceptable to large and important sections, then the Government can't agree to it. That means that if Jinnah and the Princes don't accept it, there is no settlement.

SATYENDRA: Nehru says the Sevadal won't be dissolved. They will keep their organisation.

NIRODBARAN: With *lathi*?[1]

SATYENDRA: Why *lathi*? It is non-violent.

SRI AUROBINDO: Or is the *lathi* for others to beat them with? (*Laughter*)

PURANI: Yes, they can offer their *lathi* to the opponent and ask to be thrashed.

SATYENDRA: That would be ideal non-violence.

SRI AUROBINDO: A hundred per cent!

PURANI: Somaliland is now being attacked by the Italians.

SRI AUROBINDO: I thought they had already taken it.

NIRODBARAN: The British are retiring after inflicting heavy losses.

SRI AUROBINDO: And without any loss to themselves! Bhaskar has again put an exclamation sign. (*Laughter*) They don't seem to have any force there at all.

PURANI: Only camel corps.

SRI AUROBINDO: I don't understand their war strategy. There is no head or tail to it.

PURANI: They think if they win the war, they can take the place back.

SRI AUROBINDO: Yes, but if Egypt loses, their chances of winning the war will be jeopardised. Egypt occupies an important position.

NIRODBARAN: Shyama Prasad has given a one-month time-limit to the Bengal Government.

SRI AUROBINDO: Inspired by Bose's success? But there won't be any Muslim to join him.

NIRODBARAN: Tagore has been made an Oxford Doctor and got a Latin address.

SRI AUROBINDO: And he replied in Sanskrit. Gwayer could have spoken in Irish.

---

1 A stick or staff used for defence.

9 AUGUST 1940

SATYENDRA: Everybody is silent on the Viceroy's declaration. Jinnah, Gandhi, C. R. nobody says anything. And he is interviewing the leaders all over again. He seems to be bent on expansion of his council, but perhaps nobody will accept it except the Liberals.

NIRODBARAN: Why, Savarkar has said he will.

SRI AUROBINDO: He has given qualified assent. He said some of his demands remained unsatisfied.

SATYENDRA: Our Suren has again covered his body all over.

NIRODBARAN: In anticipation of a cold!

SRI AUROBINDO: Or expecting an anticipation.

NIRODBARAN: Today when he was doing pranam at the photo in the Reception Room in that protective attire, a visitor for Darshan was looking at him very intently. Suren ought to be removed from the gate duty. Otherwise it will give a bad impression of us.

SRI AUROBINDO: The visitor was perhaps looking with admiration and saying to himself, "This man is so sick and yet has so much devotion!"

SATYENDRA: Suren and Manibhai seem to be friendly. They were talking very cheerfully.

SRI AUROBINDO: Manibhai was talking of his health and Suren of his illness?

PURANI: The British don't seem to want to defend Somaliland. They have no forces there, only some camel corps.

NIRODBARAN: What chances has the camel corps against mechanised units?

SRI AUROBINDO: The camel corps also is mechanised, they say, or perhaps they mean the camels are mechanical?

PURANI: If they don't think Somaliland is important, what about Egypt? Italians have one-and-a-half lakh troops in Libya, while the British have only a few.

NIRODBARAN: Egypt has no forces?

SRI AUROBINDO: It has a trained army. But it is neutral.

PURANI: Will it remain neutral even when it is attacked?

SRI AUROBINDO (*laughing*): In this world of Leopold, I don't know what it will do.

NIRODBARAN: The American ambassador has said that Leopold is a prisoner in his own castle.

SRI AUROBINDO: That is to gain people's sympathy.

NIRODBARAN: Also he says that Leopold informed the British about his surrender two or three days earlier.

SRI AUROBINDO: How is that? If they had been informed, they would have taken immediate steps to withdraw their troops instead of exposing them to grave peril and there was no mention of that in the papers.

NIRODBARAN: And he says further that Leopold was compelled to surrender, seeing so much destruction and suffering and the risk of complete annihilation of his army.

SRI AUROBINDO: If he was so much moved by the suffering, he could have called the Germans in at the very outset.

NIRODBARAN: That idiot about whom Charu Dutt was speaking also said that Nolini has only an assumed depth, he is a *soi-disant* philosopher or something like it. He said something about Anilbaran too.

SRI AUROBINDO: Who is this man, I would like to know, then his depth or height could be judged. It seems he has only depth. And what is his opinion about me? Third-rate too? If my influence has produced third-rate works, my work can't be any higher.

NIRODBARAN: Charu Dutt doesn't seem to consider Nishikanta's poetry in *Alakananda* as first-class.

SRI AUROBINDO: Is he a good judge of poetry?

NIRODBARAN: I don't think so.

SRI AUROBINDO: Then his opinion has no value.

NIRODBARAN: He didn't, at first reading, understand the poems. After he had read them over and over again, they were clear to him, he said.

SRI AUROBINDO: What kind of a mind these people have, I wonder!

NIRODBARAN: They are very simple poems, except for one or two.

SRI AUROBINDO: Quite so.

NIRODBARAN: And people object to Nishikanta's poems because they are all centred on the Mother and yourself, not so much because they are spiritual or lack variety.

SRI AUROBINDO: How do they know about the Mother?

PURANI: The poems can very well be taken as addressed to the Divine Mother.

SRI AUROBINDO: Yes. Besides, all the poems are not like that – "*Garur Gadi*", for instance. He has variety too. Of course they are spiritual and mystic.

EVENING

SRI AUROBINDO (*to Purani*): Do you know anything about why Baron is being recalled from Chandernagore?

PURANI: No, I only heard that he has committed some political indiscretion.

SRI AUROBINDO: It seems that recently he invited Subhas Bose to his house and for that reason the Viceroy has asked the Governor to transfer him from there.

PURANI: How could Baron do that? And how does he know Bose?

NIRODBARAN: Probably through Dilip.

SRI AUROBINDO: These people are wonderful. It will go against the Ashram. He ought to have known about Bose's activities and the consequences of his visit.

NIRODBARAN: Japan is concentrating her navy towards Indo-China.

SRI AUROBINDO: No, not concentrating, that doesn't matter. Japan is heading towards Indo-China.

NIRODBARAN: Wants to swallow it, perhaps. Being a little hasty.

SRI AUROBINDO: How? On the contrary this is the time, when other nations are engaged elsewhere. The only thing is that the Japanese are very involved in China. Don't know how effective this move will be.

10 AUGUST 1940

PURANI: It seems that when Dilip was in Calcutta, he took Bose to Baron and introduced him. That is how they know each other.

SRI AUROBINDO: Dilip has no sense of these things at all. He thinks, "You are a good man, he is a good man, both should meet each other." (*Laughter*)

PURANI: Hitler's Blitzkrieg has got a rude shock.

SRI AUROBINDO: Yes, to lose sixty planes in one attack is something. Italy also has got a knock in Libya. She lost about sixteen.

NIRODBARAN: The British superiority in the air has now been proved. If only they can achieve equality in numbers.

SRI AUROBINDO: Yes, Hitler is superior on land only.

PURANI: Somebody from Punjab, who has come for Darshan, had a severe haemorrhage from the nose. I had to call Dr. André; he gave an injection and the bleeding stopped.

SRI AUROBINDO: These people ought to pay André.

PURANI: Yes, this man will pay. It seems he has disposed of all his property and has come to stay here permanently, but he hasn't received a favourable reply. That may have helped to cause the haemorrhage.

SRI AUROBINDO: How could he make his arrangements without permission? Was he in communication with us?

PURANI: He wrote three or four letters but got no reply. I told him that he should not have acted so hastily.

SATYENDRA: People take the silence as a test.

SRI AUROBINDO: If he took it as a test the result was rather bad, as he got a haemorrhage.

SATYENDRA: Munji has asked us to accept whatever we get from the Government and fight for more.

SRI AUROBINDO: Yes, that is Tilak's policy – accept even a quarter loaf.

EVENING

The Pétain Government has acceded to Japan's demand for naval and military bases in Indo-China; at first it was reported they would resist.

SRI AUROBINDO: That means the end of Indo-China.

PURANI: Yes.

SRI AUROBINDO: The Pétain Government must have overridden Admiral Decoux's order to fight. Why do these French admirals brandish their swords and then put them back? If they resist now, there may be some chance. Otherwise it is the end of Indo-China.

PURANI: Yes. Besides, the Chinese have announced that they will resist Japan's claim. So they can combine.

NIRODBARAN: Japan is following the Russian policy. First base, then government.

SRI AUROBINDO: Yes, change of government by the Left and then "you".

SATYENDRA: The British have quietly withdrawn their forces from Shanghai.

SRI AUROBINDO: Yes, that is more dignified.

NIRODBARAN: The Pétain Government is putting one hundred people on trial for bringing France into the war! And Mandel is the main figure.

SRI AUROBINDO: Mandel is the only man, clean and honest, who has not made money from politics. Laval and others are afraid of him. He is unpopular because of his straightforwardness.

SATYENDRA: He is a Jew. He refused to join his party with Ribbentrop when the latter proclaimed eternal friendship with France in 1937.

SRI AUROBINDO: The result of his eternal friendship is the swallowing up of a part of France.

SATYENDRA: The *Indian Express* says that the Congress ought to accept the Viceroy's offer, otherwise other people will come and take it.

SRI AUROBINDO: Quite so. M. N. Roy has also advised unconditional support to the British Government. For once he has agreed with me.

NIRODBARAN: How? You didn't mean unconditional support!

SRI AUROBINDO: They ought to have done that at the beginning as Gandhi had said. They would have got much more and British public opinion also would have swung round. Even now if they accept the Viceroy's offer, it will come to the same thing. Otherwise they will either have to start civil disobedience or keep hanging.

NIRODBARAN: You said that if the British gave Dominion Status to India, a large part of their Karma would be wiped off.

SRI AUROBINDO: Yes.

NIRODBARAN: Now they have offered it but if India doesn't accept, what will be the result to British Karma?

SRI AUROBINDO: I don't know!

PURANI: But where have they offered Dominion Status?

SRI AUROBINDO: Why, it is the same thing. They have offered "free and equal partnership in the Commonwealth". That is the same as Dominion Status. They can't call it Dominion Status because Jinnah is opposed to it and the Congress too. Where it falls short is on the question of the minorities – if the minorities don't accept it, it can't be given. There is also the question of the expansion of the council, but that could be turned into a National Government later. And the other point against the offer is where they speak of their obligation to other people. I suppose they mean the native states.

NIRODBARAN: Gandhi is against abolition of the states.

SRI AUROBINDO: But Jawaharlal and all the socialists are not. So the only thing that really stands in the way is disagreement among Indians themselves.

PURANI: Yes, and we always put the blame on the English; we don't see our own faults. If we don't come to any measure of agreement, what can they do?

SRI AUROBINDO: Quite so.

PURANI: People say the British are causing and continuing the disagreement.

SRI AUROBINDO: Nonsense. As if there were no differences in India before. If people think that after the British withdrawal, they will be united, they will find it an illusion.

11 AUGUST 1940

PURANI: It seems that behind Japan's demand for naval and military bases in Indo-China, there must be Hitler's pressure on the Pétain Government to accede to the Japanese demand.

SRI AUROBINDO: Quite possible.

PURANI: Hitler may want the Japanese to act as a check against the British and keep them engaged in the East while he carries out the invasion.

SRI AUROBINDO: Perhaps. Japan is still talking only of Indo-China, the East Indies and the South Sea Isles and not talking further than that. But she may start an attack on Singapore after settling in those places. In that way the Japanese are a remarkable people. To them the first thing comes first; they can wait for the next. Once their scheme is fixed, they can wait for years to carry it out, and when the right moment comes they strike. Japan's influence in the East is, of course, good for us. It will serve as a counterpoise against

Hitler and Stalin if England goes down and in the meantime we can prepare as much as we can unless we fly at each other's throat. We heard the other day – I don't know where – maybe on the radio, that the Kuomintang met and spoke of reducing the suffering of the people. The leaders wanted to adopt a pro-Fascist policy by lining up with Germany. That means the whole of the Far East for Japan. There was no confirmation of that news.

PURANI: Everybody is becoming pro-German now. The result of the French collapse.

SRI AUROBINDO: Yes, they think England will go down but are not quite sure. This is the first time the French Government is yielding like that – so flat and miserable. It must be very decadent.

SATYENDRA: Malaviya is doing Shanti Swastyana now.

NIRODBARAN: There was in the *New Statesman and Nation* a controversy over the efficacy of prayer. A taxi-driver said that the Belgian defection was the result of prayer.

SRI AUROBINDO: A humorous taxi-driver!

SATYENDRA: And another person said that the evacuation at Dunkirk was also the result of prayer.

NIRODBARAN: Some people here said jokingly that the Mother's gift to France was responsible for its collapse, as it came one week after the gift and they hope that England won't suffer such consequences after her gift to England.

SRI AUROBINDO: It may be said that this Channel victory (sixty German planes lost) was due to that. Others may say something else. But the real purpose of the gift was to counteract the pro-Nazi propaganda in the Ashram and in that respect it has been successful.

PURANI: Hitler's 10th August has passed and nothing has happened.

SRI AUROBINDO: Yes. The threat to Indo-China may be the event of the 10th.

EVENING

SATYENDRA: One M. P. has contributed one lakh pounds to replace the sixteen British aeroplanes lost in the last German raid. Madras has given some money for two aeroplanes – whether for training or for the air force, we don't know.

SRI AUROBINDO: The Madras squadron of one aeroplane. (*Laughter*)

NIRODBARAN: Dr. Mahendra Sircar has written to Charu Dutt that the Mother's gift to the Indian Government has surprised many in Calcutta. He wants some elucidation.

SATYENDRA: Why has Mahendra Sircar suddenly taken interest?

SRI AUROBINDO: There have been many others. Somebody has come from Calcutta to get elucidation on it. Jatin Sen Gupta protested at first when we gave ten thousand francs to France. But this gift to the Indian Government he has appreciated. But it should be plain enough: I want Hitler to be knocked down.

NIRODBARAN: I don't understand how Dr. Sircar can ask that question. Is he anti-British?

PURANI: Doesn't he know what will happen to him if Hitler comes to India?

SRI AUROBINDO: He will lose his pension or Mussolini may allow it for the sake of old times!

12 AUGUST 1940

SRI AUROBINDO (*addressing Purani*): Do you remember when Bose was arrested?

PURANI: It must have been about a month back – in July.

SRI AUROBINDO: Then how can they say that Bose met Baron on the 4th? Not only that, even after the interview Baron met the Bengal Governor and expressed his confidence in Bose. What is the matter then?

PURANI: Perhaps the Indian Government has taken steps over the head of the Bengal Government. But even so, they usually inform the local Government.

EVENING

PURANI: About Baron, perhaps Bonvain is trying to stay in tune with the Pétain Government and at the same time satisfy the British. Baron spoke openly in favour of alliance with the British in Calcutta.

SRI AUROBINDO: It seems to be a mystery. The Indian Government is refusing telegrams from the French it seems. If so, it may be a retaliation against the French for their action against the British in Syria.

Have you read Gandhi's argument in favour of Ahimsa? He says that non-violence has been in progress and that De Gaulle has now advised it to the French.

PURANI: That is because they have no other way.

SRI AUROBINDO: Gandhi admits that.

Sri Aurobindo was given Moni's article to read in reply to Meghnad Saha. Nolini Sen was much hurt by Moni's personal attack against Meghnad.

SRI AUROBINDO: I have read Moni's article — (*laughing*) it is personal all through. One can't but feel the sting there and the force. But Meghnad has also made personal attacks. So neither has any reason to complain.

PURANI: No. Moni's criticism can't be without personal attack.

13 AUGUST 1940

NIRODBARAN: Azad has refused to see the Viceroy.

SRI AUROBINDO: He has refused?

NIRODBARAN: Yes, he says that as there is no common ground, no use of any interview.

SATYENDRA: They will send a formal reply after the Working Committee meeting.

NIRODBARAN: And Nehru finds a wide gulf between the Congress demand and the Viceroy's statement.

SRI AUROBINDO: Oh Nehru! But he should have seen the Viceroy. At least Gandhi would have done that.

PURANI: No. All the same, since Kher and others are meeting the Viceroy they will know what he has to say.

SRI AUROBINDO: Where is the Viceroy now? In Hyderabad?

PURANI: Perhaps. He wants twenty crores from the Nizam, it seems.

SRI AUROBINDO: Yes, that is because the Nizam is anti-British, perhaps? So the Viceroy wants to squeeze out whatever he can before the English go down. Doesn't want to leave anything for Hitler. (*Laughter*)

NIRODBARAN: But why is the Nizam anti-British?

SRI AUROBINDO: Don't know, this is a funny world – a joke.

PURANI: Montbrun has already made a broadcast from Madras. He has now left for England to fight. He wants to be somebody and if England wins, he may be that.

SRI AUROBINDO: Yes, if England wins. But that is the risk an ambitious person has to take, and he is very ambitious.

PURANI: Dara has become double now. How fat he has grown!

SRI AUROBINDO: Is there room for that? And will his room hold him?

14 AUGUST 1940

Regarding Amery's statement, Sri Aurobindo remarked that the minority question is a black spot because it leaves the power of vetoing with them.

16 AUGUST 1940

Today's evening radio says that 144 German planes have been brought down in England – the biggest number so far.

CHAMPAKLAL: That is the result of Darshan.

SRI AUROBINDO (*laughing*): The day of Hitler's triumphal entry into England!

NIRODBARAN: It seems Anandamayee of Dacca is dead.

SRI AUROBINDO: Oh! She is dead.

NIRODBARAN: It is reported in the paper.

SRI AUROBINDO: The disciples have killed her as they tried to do with the Maharshi by giving him dyspepsia?

NIRODBARAN: They say it must be due to the Divine Will.

SRI AUROBINDO: Everything is due to the Divine Will because the Divine Will is at the back of everything. But what is the Divine Will? The Will works through various factors – forces, one's own nature, etc. The murderer also can say that behind his murder there is the Divine Will. Then his being hanged also has to be taken in that light. Lele supported his queer acts by saying they were due to the Divine Will. If everything is taken like that, what is the use of doing Yoga?

(*To Purani*) I hear that the Darshan was a very happy one.

PURANI: Yes, many people say that. Plenty of people saw you smiling.

NIRODBARAN: Dilip also said it was a very happy Darshan. But they want to know what your impression was.

SRI AUROBINDO: Oh, that! Ali looked as if he was the Nizam.

PURANI: You recognised Dutt this time?

SRI AUROBINDO: Yes, I recognised him by the old cut of his face as well as by the man behind.

17 AUGUST 1940

PURANI: Italy is trying to foment trouble in Greece.

SRI AUROBINDO: Yes, and she says it is for the sake of the Albanians. Wonderful people these!

NIRODBARAN: I asked Ajit Chakravarty his opinion about Dilip's poetry and why Dilip is not appreciated in Bengal. He says that Dilip has not been able to blend *bhava* and *bhasha*[1] together and there are many lapses in his poetry. Of course, some of his pieces are very good, but they are very few. He doesn't consider that because Dilip has cut a new line he is not popular.

SRI AUROBINDO: The reason they don't like his poetry is because it is not traditional. It is mental poetry and not emotional like Nishikanta's.

SATYENDRA (*before the topic could proceed further*): We all heard Bhishma's music last night. (*All of us expressed our appreciation of it in spite of its being only raga music.*)

SRI AUROBINDO (*after listening to us quietly, without making any remarks and then smiling*): Unlike the other arts, music doesn't seem to have been modernised. There is no room for Cubism in music.

EVENING

Some friend has written to Purani that as he thinks everything is happening according to the Divine Will, there is no such thing as right or wrong.

---

1 *bhava*: mood, sentiment; *bhasha*: speech, words.

SRI AUROBINDO: Does he actually feel or perceive it or is it only a mental conception?

PURANI: Can't say. Looks as though he perceives it.

SRI AUROBINDO: What he may perceive may be the Cosmic Force. But what we seek is something higher than the Cosmic Force. One may say that the Cosmic Force is also the Divine Force or the Mother's Force. True, but the Mother's Force is acting through it under certain conditions for a certain purpose. The Cosmic Force works through Nature, which one has to observe and reject. Then it is not the question of right or wrong that has to be considered, but of Ignorance and Knowledge. The Cosmic Force works in Ignorance according to the Laws of Ignorance, whereas one has to pass from Ignorance to Knowledge.

18 AUGUST 1940

NIRODBARAN: Some time ago a long controversy was going on in Bengal regarding the place of *katha* in music: whether *katha* is greater or *sur*.[1] Though we know nothing of musical technique, we liked Bhishma's music so much that *katha* didn't seem at all necessary. Pure *sur* seems to have as much appeal.

SRI AUROBINDO: Pure music need not have any words. If words are there, they are an addition. They are not absolutely necessary. (*Sri Aurobindo repeated this twice for emphasis.*) If you say you can't have pure music without words, you can also say you can't paint a subject which is not literary.

NIRODBARAN: Tagore places a great value on words and he has developed his new Bengali music with importance given to *katha* and his own particular *sur* which nobody is allowed to vary.

SRI AUROBINDO: Is Tagore a musician?

NIRODBARAN: If I am right, Dilip also agrees with Tagore about the value of words and their place in music.

SRI AUROBINDO: Does he? That means then that he is a singer and not a musician. Like all other arts music has its own medium and it stands by itself. If it depended on words or poetry, it would be the poet's music.

SATYENDRA: Veena, sitar, etc., have no words to express, but their tunes are music all the same.

1 *katha*: words, narrative; *sur*: music, melody, tune.

NIRODBARAN: Tagore contends that *ustadi* music[1] has now become much a matter of technique. There is no life in it. Perhaps because of that he doesn't like it.

SRI AUROBINDO: If it is technique only, it is not music.

NIRODBARAN: He says Bengali music must take its own way of expression and words will have a great place.

SRI AUROBINDO: Is music to be a commentary on words?

NIRODBARAN: He thinks that *ustadi* music is dead and has no chance of revival; its age is passed.

SRI AUROBINDO: That is because classical music has degenerated. But that doesn't mean it shouldn't be revived and the remedy is not to give value to words or poetry, but to the soul of music. To leave it or forget it is not the way out. If words are indispensable for the appreciation of music, how can an Englishman listen to Italian music and like it?

SATYENDRA: Appreciation of pure music requires training.

PURANI: Everybody can't appreciate or criticise music. The ear and the aesthetic faculty have to be trained. You can see in Bhishmadev and Biren that they enter into the spirit of music. Beethoven's Symphonies are played with instruments only. When Bhishmadev sings you can see that he is conscious only of the notes and not of the words and that he tries to communicate his emotion through the notes.

NIRODBARAN: Some people say Dilip's music is spiritual and Bhishmadev's is aesthetic.

SATYENDRA: That is because Dilip sings Bhajans and religious songs.

PURANI: What I have found in Dilip's music is that the atmosphere created is due to something other than the music – his personality, maybe.

NIRODBARAN: Can pure music be spiritual?

SRI AUROBINDO: Of course.

SATYENDRA: So far as the spiritual atmosphere is concerned, it doesn't require a great musician to bring it. A spiritual person singing some devotional songs can create it.

SRI AUROBINDO: That is why I don't grant the contention of the modernist poets that in order to appreciate modern poetry you must read the poems aloud, because a clever elocutionist can

---

1 The music of the ustads or musical masters.

make much out of bad and commonplace poetry. A poem which has no rhythm will sound very beautiful if read by an elocutionist.

NIRODBARAN: The same thing is said of Dilip's poetry: that when he reads it aloud, people like it, but they call it *apathya* (unreadable) when they try to read it. That is due, I think, to his new technique. Unless one knows the *chhanda*, one will stumble. It is not Tagore's simple and smooth *chhanda*.

SRI AUROBINDO: There are two things in Dilip's poetry – subject and treatment. As regards the subject, he follows the pre-Tagore Bengali poetry – which is intellectual poetry – perhaps due to his father's influence, which I liked and miss in later poetry. He takes up an idea and puts it into poetical form. It is a poetry written from the poetic intelligence, as I say. The treatment is, as you say, his own technique which is a departure from old tradition. Tagore has brought in a new element of feeling and imagination and, as he is a genius, his poetry is beautiful. But Tagore can diffuse himself into fifty or sixty lines and even then his idea doesn't come out. After Tagore, Bengali poetry has become wishy-washy. There is no intellectual backbone.

NIRODBARAN: Motilal has a certain originality.

SRI AUROBINDO: Yes.

PURANI: Even in his poetry Tagore talks of death.

SRI AUROBINDO (*smiling*): Yes. In his Oxford convocation address he also did that. It is perhaps a form of self-defence. He may believe that by talking of death constantly, he will avoid it.

EVENING

SRI AUROBINDO (*addressing Purani*): Have you read Gandhi's new programme for mankind?

PURANI: No. What does he say?

SRI AUROBINDO: He wants to make everybody equal. Everybody will have a good house to live in and good food and, of course, khaddar. Nobody has yet been able to do this, though, not even Russia!

PURANI: We would like to see how he does it. . . .

The Pétain Government has again declared its intention to resist a Japanese move in Indo-China.

SRI AUROBINDO (*laughing*): Yes, they are adopting a see-saw policy. First they started hobnobbing with Japan, then tried to be fraternal, then tried to be friendly with China, turned again towards Japan and now combine against her. If the news is true, it means that Hitler doesn't want Japan to be master of the East.

NIRODBARAN: This eccentric Ajit Chakravarty asked Sisir –

SRI AUROBINDO: Is he an eccentric?

NIRODBARAN: No, I mean unsteady. He asked Sisir what he thinks and feels about you. Sisir replied, "That is a needless question. What did you feel?" Ajit said he felt as if you could shake the world (*Sri Aurobindo smiled*) and about Mother he felt extreme sweetness. He is also a great lover of poetry.

PURANI: He met Moni. He likes Moni's poetry better than his prose.

SRI AUROBINDO: I am afraid I can't agree. That is because he is a lover of poetry. Moni's prose has a force, especially his imaginative prose is remarkable. His prose *Hasanter Patra* (*Letters of Hasanta*) is good, but the other is better. In the prose of Hasanter Patra one cannot but feel the sting.

NIRODBARAN: Ajit likes Jyoti's prose better than her poetry.

SRI AUROBINDO: That is because her prose may be more mature. Her poetry is brilliant, but not mature yet.

NIRODBARAN: About her prose in that book *Sandhane*, Ajit said it is mature writing, though it was written earlier than *Rakta Golap*. About *Rakta Golap* he is not very keen. The style is very good, the poetry also and it is suggestive, but it is not a mature work. That is true, I think; her whole concentration was on style and the plot is a sort of mysticism.

SRI AUROBINDO: Mysticism in a novel? That is good in a short story.

PURANI: And there is plenty of talk and discussion.

SRI AUROBINDO: That is Dilip. That is better left to him. I turned the pages of his books here and there, and everywhere I found people talking and talking.

NIRODBARAN: That is the type and character of the intellectual novel, they say, which is not only story.

SRI AUROBINDO: Yes, that is the Western influence, probably. In the *New Statesman and Nation* I read somebody who said that now the novel has been made a vehicle for everything: business, politics, religion, etc.

NIRODBARAN: Ajit found a mistake in a poem of mine where I had written "Cast away on a shoreless sea". He says that "cast

K23

away" means on an island or on a shore, but not in the sense of cast adrift.

SRI AUROBINDO: It is not bound by that meaning.

NIRODBARAN: And about Dilip's poetry, he says his English is better than his Bengali.

SRI AUROBINDO: He is mistaken.

NIRODBARAN: According to him, Dilip has not been able to blend *bhava* and expression correctly. About the expression "unbargaining hyaline" which Dilip has used somewhere, Ajit says it is not good English.

SRI AUROBINDO: Can't say without knowing the context. If it is something like "unbargaining hyaline of aspiration" it is all right.

NIRODBARAN: He seems to mean that "hyaline" is a fine word, while "bargaining" is common. So the two don't blend.

SRI AUROBINDO: That is an old idea. Sometimes such combinations are used more effectively, with more force.

NIRODBARAN: It seems that, while in Shantiniketan, Ajit used to be so absorbed in classes that he would teach for three or four hours at a stretch, at the expense of the other professors.

SRI AUROBINDO: Is that why he has been driven out from there?

NIRODBARAN: Don't know; more probably due to his habits.

EVENING

Anilbaran, discussing in one of his articles the causes of the degeneration of India, has written that its vitality was lost but one can't offer any explanation as to why it was lost.

SRI AUROBINDO: Why no explanation? Things get stereotyped and tied to forms and so degeneration sets in. It is everywhere the same. After long periods of activity, the degeneration comes in unless the race finds a renewing source. For instance, when Buddhism came in as a shock, it pervaded the whole of life and brought in a new current everywhere. The saints and Bhaktas can't exert that kind of influence because their urge doesn't pervade the whole of life. It is confined to religion and hence degeneration may come in the life of a nation in spite of its saints and Bhaktas.

Anilbaran's point about Russian religion being mere superstition is only an echo.

NIRODBARAN (*after everybody had gone away*): Dilip says that for music to be spiritual it must be conscious.

SRI AUROBINDO: That is all right.

NIRODBARAN: But can't one be unconsciously spiritual while singing? Can't one write spiritual poetry without knowing it?

SRI AUROBINDO: I don't see how one can. If one writes spiritual poetry, one will be conscious of it. César Franck had a spiritual influence in his music. When Mother asked him if he knew that, he said, "Of course!" Dilip's music is spiritual due to long periods of devotional singing with words and music combined.

20 AUGUST 1940

PURANI: The Chinese Professor Tan Sen observed the 15th in Shantiniketan, it seems.

SRI AUROBINDO: Yes.

Krishnalal has drawn a horse this month. Satyendra remarked that the horse has checked the German onslaught. In the Indian tradition the vahana or vehicle of Kalki, the last Avatar, is said to be the horse.

SRI AUROBINDO: Yes, Krishnalal is very apposite and has some power of intuition. Just when the Germans began their attack, he painted an eagle, as if swooping down on its prey, and then there was the monkey picture representing the refugees. The picture of the goat represented the English waiting for the attack. And now the horse. He has a remarkable gift in drawing animals.

SATYENDRA: Here the horse has taken the classical pose.

NIRODBARAN: Dr. Amiya Sankar in his planchette sittings was told by Vivekananda's spirit that he wouldn't have his realisation in this life, that he would die about twenty-two years later, and that one year afterwards he would be born again with Vivekananda. Sri Aurobindo would still be alive and in that life Amiya Sankar would have his realisation. "Is that true?" he asks. (*There was a burst of laughter as the information was conveyed.*)

SRI AUROBINDO: Has he any justification for belief in these things?

NIRODBARAN: He says he got two things right – one about the possibility of a sea-voyage. The spirit said "Yes" and it was correct.

SRI AUROBINDO: Anyone could say that. Our Baroda instances are more striking than that.

SATYENDRA: How does he know it was Vivekananda's spirit?

SRI AUROBINDO: Quite so. Vivekananda's spirit must have other things to do by now.

NIRODBARAN: He said also that Amiya Sankar had been Sri Chaitanya's playmate. (*Laughter*)

SRI AUROBINDO: Was it found true? (*Laughter*)

SATYENDRA: Why should great souls come to such sittings?

SRI AUROBINDO: What people wonder at is that they should come and talk all sorts of rubbish. These things, as far as they are not communications from the subconscient mind, are communications of lower forces, even vital-physical ones. I remember one instance. In Calcutta I went to attend a sitting. The spirit violently objected to my presence and said that it was painful to him. In another instance, the spirit was asked to prove his presence by eating a *sandesh* which was there. Somebody took hold of the *sandesh* and asked the spirit to take it from him by force. His hand got so twisted that he cried out in pain. Evidently something was there apart from the communication of his subconscient mind.

PURANI: Moore has reviewed the second volume of *The Life Divine*.

SRI AUROBINDO: Yes, but he hasn't understood it. He wants me to go back to politics for the establishment of the New World Order, while I have said that it is not through politics that it will come.

NIRODBARAN: He seems to have said that England will form the nucleus of the New Order.

SRI AUROBINDO: If France had accepted England's offer of joint citizenship, it might have been so.

EVENING

PURANI: The Italians have occupied British Somaliland. In the popular mind this may cause some loss of prestige for the British. People will say, "Even the Italians couldn't be defeated?"

SRI AUROBINDO: But the British didn't want to defend that territory. They decided at the very start not to defend it. They say it is of no strategic importance. I expected them to withdraw; in fact I foresaw it. No, in war minor points must be sacrificed for greater ones. Egypt and Palestine are more important. I wonder if they have sufficient forces there.

PURANI: Egypt wants to defend herself now. Such neutrality as Egypt's is worse than belligerency.

SRI AUROBINDO: Yes. I have the impression that the British haven't enough forces there. In Syria they have only 200,000 troops or so. Of course, it is the French defection that has exposed their flanks.

PURANI: Yes, they relied on the French troops.

SRI AUROBINDO: Gibraltar and the Suez are points of vital importance. England by itself can be defended, perhaps, but if these are lost then it will be dangerous for England.

PURANI: If Spain doesn't come in then Gibraltar can be defended.

SRI AUROBINDO: That is the whole point.

NIRODBARAN: Now that England has regained her prestige, Spain may hesitate to join Germany. In Alexandria the French have joined De Gaulle, it seems.

SRI AUROBINDO: Yes. (*Looking at Purani*) Have you seen De Gaulle's photo? He seems a strong man and young.

21 AUGUST 1940

PURANI: Churchill in his speech appears to have said that France will be compelled to declare war against England.

SRI AUROBINDO: Has he said that? Or what has he actually said? For if he has said that, there must be some truth in it. He wouldn't have said it if he didn't know something. It is of tremendous importance for us.

NIRODBARAN: It won't come quite as a surprise. One by one the Vichy Government is taking steps leading to that.

SATYENDRA: The world seems to be getting chaotic. But if such a thing happens, the British Government will grab Pondy at once.

NIRODBARAN: The British Government has thanked the Nizam for his contribution. But the Nizam must be smarting and cursing within for the loss of his money.

SRI AUROBINDO (*laughing*): They specially thanked Sir Akbar for it.

NIRODBARAN: The rumour about the naval bases being ceded to America seems to be true, though it was rejected at first as baseless.

PURANI: And the American Navy will patrol the Canadian waters, they say.

SRI AUROBINDO (*laughing*): It is practically an alliance.

NIRODBARAN: Some sections say that this is a move towards joining the war. How slowly and carefully Roosevelt is moving!

SRI AUROBINDO: Yes, he will be freer after November. Of course, the Congress will still be there, but the Congress also will be freer. Even if he is not reelected as President, he may bind the next President to some course of action; for the next President comes in January, I believe.

NIRODBARAN: England can hold out till November, I hope.

SATYENDRA: Oh yes. In winter the operations have to be slower.

PURANI: Hitler is trying to find Britain's weak spots by these small air attacks. But if Spain and France join Hitler –

SRI AUROBINDO: Then it will be formidable.

PURANI: Hitler is trying to drag in France.

SRI AUROBINDO: In that case, it will end in a revolution in France. The French are already reluctant to fight Germany. They will be still more so against Britain.

EVENING

Purani asked Sri Aurobindo if he had finished Coomaraswamy's book on art and what he thought about it.

SRI AUROBINDO: His book is one-sided. No doubt, art is cosmic, universal; it is not concerned with personality. But the artist expresses his inspiration and in that there must be the stamp of his individuality, as you find in the case of great artists and poets. Take for instance the Greek poets or the French dramatists. They follow the same tradition, national custom, etc., but each has his own individual stamp. An artist does not express his personality, but it is stamped on his work.

PURANI: Coomaraswamy says Leonardo da Vinci followed tradition, there is no stamp of personality on his art.

SRI AUROBINDO: Not correct.

What Coomaraswamy says about the inner and the outer vision is correct and interesting. The East has followed the inner vision in art, while the West the outer; but by outer is not meant simply the surface but the deeper things of the world.

22 AUGUST 1940

EVENING

There was talk again about the Baron-Schomberg affair; it was said that it was Schomberg who had made all the mischief.

PURANI: Ali has heard from somebody that you have remarked about his progress since Darshan.
SRI AUROBINDO: When did I say that?
PURANI: That was what I was wondering about. I told him that you might have said you had been pleased with him or something like that. Alys said, "Sri Aurobindo doesn't say anything about me! Every time it is Ali and Ali. He doesn't find me good, perhaps!" (*Laughter*) I consoled her.
SRI AUROBINDO: You could have said that it goes without saying in her case.

23 AUGUST 1940

EVENING

SRI AUROBINDO: The Viceroy, it seems, has wired to Bonvain that the Governor of Bengal wants Baron back in Pondicherry. He won't accept the man who is to replace him. When Schomberg was told this news, he broke down.

It came out that Schomberg was a staunch Catholic and had taken Holy Orders and so was as good as a priest. He was therefore working under the influence of the priests here. Baron being in connection with us, the priests had turned against him.

SRI AUROBINDO: Schomberg is a Jesuit. There is a general opinion that a Jesuit can tell any lie if it serves the glory of God.

Today's news announced Trotsky's death at an assassin's hand. Somebody said, "Stalin's last enemy is gone!" He was in dread of Trotsky, it seems.

NIRODBARAN: But how is it Trotsky was thrown out by Stalin?

SRI AUROBINDO: He was a good organiser, but not a man to lead a revolution. He did not have sufficient vital force to support his action. That doesn't mean he was not a man of action, but he acted with his brain rather than with the vital force. Stalin has more vital force. He has no intellect, but has a clever and cunning brain. Lenin combined both intellect and vital force. Trotsky's actions were more of an intellectual nature. His very cut of face shows that he is more of an intellectual type. Such people work better under a leader, not by themselves. Like Subhas Bose, for instance. He did very good work under Das.

Here Purani mentioned some people in Gujarat who could work only under somebody's guidance.

SRI AUROBINDO: Charu Dutt's summary of *The Life Divine* is not bad. But there are one or two mistakes. He says that I have derived my technique from Shankara. What does he mean by technique? I don't know that I have got my technique from anybody. Again, he says that I have laid insistence on service to humanity.

PURANI: That is perhaps the old idea people are repeating.

24 AUGUST 1940

PURANI: Spain is not very eager to join Italy and Germany, it seems.

SRI AUROBINDO: No, this British resistance has removed many dangers.

PURANI: Spain is getting financial help from Britain for reconstruction of her Government, and she must be afraid of a British blockade if she joins Hitler.

SRI AUROBINDO: Yes. To get help from Hitler in financial matters is the least thing possible.

E V E N I N G

S R I   A U R O B I N D O : The Governor has warned Baron against Schomberg, saying that he is a scoundrel and will try to do harm to him. The charge against Baron is that he mixed with revolutionaries.

P U R A N I : Meaning us?

S R I   A U R O B I N D O : Who else could it be? This Viceroy seems to be *kanpatla* (credulous). What Schomberg said he quietly believed and acted on it, and now what the Bengal Governor says he believes! That is why his conferences are not successful.

P U R A N I : Yes, he is influenced by the opinion of the Civil Service.

S R I   A U R O B I N D O : This Bengal Governor seems to be a man of will.

25 AUGUST 1940

P U R A N I : Baudoin is speaking like Hitler.

S R I   A U R O B I N D O : How?

P U R A N I : He says Britain is continuing the war and will bring ruin on the world because of it. As Hitler says, "I don't see why the war should go on." (*Laughter*)

N I R O D B A R A N : Baudoin says it would have been cowardly and derogatory to leave France and fight German from the colonies.

S R I   A U R O B I N D O : It is cowardice to fight but heroism to surrender. He is another scoundrel and swindler like Laval. Many of these people had their money deposited in Germany before the war and when the war broke out Hitler stopped all payments except to these people in order to keep them in his hands.

26 AUGUST 1940

Anilbaran has again asked why the vitality of a nation is lost after a certain time and the nation degenerates. He says that for him it is inexplicable.

S R I   A U R O B I N D O : Why inexplicable? There are many factors. It would take too long to list them all, but the essential thing is that in every civilisation and culture there is a period of decline unless some new force is found, a process of new birth to give a fresh impulse to the life-force. Otherwise the old life-force gets exhausted and, if not renewed, the nation decays. The same thing happened with the Greek and Roman civilisations.

PURANI: Could it be that some higher beings took birth and built the Greek civilisation?

SRI AUROBINDO: How? The Greek civilisation was not spiritual. It was intellectual and aesthetic; it was more subtle and delicate than the Roman civilisation, which was more massive and had more strength and discipline than the Greek. That is why it lasted longer than the Greek civilisation.

EVENING

Purani spoke of some healer with occult power somewhere in Uttar Pradesh — an educated man. He had performed many miraculous cures, even cures of mad people. The cases had been verified by Abhay. But one thing peculiar was that he didn't have that descent of power after food, so there was no cure after eating.

SRI AUROBINDO: The physical may not be in a proper condition after food. Food lowers the consciousness.

29 AUGUST 1940

Purani spoke to Sri Aurobindo about a professor of psychology at Delhi College, who had promised Abhay to give his services to some national cause. Abhay now wants him at Gurukul, according to his promise. But the professor hesitates on many grounds. The main reason is that there is no freedom of expression there. So he is in difficulty over the decision.

SRI AUROBINDO: Abhay is very keen on service.

PURANI: Yes, and also on keeping to one's promise. He couldn't forgive Govindbhai's coming here, only because Govindbhai had given his promise that he would serve under Gandhi.

SRI AUROBINDO: Suppose I promise to go to Calcutta in six months. If it turns out disadvantageous, must I still go because of my promise? He should take some training under Meher Baba. (*Laughter*) What would he say to Meher Baba's bringing people all the way to India from England to take them to China and then changing the plan and turning them back? But such things are nearer to spirituality than these fixed ideas, because one is not bound to anything.

PURANI: This professor, knowing some psychology, tries to give psychological treatment by suggestions. But he is not sure if he is doing right or doing harm.

SRI AUROBINDO: All depends on the suggestions.

PURANI: Those usual things about suppression.

SRI AUROBINDO: But it is not always true that what is suppressed rushes up some time later. One has to consider the contrary thing also, that indulging them may become a habit. Just as suppressed actions may rise up later, so too by indulgence one doesn't become free of them.

2 SEPTEMBER 1940

PURANI: I read Gandhi's queer argument about non-violence with Kher and others. Kher said that during the Bombay riot even the non-violent leaders refused to risk and sacrifice their lives to stop the riot. Gandhi says, "That supports my argument." (*Laughter*) I am simply at a loss to understand how it supports his argument. Then he says, "If they had sacrificed themselves, then the riot would have stopped."

SRI AUROBINDO: "If" they had! All depends on "ifs" and expectations. Gandhi is not a psychologist. During his Dandi march, though they didn't do any acts of violence, the leaders' minds were full of violence. In fact it was because of the opportunity violence would give that they joined the movement. And then he supports prohibition. Prohibition under compulsion is violence. There is no compulsion unless there is violence.

PURANI: He says a child has to be forced to do good things and that this wouldn't be violence. But then the British Government can say that it is for our good that they are doing all these things, that it is they who have given unity to India.

SRI AUROBINDO: That is true. Only, the trouble is, we haven't got that unity. (*Laughter*)

After this there was some talk on Science, especially Relativity, which started by reference to the term "light-year" which Sri Aurobindo used in The Life Divine. *Nolini Sen had pointed out that scientists didn't use it in that sense, so the term was changed to "light-cycle". Jatin Bal supplied many quotations from Jeans, Eddington, etc., on various points. In our discussion Sri Aurobindo refused to accept Time as a dimension of Space. Purani noted, in connection with the complicated mathematical formulas involved, that scientists had first thought Science would be understood by everybody. Now only the scientists can understand anything about Science.*

SRI AUROBINDO: They are becoming metaphysical physicists. It is like poetry. Dr. Leavis said that poetry would be understood by fewer and fewer people gradually.

PURANI: Scientists say that the sum of universal energy is always the same.

SRI AUROBINDO: I do not agree. Is it proved? If not, why can't there be something behind that is constantly putting forth energy into the universe?

About the Law of Entropy Sri Aurobindo also didn't agree.

SRI AUROBINDO: One sun may be losing heat, but another sun may be created and thus perpetual creation go on. Nobody knows when creation began.

PURANI: They say, for instance, that from a machine some energy is always lost, and for that reason a machine can't operate perpetually.

SRI AUROBINDO: That is about man-made machines. Nature is cleverer than man and, besides, in future machines may be created which will go on perpetually. What happens to the energy that is lost?

PURANI: It goes to the common stock of spent energy. It is no longer available.

SRI AUROBINDO: Why? Why can't it be available in another form? What has been available once is always available.

PURANI: When you burn coal for energy, you can't get the coal back.

SRI AUROBINDO: That is true about coal because it disintegrates.

Sri Aurobindo also said that the Quantum Theory was tending towards our Indian Vayu theory without the scientists knowing it. About the deflection of starlight towards the sun, he asked:

SRI AUROBINDO: Why should it curve towards the sun?

PURANI: Because the sun contains matter, they say. Suleiman is now questioning Einstein's theory. He stands for Newton.

SRI AUROBINDO: Einstein's theory seems to me fantastic. (*At this time some dogs were barking outside.*) There, they are protesting against Einstein!

7 SEPTEMBER 1940

SRI AUROBINDO: Radhakrishnan finds contradictory statements in Buddhism about the Self. In one place, he says, it doesn't recognise the Self and in another it takes the Self as the sole refuge and giver of enlightenment.

PURANI: Yes, that is a famous quotation. But we thought that Buddhism doesn't recognise the Self.

SRI AUROBINDO: Yes, perhaps it means the phenomenal self.

SATYENDRA: Krishnaprem gives a different interpretation to Buddhism. He says Nirvana is only a half-way house.

SRI AUROBINDO: That agrees with my experience.

SATYENDRA: In one of his letters I saw that he didn't agree with you about some idea of Buddhism. I don't remember exactly what it was.

SRI AUROBINDO: What I might have said or now say about Buddhism is based on the current idea about Buddhism. Krishnaprem puts his own interpretation.

NIRODBARAN: He follows the Mahayana school.

SRI AUROBINDO: Mahayana is nearer to the Advaita school.

SATYENDRA: Even Mahayana teachings may be a modern interpretation. Nobody knows what Buddha said.

SRI AUROBINDO: Yes. My impression is that even Mahayana has no clear idea about the ultimate concepts.

8 SEPTEMBER 1940

NIRODBARAN: Charu Dutt is impressed by the fact that here there are apparently no demigods, while in Shantiniketan you find at every corner such demigods popping up their heads. Anilbaran, Nolini, etc. are inclined to keep themselves more behind and aloof than in front.

SRI AUROBINDO: I see. Anilbaran and Nolini are not likely to interfere with anybody. Suren and Ramachandra may.

CHAMPAKLAL: Here the condition or atmosphere is quite different. There is no scope for anybody's domination, even if they wanted to. Isn't that correct?

SRI AUROBINDO: Yes, the desire to dominate is in everybody, but there is no field here because of the Mother.

CHAMPAKLAL: Yes, that is what I meant.

Anilbaran couldn't understand one quotation in The Life Divine *taken from the Rig Veda:*

"By the Names of the Lord and hers they shaped and measured the force of the Mother of Light; wearing might after might of that Force as a robe the lords of Maya shaped out Form in this Being.

The Masters of Maya shaped all by His Maya; the Fathers who have divine vision set Him within as a child that is to be born."

SRI AUROBINDO: What is the difficulty? It is very simple.

PURANI: He is asking because he will have to explain it to his class. He wants to know what is meant by "Names" and how "might after might" can be worn as a robe. (*Loud laughter*)

SRI AUROBINDO: What has become of his head? It is a metaphor and why can't it be used as a metaphor? He can tell his students that these are mystic expressions and that they will have to become mystics to understand them.

PURANI: Then he will have an easy escape.

SRI AUROBINDO (*taking up the passage*): "Names" means ideas, significances, and as for "might after might", the Divine Force is of various kinds, each of which one takes up just as one wears a robe; all very simple. Ask him to use his mystic mind instead of the professorial one.

E V E N I N G

P U R A N I : It seems Bonvain is going to declare for De Gaulle.
S R I A U R O B I N D O : Yes. The British Government has put pressure on him. He must either declare for De Gaulle or the British Government will take possession of Pondicherry.

Purani then reported that there had been a meeting of the Council in which David and others had spoken about the matter; some, especially Baron and the bank manager, favoured the idea, others opposed it.

S R I A U R O B I N D O : Baron's voice seems to have been drowned out in a murmur of disapproval.
S A T Y E N D R A : But why should there be any difficulty? The Governor has been advised by Pétain: "*Marchez avec les voisins.*"[1]
S R I A U R O B I N D O : Yes, but this is not "*avec*" but "*vers les voisins*"[2], more than what was asked. But this is the first time the British Government has given such an ultimatum. They are feeling stronger, perhaps, after their alliance with America in the matter of the naval base.

9 SEPTEMBER 1940

S R I A U R O B I N D O (*to Purani*): Any more news about French India joining De Gaulle?
P U R A N I : It seems the Governor has sent the resolution to the Viceroy.
S R I A U R O B I N D O : I understand that the French officials here have made one condition with the Indian Government that if war breaks out in Indo-China they may be allowed to send troops there, and the Indian Government has consented.
P U R A N I : But how is it possible? Indo-China is under the Pétain Government.
S R I A U R O B I N D O : Yes. So they may get shot by them. And it will be bad for us.

1 "Go along with your neighbours."
2 Not "with" but "towards your neighbours".

PURANI: Scientists say that the light of a star passing close to the sun is deflected towards the sun; the light curves in this way because of the curvature of space.

SRI AUROBINDO: How does space get a curvature and manage to do all these stunts?

PURANI: Mathematically a curved space has been demonstrated.

SRI AUROBINDO: Mathematics is like reason. As by reason you can logicise anything, so by mathematics you can prove anything.

PURANI: But one has no means to verify these things. And the difficulty is that if anybody questions them, these scientists at once reply that you must first know mathematics. All these people get some idea first and then try to fit the idea into their work.

SRI AUROBINDO: What Arjava said seems to be true, that according to the way you approach Nature, Nature will answer you.

PURANI: And they say that mathematics is most impersonal.

SRI AUROBINDO: Nonsense! They used to say the same thing about Science. Algebra and geometry are like designs. They offer no theory on the conception of the world, but only a structure.

10 SEPTEMBER 1940

Yesterday again there had been a rumour that the Governor was not going to declare for De Gaulle.

PURANI: It has come in the *Hindu* like that: "The Governor announces..." So there can't be any truth in that rumour.

SRI AUROBINDO: It is true he has declared for De Gaulle and also that there won't be any mobilisation for Indo-China if a fight breaks out there. The two things we wanted have happened: that he should reject the Pétain Government and also any involvement in this Indo-China affair. But why are these people, including Dr. André, in favour of sending troops to Indo-China?

NIRODBARAN: Perhaps because Dr. André has his brother there.

SRI AUROBINDO: Oh, his brother is there?

PURANI: Yes, and many other relatives. Many people here have their relations there.

SRI AUROBINDO: But instead of sending troops, André should bring his relatives back. (*Laughter*)

NIRODBARAN: M. N. Roy has been expelled from the Congress.

SRI AUROBINDO: Yes. I don't understand the reason.

NIRODBARAN: Because he makes freedom dependent on British support.

SRI AUROBINDO: But he is talking about world freedom and it is quite true that unless Nazism is destroyed, there won't be any freedom anywhere.

PURANI: And if Hitler wins, India's freedom has no chance.

SRI AUROBINDO: Not in a century.

NIRODBARAN: Roy has also said that we must give unconditional support to gain the sympathy of the British public.

SRI AUROBINDO: He is right. What sympathy the British have at present will cool down if India persists in this attitude. They will say, "We have promised them Dominion Status after the war, what more do they want?" They can't understand fine distinctions.

11 SEPTEMBER 1940

PURANI: Udar has got an unexpurgated edition of *Mein Kampf*. If you want to see –

SRI AUROBINDO: I don't want to waste my time on it.

PURANI: Charu Dutt says that the modern poets are trying to follow Pope and Dryden in their play with words, their metrical devices, etc.

SRI AUROBINDO: How? Pope and Dryden are very clear in what they say, while you can't make out anything of the Modernists. As regards metre, Pope and Dryden are formalists and limited. One may say they don't play with words. The Modernists are unintelligible and their irregularities are eccentric. The only similarity they have is in their intellectuality and the ingenuity of their mind.

Sahana wrote an aphorism in which darkness indicates unwillingness to receive the Light. Dilip didn't agree.

SRI AUROBINDO: It is partly true. In one state it may be true, but in the state of inconscience there is a temporary obstruction which produces an incapacity to receive even if one has the will. You can say it is also an unwillingness, but one of nature, not a personal unwillingness. In other cases, the mind may be unwilling, or it may be willing but the vital may not agree. In these cases you can say that one is unwilling.

Then there was some talk about Kalidasa's Raghuvamsha and Kumarasambhava. It seems that X found Raghuvamsha full of problems, questions of morality and immorality.

SRI AUROBINDO (*to Purani*): Have you been struck by a great number of problems in Raghuvamsha? Kalidasa being concerned with morality and immorality?

Purani (*laughing*): I thought Kalidasa was the last person to be concerned with them. He was more concerned with beauty, the aesthetic aspect. No ethical question troubled him.

SRI AUROBINDO: Yes. If it was a feeling, he was concerned with the beauty of the feeling, if an idea, with the beauty of the idea.

PURANI: Some people – Bankim was one, I think – are trying to make out that *Kumarasambhava* is earlier than *Raghuvamsha*.

SRI AUROBINDO: I don't think so. *Raghuvamsha* is brilliant while *Kumarasambhava* is more mature, has more power and energy.

13 SEPTEMBER 1940

EVENING

PURANI: Anilbaran seems to hold that the individual has no selective action. He is only an instrument, a puppet, an automaton of the Divine Will. He has no individual choice.

SRI AUROBINDO: The individual is also the Supreme.

SATYENDRA: Yes, it is the Supreme that has become transcendent, universal and individual.

SRI AUROBINDO: How does Anilbaran come to his view of the individual?

PURANI: He quotes the Gita where Arjuna is said to be an instrument of the Divine.

SATYENDRA: But why then does Krishna ask him also to be *manmana, madbhakta* (my-minded, my devotee)?

SRI AUROBINDO: Quite so. And why does he ask Arjuna to get rid of Ahankara? (*Sri Aurobindo quoted the passage.*) Who is that "you" there? If he makes the individual a mere puppet, an automaton, my whole philosophy comes to nothing. Doesn't Anilbaran know that the individual has a Purusha who is free to choose, accepting or rejecting? If according to his idea everything is done by the Divine Will, then a murderer can say that it is the Divine who is committing the murder and in that case there is no necessity of doing Yoga because everything is being done by the Divine Will and so everything is perfect; there is nothing to change. And we shall have to concede Shastri's demand to supply him with two thousand books because it is the Divine Will! He says everybody doing anything here is right, because it is the universal Divine Force that is acting through him. About Arjuna, even if he was an instrument, he was acting according to his own nature, in his own way, by using his bow, and not like Bhishma and Bhima. There the selective action comes in. Besides, he has been asked *nimitta matra bhava*, to be an instrument for a particular purpose.

It is true that whatever is the ultimate Divine Will must fulfil itself, but that doesn't mean the individual has no choice and is an automaton. These are fundamental metaphysical facts true in another plane of consciousness or spirituality. When one brings them down into the practical field, they create great difficulties.

SATYENDRA: Only one who has gone into such planes of consciousness can say that everything is done by the Divine. In the plane of Ignorance, one can't say that; we would all come to Maya then.

PURANI: Mother also said that each truth has its own plane. What is true on one plane may not be true on another.

SRI AUROBINDO: The Supreme takes three positions: transcendent, universal and individual. But it is the position that makes the difference. Here, if the individual doesn't choose, where is the place of effort? Why do we insist on and demand consent? If we were to act without consent, it would create much difficulty. And, if, after proceeding on a wrong path, one realises it, he won't be able to come back because it is the Divine Will that has led him there. Then Nolin Bihari and some others would be quite right in saying that the Divine Will was behind all their actions. Even when we contradicted him, he was quite right in insisting on his own way.

PURANI: Anilbaran would say that even the selective action is chosen by the Divine.

SRI AUROBINDO: Then the individual is the Divine and there is no longer any individual and we come to Shankara. What is the meaning of my insistence on the One and the Many? Anilbaran seems to have a rigid mind. If he reads my philosophy in that way, he will never understand it. It has to be taken as a whole.

(*After some time to Purani*) You have seen that the Pétain Government is in difficulty.

PURANI: Yes. The Axis is threatening them with complete occupation. But it would be good if they did. The French will then be obliged to put up resistance again.

SRI AUROBINDO: Yes. I hope the news is true.

PURANI: People have submitted to all this mainly because of Pétain.

SRI AUROBINDO: Yes, they thought, "After all it is Pétain!"

PURANI: And now if Pétain is forced out, it will be difficult to hold the people.

SRI AUROBINDO: Then also, "After all, Pétain?" (*Laughter*)

14 SEPTEMBER 1940

PURANI: Anilbaran says you have written in *The Mother* that one has to be an instrument of the Divine.

SRI AUROBINDO: But that is about work only. An individual is not only an instrument. He is a lover (Bhakta) and knower (Jnani), as well. If I have written about the instrument, I have also written about effort and rejection in the earlier part. If he says that passivity is an intermediate stage, that is another matter. Otherwise, by simple passivity you expose yourself to various forces, as Lele did, thinking that everything is being done by the Divine.

PURANI: Besides, one can't lift one passage out of its context and apply it in a general way.

SRI AUROBINDO: I have very clearly said that the individual is not an automaton. His consent is required. He has to be a conscious, living and consenting instrument. I think Anilbaran is unconsciously influenced by the Advaita idea of the One being real and the Many being Maya. The One is real and the Many are also real, just because the One is real. If that is correct, then the individual must be real.

PURANI: Yes, otherwise there is no individuality. Each one would be like everyone else.

SRI AUROBINDO: If he says the individual is a passive automaton, one may ask, "What are *you* doing all the time?" or "There is no *you*, is there?"

PURANI: Another point he wants to know: you have spoken of two Mayas, the higher and the lower. He is asking where one goes after passing beyond both. To the Akshara?

SRI AUROBINDO: Damn the Kshara and Akshara. Why does he want to bring in the Akshara? One overpasses the higher Maya and goes to the Transcendent. First, as I said, one embraces the lower Maya to overpass it and then one overpasses the higher — Para Prakriti — after embracing it.

SATYENDRA: He seems to be influenced by the Gita.

PURANI: Yes, so he wants to know if, after overpassing these Mayas, one can remain in Akshara Purusha.

SRI AUROBINDO: He can if he wants to. But that is withdrawing from all Nature, not transcending it. You have to pass through all these aspects to go to the originating Source.

EVENING

A quotation was supplied from The Life Divine[1] *in which the individual is described as a dynamo or channel and afterwards is merged in the Cosmic. Sri Aurobindo read the passage.*

SRI AUROBINDO: There is no difficulty. I have said here, "the dynamo selected" — I haven't said who selects. It may be the Divine Will or Nature. And even when the individual is merged in the Cosmic, the individual character remains. But the question of selective action of the individual doesn't arise from this passage.

All this took place before the walk. Afterwards, when Sri Aurobindo sat on the bed, Champaklal beckoned to me to give him the chamber-pot as he occasionally needed it after the exercise. I was hesitant. Then he himself asked for it. Dr. Becharlal had not noticed it and so Champaklal gave him a call too. As Champaklal was insisting on it, all of us, including Sri Aurobindo, looked at Champaklal and laughed.

1. SABCL vol. 18, pp. 543–44.

SRI AUROBINDO: The question is now: who calls? The dynamo, Nature or Champaklal? If not Champaklal, is it I or Nature? (*Laughter*) But I think it is Champaklal because my need was not urgent. (*Laughter, and Champaklal abashed*)

Take the example of a machine. The machine is driven by an electric force. Now, is the Force driving the machine or is there a man behind it? Whichever it is, if a pig is put into the machine to be cut up, the machine will put out bacon or sausages. It won't put out anything else. You can't make the machine move like a train. It has its own characteristics according to which it will work. If such be the case with a machine, how much more so with man who is a conscious being? It makes it all the more complicated. And even if an individual is a perfect automaton, a passive instrument of the Divine Will, here too he has to act only according to that Will. He has to reject and choose amongst all other forces which are not that. Then he performs the action of rejection. He is no more an automaton. And his very calling for the Divine Grace may be an interference.

SATYENDRA: Besides, one has first to know what the Divine Will is.

SRI AUROBINDO: Quite so. It is true that ultimately everything works out according to the Divine Will and fulfils the Divine Purpose. But that doesn't mean that the individual has no choice, no selection.

SATYENDRA: These are truths of a higher spiritual consciousness where one knows what the Divine Will is and sees or perceives it acting everywhere through Nature.

SRI AUROBINDO: Yes, here in the Ignorance there are various forces and possibilities and one has to choose from all these. When the soul came into the manifestation, it was not that God threw it down on earth by force, but that the soul willingly chose to come down. There was no compulsion by the Divine.

Anilbaran may be influenced by the determinism of Nature in the Gita. But that is not the whole thing. There the Purusha also comes in. The Purusha may dissent to something but still Nature carries it out or the Purusha may assent to it while Nature refuses. That is what happens in Yoga. Nature goes on repeating its own habits and preferences against the Purusha's consent till the power of the Purusha so increases that it can assert itself over the Prakriti. Anilbaran may also be speaking from an ideal point of view, but there too discrimination by the individual comes in. Will you remember all that?

Purani (*laughing*): At least I will remember the substance.

SRI AUROBINDO: Have you read Anilbaran's article in the *Vedanta Kesari*? I just glanced through it. He says that it is the soul that enjoys and suffers – a very astounding remark to make. And he seems also to have said that the soul is wholly responsible for a new mind, life and body in the next birth. What then becomes of the Karma theory? Surely the editor will contradict him.

PURANI: I haven't read it. I will go through it. But how can he say that the Soul enjoys and suffers?

SRI AUROBINDO: In a way you can say that the soul takes up the essence or Rasa of all experiences, holds and supports them. But the way he has put it, makes the soul subject to the experiences. Anilbaran has a fighting mind, so his statements are put in such a way as to evoke protest, contradictions, etc.

If the soul or the psychic being took an entirely new mind, vital and body, then the law of Karma would not be binding in the next life. It is not a *tabula rasa* that it begins with. It collects and gathers from the past life's experiences whatever is necessary for the next life, adds what new force it can bring in and takes up a new instrument to fulfil that evolution.

15 SEPTEMBER 1940

SRI AUROBINDO (*addressing Purani*): Have you mentioned yesterday's points to Anilbaran? What does he say?

PURANI: I have told him a few of them as there was not enough time. He is coming round and was especially impressed by the example of the machine.

SATYENDRA: All these questions don't arise if one accepts Nirvana as the goal.

SRI AUROBINDO (*smiling*): Yes.

SATYENDRA: After all the explanations the mystery remains the same.

SRI AUROBINDO: Because Truth is supra-rational, hence it must be mysterious. Buddha in that way was most logical. He was concerned with how things started and got stuck together and how to unstick them and make oneself free. It is the Upanishad's standpoint – psychological. Shankara bringing in Maya created the difficulty.

SATYENDRA: Isn't there some difference between Buddha's and Shankara's ultimate goals?

SRI AUROBINDO: Yes. Shankara speaks of the One and the One-in-Many. For Buddha there is no ultimate Self of all; each by his own effort attains separate liberation. Radhakrishnan is now trying to prove that Buddhism believes in the Self. But then illogicality will come in.

SATYENDRA: The Tibetan Buddhists say that Nirvana is a half-way house.

SRI AUROBINDO: What is beyond?

SATYENDRA: That I didn't find in Madame David-Neel's book.

SRI AUROBINDO: I met a Muslim scholar in Calcutta who said that Islam also has ascending planes of experience of the Divine.

SATYENDRA: Maybe a Sufi.

SRI AUROBINDO: Bhaskarananda of Poona spoke to me of the same ascending planes.

(*After some time*) Germany is speaking of invasion of England but again says that invasion is not necessary. Their air attacks and submarine blockade will break down the English. (*Laughing*) They are preparing their people in case the idea of invasion is given up.

PURANI: Yes, it must be that.

SRI AUROBINDO: In the meantime the R.A.F. is battering the French coast and Germany too.

PURANI: I don't know how far an invasion will be successful.

SRI AUROBINDO: Now it will be difficult. Hitler had his chance after the fall of France. If he had attacked at once it would have been difficult for England to resist. Hitler really missed the bus. Now England is equally strong in air and navy. Only on land, if they come to grips, it has to be seen what the outcome will be.

PURANI: Hitler will have to pay a heavy toll for an invasion.

SRI AUROBINDO: He doesn't care about that. What he is afraid of is failure.

SATYENDRA: It seems there are eight hundred thousand Italians in Egypt.

SRI AUROBINDO: Eight hundred thousand?

SATYENDRA: So the *Indian Express* says.

PURANI: It must be eighty thousand or so.

SRI AUROBINDO: Eight thousand!

PURANI: The other French colonies are now moving towards De Gaulle.

SRI AUROBINDO: How? (*Laughter*)

PURANI: That is what somebody writes in the *Indian Express* –

SATYENDRA: Can we believe it?

CHAMPAKLAL: That is why he didn't name the *Indian Express* before!

PURANI: No, but they say there is a great tension in Syria.

EVENING

SATYENDRA: The *Indian Express* holds the opinion that the Congress should have accepted the Viceroy's extension of Council and then fought for more.

SRI AUROBINDO: That would obviously have been a practical step. A practical politician like Tilak would have done that, accepted half a loaf and fought for the rest. If you won't accept any compromise, then the only alternative would be to prepare for a revolution.

SATYENDRA: Nehru is speaking bitterly against the Government policy and saying that Congress can't remain in such inactivity for long.

SRI AUROBINDO: He is the Kerensky-type. Any resumption of Satyagraha when England is being threatened with invasion would be serious. Besides, talk of independence is absurd. England won't concede that, especially if after that you declare yourself neutral. When the British Government offered Dominion Status of the Westminster variety –

NIRODBARAN: That was as good as independence and, as in the case of Ireland, the British Government could not force India to join the war.

SRI AUROBINDO: Yes, and Egypt too. Suppose today Hertzog gets a majority and tries to make peace with Hitler; England can't do anything about it. It can only create a split separating Natal and Cape Town.

NIRODBARAN: Nolini Sen is asking whether, after the ego-sense has disappeared, any selective action can remain.

SRI AUROBINDO: After the disappearance of the ego-sense ego-movements remain and they go on, the habitual movements of the old Prakriti, but one is not bound by it as in the Ignorance.

SATYENDRA: Two liberated souls won't act in the same way. They will have some selective action.

SRI AUROBINDO: In the old Yogas one used to leave the nature-part to act in its own way, thinking that it would fall off with the falling of the body. They would either allow the Cosmic Force to act on their nature so that the Bhavas of Bala, Unmatta, etc. would result, or they would open to the Cosmic Force with a controlling influence. Or it would be the nature of their own being that would go on with its movements to exhaust the Karma.

SATYENDRA: Unless after liberation one becomes entirely passive as did Ramakrishna –

SRI AUROBINDO: Even Ramakrishna used to pray, "Give me whatever you like but not lust." So he kept a preference there. Among the saints, there is the egoism of the Bhakta. Besides, one may say that the ego-sense has gone, while in fact it may be there. We have seen a number of cases like that where people have claimed that their egos had disappeared.

NIRODBARAN: In the other state, where there is no ego-sense or ego-movement, can't there be selective action still?

SATYENDRA: That is the supramental state; before Supermind it is not possible.

SRI AUROBINDO: One can have a reflection of it. But that is a very difficult state. There the individual becomes as it were a divine personality. He acts and lives in the Divine Presence. There is no longer any selective action.

16 SEPTEMBER 1940

SRI AUROBINDO (*smiling*): England has destroyed 175 German planes.

NIRODBARAN: A very large number, as on August 15th.

PURANI: Yes.

CHAMPAKLAL: It was also the 15th yesterday.

PURANI: Anilbaran was asking, "How does the psychic carry its experiences into the next life?"

SRI AUROBINDO: By the various subtle sheaths. After the dissolution of the body these sheaths preserve their experiences and they go to rest in their own planes after which they get dissolved. From these experiences the psychic takes up the essential elements that are necessary for the soul's evolution in the next life. It is the psychic that chooses according to its need from its own inner world. It is not that the psychic takes up an entirely new body, mind, etc. or that it is once again the old personality that renews itself. You can see in the case of the Lamas that it is not the same person.

Purani gave an instance of how a Dalai Lama, as a boy, gave the correct details about a new hidden tea-bowl about which all others had forgotten.

SRI AUROBINDO: I hear these Lamas die young.

PURANI: About thirty or forty.

SRI AUROBINDO: When one dies young, one comes back to life quickly and the memory remains fresh, as in that Mathura case. Very often one's desires remain unsatisfied and attachments persist, while in old people desires have to a great extent been worked out.

PURANI: In Tibet they have developed this occult science wonderfully well. (*Purani gave some instances from Madame David-Neel's book.*) They call in a Lama during somebody's death to help the passage of the soul through the vital world.

SRI AUROBINDO: That is the most dangerous passage. It is this world of which people usually speak when they refer to heaven and hell.

PURANI: By some process the Tibetans are able to awaken some flame in the heart and after that, even if one is kept immersed in ice, it does not affect one at all.

SRI AUROBINDO: That is the Yogagni, I suppose. Here, only Kanai may be able to do that (*laughter*), but unfortunately we haven't sufficient ice to test it.

PURANI: Instead of immersing him in ice, we can put ice on him.

EVENING

SRI AUROBINDO: The number of aeroplanes shot down is now 185!

PURANI: Yes. It seems two French fleets have passed from west to east through Gibraltar. Perhaps they have been allowed by the British to proceed to Indo-China!

Tabouis has said that if the Italian navy could be destroyed, it would give a tremendous blow to the Axis.

SRI AUROBINDO: That is my view also. If they could do that, they could separate Africa and occupy the whole of it.

PURANI: She has also said that if the French had attacked the Siegfried Line, they could have broken through it.

SRI AUROBINDO: That is what I thought. Of course they would have had to sacrifice a lot of men, but it wouldn't have been as invulnerable as they thought.

NIRODBARAN: Nolini Sen is still not clear about the selection of the individual in the supramental state. He says there will be individual centres and asks whether the individual, though he will work according to the truth of his being, won't exercise some selection in the process. As each individual will work according to his own truth, there will be some selective process.

SRI AUROBINDO: In the supramental state there will be individual centres of cosmic consciousness. The Supermind will work through the cosmic in these centres according to the truth of their being.

NIRODBARAN: Is the condition of complete egolessness a supramental state?

SRI AUROBINDO: Yes, when there is the fullness of the supramental state. In the intermediate stages there may be various ways of working.

NIRODBARAN: Nolini Sen also speaks of individual truth of being. He says that since there will be various individuals, the truth of one will be different from that of another. So in their manifestation a certain selection will come in.

SRI AUROBINDO: Selection is the wrong word. It does not apply. The Supermind will work in various ways harmoniously for one purpose, without any limitation. In the lower planes there are various possibilities and the ego bound by its limitations selects out of them. If one looks at the supramental state mentally, giving it a mental and vital character, one is likely to make mistakes.

PURANI: One can say it is a specialisation.

SRI AUROBINDO: Not even that. It is a fulfilment.

18 SEPTEMBER 1940

NIRODBARAN: Gandhi says he won't embarrass the British Government; at the same time he is asking permission to start non-violent non-participation in the war. This statement seems queer.

SRI AUROBINDO: Yes, it is very funny. He may as well hope for the Viceroy and other Englishmen to walk out of India non-violently. But does he think non-participation will remain non-violent? (*Looking at Purani*) You have seen the incident at Madras? (*There was a police firing and riot in a Congress meeting.*)

PURANI: Gandhi in his interview may ask for clarification of the whole question again and, if the Government doesn't offer satisfactory reforms, he may ask that the situation be allowed to remain as it is, instead of this extension of councils, etc.

SRI AUROBINDO: That is what the Working Committee said, isn't it?

PURANI: Yes.

NIRODBARAN: It seemed from Gandhi's speech that he almost wished he had stuck to his first statement.

SRI AUROBINDO: Yes.

NIRODBARAN: People make wonderful statements. Nehru said they were not bargaining with the British Government, and now Gandhi again makes another contradictory statement.

SRI AUROBINDO: Original ideas!

EVENING

PURANI: Anilkumar has been asking me if it is true that Italy has invaded Egypt.

SRI AUROBINDO: No, not invaded. Mussolini wants to deliver Egypt. Anilkumar seems to be naive.

NIRODBARAN: He doesn't read the papers.

PURANI: This man Sumer is saying that though Spain is quiet now, it doesn't mean that Spain has no interest in the New World Order in Europe. When the time comes, Spain will take her share. He has gone to Germany. Perhaps Hitler may persuade or force him to join him.

SRI AUROBINDO: Yes. Siam is also claiming from the French her bit of territory, not by using any force but only as a concession. However, if France doesn't listen, Siam will renounce the non-aggression pact!

PURANI: It must be the Japanese pressure behind.

SRI AUROBINDO: Yes.

22 SEPTEMBER 1940

PURANI: It seems Bonvain called all the European officials today to discuss the support to De Gaulle.

SRI AUROBINDO: How do you know? It may not have been for that reason.

PURANI: What else could it be for?

SRI AUROBINDO: We are not told. It seems the representative of De Gaulle found the French people lacking in enthusiasm.

PURANI: Yes. They all want safety and self-interest. Even the Governor's statement looks dubious.

SRI AUROBINDO: How?

PURANI: He has said, "The Vichy Government has said to us, '*Marchez avec les voisins.*' According to that advice we have joined De Gaulle." (*Laughter*)

SRI AUROBINDO: He is not sure of British victory. If the British lose, then he will say to Vichy, "You asked me to be friendly with them." He wants to keep his path clear. De Gaulle is getting very good support, it seems. He wants to raise a French army and take offensive action in France.

PURANI: That would be very good. They may have many supporters there too.

SATYENDRA: But it won't be an easy job. The number of men has to be very high.

NIRODBARAN: They have one million, they say.

SRI AUROBINDO: Not only number; the men must have equipment too. De Gaulle is a man who understands the need for equipment; without it he won't do anything.

EVENING

SRI AUROBINDO (*after reading Bonvain's statement*): He can be compared with Mark Twain! (*Laughter*) Bonvain doesn't believe that England will win.

PURANI: It seems the French were asking De Gaulle's representative many questions about their future situation if England got defeated. How can one answer all that now? Besides, one must take a certain amount of risk.

SRI AUROBINDO: Quite so. He has replied to them as far as he could, but also said, "If we go on predicting we will lose everything." In times of revolution everything is unsettled; how can anything definite be said? Some risk has to be taken. When a course of action is chosen, emergencies have to be met with as they come.

SATYENDRA: According to an Italian source, the British have a 230,000-strong army in Egypt.

SRI AUROBINDO: How the devil can they give an exact figure? If it is really true, they are almost equal to the Italians. Why then don't they enter into an encounter?

SATYENDRA: I think it is either to prove their prowess or prepare their people for any reverses. (*Laughter*)

19 SEPTEMBER 1940

PURANI: It seems the Pétain Government is resisting the German demands and there is a possibility of Pétain resigning. Weygand is also dissatisfied with the ways of the Government. He intends to fly to Morocco, set up an independent government and declare for De Gaulle.

SRI AUROBINDO: Oh!

PURANI: And there have been clashes in Morocco between De Gaullites and Pétainites.

SRI AUROBINDO: Who won?

PURANI: That is not said.

SRI AUROBINDO: Where did you get all this?

PURANI: The *Indian Express.* (*Laughter*)

SRI AUROBINDO: You always keep the name out.

PURANI: But it must be in the *Hindu* also.

SRI AUROBINDO: Baron says that the Germans are trying to use the French navy and submarines. The sinking of a British ship by a French submarine near Indo-China was done by Germany, he says. And that is why Darlan has ordered those two French destroyers to proceed to Dakar.

PURANI: Something like that must be true. Otherwise they would not have escaped the British. If the French take the British side, they will be able to keep Italy out.

SATYENDRA: The British are offering no resistance to the Italians in Egypt. They don't seem to have enough forces there.

SRI AUROBINDO: No. They say they have transferred several thousand there. But it is not a question of thousands. They have one and a half million troops. Why can't they send one hundred thousand? These news correspondents are talking in terms of the old warfare. They say there are stretches of desert to cross.

SATYENDRA: What are deserts nowadays to tanks and cars?

SRI AUROBINDO: Quite so.

PURANI: Hitler seems to be putting pressure on Sumer, trying to displace the French.

SRI AUROBINDO: He doesn't require pressure. He has always been pro-Axis. He is a phalangist.

PURANI: The British have kept Spain neutral by offering joint control of Gibraltar after the war as well as now.

SRI AUROBINDO: If Hitler gets Spain, it will be only one point controlled.

EVENING

The radio reported that Sri Aurobindo had contributed Rs. 500 to the Madras War Fund as a token of his entire support to the British in their struggle for the cause of freedom. All of us were taken by surprise by this sudden disclosure though, of course, we knew Sri Aurobindo's standpoint.

NIRODBARAN: This has come as a counterblast to Gandhi's non-participation. (*Laughter*)

SRI AUROBINDO: It was not meant to be. For the money was sent some time back, before Gandhi's blast.

PURANI: The Italians have penetrated sixty miles into Egypt. The British are not offering any resistance, it seems.

SRI AUROBINDO: Yes, they say it is still only the desert the Italians are occupying. The whole of Egypt seems to be a desert, except for a small strip along the Nile. (*Laughter*) The English don't seem to have any forces there. They say they are waiting to come in contact with Italian forces. I don't understand their strategy. They talk of a blockade. But if Cairo and Alexandria are lost, then what effect would a blockade have in spite of their control of the Mediterranean? And I don't see either how they will keep that control.

SATYENDRA: They seem to have concentrated all their forces on home defence.

SRI AUROBINDO: That must be the fact.

SATYENDRA: They think that if they can prevent Germany from occupying England, everything will be all right.

SRI AUROBINDO: That is not enough. They will have to take back all these lost territories.

PURANI: Joad has written an article describing how and why he has turned from a pacifist into a supporter of the war. It is not only a war for defence, he says, but for civilisation.

SRI AUROBINDO: That is my standpoint also. They talk of independence, but nobody will remain independent if Hitler wins.

PURANI: Dr. André was asked by the pharmacist what he would do if Germany came to India. André was telling me it is a far-off thing yet.

SRI AUROBINDO: All the same, it is a pertinent question.

21 SEPTEMBER 1940

Today's Hindu *published news of Sri Aurobindo's war contribution and quoted his letter to the Madras Governor, in which Sri Aurobindo said that we give our entire support to the British in their struggle. It is not only a war for self-defence and the defence of nations threatened with world domination by Hitler, but also a war for the preservation of civilisation, etc.*

SRI AUROBINDO (*looking at Purani*): So?

PURANI: It will be published in all the papers. Gandhi will see it.

NIRODBARAN: He may find some light in his groping. (*Laughter*)

SRI AUROBINDO: It is not in his line. They call me a savant.

PURANI: Yes.

NIRODBARAN: No other savant has contributed anything yet.

SATYENDRA: The letter has come out at an opportune time.

SRI AUROBINDO: Schomberg can no longer say that the Ashram is a nest of Nazis.

SATYENDRA: This is your first public pronouncement since your retirement.

SRI AUROBINDO: Yes, though indirect and not given as a pronouncement.

SATYENDRA: No, but it was meant to be.

SRI AUROBINDO: Yes.

SATYENDRA: But as regards India, the British are not very lovable.

K25

SRI AUROBINDO: Lovable? Nobody said they were lovable. They never were. But the question is to love Hitler less. (*Laughter*)

PURANI: Some American correspondent has said the British forces are waiting in Egypt for the Italians to come out like tortoise heads, and then they will chop them off.

SRI AUROBINDO: Of course if the British can face them, the Italians will have the disadvantage of having the desert at their back.

SATYENDRA: Egypt may declare war now.

SRI AUROBINDO: Why?

SATYENDRA: The marriage of some prince of theirs is over. (*Laughter*)

PURANI: Oh, the brother of the Hyderabad princess, the legal heir to the Sultan. He would have become the next Sultan if he had been in Turkey.

SRI AUROBINDO: No.

PURANI: I see; he would have been killed!

SRI AUROBINDO: This Egyptian ministry can't raise popular enthusiasm. Nahash Pasha could have.

EVENING

SRI AUROBINDO: So New Caledonia has revolted against the Pétain Government?

PURANI: Yes.

SATYENDRA: Where is New Caledonia?

SRI AUROBINDO: It is a small island near Australia.

PURANI: There are some volunteers here who want to join De Gaulle.

SRI AUROBINDO: Have they declared themselves? They have to do that first. But do they know that they are to be shot by the Pétain Government? You have heard the story of the French Consul in Bombay? It seems that somebody painted the Croix de Lorraine on his door at night. Most Frenchmen in Bombay are for De Gaulle, while he is for Pétain. He wanted to report to Pétain against some of these sympathisers, but as he could not do it from Bombay, he went to Kabul and telegraphed from there. The reply came that the sympathisers are to be shot. Now after his return to Bombay, somebody phones him every morning saying, "Ulysse, are you still proving yourself to be a traitor to your country?" (*Laughter*)

PURANI: But the condition in France is none too happy.

SRI AUROBINDO: No. Hitler is putting pressure on Pétain. The Germans are plundering whatever they can in the non-occupied territories and withholding payment from the banks. They have released French prisoners from Germany and are sending them to Pétain to avoid a shortage of food in Germany. Pétain is being tolerated only for the sake of the colonies. It seems the Germans and Italians have already divided the colonies between themselves. Italy is to take Tunis, Corsica and Morocco, while Germany will get West Africa.

After some time Purani spoke about Tagore's new interpretation of an ancient Indian history of the Ramayana period – Itihasher Dhara. Tagore seems to hold that: (1) Rama, Vishwamitra and Janaka are the three forces combined into one that moulded the ancient social life; (2) the fact that Sita was found on cultivated ground indicates that she is a symbol of agriculture; (3) the Kshatriyas were really the ones responsible for the growth of culture and civilisation while the Brahmins were only its preservers.

SRI AUROBINDO: All these are old European ideas. He is not even being original. They are as old as the hills.

23 SEPTEMBER 1940

SRI AUROBINDO (*looking at Purani*): Is Hitler waiting for the fog?

PURANI: It seems he is more busy in the east settling Rumanian questions in the warm climate.

Japan seems to have toned down. It must be due to the Anglo-American alliance regarding the Singapore naval base.

SRI AUROBINDO: Obviously. Everything is getting queer. They make war without declaring war, alliance without calling it alliance.

SATYENDRA: What has happened to Japan's ultimatum?

SRI AUROBINDO: Modified. If this alliance takes place, it will be dangerous for Japan; for Singapore is a strong naval fortress, but at present the British have only a few ships there. An alliance with America will bring in American ships.

SATYENDRA: I don't think Hitler has given up the idea of attack. Perhaps he is delaying because of differences among his generals.

SRI AUROBINDO: He may attack. There have always been differences; in spite of them he has acted on his own. He is trying to establish his air superiority. Hitherto, all his tricks have failed.

SATYENDRA: The war will last a long time, it seems.

SRI AUROBINDO: At any rate, it won't end now.

PURANI: The Egyptian cabinet is meeting to decide what Italy's intention could be. (*Laughter*) The President has already said that their intention is very clear, so they must act at once.

SATYENDRA: Do they think the Italians are coming to embrace them?

SRI AUROBINDO: Or perhaps they think that they will blow a kiss from Sidi Barani and withdraw. (*Laughter*)

PURANI: We had a joke at Rajangam's cost. He has received a letter from France. We told him that the Vichy Government was calling him.

SRI AUROBINDO: Why from France?

PURANI: It's from a medical firm. It was posted before the Armistice.

SRI AUROBINDO: I see. But the firm may not exist now – like a star that has gone out although its light still comes to us. (*Laughter*)

EVENING

SATYENDRA: Plenty of people are writing to Doraiswamy about your war donation. They don't understand why you have done it.

PURANI: Why? The reason was given very plainly in the statement itself.

SRI AUROBINDO: Quite so.

SATYENDRA: They don't see how you can support the culture and civilisation of the British and their allies.

SRI AUROBINDO: Why not? They ought to see what Hitler is doing everywhere.

NIRODBARAN: The difficulty is that they are so biased with an anti-British feeling.

SRI AUROBINDO: But I am not biased like them.

SATYENDRA: They are political people, not Yogis.

SRI AUROBINDO: Then they should have political insight.

PURANI: The Egyptian ministers have resigned. It seems the Egyptian Government is pro-Fascist in tendency; that is why it is hesitating.

SRI AUROBINDO: If it has only a twenty-thousand strong army, of course it won't count for much; but why is the Government pro-Fascist?

PURANI: It is Mussolini's work, I suspect. Mussolini has been working and preparing the field there for a long time. He has, perhaps, promised these old Pashas high offices and posts.

SRI AUROBINDO: They must be idiots if they believe him even now.

PURANI: Yes, and the King also is centralising power in his hands.

SRI AUROBINDO: They ought to have abolished the King as was done in Turkey.

NIRODBARAN: Is it because of Egypt's neutrality that the British are not attacking the Italians?

SRI AUROBINDO: No. Egypt won't dare to prevent them unless they turn hostile.

24 SEPTEMBER 1940

The radio said that De Gaulle had gone to Dakar as there had been rumour of a revolt among the people. Sri Aurobindo remarked, "He would not act simply on a rumour." There was confused and meagre news from Dakar. It was reported that naval fighting was going on between the French and the British. Then Purani described how France had given up the fight in spite of having much material – the usual story about how the French leaders and people had betrayed the cause, etc.

SATYENDRA: France would have been in a better position if she had not joined the war.

SRI AUROBINDO: How? She would have been attacked one day. Italy was already talking of her colonies. In that case, British help wouldn't have been available. They might have hoped that Hitler would attack Russia first but it is doubtful whether Italy would have waited such a long time.

Sri Aurobindo had been styled a Brahmo leader by some American paper in connection with George Nakashima's talk on Nishtha – Margaret Wilson, daughter of the former President of the U.S.A.

SRI AUROBINDO: So I am called a savant [*British radio*], a Brahmo leader and an ascetic [*Bombay Times*]!

Some Egyptian prince had come to India, visited Hyderabad and called it "marvellous".

PURANI: If he finds Hyderabad marvellous then one wonders what Egypt may be like.

SRI AUROBINDO (*laughing*): Yes, Hyderabad is still half in the Middle Ages! You know Dara's story? One of two brothers from there came for Darshan. After going back the brothers had some quarrel over property and the one who had been here filed a suit and asked our help. He won the case. Then the other brother came for Darshan and after going back he filed another suit against the brother who had won, and he also asked our help. This brother also got a judgement in his favour. I don't understand how it was possible to have opposite judgements, when the judge was the same.

EVENING

SRI AUROBINDO: Bhaskar reports on his radio, "It must be remembered that the British have been shelling Dakar." (*Smiling*) How can we remember when we never heard of it before? There seems to be a mystery around the whole affair.

PURANI: Yes, all sorts of conflicting news is coming in. Nobody knows what the truth is.

SRI AUROBINDO: It appears from an Englishman bringing news from Rome that Hitler will try to take Gibraltar first, then cross to Morocco, capture Egypt, the Suez canal, the whole of Africa and finally invade England.

PURANI: If the French forces side with England in Africa, even now there may be a chance of victory. There are fine French forces in Morocco.

SRI AUROBINDO: Yes. If Hitler takes Gibraltar, the British can occupy Tangiers as a counterblow.

25 SEPTEMBER 1940

SRI AUROBINDO: The situation about Dakar seems to be a little clearer now. It appears that De Gaulle went there with some free French forces supported by British warships; he sent an ultimatum to the authorities but a fight is still going on as they didn't surrender. But I don't understand why De Gaulle wants to land troops at Dakar. It will be very difficult. He could have landed them in the neighbouring British territory and from there marched to Dakar.

PURANI: Yes, and in that case he might have got the support of the people without any fight.

SRI AUROBINDO: Perhaps there is no good port for landing.

26 SEPTEMBER 1940

The radio announced the cessation of fighting by De Gaulle at Dakar.

SRI AUROBINDO: Queer end of the expedition. He shouldn't have undertaken it.

NIRODBARAN: He wants to spare French blood.

SRI AUROBINDO: But the French at Dakar didn't spare it. (*The French fired at De Gaulle's forces when they tried to land.*) Neither will the British.

NIRODBARAN: De Gaulle still has some sentiment left.

SRI AUROBINDO: Gandhian sentiment of non-violence?

PURANI: Mrs. M. N. Roy has written an article in support of the war. There she says that people consider Hitler great because he is a vegetarian and because he is a bachelor. "But there may be medical reasons for it," she says. (*Laughter*)

SRI AUROBINDO: Any vegetarian who murders people will be great then?

NIRODBARAN: That is what the Jains seem to have thought. Plenty of Jain kings, while being strict vegetarians, had no hesitation in killing others.

SRI AUROBINDO: You know the story of the two Jain brothers during the invasion by Mahmud of Gazni? The brother who was the king was defeated and taken prisoner. The other brother was then made king by Gazni and his brother was handed over to him. He didn't know how to dispose of his brother. At last he found a way.

He made a pit below his throne and put his brother there. If he died, it was not his fault. (*Laughter*) It is a fact of history, not a mere story!

27 SEPTEMBER 1940

SATYENDRA: It seems Jinnah carried many files with him to his interview with the Viceroy.

SRI AUROBINDO: Files? All the speeches he delivered at the Muslim League meetings? (*Laughter*) He is making most exacting demands.

PURANI: The Secretary of State has already answered Gandhi's conscientious objection to war.

SRI AUROBINDO: What did he say?

PURANI: He has said that it is Viceroy's conscientious conviction that India's interest is also involved in the war and so nothing should interfere with India's war effort.

In the recent military pact Japan has been given the right to be the leader of Asia.

SRI AUROBINDO: Asia? How? What of Italy's intentions regarding Syria and Palestine?

PURANI: I don't see what the pact means or how Japan is going to profit by it.

SRI AUROBINDO: It means nothing. It is like the anti-Comintern pact – implying a "we all hate communism" sort of thing.

28 SEPTEMBER 1940

SRI AUROBINDO (*after inquiring whether there was any further news regarding the three-Power pact and whether Japan was declared the leader of Asia or the Far East*): Not that it makes any difference.

SATYENDRA: It is the Far East.

SRI AUROBINDO: Italy has an eye on Palestine and Hitler wants Baghdad. How can Japan be allowed the whole of Asia then?

NIRODBARAN: Russia left out of the picture?

SRI AUROBINDO: Yes, perhaps they have seen that she is not in a fighting mood at present.

It seems probable that there is some spy in De Gaulle's camp who gave information of the expedition and so the French Government was able to provide the military resistance.

NIRODBARAN: But did he expect no resistance?

SRI AUROBINDO: He expected that the people would get hold of the town.

29 SEPTEMBER 1940

Sri Aurobindo has decided not to give Abhay a copy of his letter in support of the Allies. It is widely known in the Ashram that he has written such a letter and, as a matter of fact none of us thought it was confidential; on the contrary we thought that if people knew about Sri Aurobindo's views they would be enlightened. Sri Aurobindo's objection to publicising it was that it would raise controversies and spoil the work. He didn't want to get into any controversy. When he decided that Abhay shouldn't write anything to Mahadev Desai, Purani pleaded that if Sri Aurobindo didn't want it he wouldn't write anything in Sri Aurobindo's name nor show the letter to anyone.

SATYENDRA: It will profit many people to know your points, especially Doraiswamy. He is much disturbed.

SRI AUROBINDO: If one does not want to give up his idea nothing will induce him. The facts are there speaking for themselves. There is the three-Power pact.

(*After a while, laughing*) Some Patel has written a postcard to us saying that he is convinced Hitler is right and we are wrong in supporting Britain.

NIRODBARAN: This pact seems to be directed against America.

SRI AUROBINDO: Obviously!

PURANI: It seems Spain is being persuaded to join the war and allow German troops to pass through Spain to attack Gibraltar.

SRI AUROBINDO: Indo-China's example?

PURANI: But Franco doesn't seem anxious to join the war. He has to reckon with the blockade too.

SRI AUROBINDO: Yes. The Monarchists also don't want Fascism in Spain. It is not the Republicans alone but Franco's own men who don't want war. The Phalangists, of course, want it. The Phalangists are Fascists.

SATYENDRA: Laski says that whenever the India-question is touched, he doesn't know what the devil happens to Churchill.

SRI AUROBINDO: At any rate, he is allowing discussion on equal terms with the half-naked Indian Fakir.

Satyendra (*laughing*): Yes, that was Churchill's own expression.

30 SEPTEMBER 1940

Yesterday morning, Vithalbhai suddenly disappeared somewhere, but returned at night about ten. Somebody gave the news to Sri Aurobindo.

SRI AUROBINDO: He was too disorganised and so he came back?

Sri Aurobindo asked if any of us had inquired where he had gone and why. Somebody said that perhaps he had been passing through some difficulty.

SRI AUROBINDO: He has behaved like Naik. Naik used to have such fits. I suppose it is vital restlessness and dissatisfaction.

SATYENDRA: Perhaps. Some dissatisfaction must have been growing within.

SRI AUROBINDO: He seems to have many minds. He wrote to us that he didn't want to be in any organisation. By going out he found himself disorganised, probably. Another time he wrote he wanted to see the influence of other Yogis.

Purani brought in Roosevelt in some connection.

SRI AUROBINDO: It seems this Wilkie is almost certain to be elected. Many Democrats are supporting him. All the same Wilkie doesn't appear to be of Roosevelt's standard.

PURANI: No!

EVENING

Purani narrated a story of how Reynaud was persuaded by his mistress to give up resistance in the North and withdraw to the South, as a result of which the majority of the French Army was crushed in Belgium.

SRI AUROBINDO: Where was that story?

PURANI: The *Sunday Times*.

NIRODBARAN: The *Sunday Times*? We didn't see it.

SRI AUROBINDO: No! I would like to see it.

PURANI: I will get the paper tomorrow.

1 OCTOBER 1940

PURANI: Hitler hasn't given up the idea of attacking Britain. He is concentrating his forces in Norway.

SRI AUROBINDO: Yes. About 200,000 troops are practising jumping into the sea from the rocks! Is it a preparation, in case of reversal, to swim back from England?

Any news about Gandhi's second interview with the Viceroy?

PURANI: No, there is conjecture that Gandhi may have urged the release of the politicals.

SRI AUROBINDO: That means there must have been some settlement.

SATYENDRA: The Muslim League has also refused.

SRI AUROBINDO: Yes. Jinnah wants to know what the League's status will be in case some other party comes in later. He means Congress! It is like the Berlin-Japan pact – by some other power they mean the U.S.A.

SATYENDRA: Jinnah has realised that the Viceroy doesn't want to part with power.

SRI AUROBINDO (*laughing*): To the Muslim League? No! The Government is in an impossible position. Congress wants Dominion Status now and, declaration of independence after the war; at the same time it refuses to say that it will support Britain in the war and speaks only of the defence of India. The Muslims want Pakistan with a fifty per cent representation everywhere. The Hindu Mahasabha demands one quarter of the seats to be given to Muslims.

SATYENDRA: The Muslim League wants to know the number of members in the council and the personnel having portfolios.

SRI AUROBINDO: How can the Government say this now? There seems to be a new age of inspiration, not of reason. Pakistan, Hindustan, the Khaksars, all are inspired and inspiration is sacred. Gandhi is more rational.

SATYENDRA: He has been till now. This affair about freedom of speech has spoiled his reputation a bit.

SRI AUROBINDO: Even after independence there may be civil strife and some dictatorship may be needed.

PURANI: Gandhi doesn't want war.

SRI AUROBINDO: No, no government by force. But if the Khaksars start violence how will he prevent it, or how will he prevent the goondas who take joy in beating and killing? Does Gandhi know that the Nazis are trained to beat people as part of their duty? What will he do then? The British people have two things: first, they are afraid of world opinion; second, they want to play hide-and-seek with their conscience. If it is exposed, they begin to scratch their heads. But the Nazis have no conscience to deal with and no world opinion to reckon with.

NIRODBARAN: This story about Reynaud's mistress was in the *Indian Express*.

Satyendra (*smiling*): Yes. I read it there but I thought it might have been in the *Sunday Times*, too, when Purani said that.

SRI AUROBINDO (*laughing*): Purani's subconscious thought that the *Sunday Times* was more respectable than the *Indian Express*. (*Laughter*)

EVENING

PURANI: Gandhi's freedom of speech hasn't been granted by the Viceroy.

SRI AUROBINDO: No.

PURANI: Gandhi takes up some theoretical issue. C. R. would have been much better in such cases. He has practical sense.

SRI AUROBINDO: The Viceroy has referred to conscientious objectors in England and says that they are not allowed to preach against war among munitions workers.

SATYENDRA: Gandhi says the conditions in India are different.

SRI AUROBINDO: Yes, and he says that though he won't himself preach, others must have the right to do so, if they want – people like Bose. How can any government allow that?

PURANI: The Jinnah-Viceroy correspondence is out.

SRI AUROBINDO: Yes, it is full of impossible demands. The Viceroy has answered to them, "Yes, I note them. We will consider them". All the time he must be thinking what a fool Jinnah is that he doesn't understand what impossible demands he is making.

PURANI: Gandhi speaks of freedom of speech. But even during the Congress regime, that was not given to the Socialists, even by C. R.

SRI AUROBINDO: M. N. Roy is cogent. He said, "You talk of freedom of speech, but don't tolerate anybody criticising you."

SATYENDRA: But he belongs to an organisation which is fighting.

SRI AUROBINDO: So is England. Besides, Roy is not in the Executive of the Congress so he can't criticise it. He is only a member. Congress has two contradictions. If it is an army then it's all right not to allow any freedom of speech, but if it is a democratic organisation how can freedom of speech be disallowed?

SATYENDRA: There is no review of the second volume of *The Life Divine* yet.

SRI AUROBINDO: No, they will take six months to finish it and, after finishing, they won't know what to say.

2 OCTOBER 1940

Somebody had sent a reply-paid wire to Sri Aurobindo asking for some message for Pratap Mazumdar's centenary, which they were celebrating. Naturally Sri Aurobindo refused.

SATYENDRA: They have wasted two rupees. (*Laughter*)

SRI AUROBINDO: I may send a message one day late. (*Laughter*)

PURANI: Even then they may publish it.

SRI AUROBINDO: If I say that he was an insignificant person? (*Laughter*)

PURANI: That would be a nice idea.

SRI AUROBINDO: I don't see why they are making a fuss about him. He was a second-class personality. All I know about him is that he was Keshab Sen's disciple and went to America.

PURANI: He was a good speaker.

SRI AUROBINDO: Plenty of people are good speakers!

PURANI: You have seen the Egyptian Government's queer resolution? They think that a sixty-miles' entry into their territory is not of much concern.

SRI AUROBINDO: No! It is only desert! It is like walking on the garden-path of a compound. When they actually come to the verandah, then it is of some concern and something needs to be done!

3 OCTOBER 1940

NIRODBARAN: Sikandar Hyat Khan has strongly attacked Gandhi.

SRI AUROBINDO (*smiling*): Yes.

NIRODBARAN: He says Gandhi's non-participation in the war is stabbing the British in the back.

SRI AUROBINDO: Non-violently!

SATYENDRA: Violent or non-violent, the result is the same.

NIRODBARAN: Sikandar says he can't understand Gandhi's logic. The logic of Mahatmas is different from that of ordinary mortals like him. Otherwise what could be meant by non-embarrassing the British Government and at the same time preaching India's non-participation?

SATYENDRA: I would like to know what Kripalani says about this statement of Gandhi. He has a keen intellect.

PURANI: The Sikhs also don't understand; they say, "These are intellectual quibbles." Neither can they conceive of how the defence of India can be done non-violently.

SRI AUROBINDO: That is something I can't swallow myself.

SATYENDRA: Gandhi himself can't carry Congress with him. But the question has been shelved for the present – I hope buried like Aurangzeb's musicians. (*Aurangzeb forbade all music. In spite of that, some took out a musical procession in front of his palace. He ordered all the musicians to be buried alive.*)

SRI AUROBINDO: Is music forbidden by the Koran?

SATYENDRA: I don't know.

PURANI: There is no injunction against it in the Koran, as in the case of art.

SRI AUROBINDO: Art is different; it is idolatry. But there are so many things without injunctions in the Koran. Is there an injunction against killing brothers?

PURANI: No, but if someone is a drunkard he can be killed. That is how they killed Murad. They themselves made him drunk and on that pretext killed him.

SRI AUROBINDO: What about Dara, then?

PURANI: He was a Kafir.

SRI AUROBINDO: Are Kafirs to be killed according to the Koran?

PURANI: Don't know. They find so many things in the Koran. Even the idea of non-cooperation, they say, is found in it. That was during the Khilafat agitation. They say that Mohammed was threatened with his life and he fled and that was non-cooperation.

SRI AUROBINDO: Many people have fled in such circumstances! Then I myself was a non-cooperator since I fled from Bengal! (<i>Laughter</i>)

4 OCTOBER 1940

Purani said that Girijashankar had written another instalment of Sri Aurobindo's life in Udbodhan. Nolini sent it up through Purani.

SRI AUROBINDO: Is anything written there about my life which I don't know? (<i>Laughter. Then Sri Aurobindo began to read it. After a while he gave a hilarious laugh.</i>) He says "Night by the Sea" has been addressed to my English sweetheart. (<i>Laughter</i>) And "Estelle" to a French girl! He is trying to make my biography out of my poetry! He also says that "Baji Prabhou" was written in Gujarat under the influence of Tilak and the Mahrattas. In fact it was written in Calcutta. (<i>After reading the whole instalment</i>) He has not made enough out of the poetry. He ought to have said that <i>Myrtilla</i> was addressed to a Greek girl – a girl whom I loved and buried on an island. Seshadri said about the poem "Revelation" that the girl spoken of there must be somebody I came across on the Pondicherry beach! (<i>Laughter</i>)

PURANI: What would he say about "The Hound of Heaven" then? An ordinary dog?

SATYENDRA: That is not interesting.

SRI AUROBINDO: There is nothing about my life here. It is all about my poetry, also the poetry of Tagore, Das, Monomohan, etc. He also says "Love and Death" and "Baji Prabhou" are ballad poetry. (<i>Laughter</i>) People are funny. Somebody criticising "Love and Death" said it was all Keats, and Girija says there is nothing of Keats, but it is a ballad!

SATYENDRA: As in your *Life Divine*, people find Shankara, Ramanuja, etc. (*Laughter*)

EVENING

It appeared that Veerabhadra had been going to the labourers and teaching them Hindi. Also a pamphlet had been circulated that he would deliver a speech on Gandhi, on Gandhi's birthday. If all this was true, naturally it would go very much against the Ashram. Sri Aurobindo was anxiously inquiring about it from Purani. Some days earlier Purani had spoken to Sri Aurobindo about it. Sri Aurobindo had said, "In that case Veerabhadra will have to leave the Ashram. He ought to know that the Ashram is not allowed to join in any public activity." It seems the Mother also heard about the pamphlet and told Sri Aurobindo of it. Both the Mother and Sri Aurobindo were rather concerned.

SRI AUROBINDO: There are already people here who are looking for any pretext to use against us. There was an enquiry some time back as to whether we were an enemy of the British. It was reported that we were concerned only with philosophy. Now if they get to know this? Mother has been telling me that something is going on in the subtle plane against the Ashram. Of course we knew – like that.

PURANI: I don't know why he should meddle with these things. He is a fool to do that.

SRI AUROBINDO: I may be forced to make an official statement. (*laughing*) If they made a real enquiry and cross-examined Y, for instance, then –

Later on it was found that the pamphlet had been circulated by somebody else. Veerabhadra had nothing to do with it.

SRI AUROBINDO (*smiling*): There is still another charge against him.

5 OCTOBER 1940

NIRODBARAN: Mandel is acquitted!

SRI AUROBINDO: Yes, he seems to have dangerous documents against everybody.

NIRODBARAN: Like Daladier!

PURANI: Yes, Daladier said he would drag down many others with him.

SRI AUROBINDO: If politicians were made responsible for their mistakes, then many would have to go to the scaffold. It is like the French Revolution: when a General failed, his head was cut off!

SATYENDRA: Is it some new poetry you are writing now, Sir?

SRI AUROBINDO: No, it is *Savitri*.

NIRODBARAN: Is it not finished yet?

SRI AUROBINDO: The writing is over, but every time I see it, I find imperfections. Only about two and a half cantos can be said to be finished.

SATYENDRA: It is good that it is something innocent. Otherwise every time you took up *The Life Divine* some catastrophe took place: first in 1914 and now in 1939 – both times war. (*Laughter*)

SRI AUROBINDO: *Savitri* also contains war, but it is imaginative. So I suppose the opposing forces may not object.

SATYENDRA: What would that commentator Girija make of it?

SRI AUROBINDO: He said nothing biographical about "Baji Prabhou" either. He could have said that it was the glorious account of a scuffle I had with some Mahommedan!

NIRODBARAN: But what was this man trying to prove? He seems to be trying to establish some connection between the development of your poetry and that of Tagore.

SRI AUROBINDO (*laughing*): Yes.

NIRODBARAN: He said that Tagore wrote his *"Jete nahi dibo"*[1] when you came back to India and that it was as if a new glimpse of his *"Aurobindo Rabindrer laha namaskar."*[2] I don't see any connection.

SRI AUROBINDO: Neither do I. I thought Girija idiotic when he was writing in Das's paper. *"Jete nahi dibo"* is about some daughter, isn't it?

PURANI: Yes. The daughter doesn't allow her father to return to his place of activity and then he philosophises about love, etc. What is the connection there?

SRI AUROBINDO: I don't know. He makes out that Das, Tagore, I and others were writing under the same influence, with

1. "I shall not let you go."
2. The poem composed by Rabindranath Tagore on the occasion of Sri Aurobindo's arrest: "Rabindranath, O Aurobindo, bows to thee!".

K26

the same *bhava*, on the same subject! But how can he say that some new poems were added to *Songs to Myrtilla*? None were added.

PURANI: No!

SRI AUROBINDO: In this book only earlier poems were included. He says three poems in *Myrtilla* are about a part of my life I wanted people to know about. He objects to the poem on Rajnarayan Bose being excluded from the new edition. The fact is I had no copy of it. Besides, these are the usual sorts of things critics say about a poet after his death. I am still alive. I should be immune so long as I am alive. (*Laughter*)

SATYENDRA: They construct a biography out of the poems since they can't approach dead poets. But they can approach you.

PURANI: About Shakespeare also they have built up many stories.

SRI AUROBINDO: Yes. They say his dramas are all experiences of his life. He deserted his wife, became an actor-manager, later abandoned that job. Now it is denied. They also made him out to be a usurer, a thief who killed a deer in a park and stole it. As a protest against the theory about Shakespeare's sonnets that "with this key Shakespeare unlocked his heart", Browning wrote:

"Did Shakespeare? If so, the less Shakespeare he!"

SATYENDRA: It was said that no such person as Shakespeare existed.

SRI AUROBINDO: That idea has been given up – then they said there were two Shakespeares – both at Stratford.

PURANI: Bacon also was bolstered up as the real Shakespeare.

SRI AUROBINDO: Yes. Some critic made Bacon out to be both an Elizabethan and a post-Elizabethan poet. But take the actual poetry he has written: one can see how prosaic it is!

EVENING

SRI AUROBINDO: Moore has written an article against Gandhi, taking his stand on the Gita and on me. He says that if Gandhi considers himself an instrument of God and preaches non-participation, he, Moore, is also an instrument of God entitled to object to it. (*Sri Aurobindo gave us the gist of the article.*)

PURANI: Azad and others take a different standpoint from Gandhi.

SATYENDRA: They make it a political non-participation, while Gandhi –

SRI AUROBINDO: Brings in both political and conscientious objections. (*Laughter*)

SATYENDRA: It seems Azad, C. R. and Nehru aren't very warm towards this new stand of Gandhi.

SRI AUROBINDO: That is evident from C. R.'s speech. After the rejection of the Poona offer, they didn't know what to do. So they had to take Gandhi's help. Now they are in an impossible position. It was Venkataram Shastri, I think, who has said Congress has been making mistake after mistake. After they had resigned their offices, if they had stuck to civil disobedience it would have meant something. Right or wrong, it was a line of action, a policy. But instead they have been going now this side, now that side.

SATYENDRA: Nehru also speaks of being international. Now his sister speaks in the same vein.

SRI AUROBINDO: In that case he should support Britain. Otherwise, he will only help Hitler.

NIRODBARAN: If there is any trouble in India, Hitler will be glad.

SRI AUROBINDO: Of course!

PURANI: Benoy Sarkar writes in *Rupam* about art, that the subject matter is not important. Indian art has been always concerned with the subject while what matters in art is whether it is aesthetic or not. From that point of view, pattern, design, colour, line are things that count.

SRI AUROBINDO: But that is decorative, not aesthetic.

PURANI: Yes, he takes the current modern view of art. He says one must see the balance and mass, etc., in a work of art, for instance in a Buddha seated in a triangle.

SRI AUROBINDO: That is again scientific art, not aesthetic, and besides, has modern art no subject?

PURANI: Agastya answers Sarkar by saying that by the Indianness of Indian art what is meant is not so much the subject as the tradition, the training that one follows in one's art, which is quite different from the European tradition.

SRI AUROBINDO: Apart from the subject, art has something which is extremely important, but the subject, too, has its value. If it is all mass and balance, why call in Buddha then? The image or figure of Buddha is supposed to express the calm of Nirvana. If you are not able to feel that or if the art hasn't been able to bring that out, then you don't appreciate the art.

PURANI: It is the same thing they are doing in poetry.

SRI AUROBINDO: Poetry has no subject? No meaning? Then it is what Baron makes out of it when he says, "Why do you want to understand?"

6 OCTOBER 1940

PURANI: Sarkar says that art was at first religious everywhere; only India has remained where she was, while Europe has gone forward.

SRI AUROBINDO: That is all right, but where?

PURANI: Going round!

SRI AUROBINDO: And backward. They have gone farther back than we have ever done.

PURANI: What seems to me the point is not whether art is religious; it is the inner vision, the inlook, so to say, by which an artist creates, that matters.

SRI AUROBINDO: Quite so. Sarkar is scientific.

PURANI: I remember Arjava used to see Krishnalal's pictures like that – the scheme, line, composition – the geometry of art, so to say. Poor Krishnalal couldn't make head or tail of his criticism.

SRI AUROBINDO: He practised without knowing!

NIRODBARAN: Moore's article on Gandhi is very strong.

SRI AUROBINDO (*smiling*): Have you read it?

NIRODBARAN: Yes.

PURANI: Yes, it is very strongly worded.

NIRODBARAN: But he goes a little too far. He doesn't believe that non-cooperation has done any good – on the contrary it has done much harm, he says.

PURANI: What non-cooperation has done is to show people in a combined state, united in action for a common purpose and thus it has given solidarity and a sense of unity.

SATYENDRA: It has helped to awaken the mass-consciousness tremendously.

SRI AUROBINDO: That, of course.

PURANI: Non-violence has been brought in by Gandhi as a principle, while Azad and others have accepted it only as a policy.

SRI AUROBINDO: Non-cooperation is nothing new. It is the same as the Swadeshi movement. Only, we had no non-violence. Holland is using non-violence by a violent abuse of words.

PURANI: Abhay says this is the time to preach non-violence to people in Europe when they are down with the curse of war and violence.

SRI AUROBINDO: Yes, to preach but not to practise!

 EVENING

C. R. Das has delivered a speech in answer to the Madras Governor. He says that it is easy to sneer at non-violence during war, but it was the non-violent movement that overcame the terrorist activities that had been raging before the war and converted the terrorists.

SRI AUROBINDO: That is saying too much. They were not converted: when they saw that their movement was a failure, they took this up as a policy.

SATYENDRA: When there was repression everywhere by the Government, it was only this non-violent movement that could have been produced and it helped to awaken the masses.

SRI AUROBINDO: That, yes. But that was due to the non-cooperation movement, non-violence serving only as a policy. And it succeeded because the common people thought it would give them freedom from the Zamindars. Everybody except Gandhi took it up as a policy and, if you do that, then there is no quarrel.

SATYENDRA: Gandhi himself was not so strict about non-violence before. In 1928 he said that government by use of force may be necessary. Only recently has he made non-violence an absolute faith.

SRI AUROBINDO: No, even at that time it was in his mind. If you keep it for religious and ethical matters, nothing can be said against it. But in politics even his own followers accept it with reservation.

SATYENDRA: Now all are in an uncomfortable position. It seems C. R. would be glad to go back to office.

SRI AUROBINDO: That he feels uncomfortable is quite evident. There is no strength in his speech.

SATYENDRA: If Gandhi had kept out after the Poona meeting, it would have been better for everybody.

SRI AUROBINDO: Oh yes, much better.

PURANI: This new Madras Governor gave a hint of conceding to Congress demands for a national government at the Centre. So C. R. took it up.

SRI AUROBINDO: In fact many Governors were in favour of it. This Governor came fresh from England and didn't know the official mind.

7 OCTOBER 1940

PURANI: Gandhi has made a long statement about his interview with the Viceroy. He says that the Viceroy was very patient, very courteous but unbending. Gandhi discussed all the problems with him and he listened to everything patiently as no Viceroy had done before. But he didn't go into any of the arguments.

SRI AUROBINDO: Only listened?

PURANI: He says there was a cold reserve about the Viceroy which couldn't be penetrated. From his answers it could be seen that they were all prepared beforehand and that he had made his decisions already and nothing could shake him. "And that is what is meant by a steel frame, I suppose," he says.

SRI AUROBINDO: To frame him?

PURANI: So Gandhi departed, but as a personal friend.

SRI AUROBINDO: And he saw Jonah before going, didn't he? (*Purani apparently didn't know what "Jonah" referred to.*) Jonah is the turtle that was saved by the Viceroy from the mouth of a fish and put into a pond. Jonah is a Biblical name. You don't know the story of Jonah?

PURANI: No.

SRI AUROBINDO: Jonah was a saint swallowed by a whale and he remained in its stomach for about three days, after which he was rescued. So it was quite an apposite name. Gandhi even cooed to Jonah. (*Laughter*)

PURANI: Gandhi complains that the Viceroy didn't say anything in reply to all his questions and problems.

SRI AUROBINDO: What could he say? It is very plain why he didn't. First of all, the British don't want to concede the demand for independence. What they are willing to give is Dominion Status after the war and they expect that after that India will settle down into a common relationship with the Empire. But just now a national government would virtually mean Dominion Status, with the Viceroy acting only as a constitutional head.

Nobody knows what the Congress will do after they get that power. They may be occupied only with India's defence and give Britain only such help as they can spare. And if things go wrong with the British they may even make a separate peace leaving the British in the lurch. There are left-wingers, socialists and communists whom Congress won't be able to bring to their side; neither will they dare to offend them, and if their influence is sufficiently strong the Congress may stand against the British. So it is quite natural for the British not to part with power just now. As it is also natural for us to make our claims. But since we have not enough strength to back us we have to see if there is any common meeting-ground with the Government. If there is, a compromise with the Government is the only practical step. There was such an opportunity but the Congress spoiled it. Now either you have to accept what you can get or I don't know what is going to happen.

Of course if we had the strength and power to make a revolution and get what we want, it would be a different matter. Amery and others did offer Dominion Status at one time. Now they have altered their stand because of the temper of the people. These politicians have some fixed ideas and they always go by them. Politicians and statesmen have to take account of situations and act as demanded by them. They must have insight.

PURANI: Even now if we could make common cause and demand things, they would be compelled.

NIRODBARAN. But it is because of the British divide-and-rule policy that we can't unite.

SRI AUROBINDO: Nonsense! Was there unity in India before the British rule?

NIRODBARAN: But now since our national consciousness is more developed, there is more chance of unity if the British don't bolster up Jinnah and his Muslim claims.

SRI AUROBINDO: Does Jinnah want unity? His very character shows what he wants. What he wants is independence for Muslims and, if possible, rule over India. That is the old spirit. But why is it expected that Muslims will be so accommodating? Everywhere minorities are claiming their rights. Of course there may be some Muslims who are different, more nationalistic in outlook. Even

Azad has his own terms; only he sees Indian unity first and will settle those terms afterwards.

NIRODBARAN: C. R. seems to be sure of British victory. He says Britain won't lose India to Germany.

SRI AUROBINDO: Lose to whom else? Against Germany there is one advantage: the British navy is supreme. What Germany intends is a long-term blockade of England and thus to exhaust her. But to do that she must have Mediterranean supremacy. If she gets that and can also occupy Africa, then she will have endless resources at her disposal. Germany bungled by treating conquered people like slaves and not making use of her opportunity.

PURANI: In these air raids the British have shown themselves more than equal to the Nazis.

SRI AUROBINDO: Yes. The Nazis have more enthusiasm and dash. But the British individual is more awake and has more initiative and brain-power.

PURANI: Some military correspondent writes that Britain could start an offensive and invade Germany through the Adriatic.

SRI AUROBINDO: They are looking far ahead. But where will they land their troops? Yugoslavia? That means violating Balkan independence. Rather, with their troops in Palestine they could take Syria and then, with Turkey siding with them, proceed towards Germany. That would be much easier than going through the Adriatic. The Adriatic is far more risky and difficult, for the Italians guard the coast. Turkey will side with the British if the British are powerful enough.

Rameshwar is bringing out a booklet containing Sri Aurobindo's writings on Bankim, Tilak, Dayanand and Romesh Dutt. He has asked if Romesh Dutt should not be put after Bankim. Nolini asks why Romesh Dutt should come after Bankim.

SRI AUROBINDO: I don't know. I don't know why he should be there at all. (*Laughter*)

8 OCTOBER 1940

PURANI: German troops are pouring into Rumania, it seems. Do they anticipate a British invasion through it?

SRI AUROBINDO: No, it is more a move towards the Balkans by Germany, if it is also true that Italy has concentrated troops in Albania against Greece.

PURANI: But war on two fronts will be costly for Germany.

SRI AUROBINDO: But how can the British help there? They have no army to spare unless Turkey joins and brings her troops.

PURANI: Kalelkar has rearranged the Gita text leaving out some of the portions which according to him are not essential. And he gives each chapter a separate name: for example, Utthapana Yoga.

SRI AUROBINDO: And Kalelkar Yoga? (*Laughter*) Nobody has so far tampered with the text of the Gita.

PURANI: No, they have done so with the Ramayana and the Mahabharata but not the Gita.

SRI AUROBINDO: Yes.

EVENING

PURANI: America and Russia will check Japan in her imperialist policy in the East.

SRI AUROBINDO: It seems they are not willing to go to war. They only want to help China so far.

Somebody writing about Egypt says that it is the British who don't want Egypt to take any action against Italian attacks just now. I don't see why. They may have their reasons.

PURANI: Kalelkar says that after the war it will be India's lead.

SRI AUROBINDO: Kalelkar's lead? (*Laughter*)

PURANI: He says the Western powers will be crushed. Only Russia and India will survive. They will see the futility of violence, the fruits of such atrocious wars!

SRI AUROBINDO: How is communism a substitute for violence? And why does he call it an atrocious war? In the past also there have been massacres, pillages, sackings, burnings, etc., only in a different way. In these air-attacks on England the death rate so far is less than death by motor accidents. Only the destruction of property is great.

NIRODBARAN: If Russia and India alone survive, India will be a great opportunity for Russia.

SRI AUROBINDO: It will be like the story of a lady of Niger and a tiger – in Edward Lear's limerick. You know the story?

PURANI: No.

SRI AUROBINDO: A lady of Niger went for a ride on the back of a tiger. The tiger returned with the lady sitting inside and the tiger bearing a smile on its face. (*Laughter*) There are good stories in his limericks. You know the story of the cow?

PURANI: I have heard it. Moni's favourite, I think.

SRI AUROBINDO: It can be very well applied to passive resistance. It is like this:

> There was a young man who said, "How
> Shall I melt the heart of this cow?"
>> So he sat on a stile
>> And continued to smile
> Till he melted the heart of the cow. (*Laughter*)

9 OCTOBER 1940

PURANI: It seems America's war with Japan is inevitable.

SRI AUROBINDO: Why?

PURANI: As a consequence of the opening of the Burma Road by the British.

SRI AUROBINDO: Not likely.

PURANI: And Russia also will have two ports – the Balkans and Japan.

SATYENDRA: Japan won't go to war.

SRI AUROBINDO: None of them is willing unless they are obliged to.

Have you any idea what Churchill meant when he declared that Mussolini would very soon see the surprise that the British has for him? What Churchill means in simple words is, "I will show you." (*Laughter*)

NIRODBARAN: He may have something up his sleeve. He doesn't give out empty threats.

SRI AUROBINDO: Not usually.

(*Addressing Purani with a little smile*) Baron went to see Schomberg on some business.

PURANI: I see.

SRI AUROBINDO: He said that he had come to know it was on Schomberg's demand that he had been called from Chandernagore. Schomberg with great surprise exclaimed, "Oh, what a lie, what a lie! Who told you this? It is the Governor who called you; I had nothing to do with it." "But the Governor himself told me that you did it." "What a lie! it is not true, it can't be true." And then when Baron met the Governor he told him what Schomberg had said. The Governor now exclaimed, "What lies, what lies!" (*All of us burst into laughter.*) Baron thought one of them must be lying. He forgot the possibility that both may have been lying.

PURANI: Yes. The Governor may himself have called him back in order to please his Vichy Government.

EVENING

PURANI: Veerabhadra has gone, it seems.

SRI AUROBINDO: Yes, he was asked to give up his public activity, if he wanted to stay here. He says he can't do that as public activity is part of himself. He has got permission to come to the Ashram but live outside. He is fit for nothing else but propaganda. I was many times on the point of driving him out, but he escaped.

PURANI: I wonder how he was teaching Hindi when he himself knows so little. He knows even less than Amrita, I think.

SRI AUROBINDO: It is like Amrita's teaching French in Madras. You know the joke about old French?

PURANI: No.

SRI AUROBINDO: While he was teaching in the class, the students said that what he was saying was different from the book. Amrita replied, "That is old French." (*Laughter*)

PURANI: Yes, yes, I remember Moni and others used to taunt him.

SRI AUROBINDO: It was a standing joke for a long time.

11 OCTOBER 1940

SATYENDRA: The British Government is preparing a huge scheme of insurance for all against the destruction caused by Germany.

SRI AUROBINDO: Yes, it will be a heavy bill. I don't see how they can meet it unless they socialise the whole Government. It is only by socialisation that they can succeed.

SATYENDRA: It may lead to socialism in England after the war.

SRI AUROBINDO: Yes, some form of modified socialism, of course.

PURANI: Shaw goes a step further – he wants communism.

SRI AUROBINDO: Communism exists nowhere, not even in Russia.

EVENING

PURANI: Sarat Bose has also been expelled from the Congress.

SRI AUROBINDO (*laughing*): Yes, two great Bose brothers are gone now. They may try to do some mischief now.

12 OCTOBER 1940

The Czech national committee of Bombay published a pamphlet on the oppressive rules instituted by Germany in Czechoslovakia against university education. The Mother brought a copy of it to Sri Aurobindo in the morning.

SRI AUROBINDO (*after breakfast*): Those who think that Hitler's rule in India won't make much difference from the British, can read it. Then they will see why I support the British. But this is only one example of their oppression, directed only against the university.

PURANI: I have read it. Jallianwalla Bagh seems only a small incident by its side and that was committed by a single man who was afterwards compelled to retire from his office.

SRI AUROBINDO: Yes, that was an instance of a military commander doing something on his own authority, while here it is a regime. Wherever Hitler goes, he starts that regime.

NIRODBARAN: If he could be so brutal with his own white race, what will be the fate of the coloured races?

SRI AUROBINDO: Quite so. But in Poland it is still more severe.

NIRODBARAN: Why?

SRI AUROBINDO: Because he knows the Polish people are more resistant and won't be subjugated. At one time he thought of exterminating the Poles wholesale.

PURANI: The Polish lady who wrote to Ravindra has come back from Europe. She says she has first-hand knowledge of the condition in Poland – about what Germany has done. She prays to you for Poland's amelioration.

SRI AUROBINDO: Poland's amelioration is not possible unless Hitler undergoes deterioration.

PURANI: Hitler's entry into Rumania seems to be his first step towards the Balkans.

SRI AUROBINDO: It is, like all his moves, a slow penetration from which he may go to Turkey, Egypt and Asia. What is wonderful is Stalin's attitude. He is quite silent.

NIRODBARAN: Any secret pact?

SRI AUROBINDO: Even if there were, how long would Hitler respect it if he won? Then Russia would have either to resist or be effaced. Stalin is counting on the exhaustion of the Axis and England and France. Now if Hitler takes Turkey and Egypt and Africa, that will mean practically England's defeat. Then what can Russia do? Hitler has a sufficient army to fight on two fronts while England can hardly spare her troops.

PURANI: Japan is trying to be original: she says she wants peace with America. The three-Power pact is not against America! (*Laughter*)

SRI AUROBINDO: I don't see how Japan can fight England and America when all her war supplies come from them. That is also why Spain can't join Germany.

PURANI: N. R. Sarkar has given a lecture in Madura against non-violence. He says non-violence can't prevent invasion by another power.

SRI AUROBINDO: That is my opinion too. I don't see how Satyagraha can prevent it, or does Gandhi expect that Hitler won't come to India? Hasn't he read anything about Poland?

PURANI: He must have. This Polish lady who was there must have told him. Gandhi says he does not know himself what would be the exact method. He waits for inspiration at the last moment as in all his other cases. He also says that generals don't know their moves beforehand. They wait for inspiration calmly and quietly. In violence one can't be quiet. Gandhi is disturbed by the incidents, etc.

SRI AUROBINDO: Generals get excited by violence? If so, they could never win battles. Gandhi doesn't seem to know much about human psychology. If Napoleon and Marlborough had got excited they could never have been successful.

SATYENDRA: Gandhi doesn't say he can stop an invasion but he says that non-violent non-cooperation can make it impossible for one to rule.

SRI AUROBINDO: That is another matter.

SATYENDRA: If done rightly it can melt other people's hearts as with Prahlad, he says.

SRI AUROBINDO: Prahlad is all right, but a nation of Prahlads doesn't exist. (*Laughter*)

SATYENDRA: He actually believes that Narsimha will come down.

SRI AUROBINDO (*laughing*): To tear the stomach out of the other fellow?

Satyendra (*laughing*): Yes.

SRI AUROBINDO: But at one time he thought of stopping an Afghan invasion by Charkha.

SATYENDRA: In my opinion he should have kept aloof after that Poona affair.

SRI AUROBINDO: Quite so. Gandhi's originality lies in bringing Ahimsa into politics. Otherwise non-cooperation is nothing new.

EVENING

NIRODBARAN: Tagore is having a relapse again and passing restless nights.

SRI AUROBINDO: This time it is difficult to escape, it seems, in spite of Gandhi's wish.

NIRODBARAN: I read the Czech pamphlet.

SRI AUROBINDO: How did you find it?

NIRODBARAN: Terrible!

SRI AUROBINDO: Would you like India to have that?

NIRODBARAN: O Lord, no! I was thinking the Jallianwalla Bagh affair was mild beside this.

SRI AUROBINDO: Yes, I was wondering why they made so much noise about it.

Dr. Rao had come in the morning. Nirodbaran asked him: "What does Madras think of Hitler? It seems it is anti-British." Rao said plenty of people were much surprised by Sri Aurobindo's contribution and were wondering how it was possible for Sri Aurobindo, who once had been so anti-British, to do such a thing. But there were others who supported Sri

Aurobindo. Then Sri Aurobindo explained to Rao at great length all the points and sides of the question, most of which he had mentioned in the letter. We saw that he repeated all of them deliberately, so that Rao might speak of them to others if the occasion arose. What is not included in the letter is given below.

SRI AUROBINDO: In Africa, the Germans have already exterminated one race. Now in France they are creating a distinction between white and coloured races which didn't exist before. It is only the British navy that stands against Hitler's world domination.

DR. RAO: I don't believe that he can dominate the world.

SRI AUROBINDO: Do you know that he is trying to get a foothold in South America and doing extensive propaganda there? If he gets a hold there, he can lead an attack against the U.S.A. He is practically master of Europe. If after the collapse of France he had invaded England, by now he would have been in Asia. Now another force has been set up against him. Still the danger has not passed. He has a fifty per cent chance of success. It is a question of balance of forces. Up to the time of the collapse of France he was extraordinarily successful because he sided with the Asuric Power behind him from whom he received remarkably correct messages. He is a mystic, only a mystic of the wrong kind. He goes into solitude for his messages and waits till they come.

DR. RAO: But how long can he keep these races in subjection? They will rise in revolt one day.

SRI AUROBINDO: What about Poland and Czechoslovakia? They are two of the most heroic nations in the world and yet what can they do? Besides, Hitler doesn't want to annex all these countries under direct German rule. He wants to make them protectorates under his *gauleiters*, all schools, institutions, industries serving German interests and having its culture.

DR. RAO: What is the difference between communism and Nazism?

SRI AUROBINDO: Communism is the proletariat State – no dictatorship, though Stalin is a dictator but he doesn't call himself that. Otherwise they are the same.

DR. RAO: The trouble in India is that the British Government has not kept a single promise so far. So nobody trusts it.

SRI AUROBINDO: The fact is that the British don't trust India to help them if she is given Dominion Status. Otherwise they would have given it.

DR. RAO: I don't think India will refuse to help if we get something in return.

SRI AUROBINDO: You think so? I am not sure. What do you think of the left-wingers, the communists, Subhas Bose, for instance? And it is not true that they have given nothing. It is the British character to go by stages. Whenever their self-interest is at stake they come to a compromise. You have to take account of things as they are. They gave provincial autonomy and didn't exercise any veto power. It is the Congress that spoiled everything by resigning. If without resigning they had put pressure on the Centre they would have got by now what they want. It is for two reasons I support the British in this war: first in India's own interest and secondly for humanity's sake, and the reasons I have given are external reasons; there are spiritual reasons too. You know that no propaganda of any kind is allowed by the Nazis. In that case how are you going to awaken the national sentiment?

DR. RAO: Even if Hitler wins, there is Japan who will resist him in the East.

SRI AUROBINDO: But is Japan powerful enough to do that? It is true that Japan wants to drive out all Europeans from Asia. She can have enough power for that only if she is master of the Far East including China.

DR. RAO: People say that the British won't allow the loss of India. If it comes to that, they will make peace. (*Laughter*)

SRI AUROBINDO: They said also that Britain wouldn't fight after the collapse of France.

PURANI: But why should Hitler make such a peace if he finds that he has chances of success? The trouble with us is that we want to cut off our nose to spite another's face.

SRI AUROBINDO: No, we call in a third party to cut off our nose to spite the other's face. (*Laughter*) India has always done that.

DR. RAO: If Hitler is defeated and they make another treaty of Versailles, there will be trouble again.

SRI AUROBINDO: But if they don't do that there will be another war in twenty years' time. Something has to be done.

PURANI: The best thing would be to march into Germany as they wanted to do in the last war.

DR. RAO: People in Madras regard Italy as no more considerate than Germany.

PURANI: For that reason Egypt has not declared war, they say.

SRI AUROBINDO: No, it is said that the British are holding her back. But do you know that the Italians have exterminated half the native people in Libya? Whatever independence England has given the Egyptians, they will lose if Italy comes there. Are they so foolish as not to know that? The Arabs know the Italians very well. Hence they are completely supporting Britain though they were fighting with her before.

13 OCTOBER 1940

SRI AUROBINDO: Any news about the Congress decision or is Gandhi going to ponder for another two years till the war is over and the Satyayuga comes in? (*Laughter*)

PURANI: Azad has said that there is no going back on the Bombay decision.

SRI AUROBINDO: That is all right, but what are they going to do?

PURANI: It seems Gandhi has prepared a scheme which he is going to submit to the Working Committee. It may be something like what he has advised in Hyderabad, which you may have seen – only four persons selected to go to jail and, if they are released, they will go again.

SRI AUROBINDO: But how will that redress their grievances? And will they call a meeting?

PURANI: They will have to.

SRI AUROBINDO: Then it will no longer be individual. Or they can go to Sir Akbar and sit in his bedroom and refuse to move till their demands are acceded to. (*Laughter*)

PURANI: If they call a meeting, the police may try to break it up.

SRI AUROBINDO: Yes, and then some sort of violence is inevitable. That is about the State. What about Congress? If it is something like their Salt Campaign, one can understand.

PURANI: The same procedure, I suppose: individual Satyagrahis are calling a meeting. The meeting may be banned by the Government, then there may be some riot.

SRI AUROBINDO: In that case a riot is inevitable. Gandhi is balancing on a pinpoint.

EVENING

PURANI: Hitler's intention seems to be to launch an attack in the East.

SRI AUROBINDO: Not only that. He wants to control the oilfields in Asia Minor on which the British depend.

Turkey says Germany will have two million bayonets to face to get to Anatolia. Somebody says that, though Turkey has no mechanised army, it is not very necessary because the country is not suited for mechanised units. So Germany won't be very effective. I am not so sure of that. It may be difficult – that's all. Such things were said by France, and Belgium too.

PURANI: In Bankim's "Bande Mataram" there are two versions of the line *ke bale ma tumi abala.*[1] I don't remember the other version. Nolini wants to know which version you want to keep.

SRI AUROBINDO: But I have translated the original version only.

NIRODBARAN: The other version is *abala keno ma eto bale.*[2]

SRI AUROBINDO: *Eto bale!* Oh, that is for grammar: *abala* being feminine, one can't say *abale*; all the same *abala keno ma . . . bale* is not good. It is better to be ungrammatical than to miss the point. Bankim surely knew about the grammatical error.

14 OCTOBER 1940

PURANI: Gandhi speaks of a premonition of a fast.

SRI AUROBINDO: Good Lord!

PURANI: In reply to Malaviya who had asked him not to fast whatever else he might do, Gandhi said that if he was inspired by God, he might or must.

SRI AUROBINDO: The British Government ought to set up somebody to fast against him – (*laughter*) not to give up his fast till Gandhi stops.

---

1. Who says, Mother, that you are weak?
2. Being so strong, how are you so weak?

NIRODBARAN: Linlithgow is returning, it seems.

SRI AUROBINDO: Yes.

PURANI: They talk of Samuel Hoare as the successor to Linlithgow. In the *Indian Express* there is a cartoon showing Hoare as a rabbit being stewed in his own juice. (*Laughter*)

SRI AUROBINDO: He is needed in Spain. Lothian would have been the best choice. But he is also much needed in America.

15 OCTOBER 1940

NIRODBARAN: Have you read Gandhi's article? He says there is nothing much to choose between British rule and Nazism.

SRI AUROBINDO: Yes, I have read it. Let him be under the Nazis and then he will realise the difference.

PURANI: Amarnath Jha has given a speech in South India. He says that this is not the time for non-violence. One can make a righteous war. Non-violence very often is a cloak for cowardice.

SRI AUROBINDO: Cowardice? One can't say that. Non-violent resistance can't be cowardice. You can say that non-violence may lead to cowardice on the pretext of non-resistance.

PURANI: Yes, simply out of fear of resistance people will take up an attitude of non-violence. That was why a prominent leader of Congress once said in a speech, "I prefer non-violence but if you can't accept it, at least don't sit quiet in times of trouble or danger. Do something." To this Gandhi took objection.

SRI AUROBINDO: Why? He has said that himself many times.

SATYENDRA: Yes, only now he has taken an absolute stand.

SRI AUROBINDO: My only objection is that he wants to use non-violence as a ramrod; it is not practicable under present circumstances. Individual Satyagraha may be possible because some individuals have reached that stage of evolution but as a wholesale mass movement it is not practicable. He muddles the whole thing by bringing it into politics. As a prophet of non-violence, he can practise it as a movement of ethical affirmation, a demand of the soul.

SATYENDRA: Yes, if he had led some such sort of movement with people who could strictly follow him, there would have been nothing to say. From that viewpoint, his retirement from politics after the Poona affair was the right move.

SRI AUROBINDO: Yes, it was the right thing.

SATYENDRA: But people drag him in, foist on him the leadership of the country.

NIRODBARAN: But doesn't Gandhi himself have the idea of saving India politically too? Then why should we blame others or can we say that the leadership has been foisted on him?

SRI AUROBINDO: Oh, not only saving India but the whole world. The leadership was foisted on him as people were feeling helpless without his guidance.

SATYENDRA: That is why I blame these people more. Why don't they take the leadership?

PURANI: I think C. R. could have done something with the Viceroy if it had been left to him.

SATYENDRA: Why doesn't he do it then? He got his opportunity after the Poona affair.

SRI AUROBINDO: Yes, but he is not the leader and he couldn't go to see the Viceroy as the leader.

SATYENDRA: He can stand against Gandhiji and lead the movement.

SRI AUROBINDO: Yes. But Gandhi's hold is too strong for him. Moreover, when these people are face to face with difficulties they feel themselves weak. Unlike the revolutionaries they have not got the strength to start a movement and lead it. C. R. could have made some compromise with the Viceroy except for the fact that the Viceroy isn't a man for compromise. He is, as Gandhi says, unbending; he meets you with fixed decisions. Otherwise Amery's first speech went much farther; it was quite clear in what was said. But because of the Viceroy and the officials it came to nothing.

NIRODBARAN: Now Irwin could be sent as Viceroy.

SRI AUROBINDO: Yes, he has the instinct for peace. Lothian or some other Labour member would have been the best. Lothian has a liberal mind.

SATYENDRA: It is the officials mostly that stand in the way.

NIRODBARAN: That is why some suggested that Amery should pay a personal visit.

SRI AUROBINDO: That won't be of any use. Amery is not the man. Of course one has to take account of Indian officials for any advancement unless one is so strong as to do something over the heads of these people.

PURANI: It seems there is disagreement in the Working Committee about the procedure. Some don't agree with Gandhi in wanting to inform the Government of their move beforehand. But Gandhi wants to keep them informed.

SRI AUROBINDO: He wants to assert the right of free speech. And according to his ideal of Satyagraha he is quite right. His followers take it up as a political move.

SATYENDRA: Yes, that is the trouble. Their standpoints and outlooks are quite different. Somehow I understand Gandhiji in these principles for which he stands. The only thing, as we said, is that he should have kept himself apart from politics.

PURANI: Another trouble with Gandhi is that he says that no man can be perfect unless the society around him is perfect.

SRI AUROBINDO: In that case, like Amitabha Buddha refusing to go to Nirvana till all have attained it, he will have to wait till eternity for perfection! (*Laughter*)

SATYENDRA: He thinks his life is bound up with the national life, so he can't sever himself from the nation.

SRI AUROBINDO: Yes, his life is bound up but the national life is not bound up with him – that is the trouble. Hence wholesale non-violence is not possible. He should have gone to Denmark when they wanted to adopt non-violence, though their non-violence was for a different reason, because they saw that a small army is of no use against greater powers.

SATYENDRA: Gandhiji's non-violence is of course of a different type. You offer resistance non-violently and the enemy may pass over your dead body!

SRI AUROBINDO: Somebody in England gave the same suggestion. Hitler will regret that nobody accepted it.

PURANI: Japan declares she will help the Axis in case of reverses.

SRI AUROBINDO: By telegrams?

This Japan-China war seems to be interminable; each claims big successes and yet it comes to nothing. The same with the other war.

PURANI: Yes, only air raids!

Nandalal Bose's picture of Durga in the Puja number of the Hindustan Standard *was shown to Sri Aurobindo.*

SRI AUROBINDO: It seems to be post-Ajanta decorative style. Lion stylised, peacock in front of the lion, Kartik humorous.

EVENING

PURANI: Gandhara art is supposed to be a mixture of Greek and Indian art. More of Greek influence than Indian.

SRI AUROBINDO: What Gandhara representations I have seen seem to me to be spoiled by Central Asian influence and then bungled by Indian. It is more Central Asian than Greek – it is an imitation of Greece without its mastery, as is the case with all imitation.

16 OCTOBER 1940

Purani started the talk about one Mr. Chevalier, a friend of Dr. Ramchandra, who had arrived here. He seems to have said that Dr. Ramchandra was much changed. Satyendra and Champaklal corroborated the observation. But Purani said that he had heard also some things against Dr. Ramchandra – for instance, his gardening and gardening all the time! Then there was talk that both Suren and Dr. Ramchandra were much relieved because Suren had moved to a new house.

SRI AUROBINDO: Yes, Suren has been wanting to move for a long time, and Ramchandra said that it would be difficult to check his violence if Suren was not removed.

SATYENDRA: But I see much change in him now. Of course many things turn up here from our old nature. For instance, I find in myself things that I didn't suspect existed in me. That is, perhaps, due to some special working in the Inconscient at present.

SRI AUROBINDO: Yes, many people have said that to me. It is what the psychoanalysts put so much weight upon. They call it suppression and its later effect.

SATYENDRA: But everything is not suppression.

NIRODBARAN: You said before that the work was going on in the subconscient.

SRI AUROBINDO: It is the same; it is the rising up of the subconscient from the Inconscient.

NIRODBARAN: Has everybody such dark elements in the Inconscient?

SRI AUROBINDO: There is a possibility, though they may not be manifested in a formed state.

SATYENDRA: When the subconscient rises up, it seems there is no end to it. It keeps recurring. One doesn't know how to get rid of the cycle. It is something terrible.

SRI AUROBINDO: Mind and the vital are easy to change. It is these three, the physical, the subconscient and the Inconscient, that are most difficult.

EVENING

Gandhi has elaborated his campaign of Satyagraha and elected Mr. Vinoba Bhave as the candidate to start it.

PURANI: I read that Gandhi thought of making Vinoba Prime Minister in place of Kher.

SRI AUROBINDO: No, not Kher but Dr. Khare from Central Province.

PURANI: Good Lord! I would like to see how Vinoba would carry on even for a week.

SRI AUROBINDO: He would have advised fasting a week for purification.

Purani then gave a description of Vinoba. Gandhi has elaborated on his science of fasting, saying that it is a dangerous weapon and nobody should undertake one without being a master of its technique. Then he said that his Rajkot fast was a mistake.

SRI AUROBINDO: I thought it was inspired by God!

PURANI: Yes, but in its application he committed mistakes; for instance, he shouldn't have asked the Viceroy to intervene since he considered the Prince as his son. It seems he has selected Nehru as the second candidate after Bhave.

SRI AUROBINDO: Nehru is not scientific – an anticlimax!

NIRODBARAN: No news of Tagore!

SRI AUROBINDO: Yes, he is getting better. Something strange about him: when you think he is getting better, he suddenly begins to die and when you think he is dying he gets better. (*Laughter*)

PURANI: You have read about a Polish ship escaping from Dakar almost miraculously through a ring of submarines, warships, etc.?

SRI AUROBINDO: Yes. That's the true Pole – you can't subjugate the race. By the way, have you marked the "damages and
casualties" in Bombay from the cyclone?

PURANI: Yes.

SRI AUROBINDO: They are all speaking about it in terms of war
as if there had been some air raid. (*Laughter*)

17 OCTOBER 1940

PURANI: Gandhi gave a long introduction about Vinoba, saying
he is the most fitted and ideal non-violent worker, one who has
understood and practised his non-violence in the true spirit. Vinoba
declares that non-violence will bring about a revolution in the
country.

SRI AUROBINDO: Why speeches then?

PURANI: They will be a preparation for successful non-cooperation. He also says the Charkha will bring contentment to people and
to the peasants by making them self-supporting.

SRI AUROBINDO: Then how can there be a revolution?
Discontent brings about a revolution.

PURANI: He has also read Arabic in order to understand and
make common ties and sympathies with the Muslims. He has
written a book making the Charkha the central subject, taking
spinning, cotton, etc. as various items, and written about the history,
geography and science of it.

SRI AUROBINDO: Why the Charkha then? One can write as
well on nails! That is the kind of intelligence which looks at things
from one aspect only – a one-eyed intelligence can't take a complete
view of a subject.

PURANI: Declaring Britain's war-aims, Churchill has said that
they are not fighting for the status quo nor for the old order of
things. More than that it is not possible to say.

SATYENDRA: He says that the only war aim now is to win the
war.

SRI AUROBINDO: Quite so. If he starts declaring the war aims, a
quarrel will start at once and those who are supporting Britain will
object. For war aims don't depend on Britain alone but on Europe
too. With the co-operation and consent of all these other nations
they have to be developed. Different people will prefer different

orders. For instance, the Socialists in England will want Socialism, while no one in Europe will agree to that, not even anyone in America.

NIRODBARAN: There is Satish Das Gupta in Bengal, another lieutenant of Gandhi.

PURANI: His is more of a personal attachment to Gandhi.

SRI AUROBINDO: Not because of Gandhi's ideas?

PURANI: Ideas are secondary; he is a lieutenant because of his attachment. The main thing is his personal attachment apart from any ideas.

SRI AUROBINDO: Religious devotion?

PURANI: Yes.

SATYENDRA: There are many people like that who are attached to Gandhiji because of his personal charm, his personality, not because of any idea or principle he stands for. Patel, for instance.

SRI AUROBINDO: Has none gone for his ideas?

SATYENDRA: I don't think so. It is as things are here. There are not many people here who have come for your philosophy.

SRI AUROBINDO: Why "not many"? Very few.

SATYENDRA: That was my tactfulness.

SRI AUROBINDO: Nirod didn't come for my philosophy!

NIRODBARAN: No!

SATYENDRA: Amrita, for instance, says that whatever you say he will do. If politics, then politics.

SRI AUROBINDO: There is only one man who has come for my philosophy – Veerabhadra! (*Laughter*)

PURANI: Yes, he has his own idea about it and says it is just like Shankara's.

SRI AUROBINDO: Dilip used to shudder at the idea of the Supermind. Even the psychic used to appal him.

NIRODBARAN: Though what he is aspiring for is this psychic attitude of Bhakti.

SRI AUROBINDO: He thinks the psychic has no love and emotion. What he was afraid of was that his vital movements would be taken away.

NIRODBARAN: Mahendra Sircar also came for your philosophy.

PURANI: Adwaitanand, too. Of course, such people are very few.

SATYENDRA: Very few people have any clear idea about it.

SRI AUROBINDO: Yes. I am not speaking of those who come for Yoga. What about Veerabhadra? Where is he now?

PURANI: In the town. I suppose the Vaishya Sabha is putting him up.

SRI AUROBINDO: He ought not to have any difficulty as he is a Brahmin.

PURANI: Yes, a Brahmin in South India is honoured everywhere.

SRI AUROBINDO: And he has many disciples here. If he had the *gerua* [the saffron robe] he would have still more advantage.

NIRODBARAN: But in Bengal he would have a hard time.

SATYENDRA: Why?

NIRODBARAN: In Bengal Sannyasis are not held in much esteem.

SRI AUROBINDO: Bengal has Deshpande's idea, I suppose. I remember when Deshpande returned from England some Sannyasis came to him. He drove them away, asking why able-bodied people should go about from door to door.

SATYENDRA: But in any other part of India a Sannyasi has no difficulty. Purnananda speaks very lovingly of a warm reception in Gujarat.

NIRODBARAN: He says Bengali Sannyasis are not treated well in North India by North Indian Sannyasis. "As the Bengalis don't treat us well, why should we treat them well?" they argue. There is *himsa* [jealousy] among sadhus too!

CHAMPAKLAL: Jain Sadhus beat each other!

SRI AUROBINDO: That is not unusual, quite ancient. There are funny stories in old Buddhist books about Sannyasis. In some books the Sannyasis are described as drinking and shouting in the streets. Subramaniam Bharati told me that in old Jain books he had found instances of Brahmins killing each other in South India and eating cow's meat! Nobody will believe it now.

PURANI: No!

SRI AUROBINDO: Brahmins eating meat goes as far back as the Ramayana. There is the story of Batapi, a Rakshasa, who along with his brother wanted to kill Brahmins. He turned himself into a sheep which was killed and eaten by a Brahmin. Then his brother came and chanted some mantra by which the sheep inside tore open the Brahmin's stomach and came out. He tried to play the same trick on

Agastya. But as soon as his brother chanted the mantra, Agastya chanted some other mantra and thus prevented the sheep from tearing open his stomach. (*Laughter*)

Then there is the story in Bhavabhuti where Vasishtha ate a whole sheep in front of his disciples. The disciples exclaimed, "That fellow is eating the whole sheep!"

SATYENDRA: They must have wondered at his digestive capacity.

SRI AUROBINDO: No, it was not said in praise!

NIRODBARAN: The digestive power must have deteriorated a lot among us since then!

SRI AUROBINDO: Quite so!

NIRODBARAN: Buddha couldn't digest even some pieces of pork.

PURANI: He was eighty! But it was not a sheep that Vashishtha ate; it was a cow, I think.

SRI AUROBINDO: Yes, yes, a calf, I remember now. I was surprised to find a Brahmin eating a cow!

NIRODBARAN: Weren't Brahmins eating cows at one time?

SRI AUROBINDO: Oh yes, sacrificial cows.

NIRODBARAN: It was the post-Buddhistic influence that stopped meat-eating.

SRI AUROBINDO: No, it was Jainism. In Bengal where Buddhism was once very dominant they used to eat meat. It is remarkable how Jainism spread that influence throughout the whole of India. It was because of Jainism that Gujarat is vegetarian. But some carry this abstinence from meat as far back as the Veda. There is a Sloka which says that meat cannot be eaten and they make it "must not" be eaten.

At the end Purani showed us a famous sculpture of Durga from Bihar. Sri Aurobindo said that it was very lively; even the posture of Durga indicated that. Then jocularly he said that one must have a divine quality to balance oneself on a lion like that.

18 OCTOBER 1940

There was miscellaneous talk about this and that. It started with the news of Vinoba's arrest. We said that Purani must be very glad of the news. Then the talk was about the business capacity of different persons. There was some discord between Vinoba and his co-worker Harkar in the Gandhi Ashram. Vinoba seems to have remarked that Harkar would not be able to earn even five rupees outside. This insult was only an additional reason to the many others for which Harkar left the Ashram with the resolve to show whether he could earn his living or not. He joined some business with our Kashibhai. Satyendra remarked that Kashibhai was a good man but had no business capacity. This led to the subject of X's capacity in business. Purani said that he had been on the point of being dismissed from the Navajeevan Office. He also had a tailoring shop which failed.

SRI AUROBINDO: Anything he touches will be a loss. He has a genius for that. He can work under somebody who will oblige him to work. Has he produced any more children?

PURANI: I don't know.

SRI AUROBINDO: He already had three. The way he was industriously working at it, he must have five or six now.

PURANI: T was complaining of the ill-health of the children.

SRI AUROBINDO: Both the parents suffer from ill-health, so their children must be like that. But such people live long.

CHAMPAKLAL: G also started some insurance business with motor cars, etc. It failed.

PURANI: He was also with Gandhi.

SRI AUROBINDO: What was he doing there?

PURANI: Harijan work.

SRI AUROBINDO: Means only talking! He is suited for that.

EVENING

SRI AUROBINDO (*referring to Vinoba's arrest*): The Government said that it would watch how the movement developed. But it didn't wait very long.

PURANI: Have you seen Vinoba's picture in the *Hindu*?

SRI AUROBINDO: Yes. The only notable feature is his forehead – it is like that of a scholar. He has close-cropped hair ready for jail.

SATYENDRA: From his appearance one can make out an ascetic type.

SRI AUROBINDO: Yes, ascetic and puritan, but a mental puritan. Not vital, because his lips indicate otherwise. Only his chin has not the necessary strength for vital indulgence.

PURANI: In spite of all his rigorous practical and routine life, his health is not strong.

SRI AUROBINDO: No, he is badly born, as we call it.

19 OCTOBER 1940

News of Vinoba's arrest has been contradicted on today's radio.

SRI AUROBINDO (*to Purani*): Has it been a great disappointment to you? (*Laughter*)

A number of visitors came from Gujarat by a special train — on a pilgrimage. Some were known or related to Satyendra. Sri Aurobindo inquired as to who they were. Purani answered that some were Satyendra's relatives.

SATYENDRA: They recognised me at once by my nose. Our family has this characteristic nose. (*Laughter*)

PURANI: He says that in the delineation of the gods he finds such noses!

SRI AUROBINDO: Yes, but Nandalal is making them short and crooked now.

Gurusaday Dutt is on a tour of South India promoting his Vratachari folk-dance movement and is expected here as Anilbaran's guest.

PURANI: Anilbaran wants to know your opinion about Dutt's movement.

SRI AUROBINDO: I have no opinion (*laughter*) — as I don't know what it is.

PURANI: He asks whether you consider the movement good.

SRI AUROBINDO: Any movement could be good.

PURANI: His books have been sent to you, it seems. Have you seen them?

SRI AUROBINDO: Yes, they have been sent but I have not read them.

PURANI: It seems he wants to do social service, village uplift work through his Vratachari folk dances. According to him it is the lower castes in India that have preserved the real Indian civilisation. Even the Harijans —

SATYENDRA: Not even! It is the Harijans who are the real custodians of Indian culture.

SRI AUROBINDO: All I can say is that the Pondicherry Harijans are cleaner than caste people. (*Laughter*) But is he also of the opinion that whatever is primitive and ancient is real culture and so must be revived?

PURANI: Yes.

SRI AUROBINDO: Then I can't agree with him.

NIRODBARAN: He claims also a spiritual value in his movement. He says it will help towards spiritual uplift too, which Anilbaran can't swallow. There are five ideals he has set forth: knowledge, labour, unity —

SRI AUROBINDO: Knowledge very good, unity better, and then?

NIRODBARAN: Truth and joy.

SRI AUROBINDO: Joy also? Ananda, Satyam —

NIRODBARAN: Anyone who follows these in his life will have spiritual development.

SRI AUROBINDO (*laughing*): Obviously! I suppose it is through the rhythm of the folk dance that all these will be achieved?

PURANI: Yes.

SRI AUROBINDO: He himself took part in a dance and his I.C.S. people thought he had gone mad! But I thought it was also a scout movement, not only folk dancing.

PURANI: Yes, that is also part of it.

NIRODBARAN: Anilbaran says there is this difference from the Gandhi movement, that it includes joy and beauty.

SRI AUROBINDO: Why? Gandhi finds joy and beauty in suffering!

NIRODBARAN: Dutt is very devoted to his wife's memory, it seems. He always keeps one vacant seat by his side during his meal time. He has written a book on her too. It seems Dutt got inspiration from his wife in all these movements.

SATYENDRA: Many people are devoted like that. Dr. Chandulal, for instance. He lost his wife when young and did not marry again. He wrote a poem on her.

SRI AUROBINDO: He can marry again and write another poem! (*Laughter*)

SATYENDRA: Sometimes in their devotion, external beauty of form doesn't count. In the Leila-Majnun story, somebody asked Majnun what made him love Leila so much, since Leila had no beauty. He answered that one must have Majnun's eyes to see her beauty. But I am afraid Majnun could not have done these Vratachari.

SRI AUROBINDO: Not even if Leila started it? (*Laughter*) A modernised Leila? You must make some allowance for modernism!

PURANI: One of the visitors is a retired D.S.P. It seems he was your student.

SRI AUROBINDO: I see!

PURANI: He says that after the war is over there will be a great economic strain all over the world. Whoever wins won't make much difference to the other economically because both sides will be utterly exhausted. He also thinks that some other social order will come in.

SRI AUROBINDO: A tremendous necessity of that sort will compel them to a new arrangement of society. It is Nature's push that they have not taken any account of so far. They can't go back to the old forms of government and state and society. If they do, there will be upheavals again. What they are calling a New Order will be forced on them by such a necessity. Hitler looks at it upside down. He wanted to make Germany self-sufficient and saw that it was not possible without making the world subservient to Germany. That means that self-sufficiency is not enough nowadays. Nobody can preserve himself by self-sufficiency alone. Unification becomes necessary. You see what Hitler's unification is?

PURANI: By compulsion!

SRI AUROBINDO: Not only compulsion but subservience to Germany!

PURANI: Italy and Germany are holding out threats to Greece; it is said Germany wants to march into Greece, after Rumania!

SRI AUROBINDO: But how? Through Yugoslavia? Is that why the Yugoslavian Prime Minister has gone to Turkey? They can march through Rumania too but it is difficult. Perhaps for a joint action Italy has held up her operations in Egypt.

EVENING

The newspaper said that Vinoba had given three or four speeches and had made up a programme of addressing other meetings.

SRI AUROBINDO: Vinoba is having the time of his life! His speeches are so inoffensive and colourless that I don't see how anybody can arrest him. He can't change his phrases for fear of falling into violence!

PURANI: The evening papers have put in a placard like Gandhi's new movement! Don't know what that new movement is!

SRI AUROBINDO: Because Vinoba has not been arrested? Perhaps he thinks it is a crime on the Government's part not to arrest him?

20 OCTOBER 1940

PURANI: Gandhi has declared his programme: he will start civil disobedience with twenty people of his Ashram – no outsiders – including two ladies, and he has even asked the Congress Working Committee members not to attend the meetings.

SRI AUROBINDO: And if the Government doesn't arrest them?

SATYENDRA: He may go through the whole of India and he will establish the right of free speech.

SRI AUROBINDO: But only Gandhi's followers may not be arrested. Others won't be free. He is fighting for freedom for everybody. Is this the new movement? Nothing new there!

PURANI: It seems Azad differed from Gandhi and was on the point of resigning!

SRI AUROBINDO: As far as that?

PURANI: Yes, he doesn't believe in ethical movements. He wants non-violence as a political weapon like others. But he was persuaded to stay on.

SRI AUROBINDO: But if these people are not arrested, what will be the next move?

PURANI: Gandhi doesn't say. Perhaps he will wait for inspiration.

SATYENDRA: But Pattabhi knows.

SRI AUROBINDO: How?

SATYENDRA: Yes, he seems to know all about Gandhi's scheme and writes about it in the papers.

SRI AUROBINDO: What did he write?

SATYENDRA: The *Indian Express* cut a joke at his cost.

SRI AUROBINDO: It is as somebody said, "Only God and Hitler know what Hitler will do next," so only God and Pattabhi know what Gandhi will do? (*Laughter*)

NIRODBARAN: Like Dinabandhu Mitra writing an epilogue to Bankim's novels?

SRI AUROBINDO: How is that?

NIRODBARAN: As soon as Bankim had finished a novel, Mitra used to come out with a conclusion imitating Bankim's manner, style, etc. Bankim said that he wouldn't be able to write any more because of this man.

SRI AUROBINDO: I see! He married off Ayesha to Jagat Singh?

NIRODBARAN: Something like that.

PURANI: There seems to be some truth about sixty thousand German soldiers being killed on September 15 when Hitler planned to invade England. It was reported at that time.

SRI AUROBINDO: Oh, it was reported? That staved off the invasion then? If only during embarkation sixty thousand were killed, then in crossing and landing how many more died? Everybody who wanted to invade England stumbled against England's sea power. Now I don't think there is any chance of an invasion, because all of Hitler's plans have been exposed and seen.

PURANI: Yes, the British R.A.F. is now able to know Germany's moves and preparations. Hitler now admits to Britain's naval power.

SRI AUROBINDO: Oh! it won't be long before he admits to Britain's air power too.

SATYENDRA: Russia says that Germany and England are equal in air power.

SRI AUROBINDO: Equal in force, not number.

PURANI: If they can start invading Germany –

SRI AUROBINDO: That will take about a year more. A standing army of one-and-a-half million is not enough for that.

SATYENDRA: Each side is now at a stalemate.

PURANI: Unless some unknown factor supervenes, one doesn't know how long it will go on.

SRI AUROBINDO: The only unknown factor is Russia or America coming in. America seems to have come to an understanding with Russia. That may be the reason for their sending war materials. But for America to enter the war with the complete equipment of her mechanised army will still take one or two years. In reply to Russia's note, Germany seems to have said that her step in Rumania is directed against any aggression – nothing more. If any other power threatens, Germany will fight, which means that she is quite ready to fight Russia if Russia attacks Rumania.

PURANI: If Turkey is attacked by Germany what Russia will do, I wonder.

SRI AUROBINDO: Don't know.

NIRODBARAN: Russia is also interested in Bulgaria.

SRI AUROBINDO: It was Russia under the Czar that liberated the Balkans and, if the Czar were there, they would have inclined towards Russia. Now they are afraid of both Russia and Germany.

PURANI: There was a short engagement with the Italian navy in the Mediterranean in which the British destroyed two or three Italian cruisers.

SRI AUROBINDO: Yes, only a short engagement is possible with Italy.

EVENING

The evening radio says that Yugoslavia has signed a protocol with Germany as regards economic and political matters.

SRI AUROBINDO (*to Purani*): Have you seen Yugoslavia's agreement with Germany?

PURANI: Yes, they are coming to an understanding.

SRI AUROBINDO: No, not only understanding; they have signed a protocol by which Yugoslavia is dependent on Germany economically and politically, which means everything. If the news is true, that is the beginning of the end of the Balkans, because Bulgaria won't resist. Greece will be at its wit's end without Turkey's help and what can Turkey do all alone? So Hitler comes to Asia Minor and that means India. This is what I thought, long before, that Hitler might do in the Balkans. The Asura is up to his tricks again. Now Hitler's moves are quite clear. He will try to move towards the Mediterranean, taking possession of the Suez and then Egypt with a simultaneous movement into Spain for Gibraltar with the help of Franco if willing or, if unwilling, without his help and by replacing him with Sumer. That is why he has probably asked Sumer to wait. After Egypt, he will try to take North Africa with Pétain's consent. If Pétain refuses, he may place Laval at the head. And if both refuse, then he will occupy the whole of France and the Mediterranean ports. Then through Spain he can move to Africa. All this will be most dangerous to England and the blockade won't be effective any more. In fact I felt this danger from the very beginning of the war.

NIRODBARAN: But will Russia remain quiet all through?

SRI AUROBINDO: It seems to be like that till now. Except for a short inquiry about Rumanian affairs she has done nothing. Don't know what has happened to Stalin's brain.

PURANI: Even if she comes in, it will be too late afterwards. She should come in now.

SRI AUROBINDO: Quite so. It is because of the lack of her support that these powers are breaking down. They know that England can't do anything to support them because England can't help them with land forces. Even Italy by herself outnumbers England.

NIRODBARAN: Turkey is depending too much on Russia. As nobody knows what Russia's motive is, it can't be safe for Turkey. If Russia betrays her?

SRI AUROBINDO: Exactly. You remember what that Turkish lady – Dilip's friend – said? She said that England is a decadent nation; Turkey won't profit by joining with her. And when she was asked what Turkey's fate would be if England went down, she said, "Why? We will join Russia!"

NIRODBARAN: I wonder if Stalin has made a secret pact with Hitler.

SRI AUROBINDO: That is what all suspect. But what will be the value of any such pact if England is defeated? Then Italy, Germany and Japan will all turn on Russia.

NIRODBARAN: How, if Greece and Turkey together put up resistance to Hitler?

SRI AUROBINDO: That would be an effective check. England could come in with her air and navy.

PURANI: Yes, and Italy could have a little fun from the R.A.F.

SRI AUROBINDO: But the world is under a double curse of stupidity and cowardice. This Hitler is very supple. He takes one step at a time, not the whole movement. When he saw that he had been baulked on one side, he turned to his other side, the danger I had anticipated from the very start.

NIRODBARAN: Now England has only America to rely on.

PURANI: But America is not prepared. She has only a seventy thousand strong army which she must keep for her own defence because she herself runs some danger.

SRI AUROBINDO: She is in no immediate danger unless Hitler establishes himself in South America. That is not possible as long as there is the British fleet.

NIRODBARAN: They could get help from India if they started munitions factories.

SRI AUROBINDO: Yes, they are going at a snail's pace. Starting now an aeroplane factory at Bangalore!

21 OCTOBER 1940

PURANI: Vinoba has made five speeches.

NIRODBARAN: Has there been any effect?

SATYENDRA: There is some effect among the masses. On the news of his arrest there was a partial hartal in Bombay. It seems the speeches are censored. The papers mention: "Two or three sentences are censored here." The *Indian Express* wanted to bring out a special number on this rumoured arrest but couldn't because of the censorship.

SRI AUROBINDO: It could have published the fact that nothing had happened! (*Laughter*)

PURANI: But what effect can non-violence produce? India has been traditionally non-violent from ancient times. So not much preaching is required.

SRI AUROBINDO: How? India was fighting all the time before the English rule. Everybody was fighting and there was no distinction between martial and non-martial races. It is only after the English came that people lost their fighting habits and ability.

NIRODBARAN: The Yugoslavian pact with Hitler seems a fact.

SRI AUROBINDO: Yes. However, it is good news that Turkey says she will resist. She is not depending on Russia.

NIRODBARAN: Nothing is known about Greece.

PURANI: There is no more blitzkrieg. So England can anticipate Hitler's moves now and prepare accordingly.

NIRODBARAN: But what can England do in the East unless Greece and Turkey resist?

SRI AUROBINDO: If they resist it will be an effective check. England can come with her air force and navy.

PURANI: Italy can be easily pounded.

SRI AUROBINDO: Not only Italy; from her bases, England can attack East Germany and Poland, where Hitler has factories, and then Rumania itself. The British can close its embassy in Rumania on the plea that she is now an enemy-occupied country. Then it will be an even game.

SATYENDRA: Ribbentrop is going to Moscow, it seems.

PURANI: Yes, to bring Moscow into Germany's three-Power pact.

SATYENDRA: They say Germany's relations with Russia are sound, solid –

SRI AUROBINDO: And durable – the three words meaning the same thing.

SATYENDRA: The *Indian Express* has published news of the birth of Churchill's grandson.

SRI AUROBINDO: The *Hindu* too!

SATYENDRA: Oh, I thought it was too small a news for the *Hindu*. Soon they will give the photo of the baby.

SRI AUROBINDO: War baby! (*Laughter*)

PURANI: Anilbaran wants to know what the relation is between cosmic consciousness and Overmind.

SRI AUROBINDO: Relation? What relation?

PURANI: I told him that Overmind is an instrument like Supermind.

SRI AUROBINDO: Cosmic consciousness has many levels: it can be of mind, vital and matter; of Overmind too. So what does he mean by relation between them? Cosmic consciousness is a term used in contrast to individual consciousness. Through it you get to know about the universe. Overmind is a power of cosmic consciousness just as mind, vital and body are. Only, you can have body, vital and mind without any knowledge of cosmic consciousness, while to go to or know Overmind you must have cosmic consciousness. The cosmic working can be known by entering into Overmind, but for the source you have to go to Supermind. You can know the working from Overmind knowledge but to get control or command or the final secret you must have Supermind, which is an instrument of self-determination of the Divine and has organised the cosmos.

22 OCTOBER 1940

SATYENDRA: In reply to the judge as to whether he had anything to say, Vinoba is supposed to have said that they had made a disgraceful translation.

SRI AUROBINDO: Translation?

SATYENDRA: Yes, Sir. He made speeches in Marathi and they were translated into English.

SRI AUROBINDO: Why disgraceful? Means inaccuracy in language or incorrectness in content?

SATYENDRA: Don't know.

PURANI: Though he is a scholar in Sanskrit, he has not read *Shakuntala* and considers this a great virtue! He has learned Sanskrit in order to read the Gita and the Upanishads.

SRI AUROBINDO: Not *Shakuntala* because it is erotic?

PURANI: Probably. Mahadev Desai has put forth Vinoba's philosophy in the *Hindu* today. Vinoba says: We live because we can't die. We eat and walk, etc., because we are compelled to. We sleep because sleep overcomes us.

SRI AUROBINDO: I thought it was the other way round. We die because we can't live.

PURANI: That was what I thought too.

SATYENDRA: He must have said it in relation to something. Perhaps a friend of mine holds the same view.

SRI AUROBINDO: How is that?

SATYENDRA: I spoke about it once before: he wanted to commit suicide, took a lethal dose of opium but it didn't kill him. Another friend had many accidents but death escaped him.

PURANI: He could have taken potassium cyanide!

Desai continues to say that Vinoba had differences with Ramdas. Ramdas says the doer is free while Vinoba says he is not. As I said before, according to him we sleep because we are compelled to. In everything we do there is a compulsion.

SRI AUROBINDO: One can say one is compelled to be born, at least in appearance. But does Ramdas say one is free?

PURANI: He says partially free – in the process of becoming free.

SRI AUROBINDO: That is a different matter.

PURANI: Sardesai makes out in the course of a talk that Shivaji had no political guidance from Ramdas: Ramdas refused to give any when Shivaji approached him. This is something new.

SRI AUROBINDO: What about the ochre-coloured flag? A legend?

PURANI: He says that Ramdas gave him advice about the succession to the throne when Shivaji wanted his second son to come to the throne instead of Shambhuji. Ramdas advised him to make his eldest son the rightful heir and to follow the usual royal custom.

SRI AUROBINDO: He did guide him then?

PURANI: It is only part of a talk Sardesai gave, in which he says that he will put forward only two or three points for the present. Shambhuji, he says, was not as bad as is made out.

SRI AUROBINDO: White-washing?

PURANI: Yes, and if it was eating and drinking, that was a common fault. Everybody used to do it.

SRI AUROBINDO: Queer defence! If he wants to be original he must say something unexpected.

SATYENDRA: Lothian is mentioned as a possible Viceroy of India.

SRI AUROBINDO: Oh! In that case they will have to change Amery too. But Lothian is doing much useful work in America. Can he be spared?

PURANI: Lord Lloyd is also suggested by the diehards!

SRI AUROBINDO: Good Lord! They may as well send the devil himself or Sir John Anderson. It will be disastrous! But the Labour Party may not consent. When is the present Viceroy to go?

PURANI: After six months.

SRI AUROBINDO: That's a long time!

EVENING

Armando Menezes has written another book of poems and has sent a copy to Sri Aurobindo. Purani asked if he had read it.

SRI AUROBINDO: Yes, some of the poems. There is a remarkable change. There is one written on 21st February. He has still to progress till every word becomes inevitable. His long poems are not so successful.

PURANI: Yes. He says that he is afraid to read *The Life Divine* lest he should have to make a choice between the worldly life and the spiritual. He got something at the Darshan.

SRI AUROBINDO: There are two or three poems in connection with that mood.

I have read Desai's account of Vinoba. He has combined Buddha and Plato in him. He could have added Diogenes too. It seems Vinoba doesn't like literature. Only history and philosophy interest him.

PURANI: Yes, I told you he is proud of not having read *Shakuntala*.

SRI AUROBINDO: Not only *Shakuntala*, but literature in general doesn't interest him.

PURANI: Yet he is said to be a great lover of art. Somebody told him that he is an ascetic and doesn't appreciate beauty. He replied that he loves beauty; he loves flowers and the starlit sky. He would rather tear off his skin than pluck a flower.

SRI AUROBINDO: That is the popular notion of art and artist. If you love flowers and admire the sky you are considered an artist. I saw in *Prabuddha Bharata* that Vivekananda was called a great master of art because he loved music.

SATYENDRA: Perhaps one can be an artist by appreciating art?

SRI AUROBINDO: In that case many people are artists.

NIRODBARAN: If one can sing well?

SRI AUROBINDO: Singing well doesn't make one an artist – that is my point. An artist must either create something or have an aesthetic understanding of art. Anybody can look at the moon or the sky and get an emotion.

PURANI: Now they give a new definition to art. They say art must be able to transmit emotion. Otherwise it is not art or it is art that has no value.

SRI AUROBINDO: What emotion?

PURANI: Feeling, I suppose.

SRI AUROBINDO: Feeling? What feeling?

PURANI: Such as an agriculturist or farmer can understand. That is their conception and in that they are followers of Tolstoy. You know Gandhi is greatly influenced by Tolstoy and follows his view of art, the puritanic and popular view.

SRI AUROBINDO: That puritanic element exists in many places. Even Ruskin who was considered an authority on the aesthetic element in art had puritanism in his blood. Puritanism has been brought from Europe to India. In India even ascetics were not puritans.

PURANI: Musriwalla is trying to introduce some ideas of spirituality. He has written three or four books on the lives of Buddha and others. He says that experiences are not reliable because they take place in Nature.

SRI AUROBINDO: In that case you can't realise God because the experiences will be in Nature. The only thing to do is to commit suicide to get out of Nature.

PURANI: Or sit quiet.

SRI AUROBINDO: That will be in Nature!

PURANI: Musriwalla has no idea of these things, not even elementary principles of Sankhya. He doesn't realise that in Nature one can have the contact of something of Supernature. He has no imagination, either. He says Valmiki has depicted Ayodhya as a rich, luxurious city.

SRI AUROBINDO: Should it have been described as a poor village? Then if he read Kalidasa he would squirm with agony.

PURANI: For such people everything should be simple, bare, austere and poor. I don't understand why poverty should be made to appear so great.

SRI AUROBINDO: Because Tolstoy said it and Gandhi said it after him!

PURANI: He is also against temples. There is no necessity of temples according to him. As somebody said, churches are not necessary, for the Bible can be read in the fields.

SRI AUROBINDO: Why houses then? Everybody can live in the fields like the birds and animals; it will be quite natural.

SATYENDRA: Rumania seems to be in luck. It has got not only the Germans but an earthquake too.

PURANI: Yes, like Turkey.

SRI AUROBINDO: But Turkey has no Germans!

PURANI: The Germans are trying to penetrate into Bulgaria also in the guise of tourists.

SRI AUROBINDO: Yes. Hitler didn't find Boris very –
PURANI: Pliable? No.

23 OCTOBER 1940

PURANI: Gandhi hasn't appointed any successor to Vinoba. He says that this time there won't be a continuous stream of resisters.

SRI AUROBINDO: If he appoints one every month so that they may be spread over the whole period of the war, it will be all right.

SATYENDRA: He wants to proceed very carefully this time as he doesn't want to precipitate any mass movement and thus give the Government cause for provocation.

SRI AUROBINDO: Especially as now is the best chance! (*Laughter*) But surely by a few arrests he doesn't expect to change the hearts of people like Churchill and Amery.

PURANI: He says any number of people are volunteering. But he will select only those who believe in complete non-violence and in Khadi, etc. Even these may not all be expected to be called. He evidently has some plan or is waiting for inspiration!

SATYENDRA: He may wait indefinitely but I fear the Working Committee won't.

SRI AUROBINDO (*laughing*): No! They will be wild.

PURANI: Churchill's speech is again magnificent. He has a wonderful quality of rising to the occasion. He has made a very stirring appeal to the French not to succumb to Hitler's perfidious cunning. It is mostly due to his personality that America has turned her sympathies towards Britain.

SRI AUROBINDO: Yes, but also helped by the misdeeds of Japan and Hitler. (*Laughter*) Churchill is the second great man given by his family to England at times of crises.

PURANI: Some American correspondent has said that though destruction from bombing is going on in London, people are as firm as before and taking it all coolly.

SRI AUROBINDO: It seems for the first few days they were very perturbed. That's what Mona's mother has written to her. Then they accustomed themselves to the bombing.

SATYENDRA: In such circumstances, people become fatalists.

SRI AUROBINDO: It is like the Japanese. In Japan there is a fire every week, a typhoon each fortnight and an earthquake every month. Mother said that they go to bed quite dressed and as soon as any of these things take place, they jump out of bed and rush out. (*Laughter*)

(*After some time*) Laval is at his game trying to make a pact with Hitler. I hope people understand him and won't believe in him. Those who understand Hitler ought to know that Hitler will agree to anything that suits him at the moment and afterwards swallow everything.

PURANI (*handing Sri Aurobindo Dean Inge's book on Plotinus*): It seems Krishnaprem has said that Plotinus's Nous is the same as Supermind. Somebody from outside has asked if that is true.

SRI AUROBINDO (*after looking at a few pages*): Inge takes Nous as Spirit. As far as I can make out, Nous is spiritual consciousness, not Supermind, but I will see about it again.

24 OCTOBER 1940

SRI AUROBINDO (*addressing Purani*): Laval is involved in a great labour!

Laval is trying to bring about peace in France by some agreement with Hitler. Proposals seem to be to give Nice to Italy, put Tunis under France and Italy, cede Alsace-Lorraine to Germany, Morocco to Spain, Indo-China to Japan, surrender air and navy to the Axis and have France declare war against England.

SATYENDRA: Will the French fight?

PURANI: If they had wanted to fight they could as well have gone on fighting against Germany in the first place.

SRI AUROBINDO: Quite so!

NIRODBARAN: But Hitler may hold out the threat that if they don't agree, the whole of France will be occupied.

SRI AUROBINDO: If they do agree, they will lose their colonies. This seems to be Hitler's game. It is quite clear now what happened at the Brenner Pass. They must have decided to spread out to the Balkans and then to the east to Egypt, and on this line bring France and Spain into the war. Sumer's visit and Hitler's visit to Franco must be to induce Spain. There must be an Italian brain behind this scheme. Hitler moves to the front with one objective at a time. This sort of combination is not usual for him. It must be Mussolini's calculating brain. It is a large scheme this time, not like Hitler's previous moves.

NIRODBARAN: Britain and America are proceeding with their evacuation. Do they think an attack is imminent?

SRI AUROBINDO: They must have got some private information. Even if there is a chance, Japan won't say anything. They will simply make arrests. But the old Japan during the Magi regime would have said something.

28 OCTOBER 1940

EVENING

Radio news came that Italy has invaded Greece.

SRI AUROBINDO: It is the result of their Brenner Pass meeting.

PURANI: England will now have a chance to bombard Italy from close quarters.

SRI AUROBINDO: Yes, if they know how to use this opportunity they can occupy the islands there.

PURANI: If Turkey wants to fight, she should join now.

SRI AUROBINDO: If she has any sense she ought to. The British can't send an army. Unfortunately the Greeks are not good fighters. If the Turks come in, then they can put up a fight. They have their army in Thrace.

PURANI: Turkey spoke some time ago about giving help to Greece, an alliance, probably.

SRI AUROBINDO: Alliance or understanding?

PURANI: May be understanding.

SRI AUROBINDO: Turks usually keep to their undertakings.

NIRODBARAN: Unless Russia beguiles them.

SRI AUROBINDO: But will Russia protect Turkey if she is invaded?

(*After a while*) Gandhi has been forestalled in non-violence by Poland. The Poles adopted non-violence against the Nazis and do you know the results? The Polish lady, who wants to come here and is Ravindra's friend, wrote to Gandhi an account of the German oppression against the non-violence. She has given a report in a

Telegu paper which accidentally came into Satyakarma's hands. He was very upset and spoke to the Mother. The Mother has asked Krishnayya to translate it. The Polish lady cites a few horrible instances of atrocity on men and women, young and old.

29–30 OCTOBER 1940

Very little talk these days.

PURANI: Hyderabad wants to be an independent sovereign state after the war and has asked the British to withdraw their forces and treat it as an equal. It says that if India gets Dominion Status, Hyderabad should become an independent sovereign state.

SRI AUROBINDO: An independent dominion within a dominion?

PURANI: No, an independent state altogether.

SRI AUROBINDO: Why does Hyderabad wait for the war? It can do that now.

PURANI: Yar Jung Bahadur with his assembly is the leader.

SRI AUROBINDO: Oh, him? It's an assembly of idiots! But what will happen is that the Nizam will be the first to be kicked out. He knows it very well.

PURANI: He claims that Hyderabad has always been independent. But in fact in five battles with the Mahrattas, it was utterly defeated; not a single battle went in its favour. Yar Jung says that the Nizam is contributing so much to the war fund, so he must be treated as an ally, equal in status.

SRI AUROBINDO: It is not the Nizam who is contributing but Sir Akbar who is forcing him to contribute. Otherwise the Government knows very well what the Nizam's views are.

PURANI: Sir Akbar will be coming here now.

SRI AUROBINDO: Yes.

NIRODBARAN: Nripen Sarcar is coming too. So they will meet.

PURANI: It seems Sarcar has suddenly turned religious. He has employed Sanskrit pundits and is learning Sanskrit.

SRI AUROBINDO: I see! Preparing himself for the other world. Whatever he has had to achieve he has done in this world and is now doing things for the next? (*Laughter*)

NIRODBARAN: Charu Dutt seems to have persuaded him to come here and also to buy a house to stay here for some time.

SRI AUROBINDO: Buy a house? Queer idea! Wants to do Yoga?

NIRODBARAN: Probably.

PURANI: He has spoken somewhere in the South against Hitler and the Nazis and, quoting from *Mein Kamf*, says that Hitler considers us "chattels and slaves". In a Nazi victory our lot will be like that.

SRI AUROBINDO: Quite so. That is the well-known Nazi position on the coloured races. Pétain is now taking it up in France.

PURANI: Yes, he has already started against the Jews.

SRI AUROBINDO: He is also preventing coloured people from entering the Government service.

6 DECEMBER 1940

DR. MANILAL: When the Gita says "I shall deliver you from all *papa*", does *papa* mean sin, Sir?

SRI AUROBINDO: No, from all evils. Sin is a religious conception, an offence against God. Arjuna's refusal to fight can't be called an offence against God; it is an offence against morality, you can say. Virtue and vice are moral conceptions.

MULSHANKAR: What type of Yogi is Gandhi, Sir?

SRI AUROBINDO: Yogi? He is not a Yogi; he is an ethical man.

MULSHANKAR: He is guided by voices.

SRI AUROBINDO: Then everybody who is guided by voices would be a Yogi. Then all Quakers are Yogis. Those who are possessed by strong vital forces, good or bad, can hear voices. Gandhi himself says that when he is so possessed he can't resist. These are voices which come from various sources. One voice says one thing, another contradicts it.

EVENING

Dr. Manilal was sitting with a warm cloth tied round his head to protect it against a cold draught.

SRI AUROBINDO: You have the expression of Schopenhauer on your face. (*Laughter*)

DR. MANILAL: How, Sir?

SRI AUROBINDO: The world, according to him, is full of suffering and sorrow, and life is an insanity.

DR. MANILAL: It is just the contrary with me. I thought I caught an infection of hilarity from Ravindra.

SRI AUROBINDO: Then you are trying to suppress it. (*Laughter*)

DR. MANILAL: Are German philosophers influenced by Vedanta? Vivekananda said that Max Müller was a reborn Sayanacharya.

SRI AUROBINDO: How? It is more than a compliment.

DR. MANILAL: Sylvan Levi is also a Sanskrit scholar. He came to Baroda. The Gaekwar used to refer to you, Sir, as "my secretary".

SRI AUROBINDO: Not a troublesome one? (*Laughter*)

DR. MANILAL: No, Sir. Vallabbhai once said that you were fined Rs. 50 by the Gaekwar in Kashmir.

SRI AUROBINDO: In Kashmir? No, it was in Baroda. I refused to attend office on Sundays and holidays, so he fined me Rs. 50. I said, "Let him fine me as much as he likes", and when he heard about it he stopped fining me.

7 DECEMBER 1940

DR. MANILAL: Is not the taking of life a sin, Sir?

SRI AUROBINDO: You are all the time thinking of sin. It depends on circumstances. English doctors advocate giving injections to cases of incurable suffering in order to cut short their lives.

PURANI: Gandhi also advocated it in case of the Ashram cow and there was a row among the Jains.

DR. MANILAL: What about suicide?

SRI AUROBINDO: It depends on the spirit in which it is done. If it is done in a vital spirit or with a vital motive it may be sin. Would you say that the Sannyasi who committed suicide in the story about Alexander engaged in an act of sin?

DR. MANILAL: I don't know the story.

SRI AUROBINDO: When Alexander was returning to Greece he wanted to take with him two Sannyasis. One refused, the other accompanied him. But after some time the latter had a severe attack of colic. He said his body was betraying him. So he decided to give up his body by immolating himself. In spite of pleadings he carried out his decision.

12 DECEMBER 1940

The talk started with the release of Mrs. Naidu from prison.

SRI AUROBINDO: As I remarked, the Government has not given her the chance of a rest cure in jail. The Government refuses to take up responsibility for her.

DR. MANILAL: Instead of getting a rest cure she would rather feel restless in jail after some time. She is a brilliant speaker. She can do more valuable work outside the Congress.

SRI AUROBINDO: Much more! She has done nothing in the Congress.

DR. MANILAL: I heard her in Baroda. She has a fine voice too.

The talk proceeded to B. L. Gupta, also a good speaker, a former Dewan of the late Gaekwar. Then the Gaekwar himself came into the talk, how he had been humiliated at the Durbar due to the foolishness of B. L. Gupta. It was reported that after this humiliation the Gaekwar had begun to go downhill.

DR. MANILAL: Before this he was really great. A speech he made at the Industrial Exhibition was marvellous.

SRI AUROBINDO: Which Industrial Exhibition?

DR. MANILAL: At Ahmedabad.

SRI AUROBINDO: That was the speech I prepared for him. (*Roar of laughter*)

MULSHANKAR: I heard your lecture at Bombay after the Surat Congress. You had some paper in your hand.

SRI AUROBINDO: That was the speech I made from an entire silence of the mind. It was my first experience of the kind. You didn't hear me at Baroda?

DR. MANILAL: Yes, Sir, once only. I was in the Matric class then. I remember only one sentence of that speech. Dr. Mullick had come to Baroda. The meeting was held in his honour. Professor Saha proposed you to the chair saying, "Dr. Mullick is a Bengali and Mr. Ghose is a Bengali. So I propose him to the chair." You replied, "I consent to take the chair not because Dr. Mullick is a Bengali and I am a Bengali, but because I am an Indian and Dr. Mullick is an Indian."

When did you conceive of doing the Yoga, Sir?

SRI AUROBINDO: Conceive of it? You mean when I started it?

DR. MANILAL: All right, Sir. (*Laughter*)

SRI AUROBINDO: It was Deshpande who wanted me to do Yoga. But when I came to know it would mean withdrawal from the world I didn't want to do it as I wanted to do political work. Then I took to Pranayama. But it didn't carry me far and I came to a point beyond which I couldn't proceed further. I gave it up and fell dangerously ill! I was on the point of death. I asked Barin if he knew anyone who could help me in Yoga. This was in Surat where I had attended the Surat Congress. Barin knew of Lele who was in Gwalior. He wired to him and asked him to meet us at Baroda. Pranayama had given me good health, a lot of poetry and various experiences. Now Lele took me to a quiet room upstairs in Khaserao Jadhav's house. I told him that I wanted Yoga to help me in my political work, for inspiration and power and capacity. I didn't want to give up my activities for the sake of Yoga. He said, "You are a poet; it will be very easy for you." Then he said, "Sit still and try to make your mind quiet and empty of thoughts. You will see that all your thoughts come from outside. As you perceive them, simply throw them away before they can enter into you." I tried and did it. In three days my mind became entirely quiet and vacant, without any thoughts at all, and it was in that condition of Nirvanic silence that I went first to Poona and then to Bombay. Everything seemed to me unreal; I was absorbed in the One Reality.

In that state of mind I told Lele, "I have been asked to deliver a lecture. How am I going to speak? Not a single thought is coming to me. I cannot make a speech." He held a day of prayer with other disciples for me and at the end he said, "Make a pranam to Narayana in the audience before you start, with your mind completely vacant. Then you will see that everything will come down and some power speak through you." I did as he had said and found that the whole speech came down from above; not a single thought or expression was mine. It got hold of my organ of speech and expressed itself through it from beginning to end. In my tour from Bombay to Calcutta all the speeches I made were from that condition of silence.

While I was parting from Lele I asked him what I should do, how I should be guided. He said, "Surrender yourself to the Divine and be guided by Him. If you can do that, you needn't do anything else." I replied, "I can easily do that." And when I did that, everything came from above and I was guided by that. After some time when Lele came to Calcutta, he asked me how I was getting on, whether I was meditating or not according to his advice. He had asked me to meditate twice a day and to be guided by the voice within. When I told him that I had given up meditation – in fact the meditation was going on all the time – he said, "Ah, the devil has got hold of you." (*Laughter*) He did not wait for me to explain anything to him. Since then we began to follow our own ways. Evidently he had something in him and it was he who opened up and gave me the silence experience after my failure to advance further. Only, he wanted me to follow his path. He didn't want me to have the Nirvanic experience.

EVENING

DR. MANILAL: What is the reason for your failure in the riding test in the I.C.S., Sir?

SRI AUROBINDO: I appeared late for the test.

DR. MANILAL: Why? Was it under any inspiration?

SRI AUROBINDO: No, (*laughing*) it was intentional. I wasn't dealing in inspiration then. I didn't want to be in the British Government Service. I had a strong dislike for the British.

DR. MANILAL: But then why did you appear for the I.C.S. exam at all?

SRI AUROBINDO: I had no intention to do it. It was my father who wanted me to be a civilian. I had to play this trick; otherwise my father and everybody would have howled. My poet brother was horrified to see me, along with my elder brother, smoking and playing cards at the Liberal Club after avoiding the riding test.

DR. MANILAL: Was your father alive at that time?

SRI AUROBINDO: Yes, he was arranging with Sir Henry Cotton a post for me in Bihar under Sir Henry. But he died of shock soon after.

DR. MANILAL: What shock?

SRI AUROBINDO: He asked me to return to India by a particular ship. I don't know why on that ship. The ship was wrecked off the Portuguese coast. He thought I was on it. But I hadn't sailed on it at all.

DR. MANILAL: Why?

SRI AUROBINDO: I didn't intend to.

NIRODBARAN: Did your father know of your failure in the test?

SRI AUROBINDO: No.

DR. MANILAL: Then he would have been shocked in any case.

SRI AUROBINDO: When they came to know, they all asked me to try again. But I didn't want to and I knew too that the British Government wouldn't give me another chance.

DR. MANILAL: Why?

SRI AUROBINDO: My record was too bad.

DR. MANILAL: How?

SRI AUROBINDO: They thought that I was a revolutionary, giving seditious speeches in the Indian Majlis. There was a man named Mehedi Hussain, an Indian deputy magistrate – I don't know why he went to England – who used to come to the Majlis and was supposed to be a spy. He may have reported me to the Government.

DR. MANILAL: How did you get the job in Baroda?

SRI AUROBINDO: I think I applied for it when the Gaekwar was in England. Sir Henry Cotton's brother asked me to do it and through his influence I came in contact with the Gaekwar.

DR. MANILAL: I thought that your political career began with the Bengal Partition.

SRI AUROBINDO: Oh no! It began long before in Baroda. It was our men who got hold of the movement in Bengal and gave it a revolutionary character. Otherwise it would have been a moderate movement. We were training people in our secret society started by Tilak.

DR. MANILAL: Servants of India Society? (*Laughter*)

SRI AUROBINDO: No, no, a secret society which I and some others joined along with some Rajput Thakurs. While in Bengal the revolutionary party was started by Okakura and joined by Nandy, Suren Tagore and others. The Swadeshi movement started before the Bengal Partition. I was coming and going between Bengal and Gujarat. Gujarat was very moderate at that time. With Pherozeshah Mehta it was just beginning to be revolutionary.

DR. MANILAL: What about Dadabhai Nowroji? He was an extremist.

SRI AUROBINDO: No, Moderate, ardent Moderate. Ardent of the non-ardent type. Moderate of the middle kind, like Gokhale.

13 DECEMBER 1940

DR. MANILAL: Sir, was the Mother doing your Yoga in Europe?

SRI AUROBINDO: Why my Yoga? She was doing Yoga, though the Europeans don't call it Yoga.

NIRODBARAN: There is such a striking similarity between your ideas and the Mother's.

DR. MANILAL: Yes, that is why I ask.

SRI AUROBINDO: Yoga is everywhere the same.

NIRODBARAN: Yes, but what I mean is that the Mother also stressed the need of divine manifestation, of not considering the world as Maya. Did she have any teacher?

SRI AUROBINDO: No, Jnan Chakravarty, the husband of Krishnaprem's Guru, gave her the Gita's Yoga in Paris. And she used to come in contact with Abdul Baha in Paris. As a matter of fact, it was she who was leading and organising the Bahai group in Europe. In one of their group meditations Mother had some experience which none of the others had.

DR. MANILAL: What is Bahaism, Sir? I find it mentioned in the *Sunday Times* too.

SRI AUROBINDO: I think Abdul Baha was the son or grandson of Baha-ullah who established the Bahai sect. It is a modernised and liberalised form of Mohammedanism. They believe there is truth in every religion, and they believe themselves to have gathered all the essential religious truths. This Baha-ullah was imprisoned in Turkey for thirty or forty years. He was kept in a tower; about thirty to forty thousand people used to come to see him and he used to give them his blessings standing at the tower window.

NIRODBARAN: I heard that Mother used to see you in visions, but could not make out the exact identity. She thought it might be a Chinese figure.

SRI AUROBINDO: No, it was not like that. Every day somebody used to appear to her calling himself Krishna. As soon as she saw me, she recognised that it was myself.

EVENING

DR. MANILAL: Could Hitler be called as great as Napoleon, Sir?

SRI AUROBINDO: What? How can he be compared with Napoleon? He can't stand any comparison with Napoleon. Hitler is a man of one idea; he has no other capacity or activity except that he is also a house-painter, while Napoleon had many sides: he was not only a military general, but also an administrator, organiser, legislator and many other things. It was he who organised France and Europe, stabilised the French Revolution. Besides being a legislator he established the bases of social laws, administration and finance which are followed even today. He is not only the greatest military genius in history but one of the greatest men, with manifold capacities. Hitler is a man of one idea, with no intellect, which he applies with strong force and violence; he has no control over his emotions. He hesitates in his policies which some call cautiousness. And all his power comes from the Asura by whom he is possessed and guided while Napoleon was a normal human being acting through the power of his brain which reached the highest development possible in a human being.

DR. MANILAL: Napoleon is said to have been immoral.

SRI AUROBINDO: If you mean that he was not chaste, it is true. As I said, he was a normal human being with enormous many-sided powers and capacities which very few people have possessed.

Hitler's idea of the Nazi order is also not his. It is the idea of a Jew whom he murdered later on.

PURANI: And you can see in Europe the type of New Order and civilisation he wants to establish.

NIRODBARAN: But as regards military genius they say he is as great as Napoleon.

SRI AUROBINDO: How? One can say that he has developed a new technique which he has pursued with great audacity. Even that new technique is not his. It was discovered by a Frenchman and was passed on to the German generals. They hesitated to act on it while Hitler pursued it boldly, disregarding the advice of the generals.

Hitler is a new type, an infra-rational mystic, representing the dark counterpart of what we are striving to arrive at: a supra-rational mysticism. (*Looking at Dr. Manilal*) Do you know that in his secluded residence he has a cinema and enjoys and gloats on the horrors and sufferings he has inflicted on people? That is the story told by his maidservant who was with him all the time.

16 DECEMBER 1940

Anilbaran in an article on the Gita has tried to bring into it Sri Aurobindo's ideas of transformation, The Life Divine, *etc. Sri Aurobindo commented on this.*

SRI AUROBINDO: The Gita doesn't speak of transformation. It is his own reading of the Gita. One can say that the Gita shows the way to something further or to our Yoga. What it speaks of is the need to act from a spiritual consciousness using the instruments of the human mind, vital, etc., but not of the transformation of these instruments.

PURANI: Anilbaran admits this but he says that here and there in the Gita there are hints beyond it.

SRI AUROBINDO: In that case my claim that our Yoga is new doesn't hold good, and the man who said that the Gita speaks of transformation would be right.

Purani conveyed Sri Aurobindo's views to Anilbaran. Anilbaran admitted his mistake and said that in the future he would be more cautious and accurate in his statements.

17 DECEMBER 1940

Today Anilbaran asked through Purani: "What is the limit of transformation which the Gita speaks of?"

SRI AUROBINDO: Limit of transformation? But the Gita, as I said, doesn't speak of transformation. It goes as far as the Buddhi.

PURANI: Krishna says, *puta madbhavam agatah* – "They come to My nature" – doesn't this mean transformation of nature?

SRI AUROBINDO: That is not transformation. *Puta*, being purified, you attain to My nature – the Divine nature – but such an attainment is not transformation.

PURANI: When one is acting from the Divine nature, the Divine spiritual consciousness is the background. Is it not the transformed nature?

SRI AUROBINDO: What is the Divine nature? Transformation does not mean the change of ordinary nature into it. At least that is not the sense in which I have used the term.

PURANI: The Vaishnavas speak of getting the nature of the Divine.

SRI AUROBINDO: Then is that transformation? If so, the Vaishnavas have the supramental transformation of the nature! And any change of nature can be called that. In that case, attaining a sattwic nature is also transformation.

NIRODBARAN: Most of us don't quite understand what is meant by this transformation.

SRI AUROBINDO: When there is an entire change in the basis of one's consciousness and a radical change in the dynamic movement of one's nature; in other words one is no longer acting from the ordinary or even the enlightened human consciousness and its ignorance.

NIRODBARAN: Couldn't people like Ramakrishna, who have attained to the Divine consciousness and been living in and acting from it, be said to have transformed their nature? He didn't act from a human motive or from egoism or selfishness.

SRI AUROBINDO: Was he correct in all his actions? Did he not commit any mistakes? At least he didn't claim to be in such a state. He didn't have selfishness in the ordinary human sense of the term, but was he completely free from the separative I? He himself said that the shadow or form of the I is necessary for action. In the supramental transformation the ego is not indispensable for action.

People always confuse a change of nature with transformation. If a change of nature means transformation, then many sadhaks here have got transformation.

NIRODBARAN: What then is transformation?

SRI AUROBINDO: Transformation is that state in which everything is based on the Truth-Consciousness; the whole instrumentality is that. One lives in that and acts from that; one has it both in its static and dynamic aspects.

It is said that Ramakrishna had a cold while travelling in a train. Somebody asked him to put his head out the window and his cold would be cured. He did that.

NIRODBARAN: He was quite childlike in many such matters.

SRI AUROBINDO: But was it acting from the Divine Consciousness?

DR. MANILAL: What about Buddha, Sir? Was he not transformed?

SRI AUROBINDO: He had knowledge. Knowledge is not trans-formation. People are using the word in any sense just like the word supramental. It is I who have first used it and in the special sense I have given to it. If everybody has attained to the transformation I speak of, the supramental transformation has already been done and everybody is supramental. They don't make the distinction between action from a spiritual consciousness which is above mind but acts through human instruments, and the supramental action from the Truth-Consciousness.

DR. MANILAL: There may be sadhaks here who act from the spiritual consciousness.

SRI AUROBINDO: Who? Nirod? (*Laughter*)

DR. MANILAL: Yes, Nirod and Anilbaran, etc. (*Laughter*)

PURANI: What Ramakrishna and others did came at most from the intuitive consciousness. They were open to that plane and got inspiration for action from those levels.

SRI AUROBINDO: Yes, their static consciousness may have been transformed, but it is the dynamic nature, too, that has to undergo transformation.

PURANI: That is why they called this world Ignorance. It is Sri Aurobindo, alone, who said that Ignorance is growing knowledge.

SRI AUROBINDO: If they had believed in and known about transformation, they wouldn't have condemned the world as Maya.

People get shocked when they hear that something more has to be achieved.

PURANI: Yes, they think Ramakrishna and everybody else had all the knowledge and realisation. What more can there be?

DR. MANILAL: But you have got transformation even down to the Inconscience, Sir.

SRI AUROBINDO: Have I? I am glad to hear of it.

MULSHANKAR: If you haven't, how can you write or know about it?

SRI AUROBINDO: One can't have the knowledge of a thing, without first getting the thing? If you are asking whether I have the experience of the Inconscience, I say I have and so I can write from my experience of it.

NIRODBARAN (*to Dr. Manilal*): You have an idea of peace, you know about it but you haven't got it yet.

DR. MANILAL: As I see the sea, have an idea of it and know about it without plunging into it?

SRI AUROBINDO: Even seeing it, you may not know it is the sea. As some people from Punjab saw the sea and asked, "What is that blue thing?" (*Laughter*)

EVENING

DR. MANILAL: How shall we be able to know whether one's nature has been transformed?

SRI AUROBINDO: By being transformed yourself! (*Laughter*)

MULSHANKAR: Could Buddha be said to have a transformed nature? His actions and discourses don't seem to have been inspired from the human mind.

SRI AUROBINDO: He used human reason and logic in his discourses.

DR. MANILAL: Nirod won't agree that Buddha didn't have a transformed nature, being a Buddhist himself. He will take the side of Buddha.

SRI AUROBINDO: Well?

NIRODBARAN: I didn't say that Buddha was transformed. But as for applying human reason and logic, you also do the same with us.

SRI AUROBINDO: That is because I have to speak to the human mind, so I have to apply human logic.

DR. MANILAL: By what tests or actions could one judge that one's nature is transformed? Is there no such criterion?

SRI AUROBINDO: You are asking like Arjuna in the Gita, "How does a liberated man walk or speak?" As I said, you have to be transformed yourself to know that. (*Laughter*)

DR. MANILAL (*laughing*): That is what I too said to Nirod. That shows I have become transformed.

SRI AUROBINDO: That doesn't show that.

DR. MANILAL: Are we a help or hindrance, Sir, in your work? (*Laughter*)

SRI AUROBINDO (*smiling*): You are asking a delicate personal question. You may be either or both. Or your help may be a hindrance and your hindrance a help. (*Laughter*) You have to be transformed in order to realise that.

In the last issue of the *Sunday Times* there are some stories related by Europeans about incidents of their previous births. They have given corroborative proofs by which the stories have been verified. (*Sri Aurobindo cited an example.*)

DR. MANILAL: I also heard of a story, Sir. In our part a deputy magistrate's grandson, who is now a student, related that he had been a parrot in a previous birth, residing in a particular banyan tree and bowing before the image of Vishnu. The wife of this magistrate, while passing beneath that tree, had seen a parrot and after hearing about its religious character prayed that it might be born as her grandson. The grandson related the story when he was only four years of age.

APPENDIX

Apropos of Sri Aurobindo's mention of his "experience of the Inconscience", we may quote a sonnet of his dating to the same period as these Talks.

THE INCONSCIENT FOUNDATION

My mind beholds its veiled subconscient base;
    All the dead obstinate symbols of the past,
The hereditary moulds, the stamps of race
    Are upheld to sight, the old imprints effaced.

In a downpour of supernal light it reads
    The black Inconscient's enigmatic script –
Recorded in a hundred shadowy screeds
    An inert world's obscure enormous drift;

All flames, is torn and burned and cast away.
    There slept the tables of the Ignorance,
There the dumb dragon edicts of her sway,
    The scriptures of Necessity and Chance.

Pure is the huge foundation now and nude,
A boundless mirror of God's infinitude.
                    18 October 1939, 7 February 1940

18 DECEMBER 1940

This evening Sri Aurobindo broached the subject of rebirth by addressing Dr. Manilal.

SRI AUROBINDO: Your story about the parrot being reborn as magistrate may not be true.

DR. MANILAL: Not as a magistrate but as his grandson. (*Laughter*)

SRI AUROBINDO: Oh, I see, but that doesn't matter. In one case the parrot will read law, in the other it will read ordinary books.

MULSHANKAR: Why not true, Sir? You mean that a parrot can't be born as a human?

SRI AUROBINDO: Because there is no evidence by which to verify it. It may be the simple imagination of the boy, whereas in other cases ample proof is given.

DR. MANILAL: Can't a parrot or and animal be reborn as a human? You don't believe in the evolution of life, Sir?

SRI AUROBINDO: Yes, I do.

DR. MANILAL: In a Jain story it is said that the mother of our first Tirthankara was born as a banana tree. By the side of that tree there was another tree full of thorns. Those thorns used to prick the banana tree so much –

NIRODBARAN: Good Lord! Do you believe in these stories?

DR. MANILAL: – but in spite of the pain and suffering the tree used to remain calm.

PURANI: As a reward it was reborn as a Tirthankara's mother.

SRI AUROBINDO: You are asked whether you believe in these stories.

DR. MANILAL (*looking at Nirodbaran*): Why not? When there is no proof to the contrary.

NIRODBARAN: But there is no proof in their favour either.

DR. MANILAL: Why? This story has been told by the Tirthankara himself who is a Sarvajna, that is, one who knows the past, present and future.

SRI AUROBINDO: How do you know it was told by a Tirthankara?

DR. MANILAL: Why? It is in the Shastra. (*Laughter*)

PURANI: Everything in the Shastra is true?

DR. MANILAL: Otherwise why should it be stated?

SRI AUROBINDO: For the sake of pleasure. Besides, what proof is there that it was told by a Sarvajna or that what the Sarvajna said was true?

DR. MANILAL: Why not? A Sarvajna is supposed to know everything. You don't think Sarvajnas exist?

SRI AUROBINDO: I don't know, I have never met one.

DR. MANILAL: If these stories can't be believed, then Buddha's recounting of all his past lives is also not true, not correct.

SRI AUROBINDO: How to know whether they were correct or not?

PURANI: Besides, who reports those stories? Is it Buddha himself?

DR. MANILAL: Then all that is said about Krishna and Arjuna and the Gita can't be believed.

PURANI: It is not necessary to believe everything. The point is whether or not the principle laid down there is true.

SRI AUROBINDO: Quite so. The important question is whether the truth or principle laid down in the Gita is valid, can be verified. The rest is unessential, legendary, unimportant.

DR. MANILAL: Buddha says –

NIRODBARAN: Where?

DR. MANILAL: In the book. (*Laughter*)

SRI AUROBINDO: You remind me of a British worker who said, "It must be true because I saw it in print." (*Laughter*)

DR. MANILAL: In that case all Buddhism and Jainism are false.

NIRODBARAN: Not Buddhism!

PURANI: Why false? There are records by which it could be proved that Buddha did exist whereas there is no proof of his previous births, of the existence of other Bodhisattvas. Only after Gautama Buddha appeared did we come to know that he was the thirty-second Bodhisattva, while Dipankar was the first. But all that depends on who has said it and whether there is any proof of it.

DR. MANILAL (*to Sri Aurobindo*): Do you disbelieve it?

SRI AUROBINDO: Disbelief is easy. Belief is difficult. But it does not matter at all whether Buddha and other Bodhisattvas existed. The thing is whether what has been said as regards Buddhism can be verified by experience. That is the important thing.

PURANI: They usually regard four things as possible proof of a fact – Shruti, Anumana, Anubhava, Aptavakya.

DR. MANILAL: Aptavakya alone is enough. What do you say, Sir?

SRI AUROBINDO (*beginning to shake his head*): What is meant by Aptavakya?

DR. MANILAL: Words of a realised soul.

SRI AUROBINDO: How to know if someone is realised and from whom the words come – from him or from somebody who reports them? Annie Besant, for instance, calls herself a saviour and knows all about her past, present and future –

DR. MANILAL: I think even the Theosophists don't believe in that.

NIRODBARAN: Why? Some may and some may not, just as some Jains may not believe in the Tirthankara stories. (*Laughter*)

DR. MANILAL: Oh no, every Jain believes in them.

SRI AUROBINDO: It was said that Mohammed was born some three or four thousand years prior to what is now presumed to be his date of birth. Only after sorting through all the documents and spurious evidence, has the date been cut down so many years now. So which is the Aptavakya and how to believe in it unless there is some proof to substantiate it?

DR. MANILAL: But if Purani reports something you have said, can't it be taken as true?

SRI AUROBINDO: It depends. It may or may not be true. Depends on the reporter. The report is not only from Purani, but from Purani to somebody else, and then from somebody to somebody again and so on! In that case the miracles that have been added to my life by Motilal Mehta may be considered true.

DR. MANILAL: Yes, Sir, as he was your disciple and came in direct contact with you. But miracles are associated with the life of realised souls. Alice told me once of a miracle in Hydrabad. She said that for a long time there was no rain in Hyderabad. Then she said to people, "You will see, in twenty-four hours there will be rain." (*As Dr. Manilal was narrating the story Sri Aurobindo was saying all the time, "Yes, yes."*) Then she began to pray to the Mother, pray, and pray very intensely, and then came a heavy downpour. Was it not a miracle by the Mother?

SRI AUROBINDO: Well! It was a response to Alice's prayer, but any and every prayer doesn't get such a response – it must be an intense prayer. One may go on praying and praying without any result. But it was not a miracle.

DR. MANILAL: It was not done by the intervention of the Mother?

SRI AUROBINDO: Maybe, but it was not a miracle, it was the result of a contact with some forces that brought down the rain. It was a play of forces. Any number of people have done that sort of thing. There is the story of some European who prayed to save the ship he was on in the midst of a heavy storm, and it was saved. Then the well-known story of a Christian minister who began to pray for rain. There was such a downpour that it wouldn't stop for days. Then the minister cried out, "Oh, God, this is just ridiculous." (*Sri Aurobindo said this with great amusement.*)

NIRODBARAN: What happened as a result of his outcry?

SRI AUROBINDO: That is not reported. The healing by Christ is not a miracle for that matter. Many people have done that.

CHAMPAKLAL: What is a miracle then?

SRI AUROBINDO: Something that happens contrary to any laws of nature.

DR. MANILAL: If on the new moon day, the moon can be seen?

SRI AUROBINDO: That is not miraculous – may be hypnotic! (*Laughter*)

DR. MANILAL: If not hypnotic?

SRI AUROBINDO: Then it could be a miracle.

DR. MANILAL: The raising of the table cloth from the table and suspending it in the air as narrated in the Mother's conversation?

SRI AUROBINDO: That is not a miracle either. It is simply done by putting out some force. Where there is a method, a process, it can't be called a miracle. Otherwise levitation is also a miracle.

19 DECEMBER 1940

DR. MANILAL: Gandhi has asked people to stop the satyagraha during Christmas.

SRI AUROBINDO: I see. The Government can also release the prisoners for that period.

DR. MANILAL: This may be Gandhi's first step towards a compromise.

SRI AUROBINDO: How?

DR. MANILAL: He may stop the movement and join hands with the Government.

SRI AUROBINDO: Not likely. I don't think he will.

After some time Dr. Manilal began again.

DR. MANILAL: There is then no such thing as Sarvajna, Sir! (*Laughter*)

After so much battering last night by all of us when he again raised the subject, we couldn't help but burst out laughing.

NIRODBARAN: Did you have good sleep last night? (*Laughter*)

DR. MANILAL: Is there no such thing, Sir?

SRI AUROBINDO: I don't know.

DR. MANILAL: How could the word come then? And what could be the meaning of it?

SRI AUROBINDO: It is for them to say who have used the word.

DR. MANILAL: Have you not used it?

SRI AUROBINDO: I may have.

DR. MANILAL: Are not those who have realisation Sarvajna?

SRI AUROBINDO: What realisation?

DR. MANILAL: Nirvana, for instance.

SRI AUROBINDO: Why should one who has separated himself from everything know everything?

DR. MANILAL: What then could be the meaning of Sarvajna, Sir?

NIRODBARAN: As he has said, knowledge of everything.

DR. MANILAL: What everything?

SRI AUROBINDO: Everything means everything.

PURANI: Their meaning of Sarvajnatva is knowing all the facts of existence.

SRI AUROBINDO: Even what Lloyd George had for his breakfast or knowledge of the share markets?

Then some other talk intervened. After this Dr. Manilal again resumed the topic.

DR. MANILAL: What are the meanings of the English words omniscient, omnipotent, etc.?

SRI AUROBINDO: They are applied in English to God.

DR. MANILAL: We are being asked, "Always behave as if the Mother was looking at you; because she is, indeed, always present." What could be its meaning then?

PURANI: It means the sadhak should feel as if he was before the Mother –

DR. MANILAL: Don't mix up the meaning.

SRI AUROBINDO: Does it mean that the Mother is expected to know what one is doing in the Working Committee?

DR. MANILAL: But doesn't it mean that she can know?

SRI AUROBINDO: That is a different thing. She can know if she wants to.

DR. MANILAL: She can know then everything?

SRI AUROBINDO: What do you mean by everything? She can know what is necessary for her to know. She may not know everything in her physical body, but in her universal entity she can know. Sarvajnatva doesn't mean knowledge of everything. It usually means knowledge of the Trikala. When the Gita says Sarvavid, it doesn't mean knowledge of everything.

DR. MANILAL: But Trikala would mean all time.

SRI AUROBINDO: No, it may mean that one knows whatever it is necessary to know, what one is concerned with in the past, present or future; beyond that he is not concerned with anything.

If Mother wants to know a particular thing she has to concentrate. A yogi can know, but by a process of concentration. It is a power, not a state of preoccupied knowledge of things. But that doesn't mean that he knows everything.

NIRODBARAN: When one gets into contact with the subliminal self, one can know whatever he wants without any concentration.

SRI AUROBINDO: How?

NIRODBARAN: Isn't the knowledge there automatic?

SRI AUROBINDO: What do you mean by automatic?

NIRODBARAN: I mean without any need for concentration one knows a thing directly.

DR. MANILAL: He means, for instance, that when one sees a gold ring, he will know at once that it is made of gold.

SRI AUROBINDO: But it may not be made of gold, it may only appear to be so.

NIRODBARAN: No, what I mean – suppose I see Dr. Manilal, I will at once be able to know without any concentration that –

SRI AUROBINDO: All about his life?

NIRODBARAN: No, say, what he has been doing.

DR. MANILAL: He may know about the essential parts of my being or consciousness.

SRI AUROBINDO: Why? It may be the most inessential part also.

DR. MANILAL: Or for instance, if he visits a patient, he will be able to diagnose without any exam that it is a case of T.B.

SRI AUROBINDO: It may not be a case of T.B. The subliminal consciousness is not all true knowledge. It is mixed with Ignorance. Also you have to develop the capacity to know. Even if you know, the capacity of utilisation may be absent; or if you have the knowledge, you may cure in some cases but it doesn't mean you will be successful in every case.

NIRODBARAN: In other words, awareness of the subliminal may give knowledge but not power?

SRI AUROBINDO: You have to develop the power. It doesn't come by itself. Even then, as I said, you may not be successful in every case. As, for example, when Christ came to some parts of Judea, he couldn't cure. He said, "These people have no faith."

DR. MANILAL: Faith is then always a preliminary to cure?

SRI AUROBINDO: Not necessarily. Without faith one may also be cured. Many patients get cured without their knowing about the action of the Force. Lack of faith may be an obstacle too, especially a positive disbelief.

CHAMPAKLAL: Is one born with faith?

SRI AUROBINDO: One is not born with it, but one may be born with a capacity for faith.

EVENING

DR. MANILAL: The Sarvajnas – (*Laughter. Sri Aurobindo exclaimed, "Oh!"*) – are they concerned with only a higher plane of knowledge, Sir?

SRI AUROBINDO: How do you mean?

DR. MANILAL: I mean, are they concerned only with the higher planes of existence, not our day-to-day mundane affairs?

SRI AUROBINDO: By clairvoyance also one can see things. But what is your idea about Sarvajna? Who, according to you, is Sarvajna?

K30

DR. MANILAL: Those who have realisation.

SRI AUROBINDO: What realisation?

DR. MANILAL: Of Nirvana or Kaivalyajnan.

SRI AUROBINDO: I don't know what Kaivalyajnan is.

DR. MANILAL: One who has a solitary realisation of the One.

SRI AUROBINDO: If he has a solitary realisation of the One, how can he be expected to have knowledge of the many?

DR. MANILAL: I mean the One and the many.

SRI AUROBINDO: That is not solitary. That is a comprehensive realisation.

DR. MANILAL: I mean that; it was a wrong expression.

SRI AUROBINDO: Not expression, but a wrong statement. Even if one has knowledge of the many, it doesn't mean he has knowledge of the all. That is, he may know what he has to know or wants to know.

DR. MANILAL: Like Vyasa's shadow-reader who could by studying someone's shadow tell his past and present, etc.

SRI AUROBINDO: Oh, he can say everything! (*Laughter*)

DR. MANILAL: Nirod says that by knowledge of the subliminal one can know everything. Isn't it so, Nirod?

NIRODBARAN: No, no, I must read the chapter again.

SRI AUROBINDO: What I have said in *The Life Divine* is that when you get into contact with the subliminal self, you get into contact with a greater source of knowledge. But it is not all pure and correct knowledge because the subliminal is also mixed with Ignorance and it has many parts and depths.

PURANI: What Nirod told me was something like this – by getting into the subliminal one can project into the physical whatever incident or event one comes in contact with.

SRI AUROBINDO: That is too mechanical a way of seeing it. Besides, there are so many ways of approaching and knowing the subliminal – by penetrating, by enveloping, and then there are various depths of the subliminal.

NIRODBARAN: What I wanted to say was that the knowledge of the subliminal gives one a direct automatic knowledge without any need for concentration. That is how I understood the matter.

SRI AUROBINDO: You may or may not have to concentrate.

DR. MANILAL: How far is the supramental from the subliminal, Sir?

SRI AUROBINDO: What do you mean by "far"?

DR. MANILAL: How distant, I mean.

SRI AUROBINDO: Ten thousand miles. (*Laughter*)

DR. MANILAL: There is a Jain story about two yogis who went to Mahavideha Kshetra and met Padmadevi and asked her how distant their realisation was. She said to one three years and to the other as many years as there are leaves on a tree. The latter began to dance –

SRI AUROBINDO: Oh, that is Narada's story of the Tapaswi and the Bhakta.

CHAMPAKLAL: That story you told me when I asked you on my first visit, "Shall I have realisation?"

SRI AUROBINDO: This is more pointed than the Jain story.

At this stage Dr. Manilal departed.

NIRODBARAN: But a contact with the subliminal may give me direct knowledge – say, correct diagnosis of a case as T.B. without any exam.

SRI AUROBINDO: It may, but it is only a knowledge. How will you have the power to cure? Besides, knowledge is not necessary for cure. Plenty of people can cure without knowledge.

PURANI: That is what I too told him.

NIRODBARAN: How does one get the power to cure?

SRI AUROBINDO: By getting the Force.

NIRODBARAN: But the subliminal may give me the knowledge of the right drug.

SRI AUROBINDO: If you know the right drug, will it always cure a case? Are there no failures in spite of the right drug being administered? Are all diseases curable?

NIRODBARAN: So says homoeopathy, that every disease has a right drug and is curable unless the organs are too damaged.

SRI AUROBINDO: I don't know about homoeopathy. But there are any number of instances where cases have failed in spite of the right treatment.

NIRODBARAN: Did you say in the morning that the Mother may not know something in her body but know it in her universal entity?

SRI AUROBINDO: Yes. It is not necessary for her to know in her body. There are many people whom the Mother has not met or seen but who call the Mother and get help.

CHAMPAKLAL: Yes, Mother told us such a story in the stores, that some people were calling her.

PURANI: I remember distinctly her other story while sitting among us. Suddenly she went into a trance and returned after twenty minutes or so. Then she said to us that she had gone to the Himalayas to help a Yogi who had been calling her. We saw her actually shivering due to the cold of the Himalayas. Mother said she didn't know who the Yogi was.

SRI AUROBINDO: In her sleep Mother goes to various places. It doesn't mean that she knows or remembers in her waking moments all the places and persons she visits.

NIRODBARAN: Now it is clear. But how will the knowledge in her universal entity be practically applied in her physical which may not know about that knowledge? I mean her universal entity may have the knowledge of a particular act done by such and such a person. How will she be able to say which particular person has done it?

SRI AUROBINDO: If it is necessary for her to know, she can know by concentration. The physical brain is an instrument of the true individuality. Even the Yogis are not concerned with what is happening on Jupiter or Venus.

BECHARLAL: Does an Avatar know everything?

SRI AUROBINDO: What everything? It is the same question. Did Rama know it was not a real deer?

BECHARLAL: They say that he knew it was a false deer but in order to set an example –

SRI AUROBINDO: Good Lord! You mean to say that all he has done, the fight with Ravana and the rescue of Sita, is all deception in order to set an example? Then the Ramayana and Rama lose all their value. And his lamentation for Sita is also a pretension? Does an Avatar resort to deception in order to teach people?

PURANI: What about Sita's Agniparisha?[1]

BECHARLAL: That was real, they say. But the Sita that was stolen by Ravana was not the real Sita, but her shadow. (*Laughter*)

SRI AUROBINDO: So all the time the real Sita was with Rama? And why then did Rama play that deception with Hanuman about Gandhamadan parvat? He could have told him straight away that it was in such and such a place, instead of Hanuman having to search for it everywhere.

1 Ordeal by fire.

The shadow-of-Sita story reminds me of Helen of Troy's story. Someone – perhaps Euripides – says that it was not the real Helen but her image that was taken by Paris and that after the battle was over she rejoined her husband.

21 DECEMBER 1940

DR. MANILAL: In the Gita Sri Krishna says that he knows all about Arjuna's past lives.

SRI AUROBINDO: What about it? A past life can be known.

DR. MANILAL: Then he knew all the details of his past life?

SRI AUROBINDO: Who says that? Does Krishna say that? (*Laughter*)

DR. MANILAL: He knew at least the salient features.

SRI AUROBINDO: Not necessarily; he may have known only the general features.

DR. MANILAL: Simply from general features one won't be able to make out the character and quality of a man.

SRI AUROBINDO: Why not? The first impression one gets, on knowing the general features of a man's past life, is that of character.

PURANI: He wants to say that one must be able to know what he had for his breakfast.

NIRODBARAN: What was your point in that question?

DR. MANILAL: I wanted to say that Krishna was Sarvajna. (*Laughter*)

SRI AUROBINDO: Then that girl from Mathura who knew all the details of her past life was also Sarvajna. When Arjuna said to Krishna, "Will you tell me again all you told me about Kurukshetra etc., etc.?" Krishna replied, "Good Lord, do I remember all that blessed lot now? At that time I was in Yoga."

DR. MANILAL: But he was always in Yoga.

SRI AUROBINDO: He didn't say that. He said he had forgotten.

DR. MANILAL: How could he have heard Draupadi's lamentation then during Vastraharan?

SRI AUROBINDO: His subliminal heard it! (*Laughter*)

DR. MANILAL: Is that story true, Sir, and not an allegory?

SRI AUROBINDO: Why an allegory?

DR. MANILAL: Of course you yourself have said somewhere that all these stories are true.

SRI AUROBINDO: Where have I said that? What I have said is that the Gita was recorded as a fact in the Mahabharata, intended to be a fact of life, not an allegory. But do you mean that Hanuman's taking the sun under his armpit and jumping into Lanka and burning Lanka by his tail-fire were all facts?

DR. MANILAL: What are they then? Poetry?

Purani narrated the story of the ex-Maharani of Porbandar who had come here. It is said she commuted the death-sentence of a criminal in her court because she was so moved by the piteous cry of his wife.

DR. MANILAL: Could this be called a Punya karma or Kuta karma, Sir?

SRI AUROBINDO: Which part of her action?

DR. MANILAL: This pardon and release of the murderer.

SRI AUROBINDO: It is an act of mercy. Mercy is a Punya karma.

DR. MANILAL: But can the release of an archmurderer be called Punya karma?

SRI AUROBINDO: How do you know he was an archmurderer? He may have been innocent.

DR. MANILAL: Let us take for granted he was an archmurderer.

SRI AUROBINDO: Why should you take it for granted?

DR. MANILAL: Suppose an archmurderer is released under such circumstances, he may go on committing more murders. Can that be called a Punya karma?

SRI AUROBINDO: It may be both. (*Laughter*) You are looking at it from the social point of view and don't see the character or nature of the act itself. Compassion is a virtue and an act of compassion is a virtuous act.

DR. MANILAL: Suppose a man is asked by a hunter about an antelope that has passed his way –

SRI AUROBINDO: Oh, that old story of the Yogi? A Yogi was asked by some murderers if he had seen a man running away. He said "Yes", and showed the way. The man was caught and killed. The Yogi after his death was taken to hell.

DR. MANILAL: Was he right in telling the truth?

SRI AUROBINDO: There was no necessity.

DR. MANILAL: Should one speak the truth in all circumstances?

SRI AUROBINDO: It depends on the circumstances. Every action has to be judged on its own merits.

DR. MANILAL: But in this case?

SRI AUROBINDO: He need not have told the truth as he knew what would be the consequence of his doing so.

DR. MANILAL: According to Jainism, one could have remained quiet.

SRI AUROBINDO: Quite so. In this case he told the truth, not for the sake of telling the truth but from ethical vanity.

NIRODBARAN: Or perhaps for fear of his own life.

SRI AUROBINDO: That can't be a virtue either. To endanger another's life in order to save one's own can't be a Punya karma.

EVENING

DR. MANILAL: Have you read Professor N. N. Sen's lecture at the Madras Philosophy Conference?

SRI AUROBINDO: I have waded through it.

DR. MANILAL: The *Hindu* gives a short note on it, but I don't grasp it myself very well. It says, "What is mind? No matter" and "What is matter? Never mind." Something like that.

SRI AUROBINDO: It means mind and matter are not the same.

DR. MANILAL: But one thing I can't understand, Sir, about life and existence. If a living organism consists of living cells and each living cell has a soul –

SRI AUROBINDO: A cell has a soul?

DR. MANILAL: Yes, Sir, otherwise how could it live?

SRI AUROBINDO: It lives because of the life in it, not because of the soul in it. You can ask "What is life?"

DR. MANILAL: What is life then?

SRI AUROBINDO: For that you have to read *The Life Divine* (*Laughter*)

PURANI: He wants a shortcut.

NIRODBARAN: If each cell has a soul, then there are so many thousands of souls in the body?

SRI AUROBINDO: He is referring to Nigodh or Jiva. (*Laughter*) In that case one can say everything existing has a soul. A tree has a soul, a stone has a soul. That may be but it is not self-evident.

DR. MANILAL: That is what Jainism says. (*Laughter*) J. C. Bose has shown that the tree has a nervous system.

SRI AUROBINDO: A nervous system is not a soul. It is capable of response to a stimulus. If a cell dies, what happens to the soul?

DR. MANILAL: It also dies. (*Laughter*)

SRI AUROBINDO: So body and soul are the same: both are destructible. If one dies, the other follows? That is the Western idea which makes no distinction between body and soul and life.

DR. MANILAL: What is your idea then?

SRI AUROBINDO: As I said, read *The Life Divine*. (*Laughter*)

DR. MANILAL: Is there no shortcut to it? (*Laughter*) When a person dies –

SRI AUROBINDO: A person dies? You mean the body dies?

DR. MANILAL: No, Sir! Say, when a human being dies –

SRI AUROBINDO: A human being dies? What is a human being?

DR. MANILAL: When the Atman departs – (*Laughter*)

SRI AUROBINDO: That means the body dies. If the Atman or soul departs, it does not die; it is the body that dies. Either the body dies because the soul departs or the soul departs because the body is destroyed. According to one conception the soul is a portion of the Divine, and hence indestructible, while mind, life and body are instruments of its self-expression. It is the materialist's conception that soul and body are the same so that when the body dies existence ceases.

Dr. Manilal was so thoroughly battered that he had no more words to utter after this. After a short while he made his usual pranam and departed.

22 DECEMBER 1940

DR. MANILAL: Have unicellular organisms like the amoeba no soul, Sir?

SRI AUROBINDO: No, they have a psychic spark, not a developed soul or a psychic being.

DR. MANILAL: According to Jainism there are different types or grades of lives with grades of development of senses. Thus some creatures have only one sense, such as touch; some have two, touch and smell, and so on, till we come to the human grade with five senses. Is that true, Sir?

SRI AUROBINDO: It is for the scientists to say.

DR. MANILAL: Perhaps it is the underlying principle of the evolution of life that they want to show. But is it by any sort of virtuous act that a lower form of life becomes a higher one?

SRI AUROBINDO: Virtuous act? No, it is a question of consciousness, a change from a lower to a higher consciousness.

DR. MANILAL (*after a while*): My shoulder is still resistant, Sir. The pain in the joint continues.

SRI AUROBINDO: Apply the Force.

DR. MANILAL: I have done so, Sir, but no result!

NIRODBARAN: Is the Force weak or the shoulder resistant?

DR. MANILAL: Both.

SRI AUROBINDO: I got rid of my shoulder trouble by a triple process: the Force, the doing of those movements that bring on pain, and perspiration!

DR. MANILAL: I have tried all that.

NIRODBARAN: You have added another – salicylates. (*Laughter*)

PURANI: He leaves nothing to chance – try everything so that one at least may hit.

DR. MANILAL: Yes. Fomentation, embrocation, massage, etc.

SRI AUROBINDO: Perhaps you tried too many things, each reacting with the other and producing no result.

EVENING

Sri Aurobindo had finished his lunch earlier than usual today. Mridu, the cook, came late with her preparations, so Sri Aurobindo could not take the fritters. Nirodbaran foolishly told Mridu that Sri Aurobindo had finished his meal and that was enough to send her away weeping and lamenting. She repeated the story to Dr. Manilal.

DR. MANILAL: Mridu was weeping today, Sir, because she was late and you had finished your meal.

SRI AUROBINDO: She shouldn't have been told.

NIRODBARAN: It was I who unguardedly told her about it.

SRI AUROBINDO: Oosh, these things should not be told.

DR. MANILAL: But she has already recovered. I must say she has improved. Formerly I used to hear her threatening of suicide two or three times a week. This was the first time in one month. She says she won't eat.

CHAMPAKLAL: She will eat all right.

DR. MANILAL: She counts everything – how many *luchis* she had given, how many you have taken.

SRI AUROBINDO: She won't be able to know how many I have taken and how many others have taken. But there is no reason why she should cry. It is I who ought to cry as I didn't have the fritters. (*Laughter*)

23 DECEMBER 1940

DR. MANILAL: Has Trikalajna no knowledge of the future?
SRI AUROBINDO: It means knowledge of all past, present and future.
DR. MANILAL: But if we can change the future by effort –
SRI AUROBINDO: Who says that?
DR. MANILAL: I think you have said it, Sir.
SRI AUROBINDO: I! What about it then?
DR. MANILAL: Then how can one read the future completely?
SRI AUROBINDO: What does "completely" mean?
DR. MANILAL: It means in every detail.
SRI AUROBINDO: I didn't say in every detail. As I said, one has the faculty of knowing.

After this there was miscellaneous talk about this and that, about the Philosophical Congress at Madras, etc. Radhakrishnan then came into the discussion.

NIRODBARAN: Radhakrishnan seems to have said that he doesn't believe there is anyone who can challenge Shankara. It was in a talk in Belur Math regarding Sri Aurobindo.
SRI AUROBINDO: There have been many people who have challenged Shankara.
PURANI: Yes, Vaishnavas, Ramanuja, Madhava, etc.

After this Nirodbaran referred to Professor Amarnath Jha's lecture in the Hindu *on Indian English where he has mentioned Gandhi's prose style as simple, sincere, almost Biblical.*

DR. MANILAL: I must say Gandhi has improved Gujarati literature remarkably.

On this topic Manilal had an argument with Purani. All the recent stylists of Gujarat came into it: Kanu Munshi, Musriwalla, Kalelkar, etc.

DR. MANILAL: What has happened to Kalelkar? He hasn't come back here after his first visit.

SRI AUROBINDO: Harin has frightened him away.

PURANI: What about B. K. Thakore?

DR. MANILAL: Oh yes, he is a great stylist. (*After a pause*) He is a great drunkard, too.

PURANI: I thought he had given up drink.

DR. MANILAL: Oh no, he can't do without it. He used to go every day to a Bombay station and drink heavily in the station restaurant. Of course he didn't get tipsy.

SRI AUROBINDO: If not tipsy, how is he a drunkard?

DR. MANILAL: He drinks so heavily –

SRI AUROBINDO: But drinking heavily doesn't make him a drunkard; you can call him a heavy drinker.

DR. MANILAL: He drinks in excess.

SRI AUROBINDO: What do you mean by excess? Excess for somebody else. But if the quantity doesn't affect him, it can't be excess for him.

DR. MANILAL: I submit, Sir.

SRI AUROBINDO: In Plato's *Symposium*, Socrates, Aristophanes, Agathon and others meet and discuss the nature of love, and drink wine. Everybody gets drunk except Socrates. Even after heavy drinking he keeps on discussing philosophy with some friends, while the rest fall asleep. You can't call him a drunkard!

EVENING

Dr. Manilal has wrapped a piece of cloth around his head because of the cold.

NIRODBARAN: Dr. Manilal is looking like a Maharaja.

SRI AUROBINDO: I thought he looked like a college professor.

DR. MANILAL: I feel cold in the head, Sir; that's why I have put this cloth on it. Usually I catch cold in the chest and head.

NIRODBARAN: In spite of so many layers of garments? He has at least five on.

DR. MANILAL: Only one is warm.

SRI AUROBINDO: Even there he doesn't hold the record. I remember in London that the strength of Sarat Ghose – one of the Christian Ghoses – was disputed in some talk. He began to take his garments off. He took off his coat, waistcoat, shirt, one vest, then another, and still another and so on – altogether eleven! (*Laughter*)

Purani started a talk about some evening procession of the Selvaraju family.

DR. MANILAL: Did the family ever come to you, Sir, I mean in your early days here?

SRI AUROBINDO: Come to me? It is said that the father of the family tried to kidnap me into British territory, if that is what you mean by coming to me.

DR. MANILAL: I saw the Governor today. He looks absolutely like a bulldog with a ruddy face.

PURANI: That is due to drink!

DR. MANILAL: He drinks?

SRI AUROBINDO: He is a heavy drinker, not a drunkard (*laughter*), but he goes on to the point of apoplexy.

DR. MANILAL (*after a while*): They speak of Gandharvaloka, Sir. Is there any such world?

SRI AUROBINDO: Supposed to be.

DR. MANILAL: Have you seen it, Sir?

SRI AUROBINDO: I have not been there.

DR. MANILAL: I meant: did you have any experience?

SRI AUROBINDO: It is not necessary: there are many musicians in the Ashram. (*Laughter*)

PURANI: Professor Indra Sen, who has come for the Philosophical Conference at Madras, says that nowadays anybody who has written on any subject, economics, social reform, is being called a philosopher. Gandhi and Tagore are being called philosophers.

SRI AUROBINDO: Karl Marx is also a philosopher and all the communists too.

PURANI: Yes. Indra Sen is asking if by the supramental descent the whole of humanity is going to be transformed and how humanity is going to be benefited by it. By a change in consciousness?

SRI AUROBINDO: If he means supramental transformation, no.

NIRODBARAN: I thought there would be a general heightened consciousness.

SRI AUROBINDO: Yes, in some persons.

PURANI: I told him there would be a move towards a higher consciousness through the influence of people who have attained to that consciousness.

SRI AUROBINDO: That is what I have said myself.

PURANI: He wants also to know how humanity today is better fitted for the change than before. I replied that nowadays one has to conceive of the whole of humanity as one unit: one can't think of it in separate terms or divide it into so many compartments. Nature won't allow any such division.

SRI AUROBINDO: The main question is one of the development of mind. There has been a general development more than before – of course it is nothing exceptional. I am speaking of the masses. That is the first necessary condition.

PURANI: Yes, I told him how in Buddha's time or in the classical period of the Greeks, teaching and culture were limited to a small area, the greater part of the race had no access to them. Now, communication being so easy, there is no such obstacle. One can hear Roosevelt here in India.

There was a Muslim professor who spoke in the Philosophical Congress. He spoke on Freud. He has criticised Freud's theory that everything is due to the subconscient. Freud says that Moses turned into a prophet because of his personal sufferings, the repression in his childhood. (*Laughter*)

SRI AUROBINDO: Repression complex.

PURANI: The professor says that Freud's theory doesn't explain Moses.

SRI AUROBINDO (*laughing*): Not at all. It explains Freud. (*Laughter*) He himself had so many complexes that he couldn't find any other theory than that for every human action. He says that the sense of injustice in children is born from their inability to retain their excrement. (*Laughter*) And what is surprising is that everybody in Europe believes it. His real contribution is about the subconscient. Even there some of his disciples, such as Jung, are throwing out many things.

PURANI: And the professor says that the idea that in primitive races men used to kill their fathers in order to marry their mothers is not true.

SRI AUROBINDO: Oh, that old thing!

PURANI: Everyone didn't kill his father.

SRI AUROBINDO: Neither did everyone marry his mother.

24 DECEMBER 1940

DR. MANILAL: Is there, Sir, such a condition of detachment that one is not disturbed or perturbed by anything whatsoever?

SRI AUROBINDO: Why not?

DR. MANILAL: Practicable, Sir? (*Laughter*)

SRI AUROBINDO: Is it only a theory, then? An ideal not realisable in practice? As with Tagore who is reported to have said that yogic realisations are only ideals, not realisable, not meant for practice?

DR. MANILAL: Has anybody achieved it, Sir?

SRI AUROBINDO: It is one of the aims of Yoga.

DR. MANILAL: I know, but it is possible? (*Laughter*)

SRI AUROBINDO: If it is impossible, why should it be an aim of Yoga? Merely as an ideal? Honesty is an ideal to be observed in commercial transactions. Does it mean you must observe it only when it suits you? (*Laughter*)

PURANI: Is the synopsis ready?

SRI AUROBINDO: No, I have just made a summary from which the synopsis will be made. After it is done, we can try it on Manilal and see if he understands it.

DR. MANILAL: If you make me understand, I will, Sir.

After some time Nirodbaran asked what was meant by space being coexistent with souls. Sri Aurobindo explained it but Nirodbaran could not follow.

DR. MANILAL: Souls have no space, Sir?

SRI AUROBINDO: There is a theory to that effect.

DR. MANILAL: According to Jainism they have no space.

SRI AUROBINDO: What is space then according to Jainism?

DR. MANILAL: Akasha.

SRI AUROBINDO: What is Akasha?

DR. MANILAL: Empty space.

SRI AUROBINDO: How is it empty?

DR. MANILAL: There are many atoms pervading it.

SRI AUROBINDO: Where do the atoms come from?

DR. MANILAL: They don't come from anywhere. They have been always there from time immemorial.

SRI AUROBINDO: From time immemorial? How do they get there?

DR. MANILAL: They have been there, Sir. We have to take it for granted. (*Laughter*)

SRI AUROBINDO: What is time then according to Jainism?

DR. MANILAL: There is no time; it is indivisible. What we see as present becomes past and what is future becomes present.

SRI AUROBINDO: So there is past and present.

DR. MANILAL: How, Sir? What we call "just now" has already become past. So there is no present. Mahavira and Buddha were at one time present but they no longer exist.

SRI AUROBINDO: If time were indivisible, they should exist now. You speak of from moment to moment.

DR. MANILAL: Relatively, Sir.

SRI AUROBINDO: What do you mean by relatively? Otherwise it is absolute timelessness.

(*Here there was talk about a discussion of Sri Aurobindo's* Life Divine *by philosophers.*)

DR. MANILAL: Is space indivisible?

SRI AUROBINDO: Not unless it is useful for it to be so (*laughter*), otherwise you have to go on walking for three miles without stopping.

If you have to take everything for granted, take my philosophy also for granted and don't discuss it. (*Laughter*)

DR. MANILAL: That requires a lot of Shraddha, Sir. (*Laughter*)

SRI AUROBINDO: Then should I be asked to have Shraddha, in your Jain philosophy? (*Laughter*) There are some postulates that are taken for granted. After a time they are given up in favour of some other postulates. For instance, matter was at one time thought to be the source and origin of everything. Now they have upset that theory.

Space is indivisible in the sense that existence is indivisible. If you look at existence as a whole, as the one Being, then space and time are indivisible. But if you look at the individual being, they are divided when you want to do anything. India is indivisible but it is very much divided! (*Laughter*)

EVENING

SRI AUROBINDO (*to Purani*): What is the news of the world?

PURANI (*smiling a little*): I have no news. You have read Lloyd George's speech?

DR. MANILAL: It is a very balanced speech, Sir.

SRI AUROBINDO: Very balanced? Nonsense! The one thing he lacks is balance. The one thing he has is vigour.

DR. MANILAL: He has made a strong attack on the Government. Chamberlain, Churchill and others are saying that they have committed big mistakes.

SRI AUROBINDO: Yes, everybody makes mistakes except him. Who doesn't make mistakes? Gandhi has also admitted that he has made "Himalayan blunders".

PURANI: Lloyd George is asking the Government to state its war aims and peace terms. How can one do that now?

DR. MANILAL: And he refers to his own Government in 1917.

PURANI: Yes, but that was when they were winning the war, while now they are just in the thick of the fight, with at most a fifty percent chance of success. And if they start stating war aims and peace terms now, division and quarrel will start among them giving a handle to Hitler to break up their alliance.

SRI AUROBINDO: Quite so. What peace terms did Lloyd George offer?

DR. MANILAL: It was the Versailles treaty and this war is the result. Perhaps he wants to be the Prime Minister.

SRI AUROBINDO: He is too old for that. Besides, he is most unreliable.

DR. MANILAL (*after a short while*): There is a Jain sloka which means that mind is a bondage to Mukti. Can it be true, Sir?

SRI AUROBINDO: Bondage? Instrument, if you like. But mind is not the only instrument of Mukti; it is the power of the Spirit also that brings Mukti. You can say that mind is an instrument of bondage in the sense that it is the dividing principle that separates itself from the Unity and brings in division and ignorance. Life can properly be more said to be the real instrument. The life principle is the principle of desire, a straining after various objects of desire. Life is the root of all desires with which it affects the mind. The desires of the mind are not really its desires because its business is to know, to perceive.

DR. MANILAL: Life is the seat of emotions, I thought.

SRI AUROBINDO: Emotions, sensations and several other things. That is the mistake most people usually commit, especially those influenced by Western ideas. They don't make any distinction between mind and life, they consider them the same. This President of the Philosophical Congress at Madras says that mind is hungry. Mind is not hungry; it is the life and body that are hungry.

PURANI: Professor Atreya calls Krishnamurti a philosopher.

SRI AUROBINDO (*chuckling*): Bhagwan Das also and Radhakrishnan. Is Radhakrishnan really a philosopher? Has he contributed anything new?

PURANI: No, he is only an exponent of Indian philosophy.

SRI AUROBINDO: That's what I thought. He is one of the highest authorities on Indian philosophy but I don't know that he has produced any new philosophy. He is a Shankarite, isn't he?

PURANI: Yes.

DR. MANILAL: He may have realised Shankara's philosophy.

SRI AUROBINDO: Realised? You mean he is a Yogi? Everybody knows he is not. He is only an interpreter.

DR. MANILAL: He could be both, Sir?

SRI AUROBINDO: He is *not!* What do you mean by could be? Anybody could be, you could be, Lloyd George could be. (*Laughter*)

PURANI: A Ceylonese young man, a Buddhist has come to see the Ashram. He says Buddha didn't teach that the world was full of evil.

SRI AUROBINDO: Oh!

PURANI: But I asked him whether or not Buddha said that the world is "full of sorrow" and that "one must escape from it"?

SRI AUROBINDO: Not full of evil but that it is undesirable.

PURANI: He also makes out that Buddha spoke of a divine consciousness.

SRI AUROBINDO: I see!

DR. MANILAL: He meant Nirvana, probably.

SRI AUROBINDO: Buddha didn't mean that by Nirvana. Of course he didn't say what Nirvana is.

PURANI: This man doesn't believe in the Jataka stories of Buddha.

NIRODBARAN: Tell it to Dr. Manilal.

DR. MANILAL: Why? I believe in them.

SRI AUROBINDO: That is just the point.

K31

DR. MANILAL: Are there no previous births, Sir?

PURANI: The point is whether all that is said is true.

After this Dr. Manilal was going away. Suddenly he came back and said, "Mother has said to Sir Hukum Chand, 'I know you.'"

SRI AUROBINDO: Well, what about it?

DR. MANILAL: That means there are previous births.

SRI AUROBINDO: Nobody denies it.

DR. MANILAL: Nirod doesn't believe it.

NIRODBARAN: I didn't say that.

PURANI: He doesn't deny the principle of rebirth but is doubtful about all that is said about the knowledge possessed by Yogis or Tirthankaras about so many previous births; for example, that Manilal's Adishwar knew about all his previous births and that his mother was a banana tree. (*Laughter*)

DR. MANILAL: Why, a Tirthankara is supposed to be Sarvajna.

SRI AUROBINDO: How do you know that?

DR. MANILAL: It is said in the books, Sir. (*Laughter*)

SRI AUROBINDO: Who said it?

DR. MANILAL: If it was not true and if Krishna and Arjuna didn't exist, you would not have written *Essays on the Gita*, Sir.

SRI AUROBINDO: Why not? Whether they existed or not I would still have written the book if the truth of the Gita was there.

NIRODBARAN: Sri Aurobindo himself has said in the preface that the important point is not whether Krishna and Arjuna did actually exist but whether the things said in the Gita are true.

At this point Dr. Manilal left.

SRI AUROBINDO: I have been reading today *Plotinus on Matter* by Dean Inge. It is curious that what he was trying to describe in various ways with much difficulty is what we call the Inconscient in Matter. But as he had no knowledge of the Inconscient he couldn't express it properly. Of course he is speaking of Matter as a principle, not as a form. This Dean Inge has a confused mind, he can't state his thoughts clearly and logically and bungles the whole thing. But what Plotinus says is that Matter is infinite, indeterminate and non-being – that means the Inconscient; and if Matter is raised to the level of the Spirit it could become divine, that is to say, Matter itself is the Divine.

25 DECEMBER 1940

EVENING

Dr. Manilal had a warm cloth wrapped around his head and was sitting leaning against the small book case. When Sri Aurobindo sat up on the edge of the bed, he looked at him.

SRI AUROBINDO: You are looking like one of the pictures of Ajanta, thinking the world to be a burden and being cold and miserable. (*Laughter*)

NIRODBARAN: Today he has put on one more vest.

DR. MANILAL: That can be easily taken off. I was not feeling cold but to prevent any draught I put it on.

SRI AUROBINDO: I was speaking of your expression; you were looking like an incarnation of suffering.

DR. MANILAL: But I am supposed to be very jolly, Sir.

SRI AUROBINDO: But at that moment you were not! (*Laughter*)

Some time later the Mother came and, soon after Sri Aurobindo's daily walk, Dr. Manilal left.

PURANI: Indra Sen wants to know if the cosmic descent could correspond to the yogic descent in any way.

SRI AUROBINDO: No, the yogic descent is a process of unveiling while the cosmic descent is involutionary, a process of veiling.

PURANI: Yes, I also said something like that.

26 DECEMBER 1940

We heard from Usha that Sachin's daughter had improved after receiving the Mother's flower. She has been brought to Calcutta.

SRI AUROBINDO: Have the doctors diagnosed her condition? I haven't heard anything.

DR. MANILAL: Regarding diagnosis the doctors are at sea –

SRI AUROBINDO: They generally are. (*Laughter*) If only one doctor is concerned, it is not so bad a situation.

DR. MANILAL: Can you not help us with your knowledge?

SRI AUROBINDO: That would be too much work for me.

DR. MANILAL: I don't mean in every case, only in difficult cases.

SRI AUROBINDO: It would establish a precedent. (*Laughter*)

DR. MANILAL: But you can know the right diagnosis and suitable treatment in a case.

SRI AUROBINDO: That is a medical question.

PURANI: Sri Aurobindo and the Mother can as well cure a case straight away instead of bothering about all that.

EVENING

DR. MANILAL: If Joan of Arc was a saint, how could she be burnt alive, Sir?

SRI AUROBINDO: She was declared a saint only some years ago! And what did you have in mind? Many saints have been killed, burnt, riddled with arrows.

NIRODBARAN: Christ was crucified.

DR. MANILAL: Some say it is not true. (*Laughter*)

PURANI: How? It is written in the books! (*Laughter*)

DR. MANILAL: They hold a procession now in memory of Joan of Arc.

SRI AUROBINDO: Now?

DR. MANILAL: Yes, Sir, when I was in Paris ten years ago I saw it.

SRI AUROBINDO: "Now" is not ten years ago. When you said "now", I was astonished – how could Germany allow it? It is a French national festival.

DR. MANILAL: It is said that Joan of Arc used to have some power or some power used to descend in her by which she defeated the English.

SRI AUROBINDO: Yes, what about it?

DR. MANILAL: If so, how were they able to catch and burn her? The power couldn't protect her?

SRI AUROBINDO: She had no power at that time. She herself said that she was given that power only for a short time – two years or so – and after her work was finished she wanted to go away, but the king kept her back.

DR. MANILAL: Wasn't it a sin to burn her? (*Laughter*)

SRI AUROBINDO: They didn't care a damn whether it was a sin, not having studied Jainism like Manilal. (*Laughter*)

DR. MANILAL: Tolstoy had some realisation, Sir, didn't he?

SRI AUROBINDO: How?

DR. MANILAL: Otherwise how could he write about angels etc? (*Laughter*)

SRI AUROBINDO: I suppose you know that a writer has imagination.

DR. MANILAL: But he led a moral life.

SRI AUROBINDO: Oh! Did he? He never succeeded in living a moral life – as far as I know. He became a mystic, at least tried to but never led a moral life. Are you interested in Tolstoy?

DR. MANILAL: In some principles of his.

SRI AUROBINDO: What are they?

DR. MANILAL: I have forgotten, Sir. (*Laughter*) It was long ago I read him.

SRI AUROBINDO: Principles like those of Gandhi?

DR. MANILAL: Yes, Sir.

SRI AUROBINDO: Interested in Gandhi's principles?

DR. MANILAL: Yes, Sir, in some of them when they are put into action.

SRI AUROBINDO: Which?

DR. MANILAL: Ahimsa, for instance. Of course, not Ahimsa as he preaches it. There is also truthfulness.

SRI AUROBINDO: Nothing new. Ahimsa is more than twenty-five hundred years old and truthfulness very ancient too, more than six thousand years.

DR. MANILAL: Millions and millions of years, Sir, according to Jainism. (*Dr. Manilal mentioned a book.*)

SRI AUROBINDO: I am not interested in Jain history.

PURANI: Where is the history? It is more a story like the Puranas.

The topic changed. What exactly Sri Aurobindo refers to in the following is not remembered.

SRI AUROBINDO: I have sent both the synopsis and the summary down to Nolini. I don't know how many pages they will be in type. I think there will be about two hundred pages altogether. Manilal might find them easy. (*Laughter*)

DR. MANILAL: Yes, Sir. (*Laughter*)

NIRODBARAN: It may be more difficult to understand than the text, because the argument will be more compact.

SRI AUROBINDO: Not necessarily. One may get only the salient points.

NIRODBARAN: I haven't yet got a clear idea of the Absolute. (*Laughter*)

SRI AUROBINDO (*laughing*): How could you have got a clear idea? If you had, all your troubles and difficulties would have been over.

NIRODBARAN: I mean mentally.

SRI AUROBINDO: Even mentally one can't get a clear idea.

NIRODBARAN: What I mean is whether the Absolute stands for Sachchidananda, the Supreme, the Transcendent and is also beyond all of them.

SRI AUROBINDO: Of course the Absolute is beyond all of them. But that doesn't mean the Absolute has no Sachchidananda aspect. But it is beyond all expression.

NIRODBARAN: Sachchidananda also is beyond expression.

SRI AUROBINDO: No, it is Existence, Consciousness and Bliss.

DR. MANILAL: You can't have any idea or experience of the Absolute.

SRI AUROBINDO: No, you can have an idea, even experience it, but you can't express it. When you try to express it, you limit it because expression comes from the mind and from mental ideas and thoughts.

DR. MANILAL: It is like sweetness, Sir. There are so many kinds of sweetness, but we can't define it.

SRI AUROBINDO: One can define it to a certain extent.

DR. MANILAL: How will you express the sweetness of a pomegranate, Sir?

SRI AUROBINDO: That is a question of style, but I am not going to do it; I have something more worthwhile. (*Laughter*)

PURANI: Some define the taste by colour.

SRI AUROBINDO: Yes, the modern craze!

PURANI: They will say the sweetness of an orange is yellow.

SRI AUROBINDO: Pomegranate pink and shades of pink as pink I, pink II.

DR. MANILAL: But one can get the proof and knowledge by eating.

PURANI: That is experience.

DR. MANILAL: It is knowledge.

SRI AUROBINDO: It is a knowledge of the taste, not a metaphysical knowledge. (*Laughter*)

NIRODBARAN: Nolini Sen says they are feeling a more and more intense force, peace, etc. at Calcutta in their meditation. So intense that some people wonder if it isn't the supramental force that is descending.

SRI AUROBINDO (*laughing*): No! It is the spiritual force.

NIRODBARAN: Even the children feel it.

SRI AUROBINDO: Then it must be supramental. (*Laughter*) The supramental is independent of conditions and circumstances.

NIRODBARAN: It is curious that we don't feel anything.

SRI AUROBINDO: The Supramental must have descended at Calcutta alone. (*Laughter*)

NIRODBARAN: In the circumference to start with.

SRI AUROBINDO (*after a pause*): These experiences of force, peace, etc. come easily to those who begin the Yoga in the mind or vital. Those who begin in the physical mind have a tremendous tussle. Experiences don't take place in them so easily and they come only after a long time.

NIRODBARAN: Then I must be in the physical mind. (*Laughter*)

SRI AUROBINDO: But those who open their mind or vital first are not very safe. I have seen many Yogis, not great ones, I mean those who have got some experiences and power in the vital and they are satisfied with that. They think that that is all and there is nothing beyond it. X by his sadhana has got some inert peace in the physical which he thinks to be real peace.

PURANI: Professor Indra Sen was asking me about the theory of cause and effect. I told him I had not read the new volume of *The Life Divine* but, as far as I could remember, there is a sort of a continuous process of things and events going on. You cut off from that continuity any part and say that that must be the cause of this. I don't know if I am right.

SRI AUROBINDO: What I have said in *The Life Divine* is antecedent and subsequent. What we consider to be the cause of a particular effect may not be the immediate cause. For that effect to be produced, so many forces have come into play; even the opposing forces are necessary. The human mind sees only one factor and thinks that it is the cause. But as a matter of fact, without the combination and opposition of other forces, the result would not have been possible.

The human mind can't look at anything as a whole, it sees only by parts. It is like switching on a light and thinking that the switching must be the cause of the light. But the one who designs the whole electric system has to consider many factors before light can be produced.

27 DECEMBER 1940

DR. MANILAL: My shoulder pain is still persisting, Sir.

SRI AUROBINDO: It is responding to the wind, probably.

DR. MANILAL: Just near the insertion of the deltoid, Sir. Can't turn my arm backward.

SRI AUROBINDO: Yes, yes, I also have a pain in the same place. You must have passed it on to me. (*Laughter*)

DR. MANILAL: How to get rid of it, Sir?

SRI AUROBINDO: Don't identify with it.

DR. MANILAL: But how?

SRI AUROBINDO: It is a sort of inner movement. Or else make just those movements that bring on the pain.

DR. MANILAL: That causes pain, Sir.

SRI AUROBINDO: Doesn't matter. (*Laughter*) Or try to go up out of the body. Get rid of the old Sanskaras of the body.

At this time Manilal was sipping Padodaka, the water in which the Guru's feet are washed, and applying some of it to his shoulder.

PURANI: The pain has already gone. (*Laughter*)

DR. MANILAL: It is very much there.

PURANI: No, no, I tell you it has gone.

SRI AUROBINDO: He wants to make you believe that the pain has gone but you don't believe it. Or rather you believe but your arm doesn't. You identify with the arm.

DR. MANILAL: Last evening your knee was bending more than usual Sir, wasn't it?

SRI AUROBINDO: Maybe.

DR. MANILAL: Coming almost to a right angle.

SRI AUROBINDO: I could have bent it more but I was afraid that if I tried Purani would fall on me with the chair. (*Laughter*)

Sri Aurobindo used to sit on the edge of a chair and do the bending. Purani would stand behind the chair and hold the back of it lest the chair fall forward with Sri Aurobindo's weight on its edge.

PURANI: No, I was prepared for all eventualities.

DR. MANILAL: Arthur Luther, Sir, thrust his hand into the fire.

SRI AUROBINDO: Luther? You mean Archbishop Cranmer? Your knowledge of history is extraordinary! Neither was his name Arthur. What about it?

DR. MANILAL: When his hand was burning, did he not feel pain, Sir? How could he keep his hand in the fire? Did he do it stoically?

SRI AUROBINDO: How stoically?

DR. MANILAL: I mean in spite of the pain he endured the suffering. Or did he feel no pain at all?

SRI AUROBINDO: He may not have done it stoically but out of religious feeling. One can separate oneself from the body and then pain doesn't affect one.

DR. MANILAL: Is it possible, Sir?

SRI AUROBINDO: Why not?

NIRODBARAN: Nishtha was asking again whether, since the Mother doesn't know everything, she has to tell everything to the Mother, every detail. She also says that everything comes from the Divine. In that case there is no need to do Yoga, I said. She is wondering whether it wouldn't be better for her to resume the vitamin pills she was taking before and says that the suggestion may have come from the Divine.

SRI AUROBINDO: The suggestion to stop may have come from the Divine too.

NIRODBARAN: I told her what you said to us the other day about the Mother knowing things. She thinks that mental prayer is not sincere and so won't be heard by the Divine. The prayer must come from a deeper source.

SRI AUROBINDO: Of course, the deeper the source it comes from, the better it is. But why can't the Divine hear? Is he deaf to mental prayer?

NIRODBARAN: I said any sincere prayer is heard.

SRI AUROBINDO: He may hear but whether it is answered is different.

DR. MANILAL: Why couldn't it be answered, Sir? (*Laughter*)

SRI AUROBINDO: Not couldn't be. Anything could be but it may not be. (*Laughter*)

EVENING

DR. MANILAL: According to our Jain Shastra, there are three or four signs, Sir, by which gods can be recognised. Their feet don't touch the ground, their eyes don't blink, the garlands around their necks don't dry up.

SRI AUROBINDO: You will find those signs in the Mahabharata also. There is one more sign. The gods have no shadows.

DR. MANILAL: And they don't perspire. Is that true, Sir?

SRI AUROBINDO: Ask the gods.

DR. MANILAL: You are above the gods, Sir.

SRI AUROBINDO: I am on earth.

DR. MANILAL: Some time ago the Mother said that the gods – Shiva, Vishnu, etc. – came to the meditation she was giving.

SRI AUROBINDO: Yes, and then?

DR. MANILAL: In what form did they come, Sir?

SRI AUROBINDO: What do you mean?

DR. MANILAL: In an image form?

SRI AUROBINDO: What is an image? Everything is an image. You are an image. Nirod is an image.

DR. MANILAL: I mean could they be seen as concretely as, for instance, I see Nirod?

SRI AUROBINDO: Shiva is as concrete to Vishnu as you are to Nirod. (*Laughter*)

DR. MANILAL: Were they seen with open eyes?

SRI AUROBINDO: One can see with open or closed eyes. But with what sense does one see the gods?

DR. MANILAL: I don't know, Sir. That was not made clear by the Mother.

SRI AUROBINDO: What is there to make clear? One sees them with a subtle sense, not with the material.

28 DECEMBER 1940

*In connection with the ex-Maharani's case, Purani reported that Dilip
said he had heard from very reliable sources that the Madras judges had now
become corrupt and took bribes. It was not so during Purani's time.*

SRI AUROBINDO: Everything going down?

DR. MANILAL: In Bengal also there is much corruption.

SRI AUROBINDO: In the High Court?

DR. MANILAL: Yes, Sir.

SRI AUROBINDO: I suppose it has come after the new Government – with the advent of H and B. I am wondering what Swaraj
will be like.

NIRODBARAN: Was there no corruption before?

SRI AUROBINDO: Not so much. Bengal and Pondicherry were
the only two exceptions.

NIRODBARAN: H's ministry is almost openly doing these
things.

SRI AUROBINDO: Yes, one has the impression that after this
new Government, Bengal has become quite corrupt. There is one
good thing about England: it is still free from corruption in public
life. Of course England also was at one time corrupt but it has come
out of that. Victoria's time was especially admirable.

DR. MANILAL: France and America also are said to be very
corrupt.

SRI AUROBINDO: Oh, terrible! Not a single senate member is
free from bribery and corruption.

NIRODBARAN: What about your shoulder, Dr. Manilal?

DR. MANILAL: Same!

PURANI: You shouldn't have asked. It is all right, isn't it? I see it is
all right.

SRI AUROBINDO: It is all right without his knowing it.
(*Laughter*)

DR. MANILAL: Yes, Sir. Purani knows it without my knowing
myself.

SRI AUROBINDO: Knowledge by identity! (*Laughter*)

DR. MANILAL: That would have been all right if by my eating
Purani's hunger would have been satisfied.

SRI AUROBINDO: But suppose it is by Purani's eating that your
hunger would be satisfied? (*Laughter*)

Dr. Manilal: If it were, a lot of trouble would be saved, Sir, but it isn't; my hunger is still as strong.

Sri Aurobindo: Consider it an illusion. (*Laughter*)

Dr. Manilal: I am not a Mayavadin, Sir.

Nirodbaran: Will knowledge by identity give one knowledge of diagnosis of a case?

Sri Aurobindo: If it is complete. If you identify only with the patient's mind, however, you may not know because the patient himself may not know.

Purani: What will you do with a diagnosis if you don't know the cure?

Dr. Manilal: Identify with the Mother, not the patient, then you will know everything.

Nirodbaran: But one can also know the right drug.

Sri Aurobindo: Does the right drug always cure?

Nirodbaran: Why not?

Sri Aurobindo: Is every disease curable?

Dr. Manilal: No, Sir, but why isn't it curable?

Sri Aurobindo: There are conditions.

Nirodbaran: The Divine may cure unconditionally.

Sri Aurobindo: In every case?

Nirodbaran: No, when he chooses.

Sri Aurobindo: That means a condition.

Dr. Manilal: What are the conditions? Faith, aspiration?

Sri Aurobindo: You leave out the important element – receptivity.

Dr. Manilal: Am I receptive, Sir?

Sri Aurobindo: You may be but your shoulder may not.

Dr. Manilal: How to make it receptive?

Sri Aurobindo: Surgical operation. (*Laughter*)

Dr. Manilal: With what scalpel, Sir?

Sri Aurobindo: Opening!

Nirodbaran: Do different parts have different degrees of receptivity?

Sri Aurobindo: Of course. The mind may be receptive but the vital and physical may not, or the mind and the vital may be receptive without the body being so.

Dr. Manilal: But Laxmi's case was a miracle, Sir, I must say. I thought she would pass away but now she is quite a different person, looks young and energetic.

PURANI: It is a question of faith. She has faith in the Mother.

DR. MANILAL: I also have faith.

SRI AUROBINDO: You may but what about your arm? Purani wants to make you believe that you are all right but you or your arm won't believe it.

DR. MANILAL: How can it believe when the pain is still there, Sir? Otherwise I have faith.

PURANI: You are not open to the Force then.

DR. MANILAL: All my cells are open. (*Laughter*)

NIRODBARAN: To what?

DR. MANILAL: To Sri Aurobindo's Force.

SRI AUROBINDO: Even your rheumatic cells? (*Laughter*)

DR. MANILAL: Yes, Sir.

SRI AUROBINDO: Open to rheumatism.

EVENING

Purani was coughing a little.

DR. MANILAL: You talk of Force. Why don't you apply it to your own cough?

SRI AUROBINDO: He is driving the Germans out with his air force!

29 DECEMBER 1940

DR. MANILAL: Sir, why are the flowers counted by the Mother when they are brought to her?

SRI AUROBINDO: Why shouldn't they be? The stars are counted in astronomy.

DR. MANILAL: The Mother has recently started counting them, Sir.

SRI AUROBINDO: Astronomers also have recently started doing it. (*Laughter*)

DR. MANILAL: Do they count them as beads are counted?

SRI AUROBINDO: I don't know. You can ask them. (*After a while*) He, perhaps, wants to know if there is any Punya in it. (*Laughter*)

DR. MANILAL: No, Sir. There are transformation flowers in our house. Ambu picks them and brings them to the Mother. He says the Mother counts every one of them. When I asked the reason, he said, "All I know is that it has an occult reason. I don't know any more and can't tell you any more."

SRI AUROBINDO: Nor can I. Even that much I don't know. (*Laughter*)

EVENING

DR. MANILAL: Have you read Savarkar's speech, Sir?

SRI AUROBINDO: Yes. What about it?

DR. MANILAL: What do you think of it? He says we should join the Army in order to profit by the experience.

SRI AUROBINDO: It is a point of view forcefully stated.

DR. MANILAL: Have you also read Chandravarkar's speech?

SRI AUROBINDO: No.

DR. MANILAL: He says the Morley-Minto reform scheme with its separate electorates is responsible for this Hindu-Muslim disunity.

SRI AUROBINDO: Anybody could have said that.

DR. MANILAL: Savarkar also says that the British can't be defeated.

SRI AUROBINDO: That is nonsense. They were saved by Divine intervention during this War. They would have been smashed if Hitler had invaded England at the right time, just after the fall of France.

DR. MANILAL: Why didn't the Divine intervene in France, Sir?

SRI AUROBINDO: Because the French were corrupt and had no power of resistance. The English people have still some of their old virtues left to which support could be given.

DR. MANILAL: They say that Hitler may occupy Italy if Italy meets with reverses.

SRI AUROBINDO: That is one of the possibilities. But it will be hard for Germany to keep so many people under control.

31 DECEMBER 1940

DR. MANILAL (*as Nirodbaran was bending to touch Sri Aurobindo's knee*): I see a trident, Sir, on Nirod's forehead.

SRI AUROBINDO: A trident?

DR. MANILAL: Yes, Sir.

NIRODBARAN: What does it mean?

SRI AUROBINDO: It means that you are Shiva. (*Laughter*)

NIRODBARAN (*after a while*): Some people want to know how to increase their receptivity.

SRI AUROBINDO: The answer would be followed by "How to do that?" (*Laughter*)

DR. MANILAL: One can understand how to open the lid of a vessel. One just pulls and it comes off. But (*touching his head*) how to open here?

SRI AUROBINDO: Just open it. (*Laughter*)

DR. MANILAL: Could you not smash our heads, Sir, as the blacksmith smashed Jupiter's head in the Greek story?

SRI AUROBINDO: What is that story? I don't know of any blacksmith doing that.

DR. MANILAL: That is what is given in children's books, Sir.

SRI AUROBINDO: That may be for children. What I know is that Jupiter had a severe pain in his head. Suddenly his head burst open and Minerva came out of it.

DR. MANILAL: What about Nirod's receptivity question, Sir?

SRI AUROBINDO: You have to become quiet, become wide and open or become open and wide.

NIRODBARAN: Is not wideness a result of quietness?

SRI AUROBINDO: Not necessarily; one may be wide without being quiet.

DR. MANILAL: It seems to me, Sir, quietude of the mind is most important.

SRI AUROBINDO: Not only the mind, there is the vital, then the physical – and (*nodding his head*) then the Inconscient. (*Laughter*)

DR. MANILAL: End of the story, Sir? (*Laughter*)

SRI AUROBINDO: Yes! When the Inconscient is in a proper condition of quietude, you are able to receive.

DR. MANILAL: That would mean throwing away all disturbances.

SRI AUROBINDO: Not all. There is a central quietness – when the stuff of the mind becomes quiet – a condition in which one can receive in spite of all disturbances.

DR. MANILAL: Am I receptive, Sir? (*Laughter*)

SRI AUROBINDO: Your mind may be but your body is not.

DR. MANILAL: What percentage of receptivity have I, Sir?

SRI AUROBINDO: These things don't go by percentage. Besides, receptivity is infinite.

DR. MANILAL: How to know if one is receptive?

SRI AUROBINDO: If you receive you know you are receptive. (*Laughter*)

DR. MANILAL: My shoulder is the same, Sir – painful as before.

SRI AUROBINDO: That means it doesn't receive and so is not receptive.

EVENING

DR. MANILAL: They speak of a golden lid, Sir, above the head which covers the face of the Sun. Is it a matter of experience?

SRI AUROBINDO: Of course.

DR. MANILAL: Is it in the subtle body that one feels these things?

SRI AUROBINDO: Yes, one feels a sense of boring, drilling, hammering – so many things. Never had any such an experience?

DR. MANILAL: Yes, Sir. I had it, but long ago. It was marvellous, Sir, at the time. Even while going in a carriage I used to feel the descent of Ananda, Force, etc. Now all that is past history. (*Laughter*)

SRI AUROBINDO: They were experiences in the mind. Never had any force descending into the vital?

DR. MANILAL: No, Sir!

SRI AUROBINDO: You are closed in the vital then and, when the vital opens, you may be closed in the physical. (*Laughter*)

DR. MANILAL: Tragedy after tragedy, Sir. Experience of ascent and descent also stopped, Sir.

SRI AUROBINDO: Why? Didn't you find it interesting?

DR. MANILAL: Very interesting.

1 JANUARY 1941

The radio news said that Hitler has prayed to the Almighty to protect him against his enemies, as he is a single power surrounded by enemies.

SRI AUROBINDO: Since when has he become pious?

DR. MANILAL: God must be in a fix, Sir. (*Laughter*)

SRI AUROBINDO: He is always in a fix.

DR. MANILAL: And Hitler prays to the Almighty, not just to God.

SRI AUROBINDO: He thinks himself a mighty man; God, being almighty, will be on his side, he thinks.

DR. MANILAL: On which side would Krishna be, Sir, in this war? On the British?

SRI AUROBINDO: But his army might be on the other side as in the Mahabharata. Send a letter of enquiry to his chief secretary. (*Laughter*)

DR. MANILAL: I was telling Nirod that when a medicine has both good and bad effects, it is the good aspect that acts in a disease, while the bad effect remains behind. For instance, aspirin when given in rheumatism exerts only its good effect.

SRI AUROBINDO: The bad effect has no occasion to exert itself, so it has time to lie idle! (*Laughter*)

DR. MANILAL: While if aspirin is given in normal health, it may exert a bad effect on the heart.

SRI AUROBINDO: Since it can't do good, it does harm? (*Laughter*) Is it true that sometimes a thing which is contraindicated in a disease cures the disease? Mother told me the story of a lady in Paris who was suffering from diabetes. The doctor asked her not to eat potatoes at any cost. But at that time no other vegetable than potatoes was available. So she ate them and got cured. (*Laughter*) Is it possible?

DR. MANILAL: Not impossible, Sir. I have no faith in doctors and medicines.

NIRODBARAN: But you take medicines all the same.

SRI AUROBINDO: Habit or chance! (*Laughter*)

(*After Dr. Manilal had left*) Modern science says that quantity and movement alone are real. Quality is a creation of the senses. What is seen is a configuration of the senses. The configuration of reason acting on the configuration of the senses produces what is seen! But that doesn't go far enough, for the scientific researches which deal with quantity and movement as data are also a configuration of the senses. So everything is Maya, illusion.

2 JANUARY 1941

Anilbaran has been trying to introduce The Life Divine *as a course of study in Indian universities. Some universities have refused on varying grounds. Others have given hopeful answers. He wants to make the study of religion also a part of the curriculum.*

SRI AUROBINDO: If he wants to make *The Life Divine* a text-book for the colleges, I object. It will have worse results than in Manilal's case. (*Laughter*)

Anilbaran has made a few drafts of letters to be sent to the universities for that purpose. Sri Aurobindo approved none of them. He remarked that Anilbaran had made The Life Divine *a special course of study.*

PURANI: He wants to make it compulsory.

SRI AUROBINDO: Hitlerian? No, what should be done is to introduce a course of Indian philosophy in Indian universities and *The Life Divine* can come in by the way. It can't be made a principal subject. (*Laughing*) If it is made a textbook, one indubitable effect will be that the Arya Publishing House will get a lot of money and my private purse will get fat.

DR. MANILAL: In this year's prayer,[1] we are expected to be valiant warriors, Sir. I should like to be a warrior, but a warrior, against what? Whom shall I fight?

SRI AUROBINDO: Suppose you are sent to Italy as a pilot?

DR. MANILAL: No, Sir. I can only give suggestions.

SRI AUROBINDO: You have to fight the hostile forces. But how can you do that without knowing how to use the Force?

NIRODBARAN: Dilip says that Ashok Maitra – Heramba Maitra's son, who has married a famous actress – has asked him for permission for your Darshan.

SRI AUROBINDO: Why do all these actors and actresses want to come for Darshan?

NIRODBARAN: Dilip says they are very fine people.

---

1 The Mother's New Year prayer of 1941: "The world is fighting for its spiritual life menaced by the rush of hostile and undivine forces. Lord, we aspire to be Thy valiant warriors so that Thy glory may manifest upon the earth."

SRI AUROBINDO: Everybody is fine to Dilip. How old is this Ashok Maitra?

NIRODBARAN: My age. We were in the same class in City College.

SRI AUROBINDO: You were in City College?

NIRODBARAN: Yes, one year.

SRI AUROBINDO: Not time enough to be Herambaised?

NIRODBARAN: Dilip says many good people from Madras are coming for the Darshan this time – an insurance manager, etc.

SRI AUROBINDO: He means high-placed people?

PURANI: So others who have come are bad people? (*Laughter*)

DR. MANILAL: How can bad people come? They won't get permission.

SRI AUROBINDO: Can't say that.

DR. MANILAL: But all who are permitted to come have the intention of doing Yoga and are fit for Yoga.

SRI AUROBINDO: They may be fit but they have no intention.

3 JANUARY 1941

Dr. André and we are all puzzled about Nishtha's case. She is rapidly going downhill and no definite diagnosis has been arrived at. Dr. André called Dr. Manilal for a consultation. Dr. Manilal saw her and said it was gout and that she has been asked to take chicken and fish. But the difficulty about the arrangement of cooking meat and fish couldn't easily be solved; when it was finally solved some other difficulty cropped up and Nishtha was much upset. Nirodbaran had to spend a lot of time speaking with the Mother about how things were to be managed.

SRI AUROBINDO (*after hearing the report*): Vichy negotiations finished? (*Laughter*)

NIRODBARAN: Yes. It is all about the cooking arrangement. Nishtha finished about half a chicken yesterday, though the chicken was very tough.

SRI AUROBINDO: So it is anorexia carnivora? (*Laughter*)

DR. MANILAL: Whenever I prescribe a meat diet to patients, I am not at ease with my conscience, Sir. So I avoid giving it whenever possible, saying that meat is not good for health. Is it the voice of my conscience, Sir?

SRI AUROBINDO: Sanskara!

DR. MANILAL: I thought it was my inner voice, Sir. (*Laughter*)

NIRODBARAN: Like Gandhi's?

DR. MANILAL: Is not meat injurious to the body, Sir?

SRI AUROBINDO: Depends on the person. Of course it makes the body heavy, I mean the subtle body. The other objection to a meat diet is the taking of conscious life.

DR. MANILAL: Isn't it tamasic? But Vivekananda used to recommend it.

SRI AUROBINDO: He said it is rajasic.

NIRODBARAN: It is rajaso-tamasic.

DR. MANILAL: Is it good for the spiritual life?

SRI AUROBINDO: Again it depends on the person. Vegetables are, of course, better. If there is no attachment to meat, it does not do any harm. I was very much attached to meat. In order to get rid of the attachment, I used to give up meat for a long period, then take it up again and again give it up until I got rid of the attachment.

DR. MANILAL: Why are there so many diseases now in the Ashram?

SRI AUROBINDO: The Inconscient!

NIRODBARAN: But surely not all are ill?

SRI AUROBINDO: Some have illnesses, others other things.

NIRODBARAN: Are we promised a better time after the Inconscient is conquered?

SRI AUROBINDO (*laughing*): I don't promise anything. It may be as bad.

EVENING

DR. MANILAL: Purani's cold still persisting! (*To Purani*) Why don't you apply the Force on yourself since you speak of it to others?

PURANI: I am applying it. I am already better.

SRI AUROBINDO: Applying Coué diligently!

DR. MANILAL (*laughing*): Nishtha seems to have been completely metamorphosed, Sir! She was actually running.

SRI AUROBINDO: The Divine Force is great but the force of chicken seems to be greater! (*Laughter*)

NIRODBARAN: She is doing very well with her chicken and fish. Now she waits eagerly for her meals. After finishing half a chicken, she kept the other half for the next day!

DR. MANILAL: Gouty people are usually good eaters. The Maharaja Sayajirao was also like that. He knew which things were forbidden to him but when they were served on the table, without looking this way or that, he would go on eating everything. Afterwards somebody would say, "Sir, you shouldn't have taken those things!" and he would reply, "Oh, why didn't you tell me?" (*Laughter*)

Then Dr. Manilal began to tell some stories about the Maharaja.

DR. MANILAL: I remember he once lost his wallet. He had dropped it in the bathroom. He suspected somebody and charged him with the theft. When the wallet was found, the man came to the Maharaja and gave him a bit of his mind: "You are great people; I am your poor, small officer. So you could charge me with the theft. Even when I denied it you didn't believe me," etc. The Maharaja heard all that very calmly and didn't utter a single word.

SRI AUROBINDO: Yes, but he would take his revenge afterwards.

DR. MANILAL: Yes, of course. But to listen to the abuses so calmly is unusual for a Maharaja. He was a great man except for one or two defects.

SRI AUROBINDO: More than two! (*Laughter*)

A case of pox had broken out in the Ashram. Dr. Manilal said after hearing the symptoms that it might be small-pox. Dr. André saw the case and said it was chicken-pox.

SRI AUROBINDO (*after asking Dr. Manilal about the period of infectiousness*): I had a mild attack of small-pox in Baroda and at that time there was no such illness there. A judge prepared some mango drink and asked me to take it and transferred his small-pox to me in the process. The Maharaja asked me to go to Mussouri but the illness prevented me. When I got cured, I went there but the Maharaja sent me back quickly.

Somebody named Ananda, about sixty years of age, has written to Anilbaran that he has taken up Sannyasa, is suffering from many ailments and wants to come for the Darshan.

DR. MANILAL: He will increase Nirod's work.

SRI AUROBINDO: How old is he?

PURANI: Sixty.

SRI AUROBINDO: He can postpone it for the next life. (*Laughter*)

DR. MANILAL: There are some here who wear the Sannyasi dress. So he will be one of them. Dilip also puts on Sannyasi garb.

SRI AUROBINDO: But he is not called Ananda unless you call him Dilipananda. (*Laughter*)

DR. MANILAL: You have yourself given the name Ananda to people – to that Japanese.[1]

SRI AUROBINDO: Yes, I gave him the name but not Sannyasa. (*Laughter*)

4 JANUARY 1941

DR. MANILAL: What type of diseases does the Inconscient bring out, Sir?

SRI AUROBINDO: No type! Any type. It doesn't select. Each person may have a personal selection. For instance, Nirod has a predilection for a cold.

DR. MANILAL: And I have for shoulder pain, gall-bladder trouble, angina, blood pressure – a walking museum of diseases, Sir.

SRI AUROBINDO: Then you must be a big Yogi. (*Laughter*)

DR. MANILAL: How?

SRI AUROBINDO: Barin used to say that all the big Brahmo preachers used to have a lot of ailments. So they must have been big Yogis.

NIRODBARAN: What comes after the Inconscient?

SRI AUROBINDO: Nothing. The Inconscient is the basis of matter.

NIRODBARAN: I mean, what will be the next phase of the working?

SRI AUROBINDO: Development of Supermind or of the higher planes.

NIRODBARAN: Will the troubles be less?

SRI AUROBINDO: For whom?

---

1. Sundarananda – the name given to the Japanese architect of Golconde, George Nakashima.

NIRODBARAN: General.

SRI AUROBINDO: Oh, open your Inconscient first.

NIRODBARAN: I thought it was open.

SRI AUROBINDO: Manifest it at any rate.

DR. MANILAL: What really is the Inconscient, Sir?

SRI AUROBINDO: Absence of consciousness. (*Laughter*) The world is inconscient. Consciousness grows in it but along with its development the Inconscient also remains, like a crust, so that the development is always limited. This Inconscient has to be broken in order that consciousness may enlarge. Your shoulder, for instance, is conscious of the pain but is unconscious of the Force. (*Laughter*)

DR. MANILAL: What should the shoulder do, Sir?

SRI AUROBINDO: The Inconscient in the shoulder or else the shoulder itself can become conscious and open to the Force. The Inconscient is the last obstacle.

DR. MANILAL: Have you heard of Ralph Waldo Trine, Sir?

SRI AUROBINDO: No, who is he?

DR. MANILAL: He is an American writer and mystic. His method is like Vedanta.

SRI AUROBINDO: In tune with the Infinite – something like that?

DR. MANILAL: Yes, Sir. He says that one should imagine oneself as the Brahman and try to feel the force running through all the fibres of the body.

SRI AUROBINDO: Like Coué. You had any result with it?

DR. MANILAL: For a time.

SRI AUROBINDO: It is the same with the descent and action of the Force, only it is an unconscious process, done by the power of the idea of the mind. It may help but I don't know if it goes the whole way. It may affect the mind, but after the mind, there are the vital, the physical and the Inconscient. The Inconscient has ideas of its own, as it were. If the opposite ideas are strong enough and have power over them, then a cure may result.

DR. MANILAL: You have written in *Bases of Yoga* that one should say to oneself in any trouble, "I am a child of the Mother and Sri Aurobindo."

SRI AUROBINDO: Yes, it is the same power of the idea, a question of fundamental faith not only in the mind but in every part of the being, even in the Inconscient.

DR. MANILAL: Will it take a long time, Sir, to finish the Inconscient?

Sri Aurobindo with such a smile and tone said: "Yes!" that we all roared with laughter.

EVENING

Champaklal forgot today to give the wiping cloth to Sri Aurobindo and Nirodbaran did it instead. We laughed over it. Sri Aurobindo asked why we were laughing. When we said that Champaklal had forgotten to give the cloth he said, "The Inconscient?"

NIRODBARAN: Is the Inconscient the last?

SRI AUROBINDO: I have told you many times that it is the last, but I must remind you that the work is not short and not individual; it is the principle of the Inconscient that is being worked out.

Sri Aurobindo now took up Dara's radio news. Dara had incorrectly written something like Lord Garlic.

SRI AUROBINDO: Lord Garlic and Lady Asafoetida! (*Laughter*)

NIRODBARAN (*after the news was over*): I don't quite understand your work in the Inconscient. If it is concerned with the general Inconscient, then we ought also to be benefited by it.

SRI AUROBINDO: Indirectly. (*After a while*) What I want to discourage in you all is the idea that you will get the Supermind or be on the way to it as soon as the work in the Inconscient is over.

NIRODBARAN: No, I am not asking with that motive; neither have I that ambition.

SRI AUROBINDO: You may not, others have.

DR. MANILAL: They will be at the feet of the Supermind. (*Laughter*)

SRI AUROBINDO: Not even at the tail.

DR. MANILAL: But one thing is certain, Sir, that when the Supermind is established, there will be a control over diseases.

SRI AUROBINDO: All over the world?

DR. MANILAL: Not that way, Sir; I mean mastery over disease.

SRI AUROBINDO: Whose disease?

NIRODBARAN: In the Ashram.

DR. MANILAL: Among the sadhaks. (*Laughter*)

NIRODBARAN: If it is only in the Ashram, he will be left out, so he says sadhaks.

DR. MANILAL: Even among those outside who have faith.

SRI AUROBINDO: You bring in the faith condition now.

Champaklal and Purani gave instances in which even without any faith people had been cured by a flower from the Mother.

SRI AUROBINDO: So you see (*looking at Dr. Manilal*), the problem is very complex.

DR. MANILAL: Yes, Sir, but how to explain it? (*Laughter*)

5 JANUARY 1941

NIRODBARAN: In Nishtha's case, is it the Force that has produced this rapid improvement or is it the right medicine?

SRI AUROBINDO: You can infer or believe as you like.

NIRODBARAN: If the Force, why then was there no effect for such a long time but as soon as the right medicine was given she improved?

PURANI: It may be that the right conditions were absent before and now they have been brought about and so there is a cure.

SRI AUROBINDO: But does the right medicine always cure?

DR. MANILAL: No, Sir.

NIRODBARAN: If the right medicine can be found, yes.

SRI AUROBINDO: There are many instances where the right medicine has no effect. According to the French doctor, the medicine is an excuse; it is the doctor that cures.

NIRODBARAN: If that were true, why couldn't André, who has been treating Nishtha all along, cure her before and is only now able to do it?

SRI AUROBINDO: It is the French doctor's opinion, not mine.

NIRODBARAN: What is yours then?

SRI AUROBINDO: As for me, there is the Force, the doctor and the medicine. It is the combination of all these that brings about the cure. From my point of view, a disease is a play of forces. If you make a combination of one kind of forces, it gives one result, a different combination a different result. But in Nishtha's case the main credit goes to the chicken (*laughter*) and one can say that the doctor has hit on the right medicine.

DR. MANILAL: After the Inconscient, Sir, aren't the mind and vital to be worked out?

SRI AUROBINDO: No, that has already been done; not in each and every one but in principle. In the mind and vital again there are many parts. There are also the subconscient mental, vital and physical.

DR. MANILAL: What is the difference between the Inconscient and the Subconscient?

SRI AUROBINDO: In the Subconscient, consciousness is suppressed but it is there, while in the Inconscient all is black, there is no consciousness at work, and yet consciousness is involved in it, out of which matter and everything else emerge by evolution.

DR. MANILAL: Jada is Inconscience, isn't it?

SRI AUROBINDO: No, consciousness may also be Jada; Jada is a result of Inconscience.

NIRODBARAN: What is the difference between Inconscience, Ignorance and Nescience?

SRI AUROBINDO: Ignorance is knowledge that is wrong, partial or imperfect. Nescience is absence of knowledge; knowledge develops out of Inconscience. The theory I have put forward in *The Life Divine* is that the Inconscient and the Superconscient are two sides or counterparts of the same reality, though they appear to us as opposed to each other. The Inconscient is a black trance – the dark counterpart – while the Superconscient is a luminous trance. Out of the Inconscient, knowledge emerges by evolution. In the Superconscient, knowledge is always there, it only manifests out of it. They are the two opposite poles of the manifestation of the Absolute.

Nescience may be sensitive to impulses without knowing what these impulses are, whereas Inconscience is insentient. This is the great riddle, that Inconscience can yet create perfect order. It is like the Sankhya Prakriti which is Jada and at the same time intelligent.

NIRODBARAN: What are the effects of the working out of the mind and vital?

SRI AUROBINDO: Opening to the higher consciousness and a capacity to receive it.

NIRODBARAN: Why don't we see any effect then?

SRI AUROBINDO: It is only in principle. If everybody were able to receive it, then the whole of humanity would be changed.

NIRODBARAN: But we are slightly different from humanity.

SRI AUROBINDO: But still part of humanity unless you want to say that you have achieved the Supermind.

DR. MANILAL: We ought to have at least a little taste of the Supermind since we are here. If an incense burns in a room, one gets the smell of it.

SRI AUROBINDO: But if you don't have a nose like Sayajirao? (*Laughter*)

NIRODBARAN: If the work is now in the Inconscient, why do some people, especially newcomers, get experiences? Is the work in them not in the Inconscient?

SRI AUROBINDO: It depends on what kind of experiences – inner or higher experiences or those in the vital. One may think that one has become the Supreme and the Supermind, but the fact may be otherwise.

NIRODBARAN: But don't some newcomers have psychic experiences?

SRI AUROBINDO: The work may be going on in the psychic, the Inconscient coming in between to hinder it.

PURANI: Those who have been here long may be participating in the working and in them the Inconscient may rise up.

SRI AUROBINDO: So that you may suddenly feel stupid. (*Laughter*)

PURANI: That should give some consolation!

6 JANUARY 1941

DR. MANILAL: The Mother says in her *Conversations* that one can progress without meditation.

SRI AUROBINDO: Can't say anything without the context. In that case the whole world would progress.

PURANI: No, the Mother says about those who can't meditate that through work they can progress in sadhana.

SRI AUROBINDO: That is different. There are people here who can't meditate at all but are working all the time and they receive through their work. (*Addressing Dr. Manilal*) But you have no excuse. You can meditate. You go into deep meditation, though not quite like a Tirthankara. (*Laughter*)

DR. MANILAL: I couldn't be a Tirthankara, Sir, otherwise I wouldn't have been born again.

PURANI: Why? Are Tirthankaras afraid of life?

SRI AUROBINDO: No, afraid of Pudgal.¹ (*Laughter*)

DR. MANILAL: Might I have been a Jain in my previous birth, Sir?

SRI AUROBINDO: Certainly, since you know all about Jainism but don't follow it. (*Laughter*)

DR. MANILAL: Is it a tragedy, Sir?

SRI AUROBINDO: No, your knowledge comes from a previous birth; you don't follow because it is not necessary – you have done it already.

DR. MANILAL: How to pass through the stage of sleep in meditation?

SRI AUROBINDO: Is it sleep or going within?

DR. MANILAL: Well, I don't know. Sometimes I seem to come out of a deep sleep knowing or remembering nothing about where I have been. Sometimes, I see many incoherent things but can't remember them.

SRI AUROBINDO: That is the border of the Subconscience. Before sitting, one has to fix a will to be conscious; the result comes afterwards.

CHAMPAKLAL: I also seem to be going somewhere very deep; it is very pleasant and nice there. One would like to be there for ever.

SRI AUROBINDO: That is the inner being. You feel like Shankaracharya who said, "I went somewhere to a region of Bliss. I wish I could remain there."

After this, the talk turned to the Hindu Mahasabha, whose conference was taking place in Madurai.

DR. MANILAL: The Mahasabha people are in favour of giving help to Britain but they also want India's freedom. I don't

1. Body, matter.

understand Gandhi's attitude at all. There is no question of his being insincere but his stand and actions are not very clear.

NIRODBARAN: Some say he is not sincere. As proof they cite the fact of his pledging unconditional support at the beginning and then making a somersault, saying that we are not making a bargain when it is nothing but that.

SRI AUROBINDO: The question is, when is a bargain not a bargain, like the question, when is killing not killing.

DR. MANILAL (*apropos of Abhay's father who suddenly lost his sight due to cataract*): There is no cure for a cataract except an operation when it is mature, unless Dr. Agarwal can do something. But I think gazing at the sun may sometimes destroy the eye.

SRI AUROBINDO: It depends on how one does it. Sun-gazing has been done in India since time immemorial. I myself have done it and there are people here who have regained their sight and discarded glasses by the practice.

PURANI: I have done it too. For many years I used to gaze at strong sunlight. But I gave it up after what happened once during meditation. There was a great descent of force then suddenly I felt a severe pain in my eye.

SRI AUROBINDO: It must have been an attack.

MULSHANKAR: In meditation also can the hostile forces attack?

SRI AUROBINDO: Why not? It is their business to do so at any time.

MULSHANKAR: Is there no protection from the Divine? Purani is quite strong.

SRI AUROBINDO: Strength and protection are not the same thing. So long as there is a weak spot one is liable to attack unless one puts it right oneself.

7 JANUARY 1941

DR. MANILAL: Does the killing of mosquitoes come in the way of spiritual attainment, Sir?

SRI AUROBINDO: Whose attainment? Of the mosquitos? (*Laughter*)

DR. MANILAL: No, Sir, our attainment?

SRI AUROBINDO: No, it may be for the mosquitoes because you kill them before they have exhausted their mosquito propensity. But why that question?

NIRODBARAN: Gandhian ahimsa, perhaps, or Jain virtue and vice.

SRI AUROBINDO: It may take away from ethical qualities but it has nothing to do with spiritual principles.

DR. MANILAL: In medical practice we may sometimes be liable to kill patients because of our lack of knowledge, negligence, etc. Are we responsible for the deaths?

SRI AUROBINDO: If they are due to negligence, yes, but not if they are due to lack of efficiency or knowledge. It is the spirit or intention that is more important than the act.

NIRODBARAN: But is ignorance excusable?

SRI AUROBINDO: If one is ignorant and goes on committing mistakes in his ignorance, then he can't be excused. But if his intention is good, his lack of knowledge doesn't make him responsible for his mistake. I am not speaking of those people who make experiments on patients.

8 JANUARY 1941

DR. MANILAL: The knee is bending a little more, Sir.

SRI AUROBINDO: Do you think so?

DR. MANILAL: Yes, Sir.

NIRODBARAN: Is it the Inconscient that stands in the way of a rapid cure?

SRI AUROBINDO: Partially and many things in between.

NIRODBARAN: If diseases arise from the Inconscient, then when it is worked out, all diseases should cease – Dr. Manilal's too.

SRI AUROBINDO: That depends on Manilal.

NIRODBARAN: If by Sri Aurobindo's working on the higher planes we can open more easily to them, then by his working on the Inconscient our diseases ought to be cured.

PURANI: Yes, but we can open only in the reverse way! (*Laughter*)

There was news that Hitler was trying to persuade Bulgaria to allow German passage or to join the Axis orbit.

SRI AUROBINDO: That is the danger now. I don't think an invasion of England is likely. If Britain can't help the Balkan powers with sufficient anti-tank guns, aeroplanes, etc., it will be difficult for them to resist Germany.

NIRODBARAN: Turkey may come in to help Bulgaria if the latter is attacked.

SRI AUROBINDO: Don't know. If Turkey waits till Bulgaria is attacked it will be too late. In that case Hitler may turn towards Palestine and help Italy there, and then move on to Africa. Next he will ask Spain to join him so that the English army in Africa will be caught between two forces.

PURANI: Yes, that is why England is trying to hurry up the Libyan campaign so that it can move its forces to Greece.

EVENING

Dara has reported that Roosevelt in his speech mentioned three things, one of which was freedom from care.

SRI AUROBINDO: Freedom from care? Is it material or spiritual freedom? Take for instance Manilal's shoulder. Material freedom would mean freedom from pain, while spiritual freedom would mean it does not matter even if there is pain. Which do you want, Manilal?

DR. MANILAL: Both, Sir! (*Laughter*)

Afterwards it was found that Roosevelt had said "freedom from want".

There was a difference of opinion about a case of chronic appendicitis. Dr. B. C. Roy advised an immediate operation, while others said it should be postponed for a year. Nirodbaran asked Dr. Manilal's view.

DR. MANILAL: I don't know the case, but if it is chronic it is better to remove the appendix. But it may not be appendicitis at all. Many mistaken operations have been performed even in cases of pneumonia, typhoid, pleurisy. At one time it was the fashion to blame the appendix for any trouble and remove it. Doctors sometimes make much of a little thing.

SRI AUROBINDO: I remember in England Sarat Ghose had a small pimple on his lip. A doctor was called. He examined it and said with a long face, "Very serious, very serious!" The way he said it with a grave shaking of his head was most comical!

NIRODBARAN: I had an urgent call today from X. I got a little frightened as she has been having the haemorrhage trouble. But when I went in, I saw that she had called me for just a few patches of leucoderma she had suddenly discovered under her breasts. She was on the point of weeping and asked me to tell you to stop them. She said, "God has made me sufficiently ugly. Why this further addition?" (*Laughter*)

SRI AUROBINDO: If she were a professional beauty I could understand her fear! (*Laughter*)

NIRODBARAN: You must have seen that K. S. Roy has become the leader of the Bengal Congress party.

SRI AUROBINDO (*smiling*): Yes. Y and Z have seen that the game is up now. They are the most wonderful people for creating splits. I haven't seen anyone else like them.

9 JANUARY 1941

Somebody from Bombay has written that in the old files of Indu Prakash he has found a series of six articles on Bankim written by Sri Aurobindo. Purani asked Sri Aurobindo if it was true.

SRI AUROBINDO: I may have, I don't remember. I wrote some articles on Madhusudan, I remember. In which year was it?

PURANI: In 1894, the second year of your stay in Baroda.

SRI AUROBINDO: My knowledge of Bengali was very little at that time. I couldn't have finished reading all the writings of Bankim or perhaps I wrote the articles during the first enthusiasm of my learning the language. Of course we started learning it Cambridge – the judge, Beachcroft, was one of us – under an Anglo-Indian pundit. He used to teach us Vidyasagar. One day we hit upon a sentence of Bankim's and showed it to him. He began to shake his head and said, "This can't be Bengali!" (*Laughter*)

PURANI: Nolini is very happy that he will get materials for another book.

SRI AUROBINDO (*smiling*): Can't allow publication of that. It must have been very immature.

It was decided that the man should be asked to send us copies of the articles for Sri Aurobindo's inspection. The man in his reply wanted to charge about ninety rupees for expenses.

SRI AUROBINDO: I can't pay money for these articles. They are not worth anything.

PURANI: If Sri Aurobindo wants to see them, money can be arranged from outside.

SRI AUROBINDO: Then I have no objection.

Later on it came out that Sri Aurobindo had written some articles on the Congress.

SRI AUROBINDO: Those will be interesting to see.

NIRODBARAN: How could Madhusudan write so well in Bengali?

SRI AUROBINDO: He engaged several pundits and he had the inborn poetic faculty.

PURANI: Besides, he was a linguist; he knew many European languages.

SRI AUROBINDO: Oh yes! You can see the influence of Homer, Virgil and Tasso in his writings.

DR. MANILAL: I asked Nirod if he was having experiences. He said, "No, my work is now in the physical." I asked, "What about mind and vital?" "Oh, all that is finished!" "So it will be Supermind next?" "Yes," Nirod replied. (*Laughter*)

(*After some time*) Nirod, how is your poetry getting on?

SRI AUROBINDO: He has finished his mental and vital working. (*Laughter*)

11 JANUARY 1941

There was some talk about Purushottam, a sadhak who had gone away.

DR. MANILAL: Did he have any occult knowledge?

SRI AUROBINDO: All his knowledge of previous births is humbug. What he had was some life-force which he could apply on the physical.

DR. MANILAL: What does that mean, Sir?

SRI AUROBINDO: You have to read *The Life Divine* for that.
DR. MANILAL: How could he have this fall?
SRI AUROBINDO: The physical mind.

12 JANUARY 1941

There was a long story narrated by Purani about the ex-Maharani of Baroda, how her boxes were detained and opened by a Muslim judge in Madras and handed over to the Police. The Police also detained her valuable documents.

DR. MANILAL: What type of past action makes innocent people suffer like this, Sir?
SRI AUROBINDO: Innocent people suffer everywhere! The law of Karma, perhaps. They may have been wicked in their previous lives. (*Laughter*)
NIRODBARAN: Then how can they be innocent in this life?
SRI AUROBINDO: As a reaction. In the next life they may again be wicked and fortunate. (*Laughter*)
NIRODBARAN: In her sleep X had an interesting experience of the action of the higher and the lower forces on her body in connection with her haemorrhage. The lower forces wanted to make the physical being accept the suggestion that the bleeding should start again and the higher forces repelled the suggestion.
DR. MANILAL: How can it be explained, Sir? (*Laughter*)
SRI AUROBINDO: No explanation is required. It is a fact. Usually ordinary people get suggestions of illness from the subconscious in their sleep or dreams. They don't know it and get the disease. Moreover, the physical being is habituated to these things and easily accepts the suggestions; the vital being too. But if the inner consciousness is awake, the suggestions can't act.
DR. MANILAL: I don't accept suggestions, Sir.
SRI AUROBINDO: Who is "you"?
DR. MANILAL: I, Manilal, Sir! (*Laughter*)
SRI AUROBINDO: Who is Manilal? The surface Manilal may not accept them but there are many other Manilals whom the surface Manilal doesn't know.
DR. MANILAL: Last night I got a bit depressed, Sir, because of this shoulder pain.

SRI AUROBINDO: Yes, you looked as if this world were Duhkhamaya.[1]

(*Later on, to Nirodbaran*) Now that X has got this experience she ought to be able to bring down the right kind of forces and prevent the disease from recurring.

NIRODBARAN: But how can it be practically applied?

SRI AUROBINDO: Once one has the experience, one can do it more easily. It is the power of the idea and will. If the physical consciousness is awake, it can act.

EVENING

DR. MANILAL: I am having no meditation, Sir, and no experiences. Formerly I used to feel so much peace and Ananda.

SRI AUROBINDO: That means you have progressed. You may have reached the Inconscient!

DR. MANILAL: Is the Inconscient something like Tamas?

SRI AUROBINDO: Inertia.

DR. MANILAL: How to get rid of it, Sir?

SRI AUROBINDO: By Utsaha and Kala.[2] (*Laughter*)

DR. MANILAL: If my state is due to the Inconscient, how do other people get meditation and have experiences?

SRI AUROBINDO: You have made more progress than them, progressed so much as to be as inconscient as you are. (*Laughter*) The Inconscient doesn't work in the same way with everybody. Are you becoming stupid?

DR. MANILAL: Formerly I used to feel that I was always carrying away something with me. This time nothing at all, Sir.

SRI AUROBINDO: Aparigraha![3] (*Laughter*) Are you feeling stupid, forgetting things?

DR. MANILAL: No, Sir!

SRI AUROBINDO: Then it is all right. You have been here only two months now. Nirod says he has been here for so many years and he is not getting results, only medical cases.

NIRODBARAN: Ma phalesu![4] Even in my cases I am not making any progress.

1. Full of misery.
2. Enthusiasm and time.
3. Non-acceptance.
4. Not for the results.

SRI AUROBINDO: You can't say that now there are no cases.

NIRODBARAN: No, but I am not profiting by the experience.

13 JANUARY 1941

EVENING

DR. MANILAL: There are four principles of Jainism, Sir.

SRI AUROBINDO: Yes, what are they?

DR. MANILAL: Dana, Sila, Tapa and Bhavana. Bhavana is aspiration. This concerns our Yoga, Sir.

SRI AUROBINDO: Only this one?

DR. MANILAL: Why only one, Sir? Dana also.

SRI AUROBINDO: Dana is charity. We don't insist on charity to others. Ours is self-dana.

DR. MANILAL: And Sila, Sir?

SRI AUROBINDO: What is Sila? Virtue? We don't insist on virtue. Virtue is a moral principle, not spiritual.

DR. MANILAL: Morality is a consequence of spirituality.

SRI AUROBINDO: Not necessarily. Tapa is asceticism. We have nothing to do with asceticism.

DR. MANILAL: No, Sir.

SRI AUROBINDO: So aspiration is the only common factor.

DR. MANILAL: Yes, Sir.

Shastri has recently been showing signs of unbalance. A few days ago Nirodbaran was asked by the Mother to go and see him about his health. He had not been sleeping well nor eating properly. He had been observing silence for a long time, in spite of the Mother's disapproval. The inevitable consequence happened: he lost his mental balance and this evening he came right inside the Ashram only to inquire if the Mother and Sri Aurobindo had called him. After that he seemed to have disappeared. News came later that he was wandering about in the bazar.

DR. MANILAL: I don't know anything about this story. What's the matter with him?

SRI AUROBINDO: First descent of the Supermind! (*Laughter*) Yes, that's what he said. He asked others to be valiant warriors and to write to Atreya to become one of his commanders-in-chief. (*Laughter*)

NIRODBARAN: Is it the result of the Inconscient?

SRI AUROBINDO: No, the usual story. Going into silence and shutting himself up thinking that he is doing great Yoga and that everybody is inferior to him. This kind of silence is not good for our Yoga.

DR. MANILAL: Radhanand also observes silence.

CHAMPAKLAL: No, not this kind. He has communication with selected people.

SRI AUROBINDO: Radhanand's is quite a different case. He knows what he is about. He had been doing Yoga for ages before he came here. All the cases I have seen of this nature have been due to one of two causes: excessive indulgence in sexual perversity or ambition.

DR. MANILAL: Which was it in Shastri's case?

SRI AUROBINDO: Ambition. He wanted to be a great Yogi. What happens in such cases is that they open to some intermediate zone before the vital is prepared.

DR. MANILAL: G is said to have had the Overmind experience. Is it true, Sir?

SRI AUROBINDO: True, if he had it. (*Laughter. Dr. Manilal thought that he had it, so Sri Aurobindo added:*) The question is whether he had it. (*Laughter*) It is very easy to get into some vital plane and think oneself to have had all sorts of things.

DR. MANILAL: I remember now, Sir, that Sila in Jainism is not virtue but *eka patni vrata*, being faithful to one's wife.

SRI AUROBINDO: We have no wives, so we are not required to keep that commandment. (*Laughter*)

DR. MANILAL: There are five other principles which can be said to be common with us.

SRI AUROBINDO: What are they?

DR. MANILAL: Truth.

SRI AUROBINDO: Yes.

DR. MANILAL: Brahmahcarya.

SRI AUROBINDO: Certainly.

DR. MANILAL: Aparigraha.

SRI AUROBINDO: Expected to be common, but isn't. (*Laughter*)

DR. MANILAL: I forget the other one.

NIRODBARAN: Ahimsa.

DR. MANILAL: Yes, the most important.

SRI AUROBINDO: That we half observe – for instance, the killing of mosquitoes and bugs is allowed!

14 JANUARY 1941

DR. MANILAL: By the rejection of lower impulses, Sir, is it not the rejection of immoral impulses that is in view?

SRI AUROBINDO: What is meant by immoral? What society does not like? Isn't that so?

DR. MANILAL: Yes, Sir.

SRI AUROBINDO: We have nothing to do with society. Otherwise we can't do Yoga.

NIRODBARAN: We couldn't leave our family and parents! It would be immoral. Of course in Dr. Manilal's case that problem doesn't arise. (*Laughter*)

DR. MANILAL (*massaging Sri Aurobindo's patella*): It has become more flexible, Sir.

NIRODBARAN: Not much; far less than expected. We expected a miracle from you.

DR. MANILAL: Me?

SRI AUROBINDO: Kaivalya jnana.[1] (*Laughter*)

News has been obtained that Shastri is somewhere in the town. The owner of the house in which he is lodged is in contact with the Ashram. He proposed to Shastri that he would bring him to the Ashram if he wished. Shastri replied that the Mother would send a car for him!

SRI AUROBINDO: Yes, and the next day he will ask for an elephant. (*Laughter*)

PURANI: The best thing for such people is to send them home. Then they become all right.

---

1. Knowledge of the One.

In January 1941 Nirodbaran stopped recording the talks on a regular basis. What follows are seven talks and a letter from the period 1941–48. All but one deal with a devotee from Calcutta.

10 AUGUST 1941

NIRODBARAN: A, who has come for the first time, met Dilip in Calcutta in 1937 and 1938. After Dilip's return to the Ashram for the August Darshan of 1938, A wrote him a letter. He said he was going through a severe crisis. He seemed to be enveloped by darkness twenty-four hours a day and felt that something was trying to throttle him. It is not that he did not see any daylight but that the feeling of darkness was overwhelming, and though there was no physical discomfort, the choking feeling was very real. He did not feel like doing anything though his B.A. examination was only a few months away. There was no earthly reason for his condition, he said. There was no dissension in the family, no lack of money, etc., so he wrote to Dilip that he thought it was owing to something in himself. He asked whether Sri Aurobindo could help and what he would have to do for it.

Dilip, says A, gave a beautiful, encouraging and reassuring answer. He said he sympathised with A's anguish and hoped that it would not last long. He said that he thought it was owing to something in A wanting a new birth. Till then forces of Nature had dominated him and now something in A, his Antaratma, was rebelling against that domination and naturally the old forces were reasserting themselves with redoubled vigour. Dilip said it was a very good sign and hoped that something really worthwhile would come out of the crisis. He asked A to write a letter, preferably typewritten, to Sri Aurobindo and, if he wished, to the Mother also and, if possible, to enclose a passport size photograph of himself. He assured A that Sri Aurobindo could certainly help. A did as Dilip had suggested and Dilip sent the letters to you. Dilip also enclosed for the Mother an introductory letter in which he gave his impression of A, his family background, etc., and enclosed the photograph. The Mother sent Dilip's letter back to him with this remark on the margin of the last page: "It is a beautiful face, he must be a charming boy. He may write of his experiences."

He says he got the letter in the afternoon around half-past five and as soon as he opened it and took the blessing packet in his hand,

something happened. He saw a column of white light which was at
the same time a force coming down from above, touching the
crown of his head and entering his body. Eventually it went down
to his feet. He says this was Shaktti-sanchar (a movement of force).
He has asked me to report this to you.

SRI AUROBINDO: Yes. Anything else?

NIRODBARAN: He says that he had more to report but that he is
waiting for your reaction.

11 AUGUST 1941

NIRODBARAN: A says he is very grateful to you for your con-
firming his experience. He related something about you which he
had heard from a friend of his. He went to see this friend who is a
Tantrik-cum-astrologer. He had your book *The Mother* with him.
The friend, on seeing the book, folded his hands and touched his
forehead with them in the normal Indian manner. A asked the friend
why he did so, was it the subject of the book or was it the author?
The friend simply said, "*Bhagabaner boi*" ("God's book"). Then he
became quite solemn and quietly said, "I have got his horoscope", to
which A replied, "That's interesting, God's horoscope?" The friend
chided him, "Don't be flippant, I really mean it, I have it." A realised
that the friend was serious and he also becoming so, asked him, "All
right, what is your reading?" "In 1947," answered the friend, "he
will become the *ekachatra adhipati* (unchallenged sovereign of the
whole world)."

SRI AUROBINDO: 1947? Then I will do things quicker than
Hitler! (*Turning to Dr. Manilal*) What post will you have Manilal?

DR. MANILAL: Nothing, Sir.

SRI AUROBINDO: No, you must have something to do.

DR. MANILAL: Sir, I'll be at your feet, Sir, humbly.

SRI AUROBINDO: I'll make you the Chief of the World Medical
Service.

12 AUGUST 1941

NIRODBARAN: A says that the day after he had his Diksha he
started meditating without any apparent effort, even without any

resolve to meditate. He says he got up at about four o'clock in the morning and then after having a wash he went down to his study and started to meditate. Soon he began to have experiences. He says that the first thing he noticed was that the walls of the room were vibrant, full of life and no longer made of solid matter. Two or three days later he experienced a force which was light, a kind of consciousness. After eight days he had a concrete experience of everything in the room being made of delight. He found it was the same substance of bliss which was in him and around him. He says this experience stayed with him for a month. He felt a joy always, and even for people he was not particularly fond of, he had a spontaneous sympathy and love. He felt great love even for animals he did not particularly like.

SRI AUROBINDO: He has had one of the highest experiences of Yoga.

13 AUGUST 1941

NIRODBARAN: A says that seventeen days after he had started meditating, he saw during the night when he was asleep a young woman standing by his bed. Even in his sleep he felt very alert and was sure that the apparition was not good though the woman seemed to be sad and her eyes appeared to appeal for help. A says he heard a voice within him saying, "Go away." He felt it was not his own voice and yet it sounded exactly like it. He now takes it to be a command from a deeper part of himself. The woman did not seem to hear it and became more appealing with her eyes. After a while she seemed to stir a bit as if she might go nearer the bed. The voice within A went on repeating all the while "Go away", but when the woman seemed to be on the point of moving, it shouted with great force, "GO AWAY." The woman crumpled away on to the floor without leaving any trace. A woke up, felt great relief, light and joy. He happened to look in a mirror in his room and saw a splendid light on his face.

SRI AUROBINDO: His inner being has rejected sex altogether.

NIRODBARAN: A has asked if the inner being means the psychic being.

SRI AUROBINDO: It also means the inner physical, the inner vital and the inner mental being. The psychic is the inmost being.

NIRODBARAN: A has asked if the gains in the inner consciousness are not to be worked out in the outer being.

SRI AUROBINDO: Yes, the ultimate aim is to transform the total
being and nature.

NIRODBARAN: A has requested me to convey his gratitude to
you and the Mother. (*Sri Aurobindo looked pleased.*)

28 SEPTEMBER 1941

EVENING

One L.D.M. has reviewed Sri Aurobindo's latest poems in the Hindu
*literary supplement. Dr. Manilal said at noon that it was a good review. Sri
Aurobindo expressed a little surprise and said that the* Hindu *was usually
not favourable to him. In the evening we read the paper and found that it was
a very bad review.*

SRI AUROBINDO (*to Dr. Manilal*): You said it was a good review.
There is nothing good there. In fact the writer says that this is not
poetry at all. At the end he did what they call damning with faint
praise. When I first heard about the review, my impression was
correct – that it was not favourable.

NIRODBARAN: This man doesn't seem to understand much
about poetry. He says there is no colour! Good Lord, there is any
amount of colour in "Rose of God" and in the very lines he quotes
from "Thought the Paraclete".

SRI AUROBINDO: Quite so. And he says there is no emotion or
feeling. The point is what he means by emotion.

NIRODBARAN: There is tranquillity, he says, but that, according
to him, is more an evidence of poetic failure than poetic gift!

DR. MANILAL (*rather abashed at his wrong appraisal*): Of course, I
don't understand poetry. But at the end doesn't he say that one
ought to read and reread it?

NIRODBARAN: Yes, that is the part damning with faint praise.

SRI AUROBINDO: But what does he mean by emotion?

PURANI: The usual sentimental stuff, I suppose.

SRI AUROBINDO: If he means sentimental romantic emotion,
that age has passed in poetry. Doesn't he know that? That is the
concern of drama. Nowadays poetry is concerned with Truth and

Beauty. If you are able to express them with sufficient power of language and rhythm, that is what is required of you. In drama one is concerned with drawing characters with life and its reactions. I suppose what he wants is something more like Francis Thompson's poetry.

PURANI: And Gerard Hopkins?

SRI AUROBINDO: No, for Hopkins has many compound words. The reviewer also thinks that Paraclete means advocate, and there is no advocacy in the poem!

DR. MANILAL: The dictionary also says that.

SRI AUROBINDO: Yes, that is the dictionary meaning. But one isn't always obliged to accept that meaning. Doraiswamy would then be a retired Paraclete? (*Laughter*) The Paraclete is also the Holy Ghost. What I have meant there is that thought is the intercessor between the Supreme Truth and the human consciousness. Thought flies to the Supreme Truth to connect its consciousness with the earth and after its departure all that is left behind is the Self. That is what I have meant there.

SATYENDRA: The images, he says, have an intellectual setting difficult for the reviewer to appreciate.

SRI AUROBINDO: The images I have used are, of course, not of a mental nature. What has been seen or realised is yogic through experience or vision, I have tried to express inner symbols. All the images are symbols of inner experience. And in these poems I always use yogic symbols. These experiences and visions have a form; the images have been used to give as correct a description of these forms as possible so that they may become a reality, even a being, so to say.

NIRODBARAN: That is why the reviewer says "unconventional imagery"!

SRI AUROBINDO: He means original, I suppose.

DR. MANILAL: But certainly very few people will understand the poems, Sir. I have asked many here.

SATYENDRA: The poems are like his prose works. But poems like "Baji Prabhou" Dr. Manilal will understand.

DR. MANILAL (*smiling*): Oh yes, that even I can grasp.

SRI AUROBINDO (*smiling*): You remind me of Molière. You know that story?

DR. MANILAL: No, Sir.

SRI AUROBINDO: He used to read all his plays to his maid-servant before publication. And if she understood and liked them,

Molière was satisfied. He was then certain that everybody would enjoy them. (*Laughter*)

19 AUGUST 1944

NIRODBARAN: A says that he went to see someone who was a reputable astrologer, a different person from the one about whom I spoke to you some years ago. A relation of his sent him to consult this man about her son. A had your book *Essays on the Gita* with him, and on seeing it, the astrologer made the gesture of *namaskar*. On being asked why he did so and whether it was for the author or the book, he replied, '*Bhagabaner boi.*" He also said that he not only had your horoscope but he had received your birth chart from you.

SRI AUROBINDO: How?

NIRODBARAN: A says the astrologer told the following story. Sometime before November 1926, he had written to you requesting you to send him the date and time of your birth. He also wrote that he analysed the birth charts of great people as a matter of scientific interest and not for financial gain. He asked you whether he could do the same in your case also. Then, A says, the astrologer appeared to be very moved and with obvious gratitude in his voice he said that besides sending him the date and time of your birth, you had drawn a chart for him. But you said that you would rather that he did not write and publish anything about you. The man commented: "Sri Aurobindo could have just told me not to write about him, instead he requested me not to do so. That is a sign of greatness." Asked whether he had published anything about you, he answered, "How could I after Sri Aurobindo himself said that he would not like me to do so." A asked him what his reading was. His answer was: "In 1947 his philosophy will become the basis of a new world civilisation and culture. Nothing can stop that." He added that he had read thousands of horoscopes but had never seen the same time of birth as yours. He said it has all the signs of a unique greatness. A says he emphasised unique, *ananyasadharan*.

26 JUNE 1946

One day in June 1945 around four a.m., A woke up from a sound sleep and found to his surprise something which had never happened before: Japa, the repetition of the names of the Mother and Sri Aurobindo, was occurring spontaneously within him. After some time he felt the life-force and a diffused consciousness in him rising up through his body from the feet towards the centre between the eyebrows (ajnachakra). The consciousness formed itself into a reddish golden ball and appeared right in front of that centre. A was still in bed. He saw the mosquito net, the pole holding it, the bedstead, the books on the shelves built into the walls and the walls themselves vanish into nothingness. After a while all that remained was bare Awareness. It was not awareness of anything, there was nothing to be aware of — nor did A feel he was experiencing Awareness. There was no experience but sheer consciousness. It was only later in the day when the intensity of Awareness became less and began to disappear gradually that A felt he had had an extraordinary experience. He felt a great detachment from everything and a strong disinclination to do anything. He carried on his domestic and professional duties — he was then teaching at a university in a town in north India — but had no sense of involvement in them.

A had a strong streak of inertia in his nature. He knew that Sri Aurobindo's was a dynamic Yoga and that disinclination to work was not only no part of it but a great obstacle to progress. He felt a division in his being and nature which produced in him a sense of despair. So when he came to the Ashram in June 1946, after having experienced pure Awareness, he wrote to Sri Aurobindo describing the experience and also about the strong element of inertia in his nature and asked him whether his interpretation of the experience, that it was of the silent Self, was correct and told him that he wanted to shed his inertia and prayed to the Master to assign some work to him so that he could discipline himself. A's letter to Sri Aurobindo was read out to him by me and he dictated the reply given below. After it was read back to him, he asked me to give it to A.

SRI AUROBINDO'S LETTER

Your analysis is perfectly correct.

Realisation of the silent, inactive Brahman is no bar to the dynamic side of the Yoga; often it is the first step. One must not associate it with attachment to inertia. The silent Brahman is attached to nothing. Your mind is associated with inertia and attached to it.

Work itself is no solution; the spirit behind the work is important. The real remedy is to open oneself to the Force. When one gets free through the silent Brahman, one does not go back to the old way of work. By this liberation one becomes free from the ego; one becomes an instrument of the Divine Force by receiving the Force and feels its working, then inertia goes away and work in a new way becomes possible. Until that can be, one has to work in the ordinary way. But becoming an instrument of the Divine is the proper way.

I had the realisation of sublime Nirvana first. There was complete *cittavritti nirodha*, entire silence. Then came the experience of action, not my own, but from above. One has to grow into it unless it comes easily.

27 JUNE 1948

A felt disappointed that Sri Aurobindo had not given him any guidance to do anything specific. His idea was that if Sri Aurobindo had told him to do something, whatever it might be, he would try to carry it out diligently and regularly and thus overcome the inertia in his nature. A later told me that he came to realise why Sri Aurobindo did not ask him to do anything. If he had and if A could not have fulfilled it, it would have been a failure to carry out the Guru's Adesh which might have meant spiritual disaster. A said that it was out of compassion that Sri Aurobindo did not grant his prayer for a clear "command" to do something.

A discussed the matter with the Mother at the same time as he wrote to Sri Aurobindo about his problem. The Mother also did not assign any specific task, though A had asked her for one as he was going to stay in the Ashram for nearly two months. A few days passed, but the Mother only said she would consider what A might do. On being asked a third time she simply said, "You are not used to work, A, are you?" A answered quietly, "No, Mother, I am not." And A told me that they both had a laugh.

A has reported to me that the Mother made the remark with such compassion and love and simple humour that he could not feel hurt or offended. He also said that the incident showed the Mother's great insight into people's characters. Incidentally, the Mother did tell him in response to his prayer for some guidance that if he wanted to get over his inertia he should make a resolution, for example, to read one paragraph of The Life Divine *every day and then stick to the resolution with diligence. She further told him not to worry about work during that particular stay in the Ashram but to enjoy himself.*

NIRODBARAN: A has just written that five days back he was taking a bath in the afternoon and, when he had nearly finished, feeling cool and comfortable, he started singing a bhajan of Mirabai. Towards the end the word Mira occurred and he played on it, repeating it over and over again. He says his mind suddenly became very indrawn and he felt a descent of peace. He writes that he had to go to a meeting at the Pathamandir. He says he did all that he had to do in the milling crowd of Bowbazar and College Street but the feeling of peace never left him. He has written to me to ask you whether the Mother's name – but it did not occur to him that it was the Mother's name he was repeating – has the power to bring such experiences.

SRI AUROBINDO: He has got it. Why does he ask? Of course, the Mother's name has the power.